contents

introduction 4

how the book works 5

quilting fabrics 6

tools and equipment 8

cutting out the patches 9

rotary units 11

sewing the blocks together 19

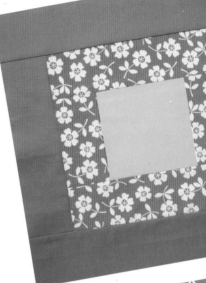

the patterns 21

templates 269

index 287

bibliography,
author biography,
and acknowledgments 288

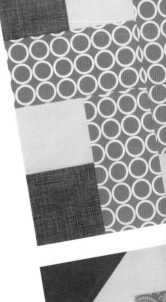

introduction

Quilting may be a centuries-old craft, but it is flourishing in the twenty-first century and has taken on a new, undeniably contemporary, guise. There is now a thriving modern community of quilt bloggers, designers, and makers across the world. Many share their ideas, tips, and techniques online, and others meet at fairs, retreats, or classes run by local quilt stores. Whether you are new to quilting or an experienced stitcher, the 365 blocks in this book— one for every day of the year—will inspire you.

ideas and inspiration

I have greatly enjoyed selecting the patterns and sourcing the fabrics to make the blocks. The designs are an eclectic mix of old and new. The historic blocks have been drawn from a wide range of sources: museum collections, 1930s newspaper columns, patchwork reference books, and my own notebooks, collated over many years. They include faithful reproductions of favorite blocks, including Cherry Basket and Bear's Paw, alongside classics, such as Birds in the Air, reinterpreted in fresh, bright fabrics. I've created many completely new figurative blocks especially for the book, and these range from cats, fruit, and flowers to a Christmas stocking and a row of beach huts. Inspiration for design is everyday, so some of my other designs are based on everyday items, such as a toy crown and package of candies, or architectural details, such as tessellated Roman flooring. Others are simply new, thrifty ways of using your tiniest scraps, which will appeal to fabric hoarders.

something for everybody

There are many ways to use the book, whether you are an absolute beginner who wants to make a block from just four squares or an experienced quilter who wants to join together forty plus patches. Some blocks will take less than half an hour to complete, others a whole afternoon. Many, such as Log Cabin or Bricks and Mortar, can be pieced quickly, because they have no seams that need to be matched precisely. Enthusiastic sewers will find plenty of ways to use their fabric stash and perfect their triangle points, while newbies can start with an entry level block and build up their skills as they progress to more complex designs. Try joining four blocks for a mini quilt or use just one block to decorate a pillow cover or tote bag. The range of designs makes the blocks ideal for sewing bees, quilt-alongs, or block swaps with your friends or within the online community.

You could, of course, take up the challenge of making a block a day for a year . . .
if you do, please let me see the results.

Lucinda Ganderton

BLOCK A DAY

365 Quilting Squares for Patchwork Inspiration!

Lucinda Ganderton

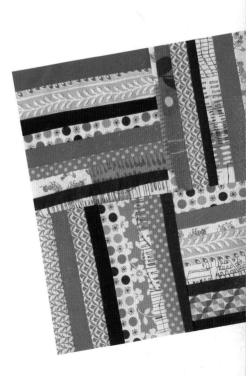

INTERWEAVE
interweave.com

First published in the United States in 2015 by

INTERWEAVE
interweave.com

Interweave
A division of F+W Media, Inc.
4868 Innovation Drive
Fort Collins, CO 80525
Interweave.com

ISBN: 978-1-63250-143-1

This book was conceived, designed, and produced by

Ivy Press
210 High Street, Lewes
East Sussex BN7 2NS, UK
www.ivypress.co.uk

Publisher Susan Kelly
Creative Director Michael Whitehead
Editorial Director Tom Kitch
Art Director Wayne Blades
Commissioning Editor Sophie Collins
Editors Theresa Bebbington & Judith Chamberlain-Webber
Technical Editors Leslie T. O'Neill, Allison Korleski & Sara Cook
Designer Ginny Zeal
Photographer Andrew Perris
Illustrators Peters & Zabransky
Editorial Assistant Jenny Campbell

Printed in China

10 9 8 7 6 5 4 3 2 1

746.46 GAN

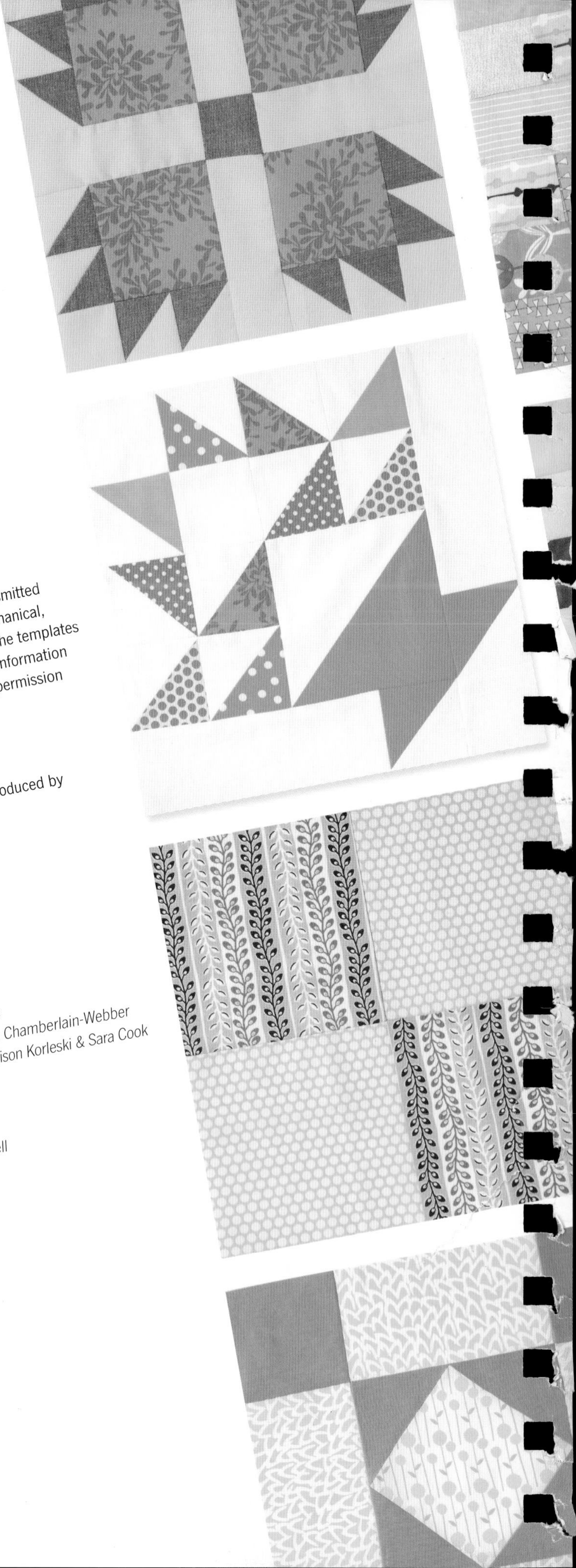

how the book works

Whether you're new to patchwork or have been making quilts for years, and whether you prefer to rotary piece your blocks or use templates, the patterns in this book have you covered. This page takes you through the way the patterns are presented and the rules we've followed to put them together consistently.

Basic techniques

Pages 6 to 8 give you all the core information you will need to get started if you are new to patchwork. This includes how to choose and prepare your fabrics as well as advice on using the tools and equipment needed for cutting out, sewing, and pressing. It is followed by a useful section on pages 9 to 20 that explains in detail how to piece all of the basic units that will be used time and again in different blocks.

Block instructions

Each block has its own short introduction, which tells you about the design, offers some ideas for an alternative look, or suggests how it might be combined with other blocks. The fabrics for each block are listed, along with the amount required, and there are reference tabs on the side of the page for quick color identification. You will find two sets of instructions for preparing the patches and making the basic unit. Which one you follow will depend on if you want to cut out the patches using the templates on pages 269 to 285 or prefer to work with the rotary cutting and unit piecing techniques (both of these methods are explained on pages 9 to 10). These instructions are followed by clear step-by-step guidelines for assembling the patches and units to make the block.

Template sizing

All of the blocks make a finished size of 12 by 12 inches, so you will be able to easily join them to make a sampler quilt. The instructions specify which of the four template sets to use or give you the precise measurements to follow to create this size. Using a 12-inch square means the block can be divided precisely by multiples of 2, 3, 4, and 6, so the blocks, based on grids of three rows of three squares or four rows of four squares, can easily be measured using the grid printed on a quilter's rule. The exceptions to this rule are the designs that are based on five rows of five squares or seven rows of seven squares, which are only template pieced because of their irregular size.

The designs are varied, so you will need to use template cutting for a handful of blocks that include acute isosceles triangles instead of right triangles. (In case you don't remember your geometry, an acute isosceles triangle has two equal sides and two equal angles of less than 90 degrees and a right triangle has a 90-degree angle.)

quilting fabrics

Patchwork was originally a thrift craft, pieced from scraps and fragments salvaged from old garments. Many quilters still incorporate family clothing into their projects, but with such an amazing range of new textiles to choose from, it's sometimes difficult to know where to start. Selecting your fabrics is one of the most creative stages of the quilting process, so take time to choose your favorites and plan how the colors and patterns will work together.

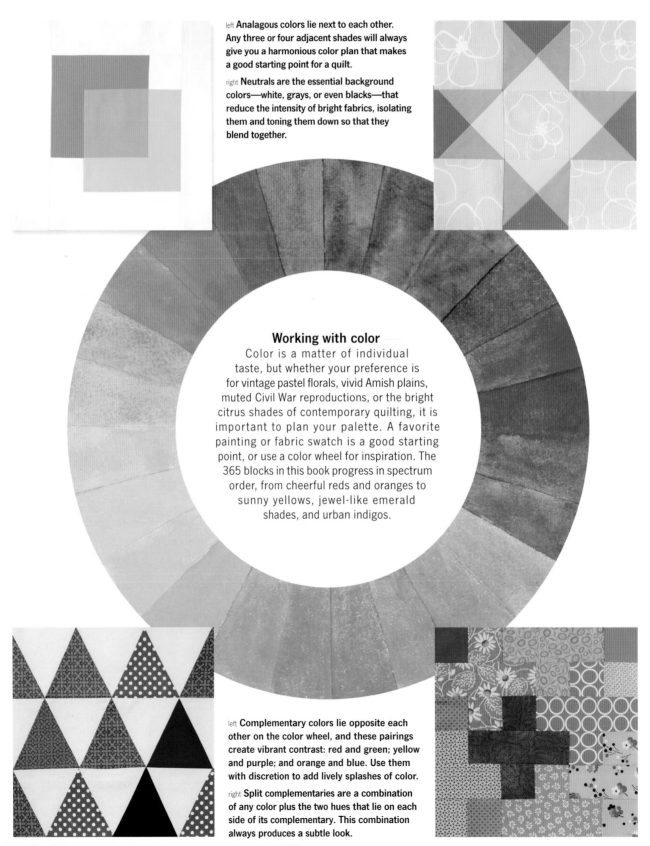

left **Analagous colors** lie next to each other. Any three or four adjacent shades will always give you a harmonious color plan that makes a good starting point for a quilt.

right **Neutrals** are the essential background colors—white, grays, or even blacks—that reduce the intensity of bright fabrics, isolating them and toning them down so that they blend together.

Working with color

Color is a matter of individual taste, but whether your preference is for vintage pastel florals, vivid Amish plains, muted Civil War reproductions, or the bright citrus shades of contemporary quilting, it is important to plan your palette. A favorite painting or fabric swatch is a good starting point, or use a color wheel for inspiration. The 365 blocks in this book progress in spectrum order, from cheerful reds and oranges to sunny yellows, jewel-like emerald shades, and urban indigos.

left **Complementary colors** lie opposite each other on the color wheel, and these pairings create vibrant contrast: red and green; yellow and purple; and orange and blue. Use them with discretion to add lively splashes of color.

right **Split complementaries** are a combination of any color plus the two hues that lie on each side of its complementary. This combination always produces a subtle look.

Light and dark

There is an important third factor to keep in mind when selecting your material. As well as the color and pattern, you will have to consider the shade of the fabrics. Make sure that there is a good balance of light, medium, and dark colors within each block, so that the framework of the design remains clear. Swap the fabrics around to be sure that they contrast well before you make your final decision, and remember that two adjacent patches in different colors will blend into each other if they are of a similar tone.

Preparing your fabric

Before you start cutting your patches, you will have to prepare the quilting fabric. Some quilters always prewash to remove the chemical dressings used in the manufacturing process and to prevent any shrinkage in the finished item. Others relish the textured surface created by washing and drying a finished quilt made from new fabric; they use dye-absorbing sheets in their wash cycle to prevent color runs. Vintage fabrics must be prewashed to freshen them up and because older dyes are not always colorfast. Whether you wash or not, the fabric should always be pressed well to remove any folds and creases. A spray of starch will help to restore body and stiffness to washed fabrics so that they are easier to handle.

Precut fabric sizes

Regular quarter yard: Cut across the width of the fabric, this narrow strip measures about 44 x 9 inches.

Fat quarter: Twice the height and half the width of a regular quarter yard, these tall rectangles measure 22 x 18 inches. They are sold either alone or in bundles of coordinating prints or colors.

Fat eighth: A smaller rectangle—half the size of a fat quarter—measuring 11 x 18 inches. This is a good way to buy the smaller amounts of fabrics needed for blocks.

Jellyroll: A roll of up to 40 different 22 x 2½-inch strips, jellyrolls are ideal for making smaller patches or Log Cabin-style blocks.

Charm packs and layer cakes: These contain 5-inch or 10-inch squares of assorted fabric, chosen to complement each other.

Prints and patterns

Spend time browsing your local quilt shop or online suppliers for ideas. Manufacturers work together with contemporary textile artists to produce seasonal collections of patchwork fabrics that are designed to work together, and you will also find precut bundles of toning fabrics (see Precut Fabric Sizes, right, for sizing hints). These usually include a mixture of toning plains, textured prints, figurative prints, flowers, and geometric patterns.

If you are choosing your own selection, start with a couple of solid colors, then add a few large and small prints that will lead your eye around the block, and maybe a stripe or checkered print. Remember that large-scale patterns lose their impact when cut into small patches, while areas of an unpromising print might create the perfect patch. If you are buying online, always check the scale; what appears like a ditsy floral on your screen may turn out to be an oversize flower print.

tools and equipment

Making quilt blocks doesn't require much equipment, although rotary techniques use a few quilting tools for accurate cutting. If you sew, you probably have all of the other basics in your sewing kit already:

Sewing tools

Scissors You will need two different pairs: small embroidery scissors for snipping threads and medium dressmaking shears reserved for cutting only fabric. If you are template piecing, keep a third pair for cutting only paper, which tends to blunt the blades.

Fabric markers These are used for drawing template outlines onto fabric and for marking seam lines. There are several types to choose from. Use air- or heat-erasable fabric markers on light colors and a sharp dressmaker's chalk pencil on dark colors. Chalk marks will brush away, air-erasable marks fade over time, and heat-erasable lines disappear when ironed.

Needles and pins Long thin needles, known as sharps, are fine for most sewing, but for hand quilting a finished project, the shorter "betweens" are better. A mixed package of needles is always useful. Decorative straight pins with glass or pearlized heads show up well against patterned fabrics. You can keep them on hand in a pin cushion.

Thread Most patchwork fabric is 100-percent cotton, so stitch with a thread that is made of pure cotton fibers. Don't skimp on the price; cheap thread not only breaks easily but doesn't slip freely through the cloth.

Starch Spray starch is useful for stiffening fine or washed fabrics so that they are easier to cut and sew, or to get rid of heavy creases.

Sewing machine A basic, reliable model with a steady straight stitch is all you need for patchwork. Use a general-purpose needle size, such as 10/70 or 12/8, and change it regularly to be sure your stitches are regular. Save time by buying a few extra bobbins and keeping them wound with different colored threads.

Iron and ironing board Keep the sole of your iron polished to prevent it from damaging your fabric, and make sure the ironing board cover is clean. Remember to turn off the steam control when pressing patches.

Rotary cutting equipment

Quilt shops often carry a fascinating array of quilting equipment, and it's tempting to buy the lot. All that you need to get started, however, is a cutting mat, a couple of rulers, and a rotary cutter. As you become more experienced, you can add more specialized tools as you need them.

Cutting mat Always cut onto a self-healing mat, which will protect both the rotary blade and your worktop. These are marked with a square grid that you can use to line up the fabric. Start with a medium-size mat, if possible, with a different color on each side, so that you can select the best contrast for your fabric.

Quilter's rulers These clear plastic rulers come in many shapes and sizes, all printed with a measurement grid for cutting squares and rectangles. A 6½-inch square ruler for cutting patches and a longer, narrower ruler (about 14 x 4½ inches) for strips are used to make all the blocks in this book.

Rotary cutter Like a pizza wheel, this tool has a round blade attached to a handle. The extremely sharp edge can cut through several layers of fabric at once, which speeds up the process of cutting identical patches. For safety's sake, only buy a cutter that has a securely retractable blade.

cutting out the patches

There are two ways of preparing your patches: the traditional way that uses templates or by the quicker rotary method with a mat, quilter's rule, and cutter. The block instructions provide both techniques, so you can choose the one that you prefer. Remember that accuracy is always vital for a professional finish, so take your time regardless of if you are cutting with templates or a ruler.

Template cutting

This hands-on method is still popular with many quilters, because it uses less fabric than rotary piecing and the templates are portable. On pages 269–85 you will find templates for all the square, rectangular, and triangular patches required for making the blocks. Each template includes a ¼-inch seam allowance, which is indicated by a broken line.

There are four sets of templates in different sizes; this is because the finished blocks are based on four different divisions of a finished 12-inch square. The four by four blocks, for example, are based on a grid of four rows of four 3-inch squares, so the basic small square unit is 3 inches plus the seam allowance. The six by six blocks are made up of six rows of six 2-inch squares, so the basic unit for this set is a 2-inch square plus the seam allowance. Always check that you are using the right size template for the block that you are making.

You can photocopy or trace the required templates and glue them to thin cardboard to make them more durable. Alternatively, trace them onto thin, clear plastic—available from quilting suppliers—that can be cut out with a sharp craft knife. After you have traced the outlines, label each one and add the arrows, which indicates the grain of the fabric. Cut carefully around the solid lines.

To make the larger templates that don't fit onto a page, copy the half-size template onto a piece of paper and cut it out. Fold in half a second piece of paper that is large enough for the whole template. Align the edge of the template indicated by the double arrow along the fold, then cut out the template through the double layer.

Lay your pressed fabric, right side up, on a flat surface. Place the template on top so that the arrow lines up horizontally or vertically with the woven threads or along a printed pattern line. Using an erasable pen or chalk pencil (see page 8), draw once around the outside for each patch you need, fitting the shapes closely together. Cut out around the drawn lines. If you want, you can mark the ¼-inch seam allowance on the wrong side of the patches to help you make accurate seams.

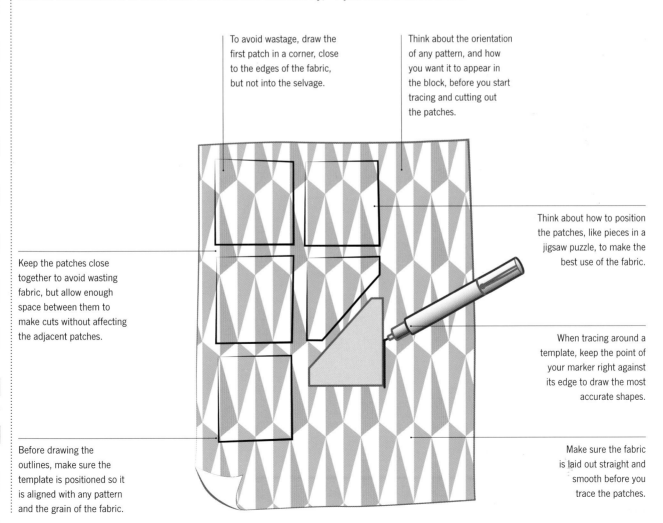

To avoid wastage, draw the first patch in a corner, close to the edges of the fabric, but not into the selvage.

Think about the orientation of any pattern, and how you want it to appear in the block, before you start tracing and cutting out the patches.

Think about how to position the patches, like pieces in a jigsaw puzzle, to make the best use of the fabric.

Keep the patches close together to avoid wasting fabric, but allow enough space between them to make cuts without affecting the adjacent patches.

When tracing around a template, keep the point of your marker right against its edge to draw the most accurate shapes.

Before drawing the outlines, make sure the template is positioned so it is aligned with any pattern and the grain of the fabric.

Make sure the fabric is laid out straight and smooth before you trace the patches.

Rotary cutting

The dimensions for each patch are set out in the block instructions. For squares, this is the length of all four sides, and for rectangles, the width is given first, then the height. To cut a single square or rectangle, lay your fabric on your cutting mat and place the ruler on top. Line the top edge up with the straight grain, or along a pattern line on striped or checkered fabrics. Hold the rotary cutter so that the blade is upright and it lies against the edge of the ruler. Press down the ruler with the palm of your other hand to keep it in position and glide the blade slowly but firmly along the side and top edges. Always cut away from yourself to avoid injury. Turn the ruler the other way around so the two grid lines that indicate your required measurements line up with the cut edges. Cut along the two remaining edges to cut out the patch.

Bulk cutting

You can make two or four identical patches at a time by folding and pressing your fabric once or twice before positioning the ruler. Cut several patches from different fabrics by stacking up several pieces, all with the grain running in the same direction. A light spray of starch will prevent the layers from shifting as you cut.

Fussy cutting
When using fabric with a distinctive motif or design, you can cut patches that use specific areas of the pattern to create a secondary pattern or effect within the block. This is known as fussy cutting. It produces an attractive result, but you will need to allow for extra fabric to space out the patches. Templates cut from plastic will help you center a motif if you're template cutting, or use the grid lines on a quilter's ruler to line it up.

The cutting mat has a grid for aligning the fabric and ruler.

Align any patterns and the grain of the fabric with the grid on the cutting mat.

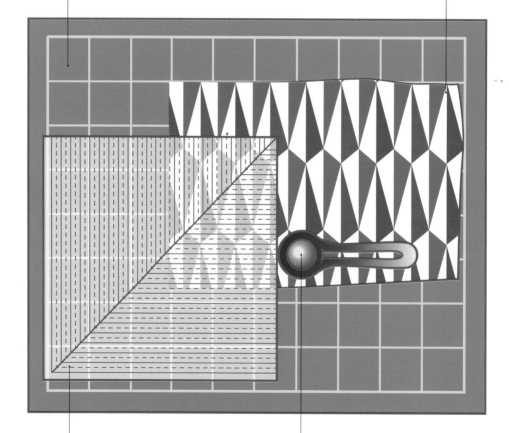

Use the marks on the square ruler to cut the square to the correct size.

Position the rotary cutter right alongside the edge of the ruler for precise cutting.

rotary units

The building blocks of the patchwork designs, rotary units are easily assembled from squares and rectangles, and you can use rotary methods to avoid sewing stretchy diagonal seams on the bias (across the grain of the fabric). Made in different sizes, they can be combined in various layouts to create most of the 365 blocks. Rotary piecing uses more fabric than template piecing, but it does save time spent cutting fabric, and the scraps can be recycled in other projects. The size and colors of the units required are given in the instructions for each block, and the measurements for the patches you will need to make the units are listed below. The seam allowance is ¼ inch throughout.

Square units

Rectangle square
- For two 4½-inch units, cut one 9 x 2½-inch main strip and one 9 x 2½-inch contrasting strip
- For two 6½-inch units, cut one 13 x 3½-inch main strip and one 13 x 3½-inch contrasting strip

Right sides together, pin and sew the two strips together; press seam over the darker fabric. Cut the resulting rectangle in half to make 4½-inch or 6½-inch squares.

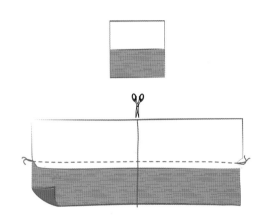

Three-patch square
- For two 4½-inch units, cut one 14 x 2½-inch main strip and one 5 x 2½-inch contrasting rectangle
- For two 6½-inch units, cut one 20 x 3½-inch main strip and one 7 x 3½-inch contrasting rectangle

Cut two 4½ or 6½-inch rectangles from the main strip. Right sides together, pin and sew the remaining fabric to the long edge of the contrasting rectangle; press seam over the darker fabric. Cut in half to make a pair of two-fabric rectangles. Join these to the main rectangles; press seam over the main rectangles.

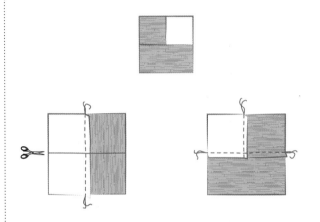

Three-stripe square
- For two 4½-inch units, cut two 9 x 1¾-inch main strips and one 9 x 2-inch contrasting strip
- For two 6½-inch units, cut two 13 x 2½-inch main strips and one 13 x 2½-inch contrasting strip

Right sides together, pin and sew the main strips to each edge of the contrasting strip; press seams over the darker fabric. Cut in half to make two 4½-inch or 6½-inch squares.

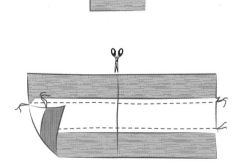

Four-patch square
- For two 4½-inch units, cut one 10½ x 2½-inch main rectangle and one 10½ x 2½-inch contrasting rectangle
- For two 6½-inch units, cut one 13 x 3½-inch main rectangle and one 13 x 3½-inch contrasting rectangle

Right sides together, pin and sew the two strips together; press seam over the darker fabric. Cut across the strip to make four 4½ x 2½-inch or four 6½ x 2½-inch rectangles. Join the rectangles in pairs, with main and contrasting patches together; press seams open.

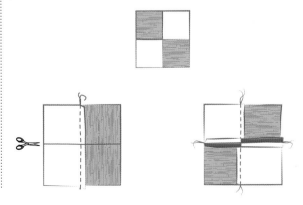

Half-square triangle

Cut one main and one contrasting square:
- For two 2¼-inch half-square triangles, cut two 3¼-inch squares
- For two 2½-inch half-square triangles, cut two 3½-inch squares
- For two 3½-inch half-square triangles, cut two 4½-inch squares
- For two 4½-inch half-square triangles, cut two 5½-inch squares
- For two 6½-inch half-square triangles, cut two 7½-inch squares
- For two 7½-inch half-square triangles, cut two 8½-inch squares

An alternative, accurate method is to cut two squares that are at least 1¼ inches larger than your finished size. Whichever method you use, you can then trim the half-square triangles precisely, to the exact measurements required, using a using a quilter's ruler; place the diagonal guideline along the seam to make sure the two sides are the same.

Draw a diagonal line from corner to corner on one of the squares, then, with right sides together, pin the two together.

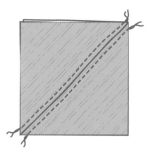

Machine stitch twice across the square along the diagonal, ¼ inch away from each side of the drawn line.

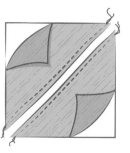

Cut along the drawn line to divide the squares into two pieces.

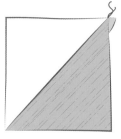

Open out the squares. Press the seams to set the stitching, then press the seam allowances over the darker fabric. Trim the "dog ears" at the corners.

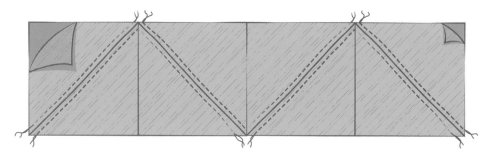

To mass-produce eight identical half-square triangles, cut one main and one contrasting rectangle. The height is the size of the square given above for each different half-square triangle, and the width is four times this measurement. Divide the wrong side of one rectangle into squares and draw diagonal lines across them. Pin the two pieces of fabric together, right sides together, and machine stitch ¼ inch from each side of the diagonal lines. Cut along the marked lines. Press the seams to set the stitching, as described above.

Pinwheel square

- For one 4½-inch unit, make four 2½-inch half-square triangles
- For one 6½-inch unit, make four 3½-inch half-square triangles
- For one 8½-inch unit, make four 4½-inch half-square triangles

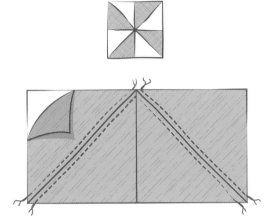

Make four identical half-square triangles from one main and one contrasting rectangle. The width of the rectangles is twice the height measurement. Divide the wrong side of one rectangle into two squares, then mark and stitch the diagonals as shown opposite. Lay out four half-square triangles as shown above. With right sides together, pin and sew the top pair together; press seam over the darker triangle. Repeat for the bottom pair. Right sides together, pin and sew the two rows together, carefully matching the corners and center seams; press seam open.

Boat square

- For one 6½-inch unit, make one 6½-inch half-square triangle and cut one 3½-inch contrasting square.

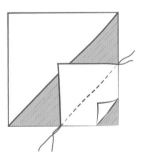

Mark a diagonal line across the wrong side of the small square. With right sides together, align and pin it to the bottom right corner of the half-square triangle up to the diagonal line, with the marked line parallel to the seam. Sew along the marked line.

Trim off the excess fabric ¼ inch from the seam (and save the scraps for a different block); press seam to one side or open, as directed for making the block.

Three-quarter square triangle

- For one 3½-inch unit, make one 3½-inch half-square triangle and cut one 3½-inch main square
- For one 4½-inch unit, make one 4½-inch half-square triangle and cut one 4½-inch main square
- For one 6½-inch unit, make one 6½-inch half-square triangle and cut one 6½-inch main square

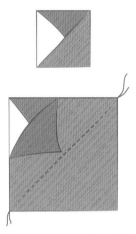

Mark a diagonal line across the wrong side of the main square. With right sides together, pin it to the half-square triangle so the line is at right angles, or perpendicular, to the seam. Stitch along the marked line.

Trim off the excess fabric ¼ inch from the seam (and save the scraps for a different block); press seam over the large triangle.

Hourglass square

- For two 3½-inch units, make two 4½-inch half-square triangles
- For two 4½-inch units, make two 5½-inch half-square triangles
- For two 6½-inch units, make two 7½-inch half-square triangles

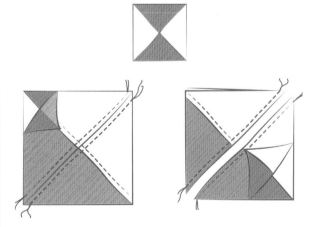

Mark a diagonal line across one half-square triangle at right angles, or perpendicular, to the seam. With right sides and opposite colors together, pin the two half-square triangles together. Stitch ¼ inch from each side of the drawn line.

Cut the unit in half along the drawn line; press seam open. Trim the squares to the size specified using a quilter's ruler and rotary cutter.

Stitch and flip

The following units are all made with a useful technique known as stitch and flip, which is a quick way to sew triangles to the corner of squares and rectangles without actually having to cut out triangular patches or sew a bias seam. You simply stitch along a marked diagonal line, trim the seam allowance, flip the triangle outward, and press toward the corner. Sew with just under a ¼ inch seam (see page 19) to keep the patches accurate.

Corner square

- For one 4½-inch unit, cut one 4½-inch main square and one 2½-inch contrasting square
- For one 6½-inch unit, cut one 6½-inch main square and one 3½-inch contrasting square

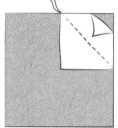

Draw a diagonal line across the contrasting square. With right sides together, pin it to the top right corner of the main square. Stitch along the line.

Trim the excess fabric ¼ inch from the seam; press seam outward.

House square

- For one 4½-inch unit, cut one 4½-inch main square and two 2½-inch contrasting squares
- For one 6½-inch unit, cut one 6½-inch main square and two 3½-inch contrasting squares

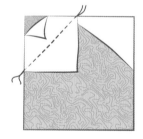

Join the first contrasting square to the top right corner of the main square, following the directions for the corner square on the left. Sew the second one to the top left corner in the same way.

Arrow square

- For one 4½-inch unit, cut one 4½-inch main square and three 2½-inch contrasting squares
- For one 6½-inch unit, cut one 6½-inch main square and three 3½-inch contrasting squares

Join the first two contrasting squares to the top right and left corners of the main square and the third square to the bottom right corner, following the directions for the corner square.

Triangle-and-square block

- For one 4½-inch unit, cut one main 4½-inch square, one 2½-inch main square, and two 2½-inch contrasting squares
- For one 6½-inch unit, cut one main 6½-inch square, one 3½-inch main square, and two 3½-inch contrasting squares

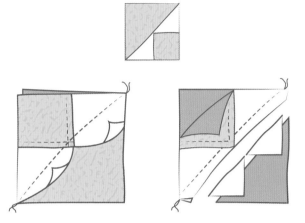

With right sides together, pin and sew the contrasting squares to the top and left edges of the small main square; press seams outward. On the wrong side of the fabric, draw a diagonal line across the contrasting squares. With right sides together and the main square in the top left corner, pin this unit to the large square. Stitch along the marked line.

Trim away the excess fabric ¼ inch from the seam; press seam across the large triangle.

Diamond square

- For one 4½-inch unit, cut one 4½-inch main square and four 2½-inch contrasting squares
- For one 6½-inch unit, cut one 6½-inch main square and four 3½-inch contrasting squares

Like the arrow square on page 14, join the first three contrasting squares to the top right, top left, and bottom right corners of the main square, then join the fourth square to the bottom left corner in the same way.

Flying geese square

- For one 4½-inch unit, cut one 4½-inch main square, one 2½-inch main square, and three 2½-inch contrasting squares
- For one 6½-inch unit, cut one 6½-inch main square, one 3½-inch main square, and three 2½-inch contrasting squares

Make a triangle-and-square block, following the directions above. Add the remaining contrasting square to the bottom right corner, following the directions for the corner square on page 14.

Hexagon square

- For one 4½-inch unit, cut one 4½-inch main square and two 2½-inch contrasting squares
- For one 6½-inch unit, cut one 6½-inch main square and two 3½-inch contrasting squares

Join the first small square to the top right corner of the large square, following the directions for the corner square on page 14, then add the second small square to the bottom left corner in the same way.

Rectangular units

Right tapered rectangle
- For one 2½ x 1½-inch unit, cut one 2½ x 1½-inch main rectangle and one 1½-inch contrasting square
- For one 4½ x 2½-inch unit, cut one 4½ x 2½-inch main rectangle and one 2½-inch contrasting square
- For one 6½ x 3½-inch unit, cut one 6½ x 3½-inch main rectangle and one 3½-inch contrasting square

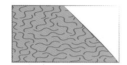

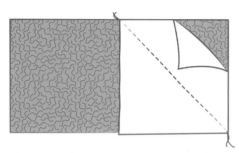

Mark a diagonal line across the square and, with right sides together, pin it to the right end of the rectangle. Sew along the marked line from center top to bottom right. Trim the excess fabric to ¼ inch from the seam; press seam outward.

Right diamond rectangle
- For one 4½ x 2½-inch unit, cut one 6½ x 3½-inch main rectangle and one 2½-inch contrasting square
- For one 6½ x 3½-inch unit, cut one 6½ x 3½-inch main rectangle and one 3½-inch contrasting square

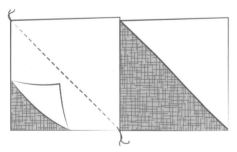

Make a right tapered rectangle, following the directions above, then add the second square to the left end in the same way, sewing from the center bottom edge to the top left corner.

Left tapered rectangle
- For one 2½ x 1½-inch unit, cut one 2½ x 1½-inch main rectangle and one 1½-inch contrasting square
- For one 4½ x 2½-inch unit, cut one 4½ x 2½-inch main rectangle and one 2½-inch contrasting square
- For one 6½ x 3½-inch unit, cut one 6½ x 3½-inch main rectangle and one 3½-inch contrasting square

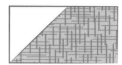

Follow the directions for the right tapered rectangle on the left, but sew the square to the left end of the rectangle and stitch from center top to bottom left.

Left diamond rectangle
- For one 4½ x 2½-inch unit, cut one 4½ x 2½-inch main rectangle and one 2½-inch contrasting square
- For one 6½ x 3½-inch unit, cut one 6½ x 3½-inch main rectangle and one 3½-inch contrasting square

Follow the directions for the right diamond to the left, but add the second square to the right end and sew from the center bottom edge to the top right corner.

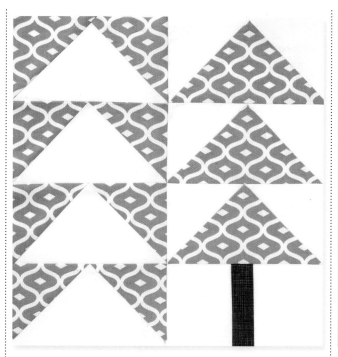

Flying geese rectangle

- For one 4½ x 2½-inch unit, cut one 4½ x 2½-inch main rectangle and two 2½-inch contrasting squares
- For one 6½ x 3½-inch unit, cut one 6½ x 3½-inch main rectangle and two 3½-inch contrasting squares

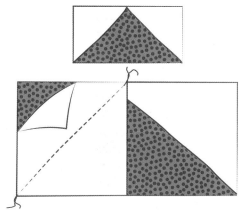

Follow the directions for the right tapered rectangle on page 16, then add the second square to the left end of the rectangle, sewing from the center top edge to the bottom left corner.

Short boat

- For one 6½ x 2½ in unit, cut one 6½ x 2½-inch main rectangle and two 2½-inch contrasting squares

Draw a diagonal line across both contrasting squares. Pin one to the right end of the rectangle. Sew along the marked line from the bottom edge to the top right corner. Trim the excess fabric to ¼ inch from the seam; press seam outward. Add the other square to the left end, sewing from the bottom edge to the top left corner.

Long boat

- For one 8½ x 2½-inch unit, cut one 8½ x 2½-inch main rectangle and two 2½-inch contrasting squares
- For one 12½ x 3½-inch unit, cut one 12½ x 3½-inch main rectangle and two 3½-inch contrasting squares

Follow the same directions for the short boat on the left.

Cat's head

- For one 6½ x 4½-inch unit, cut one 6½ x 4½-inch main rectangle and two 2½-inch contrasting squares

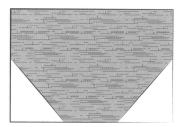

Follow the same directions for the short boat on the left.

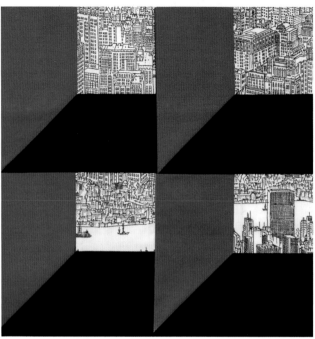

Octagon square

- For one 6½-inch unit, cut one 6½-inch main square and four 2½-inch contrasting squares

Add a contrasting square to the bottom right and left corners, following the directions for the short boat on page 17, then add the other two squares to the top right and left corners in the same way.

Perspective square

- For one 6½-inch unit, cut one 6½ x 3½-inch dark rectangle, one 6½ x 3½-inch medium rectangle, and one 3½-inch light square

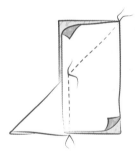

With right sides together and aligned at right end, sew a long edge of the medium rectangle to the top edge of the square, stoppin   g the stitches ¼ inch from the end of the square at the seam allowance. Fold back the unstitched part of the rectangle and add the dark rectangle to the left edge of the square in the same way, aligning the fabrics at the bottom corner.

Draw a diagonal line across the wrong side of the medium rectangle, from the end of the seam to the top right corner. Fold the loose ends of the two rectangles so that they are aligned with right sides together, pin them, and sew along the marked line, starting at the corner where the three fabrics meet. Trim the excess fabric to ¼ inch from the seam. Press the diagonal seam to one side and the straight seams outward.

sewing the blocks together

The step-by-step instructions explain the logical order in which the patches and units are pieced together to create each block. You can join them in the traditional way by hand, using backstitch or a short running stitch, or by machine. Many quilters sew with a neutral gray or beige thread, but if you are working with dark colors, match your thread to the fabric to avoid any thread color showing through.

Machine stitching

Be sure that your needle is sharp, then check the stitch tension on a scrap of fabric. The stitch length is a personal preference and can be between 10 and 14 stitches per inch. Smaller stitches are best for short seams, and they are particularly good for chain piecing (see below), because the threads won't unravel as easily when the patches are separated. There is no need to lock the ends of the seams like you would do when sewing clothes.

Seam allowance The seam allowance on all the patches is a standard ¼ inch. You can buy a ¼-inch seam foot for most machines, but first look in your accessory set, because you may already have a suitable foot marked with a line that is ¼ inch from the needle position. Match up the edge of the patches to this line as you sew to keep the seam consistent. Experienced quilters prefer to use a "scant" ¼-inch seam when piecing. This means that the seam allowance is a sliver less than ¼ inch, literally one or two threads of fabric. When the seams are pressed, a small amount of the allowance is lost within the fold, so a scant seam allows for this and gives more accurate piecing.

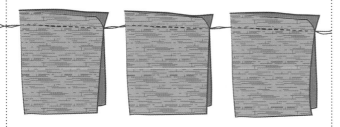

Chain piecing With this speedy technique, you join a continuous chain of patches like a row of little flags. Place or pin the patches to be joined together in pairs, with right sides together, and stack them up. Sew the first pair, then without stopping pick up the next pair and feed it under the presser foot. Continue until you have sewn all the patches, then snip the threads between them.

Diagonals and bias seams Joining two triangles to make a square, or sewing any other two diagonals requires a little extra attention. These edges are cut on the bias, or across the grain of the fabric, which means that they are stretchy and not as easy to sew as a straight seam. Handle the diagonal edges as little as possible as you work, and keep the machine at a steady pace so that they aren't pulled under the presser foot too quickly.

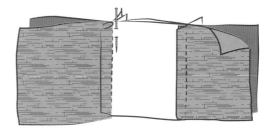

Matching seams Lining up your intersecting seams is the key to precise piecing. Hold the two edges to be joined together, right sides facing, and match the seams. When the seam allowances have been pressed to one side, in opposite directions, they will nest together; or, if they are open, they will lie flat against each other. Insert a pin along each seam and pin the corners of the units. Machine stitch, pulling out each pin just before it goes under the foot. The instructions will always tell you in which direction to press each seam afterward.

Starting again We all make mistakes, and the best way to remove a seam that's in the wrong place is to cut through the threads with a seam ripper, also known as a stitch unpicker, instead of using scissors.

Pressing

Pressing the seams as you work will keep the seams accurate and the points crisp. Pressing isn't the same as everyday ironing; don't glide the iron across the fabric, but push it down firmly to flatten the fabric without distorting the grain. Use a dry iron, because steam can also pull seams out of shape. Most patchwork fabric is 100-percent cotton, which can take a high heat, so set the temperature accordingly.

To set the stitches, first give the finished seam a press with the patches still folded together. Open them out, then press both sides of the seam allowance to one side, or open, as directed.

There are no hard and fast rules on how to press the seams, although many quilters prefer to press to one side, because the seam then has a layer of fabric underneath to strengthen the stitching. If you are sewing by hand, you should always do this. In general, the best option is to press in the directions that will create the least bulk, which often means using both techniques in a single block.

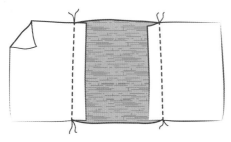

Make sure that the seam allowance lies across the darker patches, where possible, when pressing it to one side.

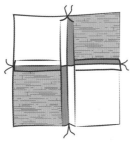

Where several seams meet up, or when you have several small patches, press the seams open to decrease the bulk. Use the tip of the iron to separate the two sides of the seam allowance.

Appliqué

Extra detail is sometimes added to a block, including the curved handle on the Basket of Cherries (page 27) and the stem on the Strawberry (page 28), by using a technique known as appliqué. A full-size template for each appliqué shape is usually given on the block page. You will need to trace or photocopy it and cut out around the outline. There are two techniques you could use for appliqué: a turned edge or iron-on adhesive.

Turned-edge appliqué Pin the template to the wrong side of the fabric and cut around it, leaving a narrow margin all around. If there are curves, fold the edges back over the paper, then snip into the curves up to the line to create a smooth fold of fabric. Tack the fabric down with small stitches and press firmly to set the creases. Unpick the thread, pin the piece to the block, and slip-stitch down by hand with matching thread.

Iron-on appliqué Reverse the template, then trace the outline onto the paper side of a piece of fusible web, a type of iron-on adhesive used in sewing. Cut out the approximate shape and press the adhesive side onto the wrong side of the appliqué fabric, using a cloth to protect the iron. Now cut neatly around the outline and peel off the backing paper. Position the appliqué piece on the block and iron it down. You can neaten the edge with a narrow machine satin stitch or by hand with blanket stitch.

rainbow circle

The seam allowance is ¼ inch throughout.

This block is a variation of Rolling Stone on page 222. The flow of color through the rainbow spectrum, from red to violet, adds to the feeling of movement around the octagon in the center. For a finished 12-inch square, the easiest way to cut the patches is with templates.

A
B
C
D
E
F
G
H
I

Fabric quantities

- Medium red fabric A: 6 x 6 inches
- Medium orange fabric B: 4 x 4 inches
- Medium yellow fabric C: 6 x 6 inches
- Medium green fabric D: 4 x 4 inches
- Medium emerald fabric E: 6 x 6 inches
- Medium turquoise fabric F: 4 x 4 inches
- Dark indigo fabric G: 6 x 6 inches
- Medium violet fabric H: 4 x 4 inches
- White fabric I: 14 x 18 inches

Prepare the patches

Template cutting
Using the 5 x 5 templates (pages 274–7):
- From fabrics A, C, E, and G, cut 1 diamond square each
- From fabrics B, D, F, and H, cut one small square each
- From fabric I, cut 16 small triangles and 5 small squares

Template piecing

With right sides together, pin and sew four fabric I small triangles to each of the four diamond squares; press seams open.

Make the block

Join the patches With right sides together, pin and sew one fabric I small square to each of the four colored small squares to make patchwork rectangles; press seams away from the white fabric.

Make three rows With right sides together, pin and sew the red diamond square to the left edge of the orange and white rectangle. Join the yellow diamond square to the right edge; press seams over the rectangle.

With right sides together, pin and sew the violet and white rectangle to the left edge of the remaining white small square. Join the green and white rectangle to the right edge; press seams away from the center square.

To make the third row, repeat the steps for the first row, using the indigo and emerald diamond squares and the turquoise and white rectangle.

Complete the square With right sides together and carefully matching seams, pin and sew the top row to the middle row. Join the bottom row to the middle row, then press seams open.

spinning heart

With a pinwheel in the center of a dark red heart, this block calls on both traditional quilting sensibilities and a modern sense of whimsy. For a scrappier look, choose different fabrics for the pinwheel and the borders.

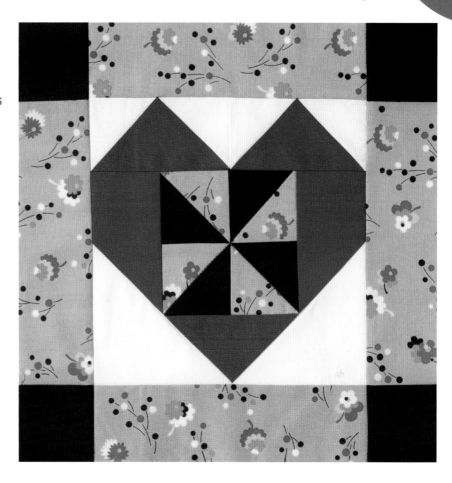

A
B
C
D

Fabric quantities

- Dark purple fabric A: 8 x 10 inches
- Medium brown print fabric B: 9 x 15 inches
- Dark red fabric C: 6 x 13 inches
- White fabric D: 6 x 7 inches

Prepare the patches

Rotary method
- From fabrics A and B, make one 4½-inch pinwheel square (see page 13)
- From fabrics C and D, make two 4½ x 2½-inch flying geese rectangles (see page 17)
- From fabric A, cut four 2½-inch squares
- From fabric B, cut four 8½ x 2½-inch rectangles
- From fabric C, cut 1 medium triangle, 1 right tapered rectangle, and 1 left tapered rectangle (6 x 6 templates)
- From fabric D, cut 2 large triangles (6 x 6 templates)

or

Template cutting
Using the 6 x 6 templates (pages 278–83):
- From fabric A, cut 4 small triangles and 4 small squares
- From fabric B, cut 4 small triangles and 4 long rectangles
- From fabric C, cut 3 medium triangles, 1 right tapered rectangle, and 1 left tapered rectangle
- From fabric D, cut 4 small triangles and 2 large triangles

Template piecing

With right sides together, pin and sew the four sets of small triangles cut from fabrics A and B. Arrange them in two rows of two squares to create a pinwheel square for the center block.

With right sides together, pin and sew two fabric D small triangles to the slanted edges of one of the fabric C medium triangles. Repeat to make the second flying geese unit.

Make the block

Prepare the patches With right sides together, sew the two tapered rectangles to the sides of the pinwheel, making sure they point inward and downward; press seams over the heart.

With right sides together, sew the flying geese units together, then join the strip to the top of the pinwheel; press seams open.

With right sides together, pin and then sew the last fabric C medium triangle to the bottom edge of the pinwheel; press seam downward. Finish the heart by sewing the two fabric D large triangles to the diagonal edges of the heart; press seams open.

Make the border With right sides together, sew one fabric B long rectangle to each side edge of the heart block and press seams over the rectangles. Join a fabric A small square to each end of the remaining two rectangles, then press seams over the rectangles. With right sides together, pin the strips to the top and bottom edges of the center panel, matching the seams, and sew; press seams open.

3 gingham

Choose two shades of the same color plus white to create an authentic checkered gingham for this one-patch block. The polka-dot fabric used here adds a graphic silk-screened look, making it a great modern quilt for a child's bedroom. If you want to rotary cut these patches, cut 3-inch squares and use a ¼-inch seam allowance.

A
B
C

The seam allowance is ¼ inch throughout.

Fabric quantities

- Dark red fabric A: 9 x 9 inches
- Medium red print fabric B: 9 x 12 inches
- White fabric C: 6 x 6 inches

Prepare the patches

Template cutting
Using the 5 x 5 templates (pages 274–7):
- From fabric A, cut 9 small squares
- From fabric B, cut 12 small squares
- From fabric C, cut 4 small squares

Make the block

Make the top, bottom, and center rows
With right sides together, pin and sew a solid A square to the left edge of a print B square. Repeat with another print B square and solid A square. Now, pin and sew one side edge each of a solid A square to a side edge of a printed B square in each joined pair, forming a row of five alternating squares; press seams over the B squares. Repeat to make another two identical rows.

Make the other middle rows With right sides together, pin and sew two white C squares to three print B squares, alternating colors; press seams over the B squares. Repeat to make another identical row.

Complete the square Lay out the five rows in their final positions, creating a checkered gingham pattern. With right sides together, match the seams, pin, and sew the top two rows together. Add the other three rows in order, pressing seams open.

4 framed windmill

The simple, traditional windmill block becomes contemporary when made in an unusual color combination. Emphasize the tones of green and orange fabrics with a complementary border.

A
B
C
D

The seam allowance is ¼ inch throughout.

Fabric quantities

- Medium orange print fabric A: 10 x 6 inches
- Light green fabric B: 10 x 6 inches
- Dark green fabric C: 9 x 12 inches
- Medium orange print fabric D: 6 x 6 inches

Prepare the patches

Rotary method
- From fabrics A and B, make four 4½-inch rectangle squares (see page 11)
- From fabric C, cut four 8½ x 2½-inch rectangles
- From fabric D, cut four 2½-inch squares

or

Template cutting
Using the 6 x 6 templates (pages 278–83):
- From fabrics A and B, cut 4 short rectangles each
- From fabric C, cut 4 long rectangles
- From fabric D, cut 4 small squares

Template piecing

With right sides together, pin and sew a fabric A short rectangle to each long edge of the fabric B short rectangles to make four rectangle squares. Press seams over the darker fabric.

Make the block

Sew the windmill With right sides together, pin and sew two pairs of rectangle squares together so that the short end of fabric A abuts the long end of fabric A; press seams over the darker fabric. Stitch the two rows together, completing the windmill.

Make the border With right sides together, pin and sew one fabric C rectangle to each side of the pinwheel; press seams over the darker fabric. Pin and sew two fabric D squares to each end of the remaining rectangles; press seams over the darker fabric. With right sides together, stitch the fabrics C and D strips to the top and bottom of the windmill; press seams over the strips.

fourth of july

A combination of prints and solids gives this patriotic block a playful look. Join multiple blocks of the same color scheme to create a secondary pattern of blue pinwheels.

Fabric quantities

- Dark blue fabric A: 7 x 8 inches
- Light blue print fabric B: 7 x 8 inches
- Dark red fabric C: 7 x 8 inches
- Light red print fabric D: 7 x 8 inches
- White fabric E: 7 x 16 inches

Prepare the patches

Rotary method
- From fabrics A and E, fabrics B and E, fabrics C and E, and fabrics D and E, make two 6½ x 3½-inch right tapered rectangles (see page 16) each

or

Template cutting
Using the 4 x 4 templates (pages 269–73):
- From fabrics A, B, C, and D, cut 2 right tapered triangles each
- From fabric E, cut 8 small triangles

A
B
C
D
E

Template piecing

With right sides together, pin and sew one fabric E triangle to the diagonal edge of each blue and red right tapered rectangle to form eight rectangles; press seams away from fabric E.

Make the block

Make four patches For the top left patch, join a fabrics B and E right tapered rectangle to a fabrics C and E right tapered rectangle, with white fabrics meeting in the center; press seam open. Repeat to make the bottom right patch. Repeat twice for the top right patch and bottom left patch, using a fabrics A and E right tapered rectangle and a fabrics D and E right tapered rectangle.

Complete the square With right sides together, sew the top left patch to the top right patch, with the dark red fabric perpendicular to the light red print fabric; press seams open. Repeat to join the bottom left patch to the bottom right patch. With right sides together, pin the two rows together, matching the red edges in the middle, and sew; press seams open.

poppy

A
B
C
D
E

This bold and cheerful flower is cleverly made with four simple house squares framed in a coordinating border. Try any color combination pulled from nature, experimenting with the hues of different seasons. The Big Flower block on page 187 uses the same flower motif on a larger scale.

Fabric quantities

- Dark red fabric A: 10 x 10 inches
- Black print fabric B: 3 x 6 inches
- Light blue print fabric C: 9 x 12 inches
- Medium blue fabric D: 6 x 6 inches
- White fabric E: 6 x 6 inches

Prepare the patches

Rotary method
- From fabrics A, B, and E, make four 4½-inch house squares (see page 14)
- From fabric C, cut four 8½ x 2½-inch rectangles
- From fabric D, cut four 2½-inch squares

or

Template cutting
Using the 6 x 6 templates (pages 278–83):
- From fabric A, cut 4 house squares
- From fabrics B and E, cut 4 small triangles each
- From fabric C, cut 4 long rectangles
- From fabric D, cut 4 small squares

Template piecing

Assemble each of the poppy petals by sewing one black print fabric B small triangle to the top right diagonal edge of each house square and the fabric E small triangle to the top left diagonal edge. Press seams open.

Make the block

Sew the poppy With right sides together and the black print triangles at the center of the block, sew the house squares together in two rows of two squares; press seams open. Sew the two rows together, then press seams open.

Make the border With right sides together, sew one blue print fabric C rectangle to each of the two sides of the poppy patch; press seams outward. Sew a medium blue fabric D square to each end of the remaining rectangles. Press seams over the rectangles, then sew them to the top and bottom of the poppy patch. Press seams open.

basket of cherries

The seam allowance is ¼ inch throughout.

First published in the 1890s, this longstanding favorite block is traditionally made in crisp white and cherry red cotton with an appliquéd handle. This block is most accurately made using templates.

Fabric quantities

- Dark red fabric A: 9 x 11 inches
- White fabric B: 12 x 17 inches

Prepare the patches

Template cutting
Using the 5 x 5 templates (pages 274–7):

- From fabric A, cut 11 small triangles plus 1 handle, using the template on page 286
- From fabric B, cut 2 medium rectangles, 2 small squares, 7 small triangles, and 1 extra large triangle

Template piecing

With right sides together, pin and sew seven sets of fabric A and fabric B small triangles to make seven half-square triangles (see page 12).

Make the block

Appliqué the handle Using the turned edge method (see page 20), appliqué the handle onto the extra large triangle, centering it along one long edge.

Sew the basket Lay the half-square triangle patches out to resemble a basket, as shown in the photograph. Starting at the top right of the basket, sew a small fabric A triangle to the top edge of a half-square triangle, right sides together. With right sides together, sew a second small fabric A triangle to the left edge of the half-square triangle; press seams open. These are the top two rows.

A
B

To make the third row, join two half-square triangles, with right sides together, then add a small fabric A triangle to the left edge. Sew the rows together, then press seams open.

To make the fourth row, join another two half-square triangles. Add a fabric B square to the right side, then a small fabric A triangle to the left. With right sides together, pin and sew to the third row, then press seams open.

With right sides together, sew the basket to the fabric B extra large triangle, making sure the handle abuts the basket.

Complete the square With right sides together, sew a half-square triangle to one short end on each of the fabric B rectangles. Join one strip to the right edge of the basket and the second strip to the bottom edge of the basket, making sure the points match. With right sides together, sew the remaining fabric B square to the half-square triangles, one at a time. Press seams open.

strawberry

The seam allowance is ¼ inch throughout.

Pick various shades of patterned red fabric to make this strawberry appear three dimensional. The curved stem is appliquéd. This block combines well with the Pear, Pineapple, and Plum blocks on pages 144, 108, and 229.

A
B
B
B
B
B
B
B
C

Fabric quantities

- Dark green print fabric A: 7 x 9 inches
- Up to 6 different dark and medium red print fabrics B: 12 x 13 inches in total
- White fabric C: 13 x 18 inches

Prepare the patches

Rotary method

- From fabric A, cut one stem using the template on page 286
- From fabrics A and C, make one 6½ x 2½-inch right diamond rectangle and one 6½ x 2½-inch left diamond rectangle (see page 16)
- From fabrics B and C, make two 2½-inch half-square triangles (see page 12)
- From fabric B, cut ten 2½-inch squares
- From fabric C, cut one 8½ x 2½-inch rectangle and two 12½ x 2½-inch rectangles
- From fabrics B and C, cut one right half triangle and one left half triangle (6 x 6 templates on page 282–3)

or

Template cutting

Using the 6 x 6 templates (pages 278–83):

- From fabric A, cut 1 right diamond, 1 left diamond, and one stem using the template on page 286
- From fabric B, cut 10 small squares, 2 small triangles, 1 right half triangle, and 1 left half triangle
- From fabric C, cut 6 small triangles, 1 right half triangle, 1 left half triangle, 1 long rectangle, and 2 full-length rectangles

Template piecing

With right sides together, pin and sew a small fabric C triangle to each of the diagonal edges of one fabric A diamond. Press seams open. Repeat to make the second strawberry leaf.

With right sides together, pin and sew the remaining two small fabric C triangles to the two small fabric B triangles; press seams open.

Make the block

Assemble the hull With right sides together, pin the left and right diamond rectangles together so they point inward and downward, as shown above, then sew; press seams open. Join the fabric C long rectangle to the top edge and press seam up. Appliqué the stem between the leaves (see page 20).

Sew the strawberry With right sides together, stitch the fabrics B and C left and right half triangles together to make two rectangles; press seams down over the red fabric.

Arrange the patches in their final positions, being careful to balance the prints and shades of red to create the illusion of a strawberry shape. With right sides together, pin and sew the patches in four columns; press seams open.

With right sides together, stitch the columns together, carefully matching the seams; press seams open.

Complete the square With right sides together, pin and sew the hull to the top edge of the strawberry and press seam open. Sew one full-length white rectangle to each side edge; press seams open.

hourglasses

The seam allowance is ¼ inch throughout.

Depending on which way you look, the vibrant colored triangles, all from the same color family, form hourglasses or bow ties. You could also use small prints.

A
B
C
D

Fabric quantities

- Light red fabric A: 6 x 12 inches
- Medium lilac fabric B: 6 x 12 inches
- Dark purple fabric C: 6 x 6 inches
- White fabric D: 16 x 22 inches

Prepare the patches

Rotary method
- From fabrics A and D and fabrics B and D, make two 4½-inch hourglass squares (see page 13) each
- From fabrics C and D, make one 4½-inch hourglass square
- From fabric D, cut four 4½-inch squares

or

Template cutting

Using the 6 x 6 templates (pages 278–83):
- From fabrics A and B, cut 4 medium triangles each
- From fabric C, cut 2 medium triangles
- From fabric D, cut 10 medium triangles and 4 large squares

Template piecing

Right sides together, sew a fabric D triangle to the right short side of of the fabrics A, B, and C triangles; press seams away from fabric D. Join in matching pairs, with triangle points in the center, to make five hourglass squares; press seams open.

Make the block

Make three rows With right sides together, sew a fabrics A and D hourglass square and a fabrics B and D hourglass square to each side of a fabric D square; press seams open. Repeat for the third row. Repeat for the center row using a fabric D square on each side of the fabrics C and D hourglass square.

Complete the square With right sides together, sew the first row to the second row, with the red hourglass in the upper left corner. Join the third row, with the red hourglass in the bottom right corner. Press seams open.

christmas stocking

The seam allowance is ¼ inch throughout.

This festive block is wonderful on its own as a cushion cover or small quilt to hang on the wall. The mixture of pink and dark red creates a rich, jewel-like look, while cool blue polka dots suggest falling snow.

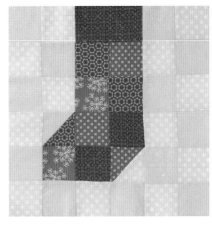

A
A
A
A
B
C

Fabric quantities

- At least 4 different medium and dark red print and pink print fabrics A: 9 x 13 inches in total
- Light blue print fabric B: 9 x 15 inches
- Light blue fabric C: 9 x 15 inches

Prepare the patches

Rotary method
- From fabrics A and B and fabrics A and C, make one 2½-inch half-square triangle (see page 12)
- From fabric A, cut ten 2½-inch squares
- From fabrics B and C, cut twelve 2½-inch squares each

or

Template cutting

Using the 6 x 6 templates (pages 278–83):
- From fabric A, cut 2 small triangles and 10 small squares
- From fabrics B and C, cut 1 small triangle and 12 small squares each

Template piecing

With right sides together, sew a fabric A small triangle to a fabric B small triangle along the long diagonal edge; press seam over fabric A. Repeat with a fabric A triangle and fabric C triangle to make a second half-square triangle.

Make the block

Sew six rows Lay out the patches in six rows of six squares with the red stocking in the center, as shown above, and alternating fabric B and fabric C squares to create a checkerboard background. One row at a time, with right sides together, pin and sew the squares to make six rows. Press the top, third, and fifth row seams to the left; press the second, fourth, and bottom rows to the right.

Complete the square With right sides together, pin and sew the rows together, matching all of the seams; press seams open.

birds in the air

The seam allowance is ¼ inch throughout.

Give a modern twist to this nineteenth-century block by making each of the corner squares a different, vibrant solid color.

A
B
C
D
E
F

Fabric quantities

- Medium turquoise fabric A: 6 x 10 inches
- Medium orange fabric B: 6 x 10 inches
- Medium red fabric C: 6 x 10 inches
- Medium pink fabric D: 6 x 10 inches
- Light green fabric E: 3 x 3 inches
- White fabric F: 12 x 15 inches

Prepare the patches

Template cutting
Using the 7 x 7 templates (pages 284–5)
- From fabrics A, B, C, and D, cut 3 small triangles and 1 large triangle each
- From fabric E, cut 1 small square
- From fabric F, cut 24 small triangles and 4 medium rectangles

Template piecing

With right sides together, sew a small colored triangle to a small white triangle and repeat 11 times to make four sets of three half-square triangles; press seams over the colored fabric.

Make the block

Sew the corner squares First form a large triangle with the smaller triangles. With right sides together, pin and sew two half-square triangles of the same color together sothat the white triangles point in the same direction, as shown above. Sew a white fabric F small triangle to the left end of the row, in the same direction as the other white triangles; press seams over the colored triangles.

With right sides together, sew a fabric F small triangle to the left side of the third half-square triangle, with the white triangles in the same direction, then press seam over the colored fabric. With right sides together, sew these two pieces to the top of the row of half-square triangles, with the edges aligned, and press seam open. With right sides together, sew a fabric F small triangle to the free edge of the colored fabric triangle at the top, forming a large triangle; press seam open.

Join the triangular piece to the large triangle in the same color, forming a square.

Repeat to make three additional sets of half-square triangles and large triangle.

Make the top and bottom rows Arrange the completed squares in the final order. With right sides together, sew one fabric F rectangle to one long edge of a large triangle. Join a second square to the other side of the fabric F rectangle, making sure both large triangles point toward the center; press seams over the rectangles.

Repeat with the remaining squares to make the opposite row.

Join the center row With right sides together, sew two more fabric F rectangles to each side of the small fabric E square; press seams over the rectangles.

Complete the square With right sides together, carefully match the seams and join the top row to the center row; press seam open. Repeat to join the bottom row to the center row.

checkerboard

The seam allowance is ¼ inch throughout.

This classic checkerboard pattern looks fresh and modern when you alternate eight different patches in the same color with a soft, solid complementary color.

Fabric quantities

- Up to 8 different dark red print fabrics A: 8 x 16 inches in total
- Light blue fabric B: 8 x 16 inches

Prepare the patches

Rotary method
- From fabrics A and B, cut eight 3½-inch squares each

or

Template cutting
Using the 4 x 4 templates (pages 269–73):
- From fabrics A and B, cut 8 small squares each

Make the block

Make four rows Arrange the squares in four rows of four patches, alternating colors, in a balanced arrangement. With right sides together, pin and sew the squares into four rows; press seams toward the red fabric.

Complete the square With right sides together, pin and sew the first row to the second row. Pin and sew the third row to the second row, then the fourth row to the third row. Press seams open.

- -

triangles

The seam allowance is ¼ inch throughout.

Half-square triangles are one of the basic units of patchwork. They can be as modern and elegant or as traditional and folksy as the fabrics you choose. This block goes for a sophisticated look by pairing floral prints from the same color palette with crisp white.

Fabric quantities

- At least 8 different medium and dark red and pink print fabrics A: 10 x 20 inches in total
- White fabric B: 10 x 20 inches

Prepare the patches

Rotary method
- From fabrics A and B, make sixteen 3½-inch half-square triangles (see page 12) each

or

Template cutting
Using the 4 x 4 templates (pages 269–73):
- From fabrics A and B, cut 16 small triangles each

Template piecing

With right sides together, pin and sew one fabric A triangle to each fabric B triangle; press seams open. Repeat to make another 15 half-square triangles.

Make the block

Sew four rows Arrange the half-square triangles in four rows of four squares, being careful to balance the colors. With right sides together, pin and sew four squares into one row; press seams to the left. Repeat to sew three more rows, pressing seams of the second and fourth row to the right and the seams of the third row to the left.

Complete the square With right sides together and carefully matching seams, pin and sew the first row and the third row to the second, and the fourth row to the third. Press seams open.

scottie dog

The seam allowance is ¼ inch throughout.

This terrier is a figurative block that harkens back to the 1930s with an angular Art Deco look. If any of your fabric is directional, like the tree print used here, make sure you cut all of your pieces on the vertical grain.

A
B
C
D

Fabric quantities

- Medium gray print fabric A: 10 x 18 inches
- White print fabric B: 12 x 14 inches
- Dark red print fabric C: 4 x 4 inches
- Dark green print fabric D: 13 x 3 inches

Prepare the patches

Rotary method
- From fabrics A and B, make four 2½-inch half-square triangles (see page 12) for the tail, ear, and snout
- From fabrics B and C, make one 2½-inch half-square triangle for one half of the bow tie
- From fabrics A, B, and C, make one 2½-inch three-quarter square triangle (see page 13) for the other half of the bow tie
- From fabric A, cut three 2-inch squares and one 6½ x 4½-inch rectangle for the body
- From fabric B, cut one 4½-inch square, three 2½-inch squares, and two 6½ x 2½-inch rectangles for the background
- From fabric D, cut one 12½ x 2½-inch rectangle for the grass

or

Template cutting
Using the 6 x 6 templates (pages 278–83):
- From fabric A, cut 1 wide medium rectangle, 3 small squares, 4 small triangles, and 1 tiny triangle
- From fabric B, cut 1 large square, 2 long rectangles, 3 small squares, 5 small triangles, and 1 tiny triangle
- From fabric C, cut 2 small triangles
- From fabric D, cut 1 full-length rectangle

Template piecing

Pair the fabric B small triangles with fabric A and C small triangles to make five half-square triangles. Combine the remaining fabric C small triangle with the two tiny triangles to make one three-quarter square triangle; press seams open.

Make the block

Arrange the patches Lay out the patches as shown above, using the fabric A small squares at the center of the dog's head and for its legs and the half-square triangles as the dog's tail, ear, snout, and bow tie.

Sew the body With right sides together, pin and sew one fabric A small square to each side of one fabric B small square; press seams open. Join the strip to the lower edge of the body.

With right sides together, pin and sew the tail patch to one fabric B square. Join one bow-tie patch to the other side of the fabric B square, then stitch the strip to the top of the body; press seams open.

Join the background strips With right sides together, pin and sew one fabric B long rectangle to the left edge of the dog; press seam open. Repeat to join the remaining fabric B long rectangle to the top edge.

Sew the head Starting at the top of the dog's head, join the six head squares in pairs: ear to one fabric B small square; fabric A small square to the top of the snout; bow tie to the bottom of the snout. Press seams open. With right sides together, pin and sew the three pairs. Join the fabric B large square to the bottom edge; press seams open.

Complete the square With right sides together, pin together the head and body sections. Sew, then press seam open. Join the fabric D full-length rectangle to the lower edge; press seam downward.

stacked squares

The seam allowance is ¼ inch throughout.

This bold, graphic design is even more modern when rendered in strong geometric prints and vibrant colors. Float just a few stacked squares across a solid background or repeat in vertical rows for an all-over pattern of square towers.

Fabric quantities

- Dark red print fabric A: 7 x 9 inches
- Medium red print fabric B: 7 x 9 inches
- White fabric C: 10 x 16 inches

Prepare the patches

Rotary method
- From fabrics A and B, cut two 2½-inch squares and two 6½ x 2½-inch rectangles each
- From fabric C, cut two 4½ x 6½-inch rectangles, two 6½ x 2½-inch rectangles, and two 2½-inch squares

or

Template cutting

Using the 6 x 6 templates (pages 278–83):
- From fabrics A and B, cut 2 small squares and 2 medium rectangles each
- From fabric C, cut 2 small squares, 2 medium rectangles, and 2 wide medium rectangles

Make the block

Sew the squares With right sides together, pin and sew the two fabric A small squares to each side of a fabric C small square; press seams over fabric A. Join the two fabric A medium rectangles to the side edges of the strip; press seams over fabric A. Repeat with fabrics B and C.

Make two rows With right sides together, pin and sew the fabric C medium rectangles to the left sides of each square. Join the fabric C wide medium rectangles to the right sides.

Complete the square Rotate one row so that the narrow fabric C rectangle is on the bottom right, as shown above. With right sides together, pin and sew the two rows together; press seam upward.

---

sliver strips

The seam allowance is ¼ inch throughout.

Mix your smallest and most treasured scraps with a neutral background color. Mixed widths and odd cuts make this block especially dynamic. Because this is an improvisational block, it is easily made with the rotary method.

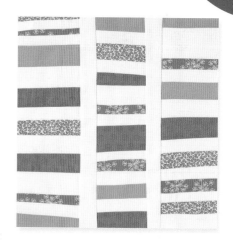

Fabric quantities

- At least 4 different medium pink and red print fabrics A: at least 3½ inches long each
- White fabric B: 14 x 14 inches

Prepare the patches

Rotary method
- From fabric A, cut twenty-three 3½-inch strips, between ¾ inch and 2 inches wide
- From fabric B, cut twenty-one 3½-inch strips, between ¾ inch and 2 inches wide, and two 1½ x 12½-inch strips

Make the block

Sew the columns With right sides together, alternate colors and widths, joining fabric A and fabric B strips to make 12½ x 3½-inch columns; press seams open.

Complete the square With right sides together, sew one column to each side of a fabric B 12½-inch-long strip. Join the second fabric B 12½-inch-long strip to the remaining column, then sew the two pieces together; press seams open.

17

string-pieced squares

The seam allowance is ¼ inch throughout.

Another thrifty block, this time made from the narrowest of random leftover strips. Save your long scraps in a bag as you work on other projects, then join together short lengths to make colorful patches. Adding in a few especially dark solids gives definition and pop to each block. Because this is an improvisational block, it is easily made with the rotary method.

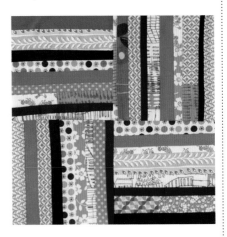

Fabric quantities

- A variety of dark and medium solid and print fabrics A: each piece at least ¾ inch wide and 6½ inches long each

Prepare the patches

Rotary method
- Cut the different fabrics into narrow strips, each ¾ inch to 1½ inches wide and 6½ inches long. You need eight to ten strips per 6½-inch square patch.

Make the block

Piece four patches With right sides together, pin and sew enough fabric A strips to measure just wider than the length of the strips, then trim to make a 6½-inch square; press seams open. Alternatively, you can use the large 4 x 4 square template on page 273 to measure each patch. Repeat to make another three squares.

Make two rows Pin and sew two of the squares together, with the stripes running in alternate directions. Repeat to make the second row. Press seams over the long edge of the final strip.

Complete the square Pin and sew the top and bottom row, keeping the stripes running in opposite directions. Clip into the center seam allowance to remove some bulk (do not go into the seam); press all seams over the straight edges.

18

nine-patch square

The seam allowance is ¼ inch throughout.

The Nine-Patch Square is the most basic quilt block, but the design possibilities are endless. Make it scrappy with eight different prints and colors, choose a monochrome palette, or try an ombre design. Tie all of the patches in one quilt together with the same center square.

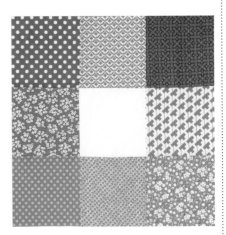

Fabric quantities

- 8 different medium red print fabrics A: 5 x 5 inches each
- White fabric B: 5 x 5 inches

Prepare the patches

Rotary method
- From fabrics A, cut eight 4½-inch squares
- From fabric B, cut one 4½-inch square

or

Template cutting
Using the 6 x 6 templates (pages 278–83):
- From fabrics A, cut 8 large squares
- From fabric B, cut 1 large square

Make the block

Make three rows With right sides together, pin and sew three of the fabric A large squares to make the top row; press seams open. Repeat to make the bottom row. To make the middle row, pin and sew the remaining two fabric A large squares to each side of the fabric B large square; press seams open.

Complete the square With right sides together and being careful to match the seams, pin and sew the top row to the middle row; press seam open. Join the bottom row to the middle row, then press seam open.

A

A

A

A

A

A

A

A

A

B

34

little prairie house

This is a scrappy take on the traditional folk art schoolhouse block. Make several house picture blocks to create your street in a quilt, or just make one to resemble your home on a cushion for your child's bedroom.

The seam allowance is ¼ inch throughout.

Fabric quantities

- Dark turquoise fabric A: 8 x 6 inches
- Medium turquoise fabric B: 5 x 14 inches
- Dark red fabric C: 7 x 10 inches
- Dark orange print fabric D: 5 x 7 inches
- Medium red fabric E: 3 x 6 inches
- White fabric F: 8 x 10 inches

Prepare the patches

Template cutting
Using the 6 x 6 templates (pages 278–83):
- From fabric A, cut 3 small squares and 1 right half triangle
- From fabric B, cut 3 small squares, 1 right half triangle, and 1 isosceles triangle
- From fabric C, cut 1 wide medium rectangle, 1 medium rectangle, and 1 small square
- From fabric D, cut 1 wide medium rectangle
- From fabric E, cut 2 small squares
- From fabric F, cut 2 small squares, 2 short rectangles, 1 left half triangle, and 1 right half triangle

A
B
C
D
E
F

Make the block

Join the chimneys With right sides together, pin and sew one fabric C small square to one fabric F small square. Sew the other fabric F small square to the fabric E small square; press seams open. Join both strips to each side of one fabric F short rectangle, with the red squares abutting the rectangle. Press seams open.

Sew the roof With right sides together, pin and sew three fabrics A and B small squares in a row, alternating colors; press seams open. Repeat with the remaining three fabrics A and B small squares. Carefully match seams and join the two rows, creating a checkerboard pattern; press seam open.

With right sides together, pin and sew the fabric B right half-triangle to the fabric F right half-triangle along the diagonal; press seam open. Join the rectangle to the right side of the checkerboard patch.

With right sides together, pin and sew the fabric A right half-triangle to the right side of the fabric B isosceles triangle and the fabric F left half-triangle to the other side, forming a square; press seams open. Join the square to the left side of the checkerboard patch.

Make the main house With right sides together, pin and sew the remaining fabric E small square to the end of the fabric F short rectangle; press seam open. With the small square at the top, join the fabric C medium rectangle to the right edge of the strip. Press seam open.

With right sides together, pin and sew the fabric C and fabric D wide medium rectangles along the long sides, then pin and sew to the three-piece patch that includes the door; press seam open.

Complete the square With right sides together, pin and sew the chimney row to the roof row, being careful to match seams; press seam open. Repeat to sew the house row to the roof row.

robin

A mosaic of patches creates a perky robin block, ideal for a festive quilt.

The seam allowance is ¼ inch throughout.

A
B
C
D
E
F
G

Fabric quantities

- Medium brown fabric A: 8 x 12 inches
- Dark purple fabric B: 5 x 9 inches
- Medium red fabric C: 3 x 3 inches
- Medium yellow fabric D: 3 x 3 inches
- White fabric E: 4 x 4 inches
- Light blue fabric F: 13 x 18 inches
- Dark purple fabric G: 13 x 18 inches

Prepare the patches

Rotary method

- From fabric A, make one 2½-inch square
- From fabrics A and C and fabrics C and F, make a 4½-inch corner square (see page 14) each
- From fabrics A and F, make three 2½-inch half-square triangles (see page 12)
- From fabrics A, B, and F, make a 4½-inch hexagon square (see page 15)
- From fabrics A and E and fabrics B and F, make a 2½-inch half-square triangle (see page 12) each
- From fabrics D and F, make a 4½ x 2½-inch right tapered rectangle
- From fabric F, cut one 4½ x 2½-inch rectangle, two 2½-inch squares, and two 12½ x 2½-inch rectangles
- From fabric G, cut two 2½ x 1-inch rectangles

or

Template cutting

Using the 6 x 6 templates (pages 278–83):
- From fabric A, cut 1 corner square, 5 small triangles, and 1 small square
- From fabric B, cut 1 hexagon and 1 small triangle
- From fabric C, cut 2 small triangles
- From fabrics D and E, cut 1 small triangle each
- From fabric F, cut 1 corner square, 1 right tapered rectangle, 2 full-length rectangles, 1 short rectangle, 2 small squares, and 5 small triangles
- From fabric G, cut 2 narrow very small rectangles

Template piecing

With right sides together, sew a fabric C triangle to the fabric A corner square; press seam open. Repeat with a fabric C triangle and fabric F corner square.

With right sides together, sew one fabric F triangle and one fabric A triangle to the fabric B hexagon to make the hexagon square; press seams open.

With right sides together, sew the fabric D triangle to the fabric F right tapered rectangle; press seam open.

With right sides together, sew a fabric F triangle to a fabric A triangle; press seam open. Repeat with two more sets of fabrics F and A triangles, a set of fabrics F and B triangles, and a set of fabrics A and E triangles to make half-square triangles.

Make the block

Sew the head and breast Arrange patches to make a robin. With right sides together, join the beak to the head; press seam open. With right sides together, join the fabrics A and E half-square triangle to a fabrics A and F half-square triangle, with the white and brown fabrics abutting; press seam open. Join the strip to the fabrics C and F corner square; press seam open. With right sides together, join the head and beak to the breast; press seam open.

Make the body With right sides together, sew the fabrics B and F half-square triangle to a fabric F square, matching the background; press seam open. Join to the hexagon square to form the wing; press seam open. With right sides together, pin and sew a fabrics A and F half-square triangle to the short side of a fabric F short rectangle, matching the background; press seam open, then join to top of the wing. Right sides together, sew fabric A and fabric F squares to fabric A and F half-square triangle, matching the background and body; press seam open; then join to bottom of the wing.

Complete the square With right sides together, pin and sew the wing to the head and breast patch; press seam open. Appliqué (see page 20) the fabric G narrow very small rectangles to a fabric F full-length rectangle as the legs, then sew the strip to the bottom edge of the bird. With right sides together, pin and sew the remaining fabric F full-length rectangle to the top edge. Press seam open.

coffee cup

The seam allowance is ¼ inch throughout.

Use graphic prints for a retro 1950s café look, complete with checkered tablecloth, or pick a floral fabric to give Coffee Cup a chintzy tea room feel. Make sure to cut all of the background pieces so that the pattern runs in the same direction.

Fabric quantities

- Dark red fabric A: 9 x 11 inches
- Black print fabric B: 6 x 9 inches
- Medium gray print fabric C: 8 x 16 inches
- Dark red print fabric D: 6 x 9 inches

Prepare the patches

Rotary method
- From fabric A, cut one 4½-inch square and six 2½-inch squares
- From fabrics B and C, make one 8½ x 2½-in long boat (see page 17)
- From fabric C, cut two 6½ x 4½-inch rectangles and one 4½ x 2½-inch rectangle
- From fabric D, cut six 2½-inch squares
- From fabric B, cut one handle using the template on page 286

or

Template cutting
Using the 6 x 6 templates (pages 278–83):
- From fabric A, cut 1 large square and 6 small squares
- From fabric B, cut 1 long boat plus 1 handle using the template on page 286
- From fabric C, cut 2 wide medium rectangles, 1 short rectangle, 2 small squares, and 2 small triangles
- From fabric D, cut 6 small squares

Template piecing

With right sides together, pin and sew the fabric C small triangles to the corresponding diagonal sides on the fabric B long boat; press seams open.

A
B
C
D

Make the block

Sew the cup With right sides together, pin and sew the short fabric C rectangle to the top edge of the fabric A large square. Appliqué (see page 20) the handle to one fabric C medium rectangle, then, matching the edges of the handle, join the rectangle to the right edge of the fabric A square. Sew the remaining fabric C medium rectangle to the left edge of the fabric A square; press seams open.

Make the saucer With right sides together, pin and sew the fabric C small squares to either side of the long boat; press seams open. With right sides together, the fabrics B and C long boat strip to the bottom edge of the cup; press seam open.

Make the tablecloth With right sides together, pin and sew six alternating fabrics A and D small squares to create a checkerboard pattern; press seams over all fabric A squares. Repeat with the remaining squares to make the second row, making sure to continue the checkerboard pattern with the row above. With right sides together and matching seams, join the two rows; press seam open.

Complete the square With right sides together, pin and sew the cup and saucer patch to the tablecloth patch; press seam open.

tee block

Quilt doyenne Nancy Cabot published this block in the *Chicago Tribune* in 1938, but it dates back to the nineteenth century. Update this traditional block by using a different solid fabric for each "T" shape. Made from standard units —half-square triangles, flying geese, and one diamond square—this block looks more complicated than it actually is.

A
B
C
D
E

Fabric quantities

- Medium orange fabric A: 6 x 12 inches
- Medium lilac fabric B: 6 x 12 inches
- Medium pink fabric C: 6 x 12 inches
- Medium red fabric D: 6 x 12 inches
- White fabric E: 18 x 24 inches

Prepare the patches

Rotary method
- From fabrics A and E; fabrics B and E; fabrics C and E; and fabrics D and E, make one 4½-inch half-square triangle (see page 12) each

- From fabrics A, B, and E; fabrics B, C, and E; fabrics C, D, and E; and fabrics D, A, and E, make two 4½ x 2½-inch flying geese rectangles (see page 17) each

- From fabrics A, B, C, D, and E, make one 4½-inch diamond square (see page 15)

or

Template cutting
Using the 6 x 6 templates (pages 278–83):
- From fabrics A, B, C, and D, cut 1 large triangle and 5 small triangles each

- From fabric E, cut 4 large triangles, 8 medium triangles, and 1 diamond square

Template piecing

With right sides together, pin and sew the large colored triangles to the large white triangles to make one half-square triangle in each color; press seams open.

With right sides together, pin and sew one fabric A small triangle and one fabric B small triangle to the diagonal sides of one fabric E medium triangle; press seams open. Repeat with the other fabrics A and B small triangles to make the second flying geese unit. Repeat to make two sets of flying geese units for each color combination: fabrics B and C, fabrics C and D, and fabrics D and A. With right sides together, pin and sew the matching sets of flying geese units; press seams open.

With right sides together, pin and sew the remaining small colored fabric triangles to each side of the fabric E diamond square; press seams open.

Make the block

Sew three rows To make the top row, pin and sew the orange, lilac, and white patches together, making sure the flying geese patch is in the middle and carefully matching seams; press seams open.

To make the middle row, repeat with the orange, red, pink, and lilac patches. Make sure the diamond square is in the middle and carefully match seams; press seams open.

To make the bottom row, repeat with the red, pink, and white patches, making sure the flying geese patch is in the middle and carefully matching seams; press seams open.

Complete the square With right sides together, pin and sew the top row to the middle row, carefully matching seams; press seam open. Repeat to sew the bottom row to the middle row.

stretched nine patch

The seam allowance is ¼ inch throughout.

This beginner block is a good choice to practice matching up the seams at square corners. If you choose a figurative print like these splashy flowers, fussy cut (see page 10) the patches so that your framed center square has an interesting design.

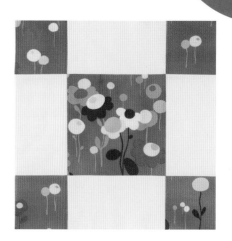

Fabric quantities

- Dark red print fabric A: 11 x 12 inches
- Cream fabric B: 8 x 14 inches

Prepare the patches

Rotary method
- From fabric A, cut one 6½-inch square and four 3½-inch squares
- From fabric B, cut four 6½ x 3½-inch rectangles

or

Template cutting
Using the 4 x 4 templates (pages 269–73):
- From fabric A, cut 1 large square and 4 small squares
- From fabric B, cut 4 short rectangles

Make the block

Sew three rows With right sides together, pin and sew two short fabric B rectangles to each side of the large fabric A square; press seams over the square.

With right sides together, pin and sew two small fabric A squares to each of the remaining fabric B short rectangles; press seams over the squares.

Complete the square With right sides together, pin and sew the two narrower strips to the long edges of the middle row, carefully matching the seams; press seams open.

equal stripes

The seam allowance is ¼ inch throughout.

This is possibly the most straightforward block you can sew, perfect for the first-time quilter. Simply join six strips together, choosing different patterns that use similar colors.

Fabric quantities

- Light pink fabric A: 3 x 13 inches
- Light pink print fabric B: 3 x 13 inches
- Medium pink fabric C: 3 x 13 inches
- Medium pink print fabric D: 3 x 13 inches
- Dark purple fabric E: 3 x 13 inches
- Dark red print fabric F: 3 x 13 inches

Prepare the patches

Rotary method
- From fabrics A , B, C, D, E, and F, cut one 12½ x 2½-inch rectangle each

Make the block

Join the first strips With right sides together, pin and sew the long edge of the fabric A rectangle to the long edge of the fabric B rectangle; press seam open.

Complete the square Repeat, joining fabric C to fabric B, fabric D to fabric C, fabric E to fabric D, and fabric F to fabric E. Stitch each seam in the opposite direction to avoid any bowing of the fabric.

windmill

In this entry-level block, four identical squares are rotated and joined together. You could keep it simple by using only solids, but here a plain fabric is paired with a pattern for more interest. Using a striped print adds a sense of movement that is well-suited to the block's name.

The seam allowance is ¼ inch throughout.

Fabric quantities

- Medium red print fabric A: 7 x 16 inches
- Dark red fabric B: 7 x 16 inches

Prepare the patches

Rotary method
- From fabrics A and B, make four 6½-inch rectangle squares (see page 11)

or

Template cutting
Using the 4 x 4 templates (pages 269–73):
- From fabrics A and B, cut 4 short rectangles each

Template piecing

With right sides together, pin and sew the long edges of rectangles A and B together, making sure the pattern of the print lies in the same direction for each square to make four rectangle squares; press seams open.

Make the block

Sew two rows With right sides together, pin two squares together, lining up one long print side with one short print side. Sew and press seams open. Repeat with the remaining two squares.

Complete the square Flip one row. With right sides together, pin and sew the two rows together so the print fabric strips are all touching, matching the center seams. Press seams open.

---

robbing peter to pay paul

The seam allowance is ¼ inch throughout.

This block is made in exactly the same way as Diagonal Cross on page 120, but the top and bottom halves are stitched together along the opposite edges for a different look. Joining several blocks edge to edge as an allover repeat creates a dramatic counterchange pattern.

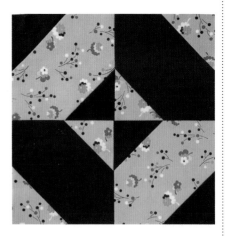

Fabric quantities

- Dark purple fabric A: 7 x 17 inches
- Medium gray print fabric B: 7 x 17 inches

Prepare the patches

Rotary method
- From fabrics A and B, make two 6½-inch hexagon squares (see page 15) with A in the center and two 6½-inch hexagon squares with B in the center

or

Template cutting
Using the 4 x 4 templates (pages 269–73):
- From fabrics A and B, cut 2 hexagons and 4 small triangles each

Template piecing

With right sides together, pin two fabric A small triangles to the diagonal edges of each fabric B hexagon and sew; press seams over the triangles. Join the fabric B small triangles to the fabric A hexagons in the same way, but press seams over the hexagons.

Make the block

Sew two rows With right sides together, pin a light quarter square with a dark quarter square so that the triangles meet at the inside bottom corner, making sure the seams match. Sew; press seams toward the darker fabric. Repeat with the remaining two quarter squares.

Complete the square With right sides together, pin and sew the two halves together with the small triangles meeting in the center, making sure the seams match. Sew; press seam open.

log cabin corner

The seam allowance is ¼ inch throughout.

This variation is also known as the Chevron or Quarter Log Cabin. Like the traditional Log Cabin block, it starts from the small dark square, joining fabric strips alternately to the top and left edges. You could use two different sets of color families when making each block and then join these squares together in different ways to create various patterns with great feelings of depth. This geometric block is easily made using the rotary method.

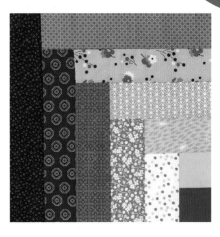

Fabric quantities

- 6 different medium and dark red or red print and solid fabrics A: 3 inches wide and 3 to 13 inches long

- 5 different light and medium blue or blue print and solid fabrics B: 3 inches wide and 3 to 11½ inches long

Prepare the patches

Rotary method
- From fabrics A, cut one 2½-inch square, one 4½ x 2½-inch rectangle, one 6½ x 2½-inch rectangle, one 8½ x 2½-inch rectangle, one 10½ x 2½-inch rectangle, and one 12½ x 2½-inch rectangle

- From fabrics B, cut one 2½-inch square, one 4½ x 2½-inch rectangle, one 6½ x 2½-inch rectangle, one 8½ x 2½-inch rectangle, and one 10½ x 2½-inch rectangle

Make the block

Join the small squares With right sides together, pin and sew the fabric B small square to the top edge of the fabric A small square; press seam up toward fabric B.

Complete the square With right sides together, sew the fabric A shortest rectangle to the left edge of the squares; press seam over the rectangle. Sew the fabric B shortest rectangle to top edge of the patch; press seam over rectangle. Continue in this way until all of the rectangles have been sewn together, always pressing the seam over the last-joined piece.

---

crown of thorns

The seam allowance is ¼ inch throughout.

Another classic block, this has acquired several other names over the decades, including Mill Wheel, Georgetown Circle, and the endearing Nest and Fledglings.

Fabric quantities

- Medium pink fabric A: 10 x 12 inches
- Medium green fabric B: 9 x 9 inches
- Light green fabric C: 5 x 9 inches
- White fabric D: 14 x 16 inches

Prepare the patches

Template cutting
Using the 5 x 5 templates (pages 274–7):
- From fabric A, cut 4 small triangles and 4 small squares
- From fabric B, cut 8 small triangles
- From fabric C, cut 4 small triangles
- From fabric D, cut 16 small triangles and 5 small squares

Template piecing

With right sides together, pin and sew a fabric D small triangle to each of the fabrics A, B, and C small triangles along the long diagonal edge to make 16 half-square triangles (see page 12); press seams toward the darker fabric.

Make the block

Sew the center row Pin and sew five alternating fabric A and fabric D small squares together; press all seams over fabric A.

Make the second and fourth rows With right sides together, sew a fabrics A and D half-square triangle to each side of a fabric A small square, with pink edges together; press seams over the square. Sew a fabrics B and D half-square triangle to each end, with a medium green edge to a white edge; press seams over fabric B.

Sew top and bottom rows With right sides together, sew a fabrics B and D half-square triangle to each side of a fabric D small square, with a green edge to a white edge; press seams over fabric B. Pin and sew a fabrics C and D half-square triangle to each end, with a light green edge to a white edge; press seams over fabric C.

Complete the square Pin and sew the first row to the second row, lining up the seams; press seams open. Repeat to join the third row to the second row, the fourth row to the third row, and the fifth row to the fourth row.

cross weave

A
B
C
D
E

Essentially four Log Cabin squares, this is a deceptively easy block to make, with only one seam to match at the center. Join multiple blocks of the same colors edge to edge to create complex designs of interwoven stripes.

Fabric quantities

- Dark red fabric A: 6 x 7 inches
- Light red fabric B: 6 x 7 inches
- Dark purple fabric C: 6 x 7 inches
- Medium orange fabric D: 6 x 7 inches
- White fabric E: 10 x 10 inches

Prepare the patches

Rotary method
- From fabrics A, B, C, and D, cut one 6½ x 2½-inch rectangle and one 4½ x 2½-inch rectangle each
- From fabric E, cut four 4½-inch squares

or

Template cutting
Using the 6 x 6 templates (pages 278–83):
- From fabrics A, B, C, and D, cut 4 short rectangles and 4 medium rectangles each
- From fabric E, cut 4 large squares

Make the block

Piece four patches With right sides together, sew a fabric A, B, C, and D short rectangle to the top of each fabric E square; press seams toward the rectangle. Sew a fabric A medium rectangle to the right long edge of the fabric D and E patch; press seam over rectangle. Repeat to make the remaining squares, joining a fabric B medium rectangle to the fabrics C and E patch; the fabric C medium rectangle to the fabrics A and E patch; and the fabric D medium rectangle to the fabrics B and E patch.

Complete the square With right sides together, sew the fabrics C, A, and E block to the fabrics B, C, and E block, with the fabrics A and B edges touching. Sew the fabrics A, D, and E block to the fabrics D, B, and E block, with fabrics A and B touching. With right sides together, sew the two rows with fabric C and D touching, matching the center seam; press all seams open.

hole in the barn door

A
B

A variation of the Churn Dash block on page 152, Hole in the Barn Door is a good showcase for quilted designs inside the red frame. The center square also offers an opportunity for fussy cutting (see page 10) a favorite print.

Fabric quantities

- Dark pink fabric A: 10 x 14 inches
- White print fabric B: 14 x 17 inches

Prepare the patches

Rotary method
- From fabrics A and B, make four 3½-inch half-square triangles (see page 12)
- From fabric A, cut four 6½ x 2-inch rectangles
- From fabric B, cut four 6½ x 2-inch rectangles and one 6½-inch square

Make the block

Piece four patches With right sides together, pin and sew a fabric A rectangle to a fabric B rectangle along the long edge; press seam over fabric A. Repeat to make three more sets of strips.

Make the rows For the top row, pin and sew a fabrics A and B half-square triangle to each short side of a fabrics A and B rectangle, with the pink triangles pointing outward and the pink strip on the bottom, as shown above. Repeat to make the bottom row. With right sides together, pin and sew the remaining fabrics A and B strips to opposite sides of the fabric B large square, making sure the pink rectangles abut the center square; press seams toward fabric A.

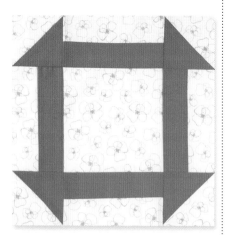

Complete the square Sew the top row to the middle row along the pink edge, lining up the seams. Flip the bottom row and sew to the middle row along the pink edge, lining up the seams. Press all seams toward fabric A.

framed pinwheel

The seam allowance is ¼ inch throughout.

Four half-square triangles come together to form a dynamic pinwheel.
The bright frame adds a splash of color.

A
B
C

Fabric quantities

- Light blue print fabric A: 6 x 12 inches
- Dark brown print fabric B: 6 x 12 inches
- Dark pink print fabric C: 12 x 13 inches

Prepare the patches

Rotary method
- From fabrics A and B, make four 4½-inch half-square triangles (see page 12)
- From fabric C, cut two 12½ x 2½-inch rectangles and two 8½ x 2½-inch rectangles

or

Template cutting
Using the 6 x 6 templates (pages 278–83):
- From fabrics A and B, cut 4 large triangles each
- From fabric C, cut 2 full-length and 2 long rectangles

Template piecing

With right sides together, sew a fabric A large triangle to a fabric B large triangle along the long diagonal edge; press seam over dark fabric B. Repeat to make another three half-square triangles.

Make the block

Piece the pinwheel square Pin and sew two half-square triangles together, joining a dark edge to a light edge; press seam toward the dark fabric. Repeat to make the second row. With right sides together, join the rows along the long edge, with the light fabric touching the dark fabric and lining up seams; press seams open.

Make the border With right sides together, sew the fabric C long rectangles to opposite sides of the pinwheel square, then sew the fabric C full-length rectangles to the top and bottom of the square. Press seams over fabric C, away from the pinwheel square.

---

counterchange

The seam allowance is ¼ inch throughout.

Though the parti-colored center design is the focus of each block,
Counterchange works particularly well when repeated edge to edge, creating
a repeat of two colored crosses. If you make each square in a different color
palette, be sure to keep a strong contrast between the light and dark fabrics.

A
B

Fabric quantities

- Dark red fabric A: 8 x 15 inches
- Dark orange print fabric B: 8 x 15 inches

Prepare the patches

Rotary method
- From fabrics A and B, make two 6½-inch three-patch squares (see page 11), using fabric A as the long rectangles
- From fabrics A and B, make two 6½-inch three-patch squares, using fabric B as the long rectangles

or

Template cutting
Using the 4 x 4 templates (pages 269–73):
- From fabrics A and B, cut 2 short rectangles and 4 small squares each

Template piecing

With right sides together, sew a fabric A small square and fabric B small square together; press seam over the darker fabric. Repeat to make another three pairs. Pin and sew one set of squares to the long edge of each rectangle, keeping fabric A on the lower left each time, then complete the three-patch squares; press seams open.

Make the block

Sew two rows As shown above, pin and sew two blocks together, with the small squares at the center and lining up the seams. Repeat for the bottom row.

Complete the square With right sides together, pin and sew the two rows together along the length of the small squares, lining up the seams; press all seams open.

massachusetts

The seam allowance is ¼ inch throughout.

This historic pattern represents the U.S. state of Massachusetts. It has an interesting counterchange design that swaps the light and dark patches in each half.

A
B
C
D

Fabric quantities

- Dark red fabric A: 6 x 18 inches
- Medium orange fabric B: 6 x 12 inches
- Medium yellow fabric C: 6 x 12 inches
- White fabric D: 12 x 18 inches

Prepare the patches

Rotary method
- From fabrics A and D and fabrics C and D, make two 4½-inch hourglass squares (see page 13) each
- From fabrics B and D, make three 4½-inch half-square triangles (see page 12)
- From fabrics A and D, cut one 4½-inch square each

or

Template cutting
Using the 6 x 6 templates (pages 278–83):
- From fabric A, cut 1 large square and 4 medium triangles
- From fabric B, cut 3 large triangles
- From fabric C, cut 4 medium triangles
- From fabric D, cut 1 large square, 3 large triangles, and 8 medium triangles

Template piecing

With right sides together, pin and sew a fabric A medium triangle to a fabric D medium triangle along a short diagonal edge; repeat with a second pair, reversing colors. Press seams open. Join the pairs, making an hourglass square. Repeat to make a second fabrics A and D hourglass square and to make two hourglass squares with fabrics C and D.

With right sides together, pin and sew three fabric B large triangles and fabric D large triangles to make three half-square triangles; press seams open.

Make the block

Join the rows For the bottom row, pin and sew the fabric A square to a matching hourglass square, with a fabric A triangle on top. Join a fabric B half-square triangle to the right side of the hourglass strip, with a fabric B triangle on top; press seams open.

For the middle row, join a fabric A hourglass square to a fabric B half-square triangle, with a fabric A triangle on the left and a fabric B triangle on top. Join a fabric C hourglass square to the half-square triangle, with a fabric C triangle on top; press seams open.

For the top row, join a fabric B half-square triangle to one side of a fabric C hourglass square, with the fabric B triangle on the bottom and a fabric C triangle on the left. Join the fabric D square to the hourglass square; press seams open.

Complete the square With right sides together, pin and sew the first row to the middle row, carefully matching the seams. Sew the top row to the middle row. Press seams open.

squared up

This smart square-within-a-square pattern is less complicated than it appears. It's easy to piece, but it lends itself to myriad color and print combinations.

The seam allowance is ¼ inch throughout.

A
B
C
D

Fabric quantities

- Light pink print fabric A: 6 x 6 inches
- Medium red fabric B: 8 x 12 inches
- Dark purple fabric C: 5 x 12 inches
- White fabric D: 10 x 12 inches

Prepare the patches

Rotary method
- From fabrics A and B, make four 4½-inch three-patch squares (see page 11)
- From fabrics C and D, make four 4½-inch rectangle squares (see page 11)
- From fabric D, cut one 4½-inch square

or

Template cutting
Using the 6 x 6 templates (pages 278–83):
- From fabric A, cut 4 small squares
- From fabric B, cut 4 small squares and 4 short rectangles
- From fabric C, cut 4 short rectangles
- From fabric D, cut 4 short rectangles and 1 large square

Template piecing

With right sides together, sew a fabric A small square to each of the fabric B small squares together; press seams open. Join the fabric B short rectangles to one long edge of each strip, with the pink square is at the top left corner, to make three three-patch squares; press seams open.

With right sides together, pin and sew the fabric B short rectangles and fabric C short rectangles together in pairs, along the long edges, to make four rectangle squares; press seams over fabric C.

Make the block

Sew three rows With right sides together, pin a three-patch square to each side of a fabrics C and D patch, with the pink squares in the center and aligned with the purple fabric; press seams open. Repeat for the third row. With right sides together, pin and sew a fabrics C and D patch to each side of the fabric D large square; press seams open.

Complete the square With right sides together, join the rows, with the purple rectangles forming a frame around the center square; press seams open.

double nine patch

This twist on the familiar nine patch features a block-within-a-block. You can use a mixture of prints and solids, but solids work best for the center square. This block is easily made with the rotary method.

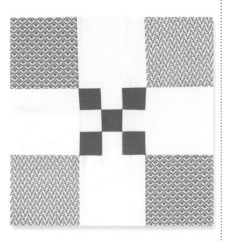

The seam allowance is ¼ inch throughout.

Fabric quantities

- Medium red fabric A: 6 x 8 inches
- At least 2 different medium red print fabrics B: 10 x 10 inches each
- White fabric C: 10 x 15 inches

Prepare the patches

Rotary method
- From fabric A, cut five 1¾-inch squares
- From fabric B, cut four 4½-inch squares
- From fabric C, cut four 4½-inch squares and four 1¾-inch squares

Make the block

Sew the center square Beginning with fabric A, pin and sew the tiny squares together in three rows of three, alternating colors; press seams over fabric A. Pin and sew the rows together along the long edges; press open.

Make three rows For the center row, with right sides together, join a fabric C large square to each side of the checkerboard center square; press seams over fabric C.

For the top and bottom rows, join a fabric A large square to each side of the remaining two fabric C large squares; press seams over fabric A.

Complete the square With right sides together, pin and sew the three rows together with the tiny squares in the center, matching the seams; press seams open.

row of geese

A center row of flying geese creates a dramatic design, especially when different colors on each side create a graphic saw tooth border. Keep the block clean by using strong solids and subtle prints.

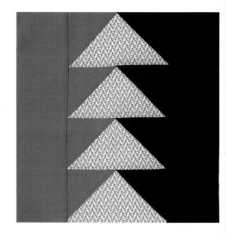

The seam allowance is ¼ inch throughout.

Fabric quantities

- Medium red print fabric A: 7 x 12 inches
- Medium red fabric B: 8 x 13 inches
- Dark purple fabric C: 8 x 13 inches

Prepare the patches

Rotary method
- From fabrics A, B, and C, make four 6½ x 3½-inch flying geese rectangles (see page 17), keeping the red fabric on the left side
- From fabrics A and C, cut one 12½ x 3½-inch rectangle each

or

Template cutting
Using the 4 x 4 templates (pages 269–73):
- From fabric A, cut 4 medium triangles
- From fabrics B and C, cut 4 small triangles and 1 full-length rectangle each

Template piecing

With right sides together, sew a fabric B small triangle to the left diagonal edge of a fabric A medium triangle; press seam over the small triangle. Sew a fabric C small triangle to the right edge of the fabric A medium triangle; press the seam over the small triangle. Repeat to make another three flying geese rectangles.

Make the block

Sew the center column Pin and sew the four flying geese together so they are pointing upward; press seams upward.

Complete the square Pin and sew the fabric B rectangle to the left edge of the flying geese rectangles and the fabric C rectangle to the right edge; press seams over strips.

pennants

Combine a row of squares with a row of flying geese and you get pennants. Make this playful block in bright spring colors and flea market prints for a delightfully retro look. Or play up the pennants by sewing them in your favorite team's colors.

Fabric quantities

- Dark red print fabric A: 8 x 10 inches
- Dark red print fabric B: 5 x 8 inches
- Medium teal print fabric C: 5 x 8 inches
- Medium teal print fabric D: 8 x 10 inches
- White fabric E: 9 x 10 inches

Prepare the patches

Rotary method

- From fabrics A and E and fabrics D and E, make two 4½ x 2½-inch flying geese rectangles (see page 17) each
- From fabrics B and E and fabrics C and E, make one 4½ x 2½-inch flying geese rectangle each
- From fabrics A and D, cut two 4½-inch squares each
- From fabric B, cut one 4½-inch square
- From fabric C, cut one 4½-inch square
- From fabric D, cut two 4½-inch squares

or

Template cutting
Using the 6 x 6 templates (pages 269–73):
- From fabrics A and D, cut 2 large squares and 4 small triangles each
- From fabrics B and C, cut 1 large square and 2 small triangles each
- From fabric E, cut 6 medium triangles

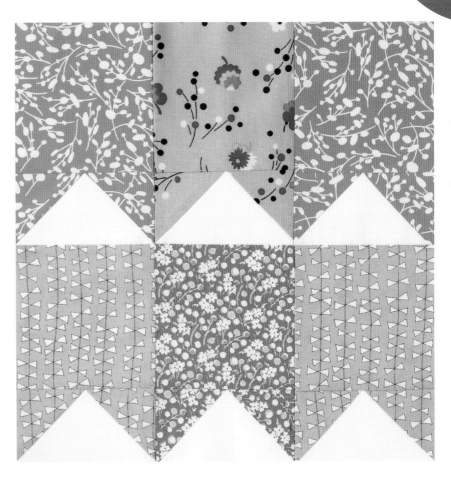

A
B
C
D
E

Template piecing

With right sides facing, pin and sew a fabric A small triangle to each diagonal edge of two fabric E medium triangles to create two flying geese rectangles; press seams away from the white fabric. Repeat with the fabric B small triangles, the fabric C small triangles, and the fabric D small triangles to make another four flying geese rectangles.

Make the block

Piece the pennants With right sides facing, pin and sew the large print squares to the matching flying geese units, making sure all of the white points face the top of the block; press seams up.

Sew two rows With right sides facing, pin and sew a fabrics A and E pennant to each side of the fabrics B and E pennant; press seams open.

With right sides facing, pin and sew a fabrics D and E pennant to each side of the fabrics C and E pennant; press seams open.

Complete the square With right sides facing, pin and sew the two rows together, carefully matching the seams; press seams open.

cactus flower

The seam allowance is ¼ inch throughout.

Cactus Flower is a hybrid block—half a sawtooth star with appliqué leaves and stem. You can use only solids, but mixing in a print will add additional depth to the design.

A
B
C
D

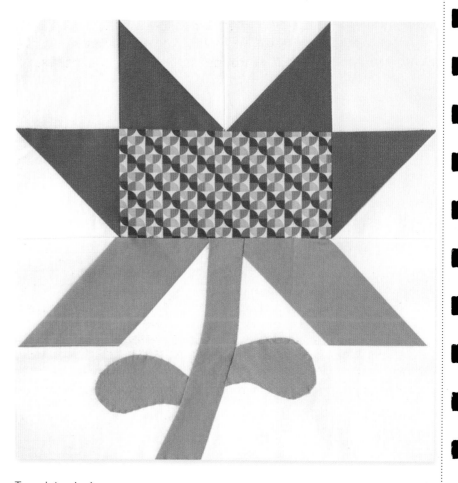

Fabric quantities

- Medium pink fabric A: 5 x 10 inches

- Light green fabric B: 10 x 12 inches

- Medium red print fabric C: 3 x 5 inches

- White fabric D: 14 x 14 inches

Prepare the patches

Rotary method

- From fabrics A and D, make four 3½-inch half-square triangles (see page 12)

- From fabrics B and D, make one 6½ x 3½-inch right diamond rectangle and one left diamond rectangle (see page 16)

- From fabric B, cut two leaves and one stem using the ≈

- From fabric C, cut one 6½ x 2½-inch rectangle

- From fabric D, cut two 3½-inch squares and one 12½ x 3½-inch strip

or

Template cutting

Using the 4 x 4 templates (pages 269–73):

- From fabric A, cut 4 small triangles

- From fabric B, cut 1 left diamond and 1 right diamond plus 2 leaves and 1 stem using the template on page 286

- From fabric C, cut 1 short rectangle

- From fabric D, cut 2 small squares, 8 small triangles, and 1 full-length rectangle

Template piecing

With right sides together, sew a fabric A small triangle to a fabric D small triangle along the long diagonal edge; press seam over fabric A. Repeat to make another three half-square triangles.

With right sides together, sew a fabric D small triangle to each side of a fabric B right diamond along the diagonal edges; press seams over fabric B. Repeat to make the left diamond rectangle.

Make the block

Assemble the flower Sew two fabrics A and D half-square triangles together with the pink triangles on the outside. Sew a fabric D square to each end; press seams over the squares. Sew the remaining two fabrics A and D half-square triangles to the short edges of the fabric C rectangle, with the white triangles on the outside; press seams over the rectangle. Pin and sew the two rows, lining up seams; press open.

Sew the leaves and stem Join the two diamond blocks so the diamonds point inward and upward; press seams open. Sew the fabric D strip to the bottom edge and press seam up. Appliqué the leaves and stem (see page 20) in the center of the patch, from top to bottom.

Complete the square With right sides together, pin and sew the top and bottom sections together; press seams open.

octagon

The seam allowance is ¼ inch throughout

This block achieves its faceted look from the balance of light and dark prints against white. Keep to one color family or bring in a second for the inner square. Joining multiple blocks edge to edge creates a diamond grid or trellis pattern.

A
B
C
D
E

Fabric quantities

- Dark red fabric A: 5 x 10 inches
- Dark pink print fabric B: 5 x 10 inches
- Medium pink fabric C: 5 x 10 inches
- Medium pink print fabric D: 5 x 10 inches
- White fabric E: 10 x 15 inches

Prepare the patches

Rotary method
- From fabrics A and E; fabrics B and E; fabrics C and E; and fabrics D and E, make four 3½-inch half-square triangles (see page 12) each

or

Template cutting
Using the 4 x 4 templates (pages 269–73):
- From fabrics A, B, C, and D, cut 4 small triangles each
- From fabric E, cut 16 small triangles

Template piecing

With right sides together, sew a fabric A triangle to a fabric E triangle along the diagonal edge; press seam away from fabric E. Repeat to make another three half-square triangles. Repeat using fabrics B and E, C and E, and D and E.

Make the block

Sew four rows Lay out the half-square triangles in their final positions, as shown above, with matching fabrics diagonally opposite one another across the block. Pin and sew in rows; press all seams open.

Complete the square Pin and sew the rows together; press seams open.

diagonal nine patch

The seam allowance is ¼ inch throughout.

The basic nine-patch layout of three rows of three squares can be interpreted in a surprisingly large number of ways. In Diagonal Nine Patch, the squares are arranged to form a diagonal line cutting through the center of the block. The large patches make this quick to sew, and it's a good starter block for learning how to match and press seams accurately.

A
B
C

Fabric quantities

- Medium red fabric A: 5 x 15 inches
- Light gray fabric B: 5 x 15 inches
- Medium gray print fabric C: 5 x 15 inches

Prepare the patches

Rotary method
- From fabrics A, B, and C, cut three 4½-inch squares each

or

Template cutting
Using the 6 x 6 templates (pages 269–73):
- From fabrics A, B, and C, cut 3 large squares each

Make the block

Make three rows For the top row, with right sides together, pin and sew a fabric A square to the right edge of a fabric B square. Join a second fabric B square to the opposite side; press seams to the right.

For the center row, with right sides together, pin and sew a fabric C square to the left edge of a fabric A square. Join a fabric B square to the right edge of the fabric A square; press seams to the left.

For the bottom row, with right sides together, pin and sew two fabric C squares together, then join a fabric B large square to the right edge of the strip; press seams to the right.

Complete the square With right sides together, pin and sew the first row and the third row to the second row; press seams open.

41 double hourglass

The seam allowance is ¼ inch throughout.

When quilt doyenne Nancy Cabot recorded this block in the 1930s, it was already considered an old design. Update this classic with a modern color palatte.

Fabric quantities

- Dark red fabric A: 12 x 12 inches
- Medium red print fabric B: 5 x 10 inches
- White fabric C: 10 x 15 inches

Prepare the patches

Rotary method
- From fabrics A and C, make four 4½-inch half-square triangles (see page 12)
- From fabric B, cut two 4½-inch squares
- From fabric C, cut three 4½-inch squares

or

Template cutting
Using the 6 x 6 templates (pages 278–83):
- From fabric A, cut 4 large triangles
- From fabric B, cut 2 large squares

- From fabric C, cut 4 large triangles and 3 large squares

Template piecing

With right sides together, pin and sew one fabric A large triangle to each of the fabric C large triangles to make four half-square triangles; press seams over the red fabric.

Make the block

Sew three rows With right sides together, sew a fabric B large square to the fabric C side of a half-square triangle, with the red triangle pointing down and right. Join a fabric C large square to the right edge of the half-square triangle; press seams open. Repeat to make the bottom row. With right sides together, pin and sew the remaining half-square triangles to the remaining fabric C square for the center row. Make sure that one red triangle points down and right and the other up and left; press seams over the center square.

Complete the square With right sides together and carefully matching seams, join the top row to the center row, making sure the fabric B square is in the upper left corner of the block. Join the bottom row to the center row, making sure the fabric B square is in the bottom right corner of the block. Press seams open.

42 three squares

The seam allowance is ¼ inch throughout.

The combination of a floral sprig print and two solid, complementary colors soften the bold geometry and large scale of this simple Log Cabin block. This block is easily made using the rotary method.

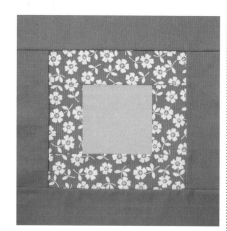

Fabric quantities

- Light blue fabric A: 5 x 5 inches
- Medium red print fabric B: 9 x 12 inches
- Dark blue fabric C: 12 x 13 inches

Prepare the patches

Rotary method
- From fabric A, cut one 4½-inch square
- From fabric B, cut two 4½ x 2½-inch rectangles and two 8½ x 2½-inch rectangles
- From fabric C, cut two 8½ x 2-inch rectangles and two 12½ x 2-inch rectangles

Make the block

Sew the center With right sides together, pin and sew the two short fabric B rectangles to the side edges of the fabric A square; press seams open.

Pin and sew the two long fabric B rectangles to the fabric A and B patch; press seams open.

Complete the square Repeat to join the fabric C rectangles.

woven heart

This woven-look heart, centered on a nine-patch square, brings a touch of Scandinavian style to any room. Use traditional shades of red and white to make a romantic statement, or you could choose softer colors for a child's or baby quilt.

Fabric quantities

- Dark red fabric A: 6 x 7 inches
- Medium red fabric B: 7 x 12 inches
- Light red print fabric C: 6 x 9 inches
- White fabric D: 11 x 13 inches

Prepare the patches

Rotary method

- From fabrics B and D, make two 6½ x 2½-inch short boats (see page 17)
- From fabric A, cut two 6½ x 2½-inch rectangles
- From fabric B, cut four 2½-inch squares
- From fabric C, cut five 2½-inch squares
- From fabric D, cut one 4½-inch square, one 12½ x 2½-inch rectangle, and one 10½ x 2½-inch rectangle

or

Template cutting

Using the 6 x 6 templates (pages 278–83):

- From fabric A, cut 2 medium rectangles
- From fabric B, cut 2 short boats and 4 small squares
- From fabric C, cut 5 small squares
- From fabric D, cut 1 large square, 4 small triangles, 1 very long rectangle, and 1 full-length rectangle

The seam allowance is ¼ inch throughout.

A
B
C
D

Template piecing

With right sides together, sew a fabric D triangle to each of the diagonal edges of the two fabric B short boats. Press the seams outward.

Make the block

Join the nine-patch square With right sides together, pin a fabric C small square to each side edge of two fabric B small squares and stitch; press seams inward. Repeat to make another row. Sew two fabric B small squares to each side edge of the remaining fabric C small square and press seams outward.

Lay the three rows of squares out in their final positions, carefully matching seams. With right sides together, sew the top and bottom rows to the middle row. Press seams outward.

Make the heart With right sides together, sew a fabric A medium rectangle to the long edge of each fabric B short boat; press seams over the rectangles. Join the white square to the left edge of one unit, short boat facing down, and press seam over the darker fabric.

With right sides together, sew the dark edge of the other fabrics A, B, and D unit to the left edge of the nine-patch square; press seam over the dark fabric. Join the two halves of the heart with a horizontal seam and press open.

Make the border With right sides together, sew the fabric D very long rectangle to the right edge of the heart and press seam outward. Join the fabric D full-length rectangle to the bottom edge and press seam outward.

concentric squares

The seam allowance is ¼ inch throughout.

Use an ombré color combination, fading the colors from the outside of the block to the inside. When the center square is the lightest color, it gives a feeling of depth to each block. This block uses the Log Cabin method of sewing strips around the center square. It is easily made using the rotary method.

A
B
C
D

Fabric quantities

- Light pink fabric A: 4 x 4 inches
- Medium red print fabric B: 6 x 13 inches
- Medium red solid fabric C: 10 x 12 inches
- Dark red fabric D: 12 x 13 inches

Prepare the patches

Rotary method
- From fabric A, cut one 3½-inch square
- From fabric B, cut one 3½ x 2-inch rectangle, two 5 x 2-inch rectangles, and one 6½ x 2-inch rectangle
- From fabric C, cut one 6½ x 2-inch rectangle, two 8 x 2-inch rectangles, and one 9½ x 2-inch rectangle

- From fabric D, cut one 9½ x 2-inch rectangles, two 11 x 2-inch rectangles, and one 12½ x 2-inch rectangle

Make the block

Sew the first round Press seams outwards as you sew. With right sides together, pin and sew the 3½ x 2-inch fabric B rectangle to the top edge of the fabric A square. Add one 5 x 2-inch fabric B rectangle to the right edge of the square and a second to the bottom edge. Complete the round by sewing the 6½ x 2-inch fabric B rectangle to the left edge.

Add the second round Working clockwise, in the same way, sew the 6½ x 2-in fabric C rectangle to the top edge of the square, the 8 x 2-inch fabric C rectangles to the right

and bottom edges, and the 9½ x 2-inch fabric C rectangle to the left edge.

Complete the square Start by joining a 9½ x 2-inch fabric D rectangle to the top edge, then add the 11 x 2-inch fabric D rectangles to the right and bottom edges. Sew the 12½ x 2-inch rectangle to the left edge to finish the block.

---

buckeye beauty

The seam allowance is ¼ inch throughout.

This historical block uses four-patch squares to form secondary patterns in a quilt. When several are joined together, the blocks create strong diagonal lines across a quilt top. Use strong patterns for the large triangles that form the centered hourglass.

A
B
C
D

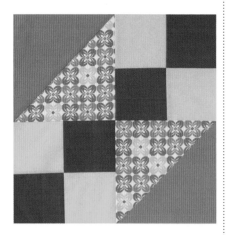

Fabric quantities

- Medium red fabric A: 8 x 8 inches
- Medium red print fabric B: 8 x 8 inches
- Light pink fabric C: 8 x 8 inches
- Dark pink fabric D: 8 x 8 inches

Prepare the patches

Rotary method
- From fabrics A and B, make two 6½-inch half-square triangles (see page 12)
- From fabrics C and D, make two 6½-inch four-patch squares (see page 11)

or

Template cutting
Using the 4 x 4 templates (pages 269–73):
- From fabrics A and B, cut 2 large triangles each

- From fabrics C and D, cut 4 small squares each

Template piecing

With right sides together, pin and sew the two fabric A large triangles to the two fabric B large triangles to make two half-square triangles; press seams over the solid fabric.

With right sides together, pin and sew one fabric C small square to each of the fabric D small squares to make four rectangles. Join two rectangles, alternating the colors, to make one four-patch square; press seams over the dark fabric. Repeat to make the second four-patch square.

Make the block

Sew two rows With right sides together, pin and sew one four-patch square to one half-square triangle, making sure the print

triangle points down and right; press seam open.

Repeat with the second set of squares, making sure the print triangle points up and left; press seam open.

Complete the square With right sides together and being careful to match the seams, join the two rows. The fabric B triangles and the fabric D squares should meet in the middle; press seam open.

floating pinwheel

The pinwheel floats in a neutral background with a scrappy frame, but you can try making it entirely from low-volume prints to make it feel even more modern.

Fabric quantities

- Dark red print fabric A: 8 x 10 inches
- Dark blue fabric B: 4 x 8 inches
- Medium green print fabric C: 9 x 6 inches
- Light green print fabric D: 9 x 6 inches
- White fabric E: 9 x 10 inches

Prepare the patches

Rotary method

- From fabrics A and B, make one 4½-inch pinwheel square (see page 13)
- From fabric A, cut four 2½-inch squares
- From fabrics C and D, cut two 8½ x 2½-inch rectangles each
- From fabric E, cut two 4½ x 2½-inch rectangles and two 8½ x 2½-inch rectangles

or

Template cutting
Using the 6 x 6 templates (pages 278–83):
- From fabric A, cut 4 small triangles and 4 small squares
- From fabric B, cut 4 small triangles
- From fabric C, cut 2 long rectangles
- From fabric D, cut 2 long rectangles
- From fabric E, cut 2 short rectangles and 2 long rectangles

The seam allowance is ¼ inch throughout.

Template piecing

With right sides together, pin and sew four sets of triangles, one blue and one red, to make half-square triangles (see page 12); press seams open. Join the squares to finish the pinwheel square; press seams open.

Make the block

Frame the pinwheel square With right sides together, pin and sew the two fabric E short rectangles to the top and bottom of the pinwheel square; press seams outward. With right sides together, pin and sew the two fabric E long rectangles to the sides of the pinwheel square; press seams outward.

Make the border With right sides together, pin and sew the two fabric D long rectangles to the sides of the frame; press seams outward. Sew two fabric A small squares to each end of the two fabric C long rectangles; press seams over the rectangles. With right sides together, pin and sew strips to the top and bottom of the frame.

A
B
C
D
E

46

47

five of diamonds

Combine a tone-on-tone red print with red and white fabrics for the playing card-like effect that gives this block its name, or choose coordinating prints for a softer look. For a scrappy design, cut each diamond from a different fabric.

The seam allowance is ¼ inch throughout.

Fabric quantities

- Dark red fabric A: 10 x 5 inches
- Medium red print fabric B: 10 x 10 inches
- White fabric C: 15 x 10 inches

Prepare the patches

Rotary method
- From fabrics A and C, make five 4½-inch diamond squares (see page 15)
- From fabric B, cut four 4½-inch squares

or

Template cutting
Using the 6 x 6 templates (pages 278–83):
- From fabric A, cut 5 diamond squares

- From fabric B, cut 4 large squares
- From fabric C, cut 20 small triangles

Template piecing

With right sides together, pin and sew two small triangles to opposite edges of a diamond square; press seams over the triangles. Add two more triangles to the remaining edges, then press seams over the triangles. Sew the remaining four diamond squares in the same way.

Make the block

Make the top and bottom rows With right sides together, pin and sew one diamond square block to the side edges of one fabric B square; press seams over the square. Repeat to sew the bottom row.

Make the center row With right sides together, pin and sew the remaining fabric B squares to the sides of the last diamond square; press seams over the square.

Complete the square Pin the top row to the center row, right sides together and with seams matching, then sew. Join the bottom row in the same way; press both seams open.

48

posy basket

This traditional folk art block gets a modern spin when you make the posy basket white and set it against scraps of vibrant solids. This block is most accurately made from templates.

The seam allowance is ¼ inch throughout.

Fabric quantities

- At least 5 different dark red, pink, and purple fabrics A: 9 x 18 inches in total
- White fabric B: 9 x 12 inches

Prepare the patches

Rotary method
- From fabrics A and B, make twelve 3-inch half-square triangles (see page 12)
- From fabric A, cut eleven 3-inch squares
- From fabric B, cut two 3-inch squares

or

Template cutting
Using the 5 x 5 templates (pages 274–7):
- From fabric A, cut 11 small squares and 12 small triangles

- From fabric B, cut 2 small squares and 12 small triangles

Template piecing

To make 12 sets of half-square triangles, pin and sew together the small colored A triangles to the small white B triangles along the diagonal edges; press seams over the colored fabrics.

Make the block

Arrange the patches Lay the solid squares and the half-square triangle patches out in five rows of five squares, following the photograph to create the basket design. Make sure that the different shades of fabric A are well balanced. Note their order on paper, so that you won't lose track of the positions as you stitch them together.

Make the rows With right sides together, pin and sew each of the five rows together. Press seams on the top, center, and bottom rows to the right; press seams on the second and fourth rows to the left.

Complete the square With right sides together and seams matching, pin the top two rows together; press seam open. Repeat to join the remaining rows.

sawtooth star

This traditional star block has many names: Sawtooth Star, Squares and Points, Eight Point Star, and Variable Star. To make it vibrant, cut the center square from a strong geometric print with a matching background and analogous points.

The seam allowance is ¼ inch throughout.

A
B
C

Fabric quantities

- Medium coral fabric A: 12 x 16 inches
- Medium yellow fabric B: 8 x 8 inches
- Medium coral print fabric C: 5 x 5 inches

Prepare the patches

Rotary method
- From fabrics A and B, make four 6½ x 3½-inch flying geese rectangles (see page 17)
- From fabric A, cut four 3½-inch squares
- From fabric C, cut one 6½-inch square

or

Template cutting
Using the 4 x 4 templates (pages 269–73):

- From fabric A, cut 4 medium triangles and 4 small squares
- From fabric B, cut 8 small triangles
- From fabric C, cut 1 large square

Template piecing

With right sides together, pin and sew two fabric B small triangles to both diagonal sides of each of the fabric A medium triangles to make four flying geese rectangles; press seams outward.

Make the block

Sew three rows With right sides together, pin and sew two fabric A small squares to both short ends of two flying geese units; press seams over the squares.

With right sides together, pin and sew the other two flying geese units to the sides of the fabric C square; press seams over the square.

Complete the square With right sides together and carefully matching seams, with the flying geese pointing toward the center square, join the top row to the center row. Repeat to join the bottom row; press seams open.

---

star flower

This is a sweet and simple block that is quick to sew. Not only is it good for beginners, but it also makes a high impact in a wide range of colors. Try analogous prints that mimic flowers in your own yard or combine complementary colors for a more modern feel.

The seam allowance is ¼ inch throughout.

A
B
C

Fabric quantities

- Medium pink print fabric A: 12 x 13 inches
- White print fabric B: 10 x 10 inches
- Medium yellow fabric C: 5 x 5 inches

Prepare the patches

Rotary method
- From fabrics A and B, make four 4½-inch house squares (see page 14)
- From fabric A, cut four 4½-inch squares
- From fabric C, cut one 4½-inch square

or

Template cutting
Using the 6 x 6 templates (pages 278–83):
- From fabric A, cut 4 large squares and 8 small triangles

- From fabric B, cut 4 houses
- From fabric C, cut 1 large square

Template piecing

With right sides together, pin and sew two fabric A small triangles to each of the diagonal edges on each of the four fabric B houses; press seams open.

Make the block

Sew two rows With right sides together, pin and sew two fabric A large squares to each side of two of the house units, making sure the roofs point out; press seams open.

Make the center row With right sides together, pin and sew the remaining house units to the sides of the fabric C square, making sure the roofs point out.

Complete the square With right sides together and being careful to match seams, join the top row to the center row, making sure the roofs point away from the square. Repeat to join the bottom row; press seams open.

diamond pinwheel

The seam allowance is ¼ inch throughout.

The pinwheel in this block appears to be turning inside the on-point square. Shown in a muted palette of autumnal shades, the deep brown gives solidity to the overall design. Try using lighter shades to change the look.

A

B

C

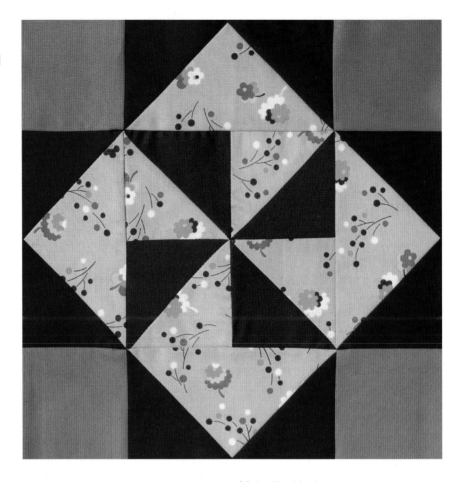

Fabric quantities

- Dark purple fabric A: 10 x 13 inches
- Gray print fabric B: 11 x 17 inches
- Dark orange fabric C: 8 x 8 inches

Prepare the patches

Rotary method
- From fabrics A and B, make one 6½-inch pinwheel square (see page 13) and four 6½ x 3½-inch flying geese rectangles (see page 17)
- From fabric C, cut four 3½-inch squares

or

Template cutting
Using the 4 x 4 templates (pages 269–73):
- From fabric A, cut 12 small triangles
- From fabric B, cut 4 medium triangles and 4 small triangles
- From fabric C, cut 4 small squares

Template piecing

With right sides together, sew a fabric A small triangle to the left diagonal edge of a fabric B medium triangle; press seam across the small triangle. Sew a second fabric A triangle to the right edge of the medium triangle; press seam across the small triangle. Repeat to make another three flying geese rectangles.

To make the pinwheel square, with right sides together, sew a pair of fabrics A and B small triangles together along their long diagonal edge to make a half-square triangle (see page 12); press seam over fabric A. Repeat to make another three half-square triangles.

With right sides together, sew two squares together along a light and dark edge; press seam toward the dark fabric. Repeat to make the second row, then join the rows along the long edge, with the light fabric touching the dark fabric; press seams open.

Make the block

Sew three rows For the top and bottom rows, sew a fabric C square to each short end of two flying geese rectangles; press seams open.

For the center row, sew a flying geese rectangle to each side edge of the pinwheel square, with the flying geese pointing outward; press seams open.

Complete the square With right sides together, pin and sew the three rows together, lining up the seams; press seams open.

large and small geese

The seam allowance is ¼ inch throughout.

This block plays with scale and the patchwork technique for making flying geese patches. Make the larger ones with half-square triangles, then make the smaller ones using the traditional method. When you join several of these blocks together, you can make a dynamic allover pattern.

Fabric quantities

- Medium gray fabric A: 5 x 15 inches
- At least 3 different medium orange print fabrics B: 5 x 15 inches in total
- Light green print fabric C: 6 x 9 inches
- White fabric D: 9 x 15 inches

Prepare the patches

Rotary method
- From fabrics A and B, make six 4½-inch half-square triangles (see page 12)
- From fabrics C and D, make six 4½ x 2½-inch flying geese rectangles (see page 17)

or

Template cutting
Using the 6 x 6 templates (pages 278–83):
- From fabrics A and B, cut 6 large triangles each
- From fabric C, cut 12 small triangles
- From fabric D, cut 6 medium triangles

A
B
B
B
C
D

Template piecing

With right sides together, pin and sew one fabric A large triangle to each of the fabric B large triangles to make six half-square triangles; press seams over the gray fabric. Join in mismatched pairs to make three flying geese rectangles; press seams open.

With right sides together, pin and sew two fabric C small triangles to the diagonal sides of each of the fabric D medium triangles to make six flying geese rectangles; press seams over fabric C.

Make the block

Sew two columns With right sides together and carefully matching the center seams, pin and sew the three larger flying geese rectangles in a column, making sure they all point in the same direction; press seams open.

With right sides together, join the six smaller flying geese rectangles in a column, making sure they all point in the same direction; press seams open.

Complete the square With right sides together, join the two columns, making sure the flying geese rectangles point in opposite directions; press seams open.

little bows

The seam allowance is ¼ inch throughout.

When joined together, several of these blocks create zigzag lines across your quilt top. This block works best with solid colors or small prints on a neutral background. Use similar shades for a subtle look, or raid your scrap basket to give it an improvized look.

Fabric quantities

- At least 8 different medium red, orange, and pink solid and print fabrics A: 9 x 9 inches in total
- White fabric B: 13 x 24 inches

Prepare the patches

Rotary method
- From fabrics A and B, make sixteen 4½ x 2½-inch right tapered rectangles (see page 16)
- From fabrics A and B, make two 2½-inch half-square triangles (see page 12)
- From fabric B, cut two 2½-inch squares

or

Template cutting
Using the 6 x 6 templates (pages 278–83):
- From fabric A, cut 18 small triangles
- From fabric B, cut 16 right tapered rectangles, 2 small triangles, and 2 small squares

Template piecing

With right sides together, pin and sew one fabric A small triangle to each of the right tapered rectangles to make 16 patchwork rectangles.

With right sides together, pin and sew one fabric A small triangle to each of the two fabric B small triangles to make two half-square triangles.

Make the block

Sew the patchwork squares With right sides together, pin and sew the patchwork rectangles into eight squares, matching the center seams and making sure the fabric A triangle points meet in the middle; press seams open.

With right sides together, pin and sew one half-square triangle to each of the fabric B small squares; press seams open.

Sew the rows Arrange the patches so that three patchwork squares are in the top and the bottom rows. With right sides together, pin and sew the squares, making sure the points of the fabric A triangles meet; press seams open.

With right sides together, pin and sew the remaining patchwork squares together, making sure the points of the fabric A triangles meet. Join the two half blocks on each side of the row; press seams open.

Complete the square With right sides together and carefully matching seams, pin and sew the top row to the center row; press seam upward. Repeat to join the bottom row to the middle row.

A
A
A
A
A
A
A
A
A
A
B

arrow block

The seam allowance is ¼ inch throughout.

Arrow is made in the same way as Row of Geese on page 46, but it has a different look. Changing the colors and the tonal balance completely alters the look of a block. Choose a wide striped pattern to make a strong border for the arrows.

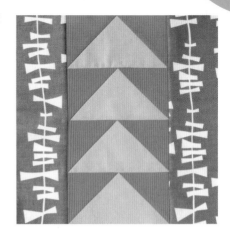

A
B
C

Fabric quantities

- Light green fabric A: 6 x 10 inches
- Dark orange fabric B: 8 x 8 inches
- Dark gray print fabric C: 8 x 13 inches

Prepare the patches

Rotary method
- From fabrics A and B, make four 6½ x 3½-inch flying geese rectangles (see page 17)
- From fabric C, cut two 12½ x 3½-inch rectangles

or

Template cutting

Using the 4 x 4 templates (pages 269–73):
- From fabric A, cut 4 medium triangles
- From fabric B, cut 8 small triangles
- From fabric C, cut 2 full-length rectangles

Template piecing

With right sides together, pin and sew two fabric B small triangles to the two diagonal edges on each fabric A medium triangle to make four flying geese rectangles; press seams away from the fabric A triangles.

Make the block

Join the flying geese rectangles With right sides together, pin and sew the four flying geese rectangles into a column, making sure they point up; press seams up.

Complete the square With right sides together, pin and sew a fabric C rectangle to each side of the flying geese column; press seams over the rectangles.

---

aunt eliza's star

The seam allowance is ¼ inch throughout.

This star in this block can be obvious, made with brightly contrasting solids, or subtle and hard to see when made with low-volume prints. Aunt Eliza's Star is also ideal for using up your favorite scraps.

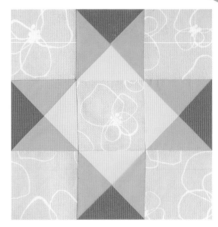

A
B
C
D

Fabric quantities

- Medium red fabric A: 6 x 12 inches
- Medium orange fabric B: 12 x 12 inches
- Medium yellow fabric C: 6 x 12 inches
- Light blue print fabric D: 10 x 15 inches

Prepare the patches

Rotary method
- From fabrics A, B, and C, make four 4½-inch hourglass squares (see page 13)
- From fabric D, cut five 4½-inch squares

or

Template cutting
Using the 6 x 6 templates (pages 278–83):
- From fabrics A and C, cut 4 medium triangles each

- From fabric B, cut 8 medium triangles
- From fabric D, cut 5 large squares

Template piecing

With right sides together, pin and sew one fabric B medium triangle to each of the four fabric A medium triangles along a short diagonal edge; press seams open. Repeat with the fabric B and fabric C medium triangles. Join the units to make four fabrics A, B, and C hourglass squares, making sure the yellow triangles are on the bottom.

Make the block

Sew three rows With right sides together, pin and sew a fabric D large square to each fabric B side of one of the hourglass squares; press seams open. Repeat to make the bottom row.

With right sides together, pin and sew the fabric C side of two hourglass squares to the remaining fabric D large square.

Complete the square With right sides together and carefully matching seams, pin and sew the top row to the middle row, making sure the yellow triangle adjoins the center square. Repeat to join the bottom row. Press seams open.

harlequin triangles

This modern block is simple, but it uses half-square triangles in a particularly effective way. Use a variety of solid colors and mix up light and dark shades to add highlights and lowlights throughout the block.

The seam allowance is ¼ inch throughout.

Fabric quantities

- At least 12 different fabrics A: 16 x 16 inches in total

Prepare the patches

Rotary method
- From fabrics A, make sixteen 4½-inch half-square triangles (see page 12)

or

Template cutting
Using the 4 x 4 templates (pages 269–73):
- From fabrics A, cut 32 small triangles

Template piecing

With right sides together, pin and sew two fabric A small triangles together to make a half-square triangle. Repeat to make 15 more half-square triangles.

Make the block

Sew four rows Arrange the half-square triangles in four rows of four patches, laying them out in different directions and balancing colors so that any triangles cut from the same color square are not adjacent.

With right sides together, pin and sew the first four patches into a row. Repeat to make three more rows; press seams to the side, alternating directions with each row.

Complete the square With right sides together, pin and sew the first row to the second row; press seams open. Repeat to join the remaining three rows.

---

hexagons and hourglasses

Four hourglass squares in analogous colours make a striking star with an airy, modern feel. The diamond square at the center of the block provides a good space for quilted embellishment.

The seam allowance is ¼ inch throughout.

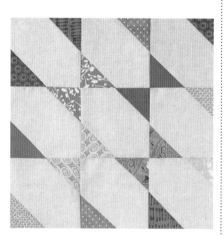

Fabric quantities

- At least 8 different medium and dark red, orange, red print, and orange print fabrics A: 6 x 12 inches in total

- 2 different green print fabrics B: 3 x 6 inches in total

- Light beige fabric C: 15 x 15 inches

Prepare the patches

Rotary method
- From fabrics A and C, make six 4½-inch hexagon squares (see page 15) with 2 different red triangles on each

- From fabrics A, B, and C, make three 4½-inch hexagon squares with 2 different red and green triangles on each

or

Template cutting
Using the 6 x 6 templates (pages 278–83):
- From fabric A, cut 15 small triangles

- From fabric B, cut 3 small triangles

- From fabric C, cut 9 hexagons

Template piecing

With right sides together, sew two different red fabric A small triangles to the diagonal edges of six hexagons; press seams open. With right sides together, sew two different red and green fabric A and fabric B small triangles to the diagonal edges of three hexagons; press seams open.

Make the block

Sew three rows Arrange the hexagon squares in three rows of three patches, matching the triangle fabrics where they meet. With right sides together and matching seams, join the first three patches; press seams open. Repeat to sew the second and third rows.

Complete the square With right sides together and matching seams, pin and sew the first row to the second row, then the third row to the second row; press seams open.

orange tree

The Orange Tree is a historic block with folkart roots. Intricately pieced trees like this were popular in the nineteenth century. Usually they were pines, made from all green fabrics, so the oranges in this tree modernize it.

The seam allowance is ¼ inch throughout.

A
B
C
D
E

Fabric quantities

- Dark green fabric A: 8 x 12 inches
- Medium green fabric B: 8 x 8 inches
- Medium orange print fabric C: 3 x 9 inches
- Medium brown fabric D: 5 x 10 inches
- White fabric E: 16 x 21 inches

Prepare the patches

Rotary method
- From fabrics A and E, make twelve 2½-inch half-square triangles (see page 12)
- From fabrics B and E, make eight 2½-inch half-square triangles
- From fabrics D and E, make two 2½-inch half-square triangles and one 4½-inch half-square triangle
- From fabric C, cut three 2½-inch squares
- From fabric E, cut three 2½-inch squares and two 4½ x 2½-inch rectangles

or

Template cutting
Using the 6 x 6 templates (pages 278–83):
- From fabric A, cut 12 small triangles
- From fabric B, cut 8 small triangles
- From fabric C, cut 3 small squares
- From fabric D, cut 2 small triangles and 1 large triangle
- From fabric E, cut 22 small triangles, 3 small squares, 2 short rectangles, and 1 large triangle

Template piecing

With right sides together, pin and sew a fabric E small triangle to a fabric A small triangle; press seams open. Repeat with the remaining small triangles to make a total of 12 fabrics A and E half-square triangles, 8 fabrics B and E half-square triangles, and 2 fabrics D and E half-square triangles.

With right sides together, pin and sew the fabric D large triangle to the fabric E large triangle; press seams open.

Make the block

Sew six rows Arrange the patches in six rows, as shown above, to create an orange tree.

To make the top row, with right sides together, pin and sew the first six patches, starting with a fabric E small square; press seams to the right.

To make the second row, with right sides together, pin and sew the next six patches, making sure the first fabric A triangle points up and right; press seams to the left. With right sides together and matching seams, join the second row to the first row and press seam open.

To make the third row, with right sides together, pin and sew the next five patches, making sure the first fabric A triangle points up and right; press seams to the right.

To make the fourth row, with right sides together, pin and sew the next five patches, making sure the first fabric A triangle points up and right; press seams to the left. With right sides together and matching seams, join the fourth row to the third row and press seam open. Sew one fabric E short rectangle to the right side of the two rows; press seam open.

To make the fifth row, with right sides together, pin and sew the next four patches, making sure the first fabric A triangle points up and right; press seams to the right.

To make the sixth row, with right sides together, pin and sew one fabric E small square to the left side of the remaining fabrics B and E half-square triangle. Join the second fabric E short rectangle to the right side; press seams to the left. With right sides together and carefully matching seams, join the sixth row to the fifth row and press seam open. Add the fabrics D and E half-square triangle to the right side of the two rows.

Complete the square With right sides together, join the last two rows to the fourth row and press seam open.

two-way star

The seam allowance is ¼ inch throughout.

The Two-Way Star can be viewed as one eight-point star or two four-point layered stars, rotating in opposite directions. The white makes this an airy, modern block.

A
B
C
D

Fabric quantities

- Medium orange fabric A: 6 x 12 inches
- Medium turquoise fabric B: 6 x 6 inches
- Medium lime fabric C: 6 x 6 inches
- White fabric D: 12 x 24 inches

Prepare the patches

Rotary method
- From fabrics A, B, and D, make two 4½-inch three-quarter square triangles (see page 13)
- From fabrics A, C, and D, make two 4½-inch three-quarter square triangles
- From fabric D, cut five 4½-inch squares

or

Template cutting
Using the 6 x 6 templates (pages 278–83):
- From fabric A, cut 4 large triangles
- From fabrics B and C, cut 2 medium triangles each
- From fabric D, cut 4 medium triangles and 5 large squares

Template piecing

With right sides together, sew a fabric D triangle to each of the fabric B triangles along a short side; press seams over the B fabric. Join the patchwork triangles to two fabric A triangles to make two three-quarter square triangles. Repeat with fabrics D, C, and A triangles to make another two three-quarter square triangles.

Make the block

Sew three rows With right sides together, pin and sew one white square to the left side of a fabrics A, B, and D three-quarter square triangle, with the triangles pointing up. Join a second white square to the right side; press seams open. Repeat to make the bottom row. To make the middle row, pin and sew an A, C, and D three-quarter square triangle to the remaining square, with the triangle pointing left. Join the remaining three-quarter square triangle to the right side of the square, with the triangles pointing right; press seams open.

Complete the square With right sides together, sew the top and bottom rows to the middle row; press seams open.

fast forward

The seam allowance is ¼ inch throughout.

Choose two opposite colors, such as orange and turquoise, for a lively pair of patches. Match a solid fabric to a small print to keep this block from getting too busy. Stacked, these two patches would make a dramatic border for other geometric blocks.

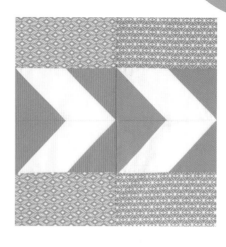

Fabric quantities

- Dark orange fabric A: 3 x 6 inches
- Light orange print fabric B: 6 x 7 inches
- Dark turquoise fabric C: 3 x 6 inches
- Light turquoise print fabric D: 6 x 7 inches
- White fabric E: 7 x 12 inches

Prepare the patches

Rotary method
- From fabrics A and E, make one each 6½ x 3½-inch right diamond rectangle and left diamond rectangle (see page 16)
- From fabrics B and D, cut two 6½ x 3½-inch rectangles each
- From fabrics C and E, make one each 6½ x 3½-inch right diamond rectangle and left diamond rectangle

or

Template cutting
Using the 4 x 4 templates (pages 269–73):
- From fabrics A and C, cut 4 small triangles each
- From fabrics B and D, cut 2 short rectangles each
- From fabric E, cut 2 right diamonds and 2 left diamonds

Template piecing

With right sides together, sew two fabric A small triangles to each diagonal edge of a fabric E right diamond and left diamond; press seams open. Repeat with fabric C small triangles.

Make the block

Join three rows With right sides together, sew the matching left and right diamonds into a square, creating an arrow with each pair; press seam open. Join matching short rectangles to the top and bottom of each arrow; press seams over rectangles.

Complete the square With right sides together, join the two halves, with arrows pointing right; press seam open.

---

open star

The seam allowance is ¼ inch throughout.

Four hourglass squares in different colors make a simple design. Join blocks with sashing between the rows of stars or sew them edge to edge for on-point squares.

Fabric quantities

- Medium pink fabric A: 6 x 6 inches
- Medium red fabric B: 6 x 6 inches
- Medium orange fabric C: 6 x 6 inches
- Burgundy fabric D: 6 x 6 inches
- White fabric E: 12 x 22 inches

Prepare the patches

Rotary method
- From fabrics A, B, and E; fabrics B, C, and E; fabrics C, D, and E; and fabrics D, A, and E, make one 4½-inch hourglass square (see page 13) each
- From fabric E, cut five 4½-inch squares

or

Template cutting
Using the 6 x 6 templates (pages 278–83):

- From fabrics A, B, C, and D, cut 2 medium triangles each
- From fabric E, cut 8 medium triangles and 5 large squares

Template piecing

With right sides together, sew a fabric E triangle to each colored triangle. Join a fabric A unit to a fabric B unit; a fabric B unit to a fabric C unit; a fabric C unit to a fabric D unit; and a fabric D unit to a fabric A unit to make four hourglass squares; press seams open.

Make the block

Sew three rows Arrange the squares in rows, with colors matching in corners, as shown above. For the top row, with right sides together, sew a white square to the fabric A side of a fabrics A and B hourglass square; join a white square to the fabric B side; press seams open.

For the center row, sew a fabrics A and D hourglass square to the left side of a white square, matching the white, then join a fabrics B and C hourglass square; press seams open.

For the bottom row, sew a white square to the fabric D side of a fabrics C and D hourglass square, then join a white square to the fabric C side; press seams open.

Complete the square With right sides together and matching the seams, sew the first and third rows to the second; press seams open.

interlocking crosses

A
B
C
D
E
F
G
H
I
J
K

This block is a small section of an overall design of tessellated or interlocking cross motifs. It works equally well with scraps for an improvized look or a range of solid colors for a more graphic pattern that emphasizes the cross shape.

Fabric quantities

- Medium orange print fabric A: 7 x 6 inches
- Dark red print fabric B: 7 x 6 inches
- Medium red fabric C: 3 x 3 inches
- Light blue print fabric D: 6 x 6 inches
- Medium turquoise print fabric E: 6 x 6 inches
- Medium turquoise print fabric F: 3 x 6 inches
- Dark turquoise print fabric G: 7 x 6 inches
- Dark turquoise print fabric H: 3 x 3 inches
- Light orange print fabric I: 3 x 3 inches
- Medium orange print fabric J: 6 x 6 inches
- Dark orange print fabric K: 6 x 6 inches

Prepare the patches

Rotary method
- From fabrics A, B, and G, cut two 2½-inch squares and one 6½ x 2½-inch rectangle each
- From fabrics C, H, and I, cut one 2½-inch square each
- From fabrics D, E, J, and K, cut two 2½-inch squares and one 4½ x 2½-inch rectangle each
- From fabric F, cut two 2½-inch squares

or

Template cutting
Using the 6 x 6 templates (pages 278–83):
- From fabrics A, B, and G, cut one medium rectangle and two small squares each
- From fabrics C, H, and I, cut one small square each
- From fabrics D and J, cut one short rectangle and two small squares each
- From fabric F, cut two small squares
- From fabrics E and K, cut one medium rectangle and one small square each

Make the block

Join six rows Arrange six rows of patches in an interlocking pattern, as shown above, making sure the crosses are formed by placing squares and rectangles in the same fabrics across two or three adjacent rows.

With right sides together, pin and sew together the first row of patches. Repeat to sew each of the remaining five rows; press seams to the right or left, alternating the direction with each row.

Complete the square With right sides together and carefully matching the seams, join the second row to the top row, the third row to the second row, and continue until all the rows are joined; press seams open.

log cabin square

The seam allowance is ¼ inch throughout.

This is one of the most versatile quilting blocks, which is easily made with the rotary method. Sewn with autumnal prints, it is traditional and folksy, but it can also look modern and breezy, depending on your choice of fabrics and color palette. It is a great block for beginner quilters, because you simply add rounds of strips to the center square.

A
B
C
D
E
F

Fabric quantities

- Dark rust print fabric A: 6 x 13 inches
- Light orange print fabric B: 3 x 7 inches
- Light orange fabric C: 3 x 7 inches
- Light orange print fabric D: 6 x 11 inches
- Light orange print fabric E: 6 x 11 inches
- White fabric F: 5 x 5 inches

Prepare the patches

Rotary method
- From fabric A, cut one 4½ x 2½-inch rectangle and one 12½ x 2½-inch rectangle
- From fabrics B and C, cut one 6½in x 2½-inch rectangle each

- From fabrics D and E, cut one 8½ x 2½-inch rectangle and one 10½ x 2½-inch rectangle each
- From fabric F, cut one 4½-inch square

Make the block

Sew the first round Press seams outward as you sew. With right sides together, pin and sew the shorter fabric A rectangle to the right edge of the fabric F square. Join the fabric B rectangle to the bottom edge of the fabrics A and F unit, then join the fabric C rectangle to the left edge of the fabrics A, B, and F unit. Complete the first round of strips by sewing the shorter fabric D rectangle to the top edge of the fabrics A, B, C, and F unit.

Sew the second round Press seams outward as you sew. With right sides together, pin and sew the shorter fabric E rectangle to the right edge of the fabrics A, B, C, D, and F unit. Join the second fabric D rectangle to the bottom edge, then the second fabric E rectangle to the left edge.

Complete the square Finish the block by joining the second fabric A rectangle to the top edge. Press seam outward.

---

framed square

The seam allowance is ¼ inch throughout.

When you combine small-scale prints with matching solid fabrics to frame them, your eye is drawn into the block. This quick-to-piece block is suitable for beginners.

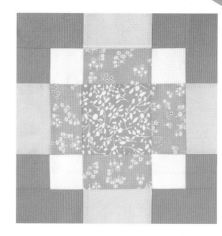

A
B
C
D
E

Fabric quantities

- Medium orange fabric A: 8 x 12 inches
- Light turquoise fabric B: 6 x 10 inches
- Medium gray print fabric C: 6 x 10 inches
- Medium orange print fabric D: 5 x 5 inches
- White fabric E: 6 x 6 inches

Prepare the patches

Rotary method
- From fabrics A and E, make four 4½-inch three-patch squares (see page 11)
- From fabrics B and C, make four 4½-inch rectangle squares (see page 11)
- From fabric D, cut one 4½-inch square

or

Template cutting

Using the 6 x 6 templates (pages 278–83):
- From fabric A, cut 4 small squares and 4 short rectangles
- From fabrics B and C, cut 4 short rectangles
- From fabric D, cut 1 large square
- From fabric E, cut 4 small squares

Template piecing

With right sides together, sew a fabric E small square to each fabric A small square; press seams over orange fabric. Join the fabric A rectangles to each strip to make four three-patch squares; press seams over the rectangles.

With right sides together, sew a fabric B short rectangle to each fabric C short rectangle to make four rectangle squares. Press seams over fabric C.

Make the block

Sew three rows With right sides together, sew a three-patch square to each side of a fabrics B and C square, with the white square and gray print at the bottom; press seam open. Repeat for the bottom row. For the center row, join a fabrics B and C rectangle square to each side of the fabric D square, with the gray and orange prints adjoining. Press seams open.

Complete the square With right sides facing, sew the three rows together; press seams open.

corner star

The seam allowance is ¼ inch throughout.

This design is a star within an octagon, and when you choose bright orange or red fabrics, it looks almost like a stylized sun. This version is made with just two fabrics: a modern print and crisp white.

A

B

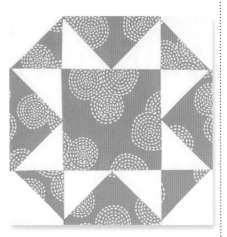

Fabric quantities

- Dark orange print fabric A: 15 x 16 inches
- White fabric B: 10 x 13 inches

Prepare the patches

Rotary method
- From fabrics A and B, make four 6½ x 3½-inch flying geese rectangles (see page 17) and four 3½-inch half-square triangles (see page 12)
- From fabric A, cut one 6½-inch square

or

Template cutting
Using the 4 x 4 templates (pages 269–73):
- From fabric A, cut 1 large square, 4 medium triangles, and 4 small triangles

- From fabric B, cut 12 small triangles

Template piecing

With right sides together, pin and sew two fabric B small triangles to each diagonal edge of the fabric A medium triangles to make four flying geese rectangles; press seams open.

With right sides together, pin and sew one fabric B small triangle to each of the fabric A small triangles to make four half-square triangles; press seams open.

Make the block

Join three rows With right sides together, sew a half-square triangle to each side of one flying geese rectangle, with the points toward the center of the block and the orange triangles at the corners; press seams over the squares. Repeat for the bottom row.

With right sides together, sew the remaining flying geese rectangles to the sides of the center square, making sure they point toward the square; press seams over the square.

Complete the square With right sides together, pin and sew the top row to the center row, matching seams carefully. Join the bottom row to the center row. Press seams open.

nine-patch cross

The seam allowance is ¼ inch throughout.

The nine-patch design is a versatile pattern that can be arranged in a variety of ways. Here, the five colored squares form a cross in the center of the block. Use several different prints, a mixture of prints and solids, or just one fabric for the cross, to create a bold, large-scale motif.

A

A

A

A

A

B

Fabric quantities

- 5 different medium orange print fabrics A: 10 x 15 inches in total
- White fabric B: 10 x 10 inches

Prepare the patches

Rotary method
- From fabrics A, cut five 4½-inch squares
- From fabric B, cut four 4½-inch squares

or

Template cutting
Using the 6 x 6 templates (pages 278–83):
- From fabrics A, cut 5 large squares
- From fabric B, cut 4 large squares

Make the block

Sew three rows To make the top row, with right sides together, pin and sew one fabric B large square to each side of a fabric A large square; press seams toward the orange fabric. Repeat to make the bottom row.

For the middle row, with right sides together, pin and sew three fabric A squares in a row; press seams open.

Complete the square With right sides together and carefully matching the seams, pin and sew the top and bottom rows to the middle row; press seams open.

goose star

The seam allowance is ¼ inch throughout.

Another traditional block, this framed sawtooth star is given a modern edge with a bold palette of solid colors. Put the darkest color at the center and the lightest color at the border to give depth to the Goose Star.

A
B
C
D

Fabric quantities

- Medium purple fabric A: 5 x 5 inches
- Medium red fabric B: 8 x 12 inches
- Light orange fabric C: 8 x 12 inches
- White fabric D: 12 x 12 inches

Prepare the patches

Rotary method
- From fabrics B and D, make four 4½ x 2½-inch flying geese rectangles (see page 17)
- From fabrics C and D, make four 4½ x 2½-inch flying geese rectangles
- From fabrics B, C, and D, make four 4½-inch four-patch squares (see page 11)
- From fabric A, cut one 4½-inch square

or

Template cutting
Using the 6 x 6 templates (pages 278–83):
- From fabric A, cut 1 large square
- From fabrics B and C, cut 4 medium triangles and 4 small squares each
- From fabric D, cut 8 small squares and 16 small triangles

Template piecing

With right sides together, pin and sew one fabric D small triangle to each diagonal edge of the fabric B medium triangles to make four flying geese rectangles. Repeat with the fabric C medium triangles to make another four flying geese rectangles; press seams outward.

With right sides together, pin and sew one fabric D small square to each of the fabric B and fabric C small squares. Sew two patchwork rectangles together to make a four-patch square, alternating the white fabric with the colored fabric; press seams open. Repeat to make another three four-patch squares.

Make the block

Join the flying geese rectangles With right sides together, pin and sew the two different flying geese rectangles together in pairs, making sure they point toward the center of the block and the fabric B flying geese are in the center; press seams over fabric B.

Make three rows With right sides together, pin and sew one four-patch square to the left side of a flying geese pair, making sure the colors match. Join another four-patch square to the right side; press seams open. Repeat to sew the bottom row.

To make the center row, pin and sew one flying geese pair to each side of the fabric A square, making sure they point toward the center of the block; press seams open.

Complete the square With right sides together, pin and sew the top row to the center row. Join the bottom row to the center row. Press seams open.

corners

This simple log cabin-style block is very quick to make because there are no seams to match. It is easily made with the rotary method.

The seam allowance is ¼ inch throughout.

Fabric quantities

- Medium purple print fabric A: 5 x 11 inches
- Medium orange fabric B: 6 x 7 inches
- Medium orange print fabric C: 3 x 9 inches
- Medium purple fabric D: 6 x 11 inches

Prepare the patches

Rotary method
- From fabric A, cut one 4½-in square, one 10½ x 2½-inch rectangle, and one 12½ x 2½-inch rectangle
- From fabric B, cut one 4½ x 2½-inch rectangle and one 6½ x 2½-inch rectangle

- From fabric C, cut one 6½ x 2½-inch rectangle and one 8½ x 2½-inch rectangle
- From fabric D, cut one 8½ x 2½-inch rectangle and one 10½ x 2½-inch rectangle

Make the block

Join the rounds Pressing all seams outward and starting at the bottom right corner, pin and sew the short fabric B rectangle to the top of the fabric A square, then sew the fabric B long rectangle to the left edge.

Pressing all seams outward, first sew the fabric C short rectangle to the top edge of the fabric B short rectangle, then the fabric C long rectangle to the left edge of the fabric B long rectangle.

Pressing all seams outward, first sew the fabric D short rectangle to the top edge

of the fabric C short rectangle, then the fabric D long rectangle to the left edge of the fabric C long rectangle.

Complete the square Pressing all seams outward, first sew the fabric A short rectangle to the top edge of the fabric D short rectangle, then the fabric A long rectangle to the left edge of the fabric D long rectangle.

---

sawtooth

A variety of gray textures blend together wonderfully to make a neutral background for vibrant orange fabrics.

The seam allowance is ¼ inch throughout.

Fabric quantities

- 4 different dark orange print fabrics A: 10 x 18 inches in total
- 5 different medium gray print fabric B: 10 x 10 inches in total
- Medium gray print fabric C: 13 x 4 inches

Prepare the patches

Rotary method
- From fabrics A and B, make eight 3½-inch half-square triangles (see page 12)
- From fabric A, cut four 3½-inch squares
- From fabric C, cut one 12½ x 2½-inch rectangle

or

Template cutting

Using the 4 x 4 templates (pages 269–73):
- From fabric A, cut 4 small squares and 8 small triangles
- From fabric B, cut 8 small triangles
- From fabric C, cut 1 full-length rectangle

Template piecing

With right sides together, pin and sew one fabric A small triangle to each of the fabric B small triangles to make eight half-square triangles.

Make the block

Piece the main column With right sides together, pin and sew one half-square triangle to each side of one fabric A small square, being careful to match the orange triangles; press seams open. Repeat with the remaining six half-square triangles and three fabric A squares.

With right sides together and carefully matching seams, sew the first row to the second row, the third row to the second row, and the fourth row to the third row, making sure all of the orange triangles point in the same direction; press seams open.

Complete the square With right sides together, pin and sew the fabric C full-length rectangle to the right edge of the block; press seam open.

flying cross

The pinwheel is given a strong sense of movement by the triangles outside the center square. Matching the background and print colors give it a traditional charm.

Fabric quantities

- Medium orange print fabric A: 10 x 10 inches
- Light yellow fabric B: 5 x 10 inches
- Light blue fabric C: 10 x 13 inches
- Medium blue fabric D: 8 x 8 inches

Prepare the patches

Rotary method
- From fabrics A and B, make four 3½-inch half-square triangles (see page 12)
- From fabrics A and C, make four 3½-inch half-square triangles
- From fabric C, cut four 3½-inch squares
- From fabric D, cut four 3½-inch squares

or

Template cutting
Using the 4 x 4 templates (pages 269–73):
- From fabric A, cut 8 small triangles
- From fabric B, cut 4 small triangles
- From fabric C, cut 4 small triangles and 4 small squares
- From fabric D, cut 4 small squares

A
B
C
D

Template piecing

With right sides together, pin and sew one fabric A triangle to each of the fabric B triangles to make four half-square triangles. Sew one fabric A triangle to each of the fabric C triangles to make four half-square triangles.

Make the block

Sew four rows For the top row, with right sides together, sew a fabric D square to the left side of a fabrics A and C half-square triangle, with the print triangle pointing down and right. Sew a fabric C square to the right edge, then join a fabric D square; press seams open. Repeat to make the bottom row.

To make the two middle rows, join a fabric C square to the left edge of a fabrics A and B half-square triangle, with the print triangle pointing down and left. Sew a fabrics A and B half-square triangle to the right side, with the print triangle pointing up and left. Join a fabrics A and C half-square triangle to the right edge of the row, with the print triangle pointing down and left; press seams open. Repeat to make the second middle row.

Complete the square Arrange the rows with the pinwheel in the center. With right sides together and matching seams, sew the second row to the first row; press seam open. Repeat to join the third row to the second, and the fourth row to the third.

pinwheel check

Two-colored sails on the pinwheels add animation to the block, although you could use one larger triangle instead for simpler piecing. Join edge to edge for a checkered look across an entire quilt.

A
B
C
D

The seam allowance is ¼ inch throughout.

Fabric quantities

- Medium orange fabric A: 6 x 10 inches
- Medium orange print fabric B: 6 x 10 inches
- Gray print fabric C: 10 x 10 inches
- Dark red fabric D: 7 x 14 inches

Prepare the patches

Rotary method
- From fabrics A, B, and C, make eight 3½-inch three-quarter square triangles (see page 13)
- From fabric D, cut two 6½-inch squares

or

Template cutting
Using the 4 x 4 templates (pages 269–73):

- From fabrics A and B, cut 8 tiny triangles each
- From fabric C, cut 8 small triangles
- From fabric D, cut 2 large squares

Template piecing

With right sides together, sew a pair of fabrics A and B tiny triangles together along one short edge, with fabric A at the left; press seam open. Sew this larger triangle to the fabric C triangle along the long edge; press seam over fabric C. Repeat to make eight three-quarter square triangles.

Make the block

Sew the pinwheel squares Pin and sew two three-quarter square triangles together along a light and dark edge; press seam toward

fabric C. Repeat to make the second row. With right sides together, join the rows along the long edge, with the light fabric touching the dark fabric; press seams open.

Complete the square Join the pinwheel squares to the fabric D large squares; press seam over fabric D. Join the two rows together, matching seams; press seams open.

---

brave world

Like Colorado Beauty on page 78, this modernized block also features a white pinwheel at the center. If joining several edge to edge, make the blocks in a variety of single colors; you'll still get the multicolored version when the blocks are aligned.

A
B
C
D
E

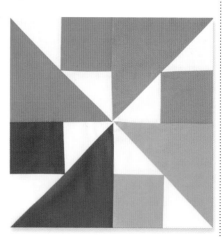

The seam allowance is ¼ inch throughout.

Fabric quantities

- Medium red fabric A: 8 x 8 inches
- Medium lilac fabric B: 8 x 8 inches
- Medium orange fabric C: 8 x 8 inches
- Medium mauve fabric D: 8 x 8 inches
- White fabric E: 9 x 9 inches

Prepare the patches

Rotary method
- From fabrics A and E; fabrics B and E; fabrics C and E; and fabrics D and E, make one 6½-inch triangle-and-square block (see page 15) each

or

Template cutting
Using the 4 x 4 templates (pages 269–73):
- From fabrics A, B, C, and D cut 1 large triangle and 1 small square each
- From fabric E, cut 8 small triangles

Template piecing

To make the triangle-and-square blocks, join a fabric E small triangle to the left edge of the fabric A small square; press seam over the triangle. Join another fabric E small triangle to the bottom edge; press seam outward. Sew the unit to the long diagonal edge of the fabric A large triangle; press seam over triangle. Repeat to make another three triangle-and-square blocks, one in each color.

Make the block

Sew two rows Lay out the four triangle-and-square blocks in their final positions, with the fabric E triangles rotating in the same direction around the center point, as shown above. With right sides together, pin and sew two squares; press seams open. Repeat for the second row.

Complete the square With right sides together, pin and sew the rows together, making sure the fabric E triangles form the pinwheel in the center; press seams open.

friendship star

The seam allowance is ¼ inch throughout.

A variation on the star motif, the Friendship Star dates to the nineteenth century. Made with retro prints and a 1950s color palette, it's ideal for modern decor.

A
B
C
D

Fabric quantities

- Medium yellow fabric A: 6 x 12 inches
- Medium gray print fabric B: 6 x 12 inches
- Dark gray print fabric C: 5 x 5 inches
- Light beige print fabric D: 10 x 10 inches

Prepare the patches

Rotary method
- From fabrics A and B, make four 4½-inch half-square triangles (see page 12)
- From fabric C, cut one 4½-inch square
- From fabric D, cut four 4½-inch squares

or

Template cutting
Using the 6 x 6 templates (pages 278–83):
- From fabrics A and B, cut 4 large triangles each

- From fabric C, cut 1 large square
- From fabric D, cut 4 large squares

Template piecing

With right sides together, pin and sew one fabric A large triangle to each of the fabric B large triangles to make four half-square triangles; press seams open.

Make the block

Sew three rows With right sides together, pin and sew one fabric D large square to each side of one half-square triangle, making sure the yellow triangle is pointing down and left; press seams open. Repeat to make the bottom row.

With right sides together, pin and sew one half-square triangle to each side of the fabric C large square. The yellow triangle on the left side should be pointing down and right, and the yellow triangle on the right side should be pointing up and left.

Complete the square With right sides together and carefully matching seams, pin and sew the top row to the center row. Join the bottom row to the center row, making sure the yellow triangle adjoins the center square. Press seams open.

zigzag stripe

The seam allowance is ¼ inch throughout.

Zigzag Stripe makes a striking border as well as a lively allover design. Try making this block in graduated colors that drift from light to dark. Alternatively, accentuate the stripes by using contrasting prints. This block is most accurately made from templates.

A
B
C

Fabric quantities

- Medium orange print fabric A: 8 x 16 inches
- Medium yellow print fabric B: 8 x 8 inches
- White fabric C: 8 x 8 inches

Prepare the patches

Template cutting
Using the 4 x 4 templates (pages 269–73):
- From fabric A, cut 4 right diamonds and 4 left diamonds
- From fabric B, cut 2 right diamonds and 2 left diamonds
- From fabric C, cut 8 small triangles

Make the block

Piece the columns For the first column, with right sides together, pin and sew a fabric A right diamond to each diagonal edge of a fabric B right diamond. Join a fabric C small triangle to the top and bottom diagonal edges to create the first rectangular column; press seams up. Repeat for the third column.

For the second column, with right sides together, pin and sew a fabric A left diamond to each diagonal edge of a fabric B left diamond. Join a fabric C small triangle to the top and bottom diagonal edges to create the third rectangular column; press seams down. Repeat for the fourth column.

Complete the square With right sides together, pin and sew the first and second columns together, carefully matching the seams. Join the third and fourth columns. Press seams open.

framed checkerboard

Alternating light and dark squares form a classic pattern found around the world. This framed version makes an ideal play quilt for a small child.

The seam allowance is ¼ inch throughout.

Fabric quantities

- Light turquoise print fabric A: 6 x 12 inches
- Medium orange print fabric B: 6 x 12 inches
- Dark blue print fabric C: 9 x 12 inches
- Dark orange fabric D: 6 x 6 inches

Prepare the patches

Rotary method
- From fabrics A and B, make four 4½-inch four-patch squares (see page 11)
- From fabric C, cut four 8½ x 2½-inch rectangles
- From fabric D, cut four 2½-inch squares

or

Template cutting
Using the 6 x 6 templates (pages 278–83):

- From fabrics A and B, cut 8 small squares each
- From fabric C, cut 4 long rectangles
- From fabric D, cut 4 small squares

Template piecing

With right sides together, pin and sew eight pairs of fabric A and fabric B small squares; press seams over fabric A. Join two pairs of rectangles, alternating colors, to make four four-patch squares; press seams open.

Make the block

Sew the checkerboard With right sides together, pin and sew two four-patch squares together, continuing to alternate the colored squares; press seam open. Repeat to make another row. With right sides together, pin and sew the two rows together, carefully matching seams and continuing the checkerboard pattern; press seam open.

With right sides together, pin and sew a fabric D small square to each side of two fabric C long rectangles; press seams open.

Complete the square With right sides together, sew a fabric C long rectangle to each side of the center block; press seams open. Join the fabrics C and D strips to the top and bottom; press seams open.

duck and ducklings

The ducklings are the triangles pointing to the center square, which is the duck. Try this block with a variety of polka dots in analogous colors to get a fresh look.

The seam allowance is ¼ inch throughout.

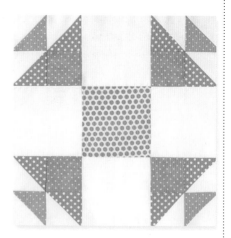

Fabric quantities

- Dark orange print fabric A: 6 x 6 inches
- Medium orange print fabric B: 8 x 8 inches
- Medium orange print fabric C: 4 x 8 inches
- Tangerine print fabric D: 5 x 5 inches
- White fabric E: 12 x 18 inches

Prepare the patches

Rotary method
- From fabrics B and E, make eight 2½-inch half-square triangles (see page 12)
- From fabrics C and E, make four 2½-inch half-square triangles
- From fabric A, cut four 2½-inch squares
- From fabric D, cut one 4½-inch square
- From fabric E, cut four 4½-inch squares

or

Template cutting
Using the 6 x 6 templates (pages 278–83):
- From fabric A, cut 4 small squares
- From fabric B, cut 8 small triangles
- From fabric C, cut 4 small triangles
- From fabric D, cut 1 large square
- From fabric E, cut 4 large squares and 12 small triangles

Template piecing

Sew a fabric E small triangle to each fabric B small triangle and fabric C small triangle to make 12 half-square triangles; press seams open.

Make the block

Join the patches Sew a fabrics C and E half-square triangle to a fabrics B and E half-square triangle, facing the same way; press open. Repeat three times. Sew a fabrics B and E half-square triangle to each fabric A square; press open. Sew the strips into four squares, with fabric E in the outer corners; press open.

Complete the square Sew a patchwork square to each side of a fabric E square, with fabric A toward the center; press seams open. Repeat for the bottom row. For the center row, sew a fabric E square to each side of the fabric D square; press seams open. Sew the rows together, matching the seams; press seams open.

bird flock

The seam allowance is ¼ inch throughout.

Bird Flock is a traditional design inspired by nature. **Make four identical blocks and join them so that the dark squares meet at the center, or sew them together in rows, so the half-square triangles all point in the same direction.**

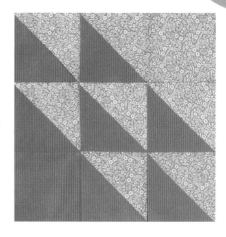

A
B

Fabric quantities

- Dark orange fabric A: 12 x 17 inches
- Light orange print fabric B: 12 x 17 inches

Prepare the patches

Rotary method
- From fabrics A and B, make seven 4½-inch half-square triangles (see page 12)
- From fabrics A and B, cut one 4½-inch square each

or

Template cutting
Using the 6 x 6 templates (pages 278–83):
- From fabrics A and B, cut 7 large triangles and 1 large square each

Template piecing

With right sides together, pin and sew a fabric A large triangle to each of the fabric B large triangles to make seven half-square triangles.

Make the block

Sew three rows For the top row, with right sides together, pin and sew two half-square triangles together, making sure both dark orange triangles point down and left; press seam open. Join the fabric B large square on the right side; press seam open.

For the center row, with right sides together, pin and sew three half-square triangles together, making sure all dark orange triangles point down and left; press seams open.

For the bottom row, with right sides together, pin and sew two half-square triangles together, making sure all dark orange triangles point down and left; press seams open. Join the fabric A large square on the left side; press seam open.

Complete the square With right sides together, pin and sew the top and bottom rows to the center row, carefully matching seams; press seams open.

- -

all square

The seam allowance is ¼ inch throughout.

In this basic, beginner-friendly block, two different color palettes of the same fabric link the squares together. The loosely drawn print softens the strong lines. **Join several blocks edge to edge for an overall checkerboard look, or make each square in a different print and color.**

A
B
C

Fabric quantities

- Medium gray print fabric A: 12 x 13 inches
- Medium orange print fabric B: 9 x 13 inches
- White print fabric C: 3 x 6 inches

Prepare the patches

Rotary method
- From fabric A, cut four 4½ x 2½-inch rectangles and six 2½-inch squares
- From fabric B, cut four 4½ x 2½-inch rectangles and four 2½-inch squares
- From fabric C, cut two 2½-inch squares

or

Template cutting
Using the 6 x 6 templates (pages 278–83):
- From fabric A, cut 4 medium rectangles and 6 small squares

- From fabric B, cut 4 medium rectangles and 4 small squares
- From fabric C, cut 2 small squares

Make the block

Piece four patches With right sides together, pin and sew two fabric A small squares to each side of the fabric C small squares; press seams open. Join two fabric A medium rectangles on the sides of both strips to make two gray-and-white squares; press seams open.

With right sides together, pin and sew two fabric B small squares to each side of the two fabric A small squares; press seams open. Join two fabric B medium rectangles on the top and bottom edges of both strips to make two orange-and-gray squares; press seams open.

Sew two rows With right sides together, pin and sew a gray-and-white square to an orange-and-gray square; press seam open. Repeat to make the second row.

Complete the square With right sides facing, pin and sew the two rows together, carefully matching the center seam and alternating colors; press seam open.

double four patch

One of the most basic blocks, Double Four Patch uses only squares in two sizes: the large squares are a good way to show off favorite prints. You can join blocks together to create a secondary pattern of rows of diagonal squares.

A
B
C

The seam allowance is ¼ inch throughout.

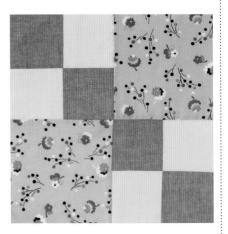

Fabric quantities

- Dark orange fabric A: 8 x 8 inches
- Medium yellow fabric B: 8 x 8 inches
- Medium turquoise print fabric C: 7 x 14 inches

Prepare the patches

Rotary method
- From fabrics A and B, make two 6½-inch four-patch squares (see page 11)
- From fabric C, cut two 6½-inch squares

or

Template cutting
Using the 4 x 4 templates (pages 269–73):
- From fabrics A and B, cut 4 small squares each
- From fabric C, cut 2 large squares

Template piecing

With right sides together, join a fabric A square to a fabric B square; press seam over fabric A. Repeat to make another three pairs.

Join two pairs together at the long edge to make a four-patch square, making sure the colors alternate; press seam open. Repeat to make another four-patch square.

Make the block

Sew two rows With a fabric A square at the top left, join each four-patch square to a fabric C square; press seam over fabric C.

Complete the square With right sides together, pin and sew the rows together, matching the seams in the center; press seam open.

---

zigzag border

Half-square triangles are combined to make a scrappy zigzag. Use a variety of prints, but keep to the same shade for visual cohesion. Join the blocks in horizontal rows to frame a quilt.

A
A
A
A
B
C

The seam allowance is ¼ inch throughout.

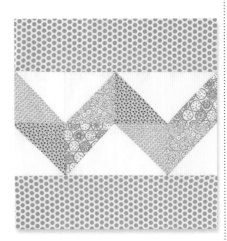

Fabric quantities

- At least 4 different orange print fabrics A: 12 x 12 inches in total
- Medium orange print fabric B: 10 x 13 inches
- White fabric C: 12 x 12 inches

Prepare the patches

Rotary method
- From fabrics A and C, make eight 3½-inch half-square triangles (see page 12)
- From fabric B, cut two 12½ x 3½-inch rectangles

or

Template cutting
Using the 4 x 4 templates (pages 269–73):
- From fabrics A and C, cut 8 small triangles each
- From fabric B, cut 2 full-length rectangles

Template piecing

With right sides together, sew one fabric A and one fabric C small triangle together along the diagonal edge to make a half-square triangle; press seam over fabric A. Repeat to make another seven half-square triangles.

Make the block

Piece the center panel Lay out the half-square triangles in two rows of four squares to create the zigzag, making sure

no two identical patches are touching. With right sides together, sew in vertical pairs; press seams open. Join the pairs at the long edges, making sure the seams match; press seams open.

Complete the square With right sides together, pin and sew the fabric B full-length rectangles to the top and bottom of the panel; press seams over fabric B.

kitten

This version is a ginger cat, but you could make the block in various colors to match your favorite pet. Pieced somewhat like a jigsaw, the block is made in two halves with green grass added at the end.

The seam allowance is ¼ inch throughout.

A
B
C
D

Fabric quantities

- Dark orange fabric A: 10 x 12 inches
- Light orange print fabric B: 8 x 9 inches
- Light blue print fabric C: 11 x 13 inches
- Medium green print fabric D: 3 x 13 inches

Prepare the patches

Rotary method
- From fabrics A and C, make one 6½ x 2½-inch short boat (see page 17)
- From fabrics A and C, make one 2½-inch half-square triangle (see page 12)
- From fabrics A, B, and C, make one 6½ x 4½-inch cat's head (see page 17)
- From fabric A, cut two 2½-inch squares
- From fabric B, cut one 4½-inch square, one 4½ x 2½-inch rectangle, and one 2½-inch square
- From fabric C, cut two 4½ x 2½-inch rectangles, two 2½-inch squares, and one 10½ x 2½-inch rectangle
- From fabric D, cut one 12½ x 2½-inch rectangle

or

Template cutting
Using the 6 x 6 templates (pages 278–83):
- From fabric A, cut 1 cat's head, 2 small squares, and 3 small triangles
- From fabric B, cut 1 large square, 1 short rectangle, 1 small square, and 1 small triangle
- From fabric C, cut 1 short boat, 1 long rectangle, 2 short rectangles, 2 small squares, and 2 small triangles
- From fabric D, cut 1 full-length rectangle

Template piecing

To make the ears, sew two fabric A small triangles to the diagonal edges of the fabric C short boat; press seams over fabric A.

For the head, join a fabric C small triangle to the bottom left corner of the fabric A cat head, and a fabric B small triangle to the bottom right corner; press the seams over the triangles.

To make the tail tip, join the remaining fabrics A and C small triangles along the long diagonal edge to make a half-square triangle; press seam over fabric C.

Make the block

Arrange the patches Lay out all the fabric pieces like a jigsaw puzzle, as shown above.

Sew the left half With right sides facing, pin and sew the ears to the top of the head at the long edges; press seam over the head.

Join a fabric A small square to a fabric C small square; press seam over fabric A. With fabric A at the bottom left, sew the strip to a long edge of the fabric B short rectangle; press seam over fabric B. Join a fabric C short rectangle to the left edge of this square; press seam over fabric C.

Sew the rectangle unit to the bottom edge of the head; press seam open.

Sew the right half With right sides together, pin and sew the fabrics A and C half-square triangle for the tail tip to a fabric B small square; press seam over fabric B. Sew a fabric C short rectangle to the left edge; press seam over fabric C. Join this square to the top of the fabric B large square; press seam over fabric B.

Join the remaining fabrics A and C small squares; press seam over fabric C. With the fabric A square on the right, join to the bottom edge of the fabric B large square; press seam over B. Join the fabric C strip to the right edge; press seam over C.

Complete the square With right sides together, join the two halves, matching the seams; press seam open. Join the fabric D full-length rectangle to the bottom edge; press seam over D.

bear's paw

A traditional block, Bear's Paw recalls life in a forest clearing, where wandering bears might leave a trail of paw prints behind them. The same design is known as Duck's Foot in the eastern United States. Vary the block by making it in a single color against a white background, or use a different solid color for each paw.

A

B

C

Fabric quantities

- Dark orange fabric A: 8 x 19 inches
- Medium orange print fabric B: 8 x 8 inches
- Medium yellow fabric C: 14 x 19 inches

Prepare the patches

Rotary method
- From fabrics A and C, make sixteen 2¼-inch half-square triangles (see page 12)
- From fabric A, cut one 2¼-inch square
- From fabric B, cut four 4-inch squares
- From fabric C, cut four 2¼ x 5¾-inch rectangles and four 2¼-inch squares

or

Template cutting
Using the 7 x 7 templates (pages 284–5):
- From fabric A, cut 16 small triangles and 1 small square
- From fabric B, cut 4 large squares
- From fabric C, cut 16 small triangles, 4 long rectangles, and 4 small squares

Template piecing

With right sides together, pin and sew a fabric A triangle to a fabric C triangle along the diagonal edge to make one half-square triangle; press seam over fabric A. Repeat to make another 15 half-square triangles.

Make the block

Sew the corner squares Lay four half-square triangles along the left and top edges of a fabric B large square, so all point to the center. Sew the top and side pairs, then sew the top pair to the fabric B large square. Join the fabric C small square to the top of the left pair and sew to the left edge. Repeat to make four squares.

Make the top and bottom rows Join a finished "paw" to each long edge of a fabric C long rectangle; press seams inward. Repeat.

Sew the center row Sew the short edge of two fabric C long rectangles to the side edge of a fabric A small square; press seams outward.

Complete the square Sew the top and bottom rows to the center row; press seams inward.

yankee puzzle

Sixteen half-square triangles combine in this carnival of a block. Just one of many versions, this block will look different depending on how the colors are arranged within the design.

The seam allowance is ¼ inch throughout.

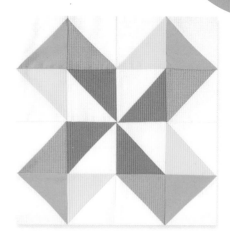

A
B
C
D
E

Fabric quantities

- Medium orange fabric A: 5 x 10 inches
- Medium pink fabric B: 5 x 10 inches
- Light yellow fabric C: 5 x 10 inches
- Medium red fabric D: 5 x 10 inches
- White fabric E: 10 x 20 inches

Prepare the patches

Rotary method
- From fabrics A and E; fabrics B and E; fabrics C and E; and fabrics D and E, make four 3½-inch half-square triangles (see page 12) each

or

Template cutting
Using the 4 x 4 templates (pages 269–73):

- From fabrics A, B, C, and D, cut 4 small triangles each
- From fabric E, cut 16 small triangles

Template piecing

With right sides together, sew a fabric E small triangle to each colored small triangle along the long diagonal edges to make 16 half-square triangles; press seams over the dark fabric.

Make the block

Sew four patches With right sides together, join the orange and pink half-square triangles, with fabric A on the left and both fabric E triangles outward; press seam over the dark fabric. Repeat to join the yellow and red half-square triangles with fabric C on the left and both fabric E triangles pointing down and left. Join the fabrics A, B, and E patch to the top of the C, D, and E patch; press seams open. Repeat to make four patches.

Complete the square Sew the patches together in pairs, with the orange triangles in the outside corners; press seams over fabric E. Flip one pair and sew the rows together, lining up seams; press seams open.

---

alternate stripes

The seam allowance is ¼ inch throughout.

This informal block could be totally scrappy, using a random collection of prints and plains, or keep to a narrow color palette for a more sophisticated look. Using color opposites here—burnt orange and tangerine with turquoise and white—makes these colors sing out. You could stitch multiples of this block edge to edge for an overall pattern of striped rows. This improvisational block is easily made with the rotary method.

A
B
C
D
E

Fabric quantities

- Dark orange print fabric A: 5 x 7 inches
- Dark orange print fabric B: 5 x 7 inches
- Dark orange print fabric C: 5 x 7 inches
- Medium turquoise print fabric D: 5 x 7 inches
- White fabric E: 10 x 14 inches

Prepare the patches

Rotary method
- From fabrics A, B, C, and D, cut one 6½ x 2½-inch rectangle and one 6½ x 1½-inch rectangle each

- From fabric E, cut four 6½ x 2½-inch rectangles and four 6½ x 1½-inch rectangles

Make the block

Join the stripes With right sides together, sew a wide fabric E rectangle to each fabrics A, B, C, and D narrow rectangle along the long edges; press seams over the print fabrics.

Sew a fabric E narrow rectangle to each fabrics A, B, C, and D wide rectangle along the long edges; press seams over the print fabric.

Make two columns Lay out the pairs of stripes in two columns, with the white wide rectangles on the left and the print patches opposite the white patches.

With right sides together, pin and sew the patches on the left along the long edges to make a column; press seams over the print fabrics. Repeat to make the right column.

Complete the square With right sides together, pin and sew the two columns together, matching the seams; press seams open.

colorado beauty

The seam allowance is ¼ inch throughout.

Another traditional block, this is much easier to piece than it may seem at first glance. Like other classics, it's been given a fresh new look by making each quarter square in a different saturated color. Note how the negative space at the center forms a white pinwheel, set within a multicolored diagonal cross.

A
B
C
D
E

Fabric quantities

- Medium mauve fabric A: 7 x 8 inches

- Medium orange fabric B: 7 x 8 inches

- Medium red fabric C: 7 x 8 inches

- Medium purple fabric D: 7 x 8 inches

- White fabric E: 8 x 16 inches

Prepare the patches

Rotary method
- From fabrics A and E; fabrics B and E; fabrics C and E; and fabrics D and E, make one 6½ x 3½-inch flying geese rectangle (see page 17) and one 6½ x 3½-inch left diamond rectangle (see page 16) each

or

Template cutting
Using the 4 x 4 templates (pages 269–73):
- From fabrics A, B, C, and D, cut 1 medium triangle and 1 left diamond each

- From fabric E, cut 16 small triangles

Template piecing

With right sides together, sew a fabric E small triangle to the left diagonal edge of a fabric A medium triangle. Sew a second fabric E triangle to the right edge of the fabric A medium triangle to complete a flying geese rectangle; press seams across the small triangles. Repeat to make one flying geese rectangle from each color.

Join a fabric E small triangle to the diagonal edges of each left diamond to make a left diamond rectangle; press seams inward over the diamond patch. Repeat to make one left diamond rectangle from each color.

Make the block

Sew four patches With right sides together and matching the colors, join the long edges of the diamond rectangles and the flying geese rectangles, making sure each colored flying geese triangle is pointing outward; press seams over the flying geese.

Make two rows Lay out squares in their final positions, as shown above. With right sides together, pin and sew in pairs; press seams open.

Complete the square With right sides together, pin and sew the two rows together, matching the seams; press seams open.

fall leaf

A classic leaf motif, Fall Leaf is based on three-quarters of a Sawtooth Star (see page 55) block with an appliqué stem. The gray background makes it look as if the leaf is tumbling through the sky. Although you could make the leaf in one fabric, the block works particularly well in tonal prints. Make a seasonal quilt in shades of russet, gold, and brown, or use bright greens for spring and summer foliage.

The seam allowance is ¼ inch throughout.

Fabric quantities

- Dark orange print fabric A: 10 x 10 inches
- Dark orange print fabric B: 5 x 10 inches
- Dark orange print fabric C: 5 x 10 inches
- Light gray fabric D: 12 x 18 inches

Prepare the patches

Rotary method
- From fabrics A, B, and D and fabrics A, C, and D make one 6½ x 3½-inch flying geese rectangle (see page 17) each
- From fabrics B and D and fabrics C and D, make one 3½-inch half-square triangle (see page 12) each
- From fabrics A, B, and C, cut one 3½-inch square each
- From fabric D, cut three 3½-inch squares and one 6½-inch square
- From fabric A, cut 1 stem using the template on page 286

or

Template cutting
Using the 4 x 4 templates (pages 269–73):
- From fabrics A, B, and C, cut 1 small square and 2 small triangles each
- From fabric D, cut 1 large square, 2 medium triangles, 3 small squares, and 2 small triangles
- From fabric A, cut 1 stem using the template on page 286

Template piecing

With right sides together, pin and sew a fabric A small triangle to a diagonal edge of a fabric D medium triangle. Sew a fabric B small triangle to the opposite edge of the medium triangle to complete the flying geese rectangle; press seams across the medium triangle. Repeat using fabrics A, C, and D.

With right sides together, sew a fabric B small triangle to a fabric D small triangle along the long diagonal edges to make a half-square triangle; press seam toward the darker fabric. Repeat using fabrics C and D.

Make the block

Appliqué the stem Using a ¼-inch seam allowance, press under the side and bottom edges of the stem, then pin to the fabric D large square with the top end overlapping the top right corner. Sew in place (see page 20).

Make the leaf Lay out the patches in their final positions, as shown above. With right sides together, join the top left fabric D square to the fabrics C and D half-square triangle, as shown above. Join the fabrics A and B squares together, then sew them to the bottom of the fabrics A, B, and D flying geese rectangle. Sew this patch to the right edge of the fabrics C and D unit.

Sew the C small square to the top of the fabrics B and D half-square triangle, with the print triangle pointing up and right. Sew both to the right edge of the stem.

With right sides together, join the patch that makes up the top of the leaf to the top edge of the stem square.

Complete the square Sew the final two fabric D squares to each end of the fabrics A, C, and D flying geese rectangle, then sew the strip to the right edge of the patchwork piece; press seams open.

A
B
C
D

chicken

This stylized chicken block would look at home in the kitchen.

The seam allowance is ¼ inch throughout.

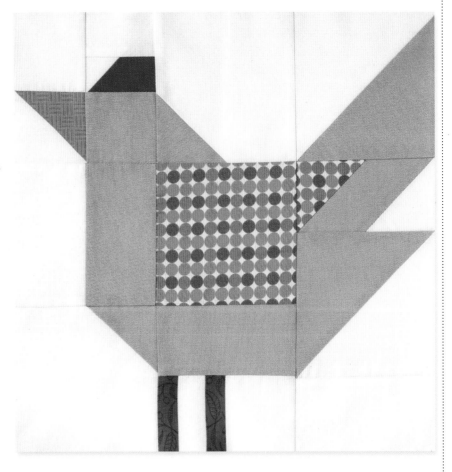

Fabric quantities

- Medium yellow fabric A: 6 x 15 inches
- Dark orange print fabric B: 3 x 3 inches
- Dark red fabric C: 2 x 3 inches
- Medium orange print fabric D: 5 x 8 inches
- Medium green fabric E: 2 x 3 inches
- White fabric F: 8 x 19 inches

Prepare the patches

Rotary method

- From fabrics A and F, make two 4½-inch half-square triangles (see page 12) for the tail, two 4½-inch corner squares (see page 14), and two 4½-inch rectangle squares (see page 11)
- From fabrics A, D, and F, make one 4½ x 2½-inch left diamond rectangle (see page 16)
- From fabrics B and F, make one 2½-inch half-square triangle (see page 12)
- From fabrics C and F, make one 2½ x 1½-inch left tapered rectangle (see page 16)
- From fabric A, cut one 2½-inch square
- From fabric D, cut one 4½-inch square
- From fabric E, cut two 2½ x 1-inch rectangles
- From fabric F, cut one 2½ x 1½-inch rectangle, one 2½-inch square, and one 4½ x 2½-inch rectangle

or

Template cutting

Using the 6 x 6 templates (pages 278–83):

- From fabric A, cut 2 large triangles, 2 short rectangles, 1 left diamond, 1 small square, and 2 small triangles
- From fabric B, cut 1 small triangle
- From fabric C, cut 1 small left tapered rectangle
- From fabric D, cut 1 large square and 1 small triangle
- From fabric E, cut 2 narrow very small rectangles
- From fabric F, cut 2 large triangles, 2 small triangles, 2 corner squares, 3 short rectangles, 1 small square, 1 very small triangle, and 1 very small rectangle

Template piecing

To make the comb, with right sides together, join the fabric F very small triangle to the fabric C small tapered rectangle; press seam open.

To make the beak, join the fabrics B and F small triangles along the long diagonal edges to make one half-square triangle; press seam open.

To make the tail, join the fabrics A and F large triangles along the long diagonal edges to make one half-square triangle; press seams over fabric A. With fabric D at left, join a fabric D small triangle and a fabric F small triangle to the diagonals of the fabric A diamond; press seams open.

To make the two corner squares, sew a fabric A small triangle to the diagonal edge of each of the fabric F corner squares; press seams over fabric A.

To make the breast and belly rectangle squares, join the long edges of the fabrics A and F short rectangles; press seams open.

Make the block

Assemble the chicken Lay out all of the pieces, as shown above.

Make the left column For the head, sew the fabric F small square to the top edge of the beak half-square triangle. Join the very small F rectangle to the top edge of the comb; press seam open. Sew to the top edge of the fabric A small square. Sew these two rectangles together vertically. Join the fabrics A and F rectangle square to the lower edge, with F on the left, then join the fabrics A and F corner square to the bottom. Press all seams open.

Make the center column Sew the fabrics A and F corner square to the top edge of the fabric D square; press seam downward. Join the fabrics A and F rectangle square to the bottom edge; press seam down. Appliqué (see page 20) the fabric E rectangles to the white rectangle for the legs.

Make the right column Join a large fabrics A and F half-square triangle to each long edge of the diamond for the tail, with the fabric F triangles pointing out; press over fabric A. Join the F rectangle to the bottom edge; press seam down.

Complete the square Sew the columns together, matching the seams; press seams open.

rooster

This colorful companion for Chicken on page 82 can be combined with other animal blocks in a quilt.

The seam allowance is ¼ in throughout.

Fabric quantities

- Medium yellow fabric A: 8 x 10 inches
- Dark orange fabric B: 4 x 4 inches
- Dark red fabric C: 2 x 3 inches
- Medium red print fabric D: 5 x 9 inches
- Medium green print fabric E: 8 x 9 inches
- White fabric F: 14 x 15 inches

Prepare the patches

Rotary method
- From fabrics A and F, make two 4½-inch rectangle squares (see page 11) and three 4½-inch corner squares (see page 14)
- From fabrics A, E, and F; fabrics D, E, and F; and fabrics E and F, make one 4½ x 2½-inch right diamond rectangle (see page 16) each
- From fabrics B and F, make one 2½-inch half-square triangle (see page 12)
- From fabrics E and F, make one 4½ x 2½-inch right tapered rectangle (see page 16)
- From fabric A, cut one 2½-inch square
- From fabrics C and F, make one 2½ x 1½-inch right tapered rectangle (see page 16)
- From fabric D, cut one 4½-inch square
- From fabric E, cut two 2½ x 1-inch rectangles
- From fabric F, cut one 2½ x 1½-inch rectangle and one 2½-inch square

or

Template cutting
Using the 6 x 6 templates (pages 278–83):
- From fabric A, cut 2 short rectangles, 1 small square, and 4 small triangles
- From fabric B, cut 1 small triangle
- From fabric C, cut 1 small right tapered rectangle
- From fabric D, cut 1 large square and 1 small triangle
- From fabric E, cut 1 right tapered rectangle, 3 right diamonds, and 2 narrow very small rectangles

- From fabric F, cut 3 corner squares, 2 short rectangles, 1 small square, 6 small triangles, 1 very small triangle, and 1 very small rectangle

Template piecing

To make the tail, join a fabric F small triangle to the diagonal edge of the fabric E right tapered rectangle; press seam open. Join a fabric F small triangle to the left side of the each fabric E right diamond, then add fabrics A, D, and F small triangles to the right sides; press seams open.

Join a small fabric A small triangle to the diagonal of each of the fabric F corner squares; press seams over A fabric. To make the comb, join the fabric F very small triangle to the fabric C small right tapered rectangle; press seam open.

Make the block

Assemble the rooster Lay out all of the pieces, as shown above.

Make the left column With right sides together, join the fabrics F and E diamond triangle to the top of the tapered rectangle.

Sew the F, E, and D right diamond rectangle to the bottom edge; press seams open. Join the fabrics F, E, and A right diamond rectangle to the top of the corner square and join to the bottom edge of the other tail units; press seams open.

Make the center column With right sides together, sew the A and F corner square to the top of the fabric D large square, then sew a fabrics A and F rectangle square to the bottom edge; press seams down. Appliqué (see page 20) the fabric E rectangles to the white rectangle to make the legs.

Make the right column With right sides together, sew the fabric F very small rectangle to the top edge of the comb; press seam over fabric C. Add the fabric F small square to the right edge; press seam over fabric F. Join the fabric A small square to the fabrics B and F half-square triangle, then join to the comb; press seams open.

Sew the fabrics A and F rectangle square to the lower edge of the head unit, with fabric A on the left. Join the fabrics A and F corner square to the bottom edge; press seams open.

Complete the square Sew the columns together, matching the seams; press seams open.

89

wishing ring

The seam allowance is ¼ inch throughout.

Wishing Ring is romantically named, evoking a talisman that safeguards a special wish or hope for the future. It was first documented in 1934, but it is probably older.

A
B
C
D

Fabric quantities

- Dark turquoise print fabric A: 11 x 12 inches
- Light turquoise print fabric B: 12 x 13 inches
- Dark orange print fabric C: 9 x 9 inches
- White fabric D: 5 x 13 inches

Prepare the patches

Template cutting
Using the 5 x 5 templates (pages 274–7):
- From fabric A, cut 8 small squares and 4 small triangles
- From fabric B, cut 4 small squares and 8 small triangles
- From fabric C, cut 4 small squares
- From fabric D, cut 1 small square and 4 small triangles

Template piecing

With right sides together, sew a fabric A triangle to each fabric B triangle along the long diagonal edges; press seams over darker fabric. Repeat to make another three fabrics A and B half-square triangles and four fabrics B and D half-square triangles.

Make the block

Make the ring panel With right sides together, sew a fabric C small square to each side of a fabric D small square; press seams over fabric C.

Sew the fabrics A and B half-square triangles to each side of the remaining two fabric C squares, with the fabric B triangles pointing outward. Sew these rectangles to the top and bottom edges of the fabrics C and D patch, again with the fabric B triangles pointing outward; press all seams open.

Complete the square Sew the fabric A small squares to each side of the fabric B small squares; press seams outward. Sew a patch to the left and right edges of the ring panel; press seams outward.

Sew the fabrics B and D half-square triangles to the short ends of the remaining fabrics A, B, and A strips, with the fabric E triangles pointing outward; sew these strips to the top and bottom edges of the center panel. Press all seams open.

90

stacked rectangles

The seam allowance is ¼ inch throughout.

This simple block is made from four identical squares but in different colors. To create a minimalist feel, use a narrow color range—here, it is dark gold through rusty orange. If you are using a striped fabric, you can vary the look by cutting some patches horizontally and others vertically.

A
A
A
A
A
A
A
A
A
A
B

Fabric quantities

- Up to 12 different light and medium orange print fabrics A: 10 x 18 inches in total
- White fabric B: 9 x 12 inches

Prepare the patches

Rotary method
- From fabric A, cut twelve 4½ x 2½-inch rectangles
- From fabric B, cut twelve 2½-inch squares

or

Template cutting
Using the 6 x 6 templates (pages 278–83):
- From fabric A, cut 12 short rectangles
- From fabric B, cut 12 small squares

Make the block

Sew four patches With right sides together, sew a fabric B square to one short end of each fabric A rectangle; press seams over fabric A.

Lay out the rectangles in four squares of three rows each, alternating the fabrics in each row, as shown above, so that the white squares do not meet. Join the rows; press seams over the center row.

Complete the square With right sides together, pin and sew two patches, matching the seams and alternating fabrics A and B; press seams open.

With right sides facing, sew the top and bottom rows together, matching the center seam; press seam open.

scrappy nine patch

The seam allowance is ¼ inch throughout.

The Scrappy Nine Patch is constructed the same way as a regular nine-patch block after you've made your patchwork squares. A textured charcoal print makes a perfect foil for the bright, scrappy patches in this checkerboard block. Make sure all of the stripes run horizontally to create the secondary pattern of random stripes. This improvisational block is easily made with the rotary method.

Fabric quantities

- Assorted scrap fabrics A: each piece 5 inches long and at least ½ inch wide, with enough pieces to make a 5 x 25-inch block
- Black print fabric B: 10 x 10 inches

Prepare the patches

Rotary method
- From fabric A, cut each scrap down to 4½ inches long
- From fabric B, cut four 4½-inch squares

Make the block

Make five scrappy patches With right sides together, sew all of the fabric A scraps together along the long sides until the piece measures 25 inches long. Press seams to one side. Cut out five 4½-inch squares.

Sew three rows With right sides facing, pin and sew a fabric A square to each side of a fabric B square, making sure the scraps are horizontal. Press seams over fabric B. Repeat to make the third row.

With right sides facing, pin and sew a fabric B square to each side of the remaining fabric A square. Press seams over fabric B.

Complete the square With right sides facing, pin and sew the first and the third rows to the second row, carefully matching seams. Press seams open.

hen and chicks

The seam allowance is ¼ inch throughout.

Another classic block, Hens and Chicks is usually made with dark fabric against a light background. Here, it's reversed; the plain white fabric and textured monochrome print emphasize the structure and symmetry of the design. This block is best made using templates.

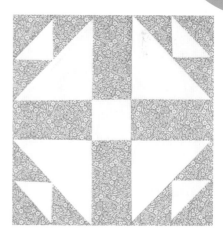

Fabric quantities

- Dark orange print fabric A: 15 x 16 inches
- White fabric B: 13 x 16 inches

Prepare the patches

Template cutting
Using the 5 x 5 templates (pages 274–7):
- From fabric A, cut 4 short rectangles and 12 small triangles
- From fabric B, cut 4 large triangles, 1 small square, and 4 small triangles

Template piecing

With right sides together, sew one fabric B small triangle to one fabric A small triangle along the diagonal edges; press seam over fabric A. Join two fabric A small triangles to each remaining edge of the fabric B small triangle, lining up the points. With right sides together, sew this new triangle to a fabric B large triangle along the diagonal edges, making a flying geese square (see page 15); press seams over the fabric B triangle. Repeat to make another three flying geese squares.

Make the block

Sew the top and bottom rows With right sides together, sew a flying geese square to each long edge of a fabric A short rectangle, making sure the triangles point inward and downward; press seams over rectangles. Repeat to make the bottom row.

Sew the middle row Join the short end of a fabric A short rectangle to each side of the fabric B small square, pressing seams over the rectangles.

Complete the square With right sides together, pin and sew each row, lining up the edges and points; press seams open.

thrift block

A
B
C
D

The seam allowance is ¼ inch throughout.

Also known as Diamond Square, this block combines with Hourglasses (see 29) for a star quilt. A light fabric around a dark square emphasizes the diamond shape.

Fabric quantities
- Dark orange fabric A: 6 x 6 inches
- Medium yellow fabric B: 6 x 14 inches
- Medium turquoise print fabric C: 8 x 8 inches
- Dark red print fabric D: 7 x 7 inches

Prepare the patches

Rotary method
- From fabrics A and B, make four 6½ x 3½-inch flying geese rectangles (see page 17)
- From fabric C, cut four 3½-inch squares
- From fabric D, cut one 6½-inch square

or

Template cutting
Using the 4 x 4 templates (pages 269–73):

- From fabric A, cut 8 small triangles
- From fabric B, cut 4 medium triangles
- From fabric C, cut 4 small squares
- From fabric D, cut 1 large square

Template piecing

With right sides together, sew a fabric A small triangle to the left diagonal edge of a fabric B medium triangle; press seam over the small triangle. Sew a second fabric A triangle to the right edge of the fabric B triangle; press seam over the small triangle. Repeat to make another three flying geese rectangles.

Make the block

Join the top and bottom row With right sides together, join a fabric C square to each short edge of a flying geese rectangle; press seams open.

Join the center row With right sides together, sew the remaining flying geese rectangles to the side edges of the fabric D large square; keep fabric B pointing away from the center square.

Complete the square With right sides together, lining up the seams and making sure all the flying geese blocks point outward, pin and sew the rows together. Press all seams open.

- -

framed four patch

A
B
C

The seam allowance is ¼ inch throughout.

Sometimes the simplest blocks can also be the most effective. This is a great way to combine large- and small-scale prints without one overwhelming the other. The dark turquoise print was chosen to match the center of the daisies on the large print, and it makes a good contrast to the ditsy floral background.

Fabric quantities
- Dark turquoise print fabric A: 4 x 8 inches
- Dark orange print fabric B: 4 x 8 inches
- Medium yellow print fabric C: 13 x 16 inches

Prepare the patches

Rotary method
- From fabrics A and B, cut two 3½-inch squares each
- From fabric C, cut two 6½ x 3½-inch rectangles and two 12½ x 3½-inch rectangles

or

Template cutting
Using the 4 x 4 templates (pages 269–73):
- From fabrics A and B, cut 2 small squares each
- From fabric C, cut 2 short rectangles and 2 full-length rectangles

Make the block

Sew the four-patch square With right sides together, sew a fabric A small square to a fabric B small square along one edge; press seam over fabric A. Repeat with the remaining pair of fabrics A and B small squares. With right sides together, pin the two rectangles together along one long edge, making sure the colors alternate. Sew together; press seam open.

Complete the square With right sides together, pin and sew the fabric C short rectangles to the top and bottom of the square, pressing seams over the rectangles. Pin and sew the fabric C full-length rectangles to each side, pressing seams over the rectangles.

light and shade

The seam allowance is ¼ inch throughout.

Made in gray and yellow fabrics, this Log Cabin symbolizes bright sunshine and shadows. The term "log cabin" denotes any block where overlapping strips at the corners echo the timber construction of a log cabin. This geometric block is easily made using the rotary method.

Fabric quantities

- Light gray print fabric A: 5 x 5 inches
- Light yellow fabric B: 4 x 4 inches
- Medium yellow print fabric C: 7 x 5 inches
- Medium gray print fabric D: 8 x 5 inches
- Light orange print fabric E: 10 x 5 inches
- Dark gray print fabric F: 11 x 5 inches
- Medium orange print fabric G: 13 x 5 inches

Prepare the patches

Rotary method

- From fabric A, cut one 2 x 3½-inch rectangle and one 2 x 5-inch rectangle
- From fabric B, cut one 3½-inch square
- From fabric C, cut one 2 x 5-inch rectangle and one 2 x 6½-inch rectangle
- From fabric D, cut one 2 x 6½-inch rectangle and one 2 x 8-inch rectangle
- From fabric E, cut one 2 x 8-inch rectangle and one 2 x 9½-inch rectangle
- From fabric F, cut one 2 x 9½-inch rectangle and one 2 x 11-inch rectangle
- From fabric G, cut one 2 x 11-inch rectangle and one 2 x 12½-inch rectangle

A
B
C
D
E
F
G

Make the block

Join round one Sew the fabric A short rectangle to the left edge of the fabric B square, then join the fabric A long rectangle to the bottom edge. Press every seam outward, away from the fabric B square in the center. Sew the fabric C short rectangle to the right edge of the patch and the fabric C long rectangle to the top edge; press seams outward.

Join round two Sew the fabric D short rectangle to the left edge of the patch and the fabric D long rectangle to the bottom edge. Sew the fabric E short rectangle to the right edge of the patch and the fabric E long rectangle to the top edge. Press seams outward.

Complete the square Sew the fabric F short rectangle to the left edge of the patch and the fabric F long rectangle to the bottom edge. Sew the fabric G short rectangle to the right edge of the patch and the fabric G long rectangle to the top edge. Press seams outward.

maple leaf

The seam allowance is ¼ inch throughout.

Maple Leaf is a good companion to its variation, Autumnal Leaf on page 81. Use a single print or variety of orange or red solids and prints to echo the wide spectrum of fall colors.

A
B
C
D
E
F

Fabric quantities

- Dark red fabric A: 6 x 6 inches, plus bias scrap for stem

- Medium red print fabric B: 6 x 6 inches

- Medium red fabric C: 5 x 5 inches

- Dark orange print fabric D: 5 x 5 inches

- Medium orange print fabric E: 5 x 5 inches

- Light blue print fabric F: 12 x 12 inches

Prepare the patches

Rotary method

- From fabrics A and F and fabrics B and F, make two 4½-inch half-square triangles (see page 12) each

- From fabrics C, D, and E, cut one 4½-inch square each

- From fabric F, cut two 4½-inch squares

- From fabric A, cut one 6 x 1½-inch bias strip for the stem

or

Template cutting

Using the 6 x 6 templates (pages 278–83):

- From fabric A, cut 2 large triangles and one 6 x 1½-inch bias strip for the stem

- From fabric B, cut 2 large triangles

- From fabrics C, D, and E, cut 1 large square each

- From fabric F, cut 2 large squares and 4 large triangles

Template piecing

With right sides together, sew a fabric A large triangle to a fabric F large triangle along the long edge; press seam over the dark fabric. Repeat to make another fabrics A and F half-square triangle and two fabrics B and F half-square triangles.

Make the block

Sew three rows Join a fabrics A and F half-square triangle and a fabrics B and F half-square triangle, abutting a fabric F edge to the fabric B edge; press seams open. Join a fabric F large square to the right edge; press seam open.

Join the fabric C large square and the fabric D large square. Add a fabrics B and F half-square triangle to the right edge, making sure fabric B points upward and to the left; press seams open.

Appliqué (see page 20) the stem diagonally across a fabric E large square. Join the fabric E large square to the right edge, then join a fabrics A and F half-square triangle; press seams open.

Complete the square With right sides facing, pin and sew the first and the third rows to the second row, carefully matching seams. Press seams open.

pinwheel

The seam allowance is ¼ inch throughout.

The familiar pinwheel motif, made up of eight triangles rotating around a center point, is a key part of many quilt blocks. Used on its own, a bold scale is wonderful for using larger directional prints, such as this vibrant floral.

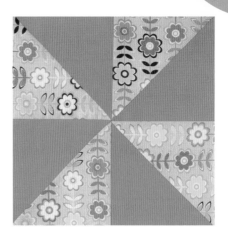

A
B

Fabric quantities

- Medium orange fabric A: 8 x 16 inches
- Medium orange print fabric B: 8 x 16 inches

Prepare the patches

Rotary method
- From fabrics A and B, make four 6½-inch half-square triangles (see page 12)

or

Template cutting
Using the 4 x 4 templates (pages 269–73):
- From fabrics A and B, cut 4 large triangles each

Template piecing

With right sides together, sew the A and B large triangles together along the diagonal edge to make a half-square triangle; press seam over fabric A. Repeat to make another three half-square triangles.

Make the block

Sew two rows Pin and sew two half-square triangles together along a light and dark edge; press seam toward fabric A. Repeat to make second row.

Complete the square With right sides together, join the rows along the long edge, with the light fabric touching the dark fabric and lining up seams; press seam open.

chinese coin

The seam allowance is ¼ inch throughout.

Triangles and squares combine to make an intricate-looking pattern, but it's easier to piece together than it looks. When multiples are joined end to end, this block creates a pleasing trellis pattern. Using a geometric print can reinforce the gridlike feel. This block is most accurately made using templates.

A
B
C
D

Fabric quantities

- Medium pink fabric A: 8 x 8 inches
- Medium orange print fabric B: 10 x 10 inches
- Light orange print fabric C: 8 x 8 inches
- White fabric D: 11 x 16 inches

Prepare the patches

Template cutting
Using the 5 x 5 templates (pages 274–7):
- From fabrics A and C, cut 4 small squares each
- From fabric B, cut 8 small triangles
- From fabric D, cut 4 large triangles and 5 small squares

Template piecing

With right sides together, pin and sew a fabric B small triangle to each of two adjacent sides of a fabric A small square; press seams over the squares. Join to a fabric D large triangle along the long diagonal edges; press seams over fabric B. Repeat to make another three triangle-and-square patches.

Make the block

Sew the top and bottom rows With right sides together, join a fabric C small square to a fabric D small square along one edge; press seam over fabric C. Repeat.

Join a triangle-and-square patch to each long side of the fabrics C and D strip, with fabrics A and C touching and all seams lined up; press seams over the triangle blocks. Repeat to make the bottom row.

Sew the center row Alternating colors, join the remaining fabric C and fabric D small squares, starting with fabric D; press all seams over fabric C.

Complete the square Pin and sew the three rows together, keeping the fabric A squares toward the center and lining up all seams; press seams open.

candies

This playful block combines hourglass blocks and simple rectangles to create a wonderful effect. Sew several blocks edge to edge in an otherwise plain quilt top for a minimal look with maximum visual impact.

The seam allowance is ¼ inch throughout.

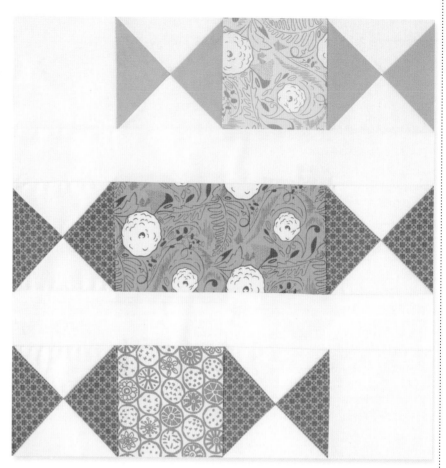

Fabric quantities

- Light orange fabric A: 6 x 6 inches
- Dark orange print fabric B: 12 x 12 inches
- Medium yellow print fabric C: 4 x 4 inches
- Medium orange print fabric D: 4 x 8 inches
- Medium orange print fabric E: 4 x 4 inches
- White fabric F: 16 x 24 inches

Prepare the patches

Rotary method
- From fabrics A and F, make two 3½-inch hourglass squares (see page 13)
- From fabrics B and F, make four 3½-inch hourglass squares
- From fabrics C and E, cut one 3½-inch square each
- From fabric D, cut one 6½ x 3½-inch rectangle
- From fabric F, cut two 3½-inch squares and two 12½ x 2-inch rectangles

Make the block

Join the top row With right sides together, pin and sew the fabric A tiny triangles of two hourglass squares to each side edge of the fabric C square. Join a fabric F small square to the left edge of the left hourglass; press seams open.

Join the middle row With right sides together, pin and sew the fabric B tiny triangles of two hourglass squares to each short edge of the fabric D rectangle; press seams open.

Join the bottom row With right sides together, pin and sew the fabric B tiny triangles of the other two hourglass squares to each side edge of the fabric E square. Join the second fabric F small square to the right edge of the right hourglass.

Complete the square Trim the fabric F full-length rectangles down to 1½-inch wide. With right sides together, pin and sew the full-length fabric F rectangles to the bottom edges of the top and middle rows and press seams over rectangles. Join the three rows together on the long edges and press seams toward the strips.

nine-patch snowballs

The seam allowance is ¼ inch throughout.

Thrifty quilters hoard even their smallest scraps, and this block is a good way to use them. Joining multiple blocks edge to edge creates a pattern of octagons alternating with nine-patch squares.

Fabric quantities

- A variety of medium print fabrics A: at least 13 x 18 inches in total

- White fabric B: 7 x 14 inches

Prepare the patches

Rotary method
- From fabrics A, cut eighteen 2½-inch squares

- From fabrics A and B, make 2 octagon squares (see page 18)

or

Template cutting
Using the 6 x 6 templates (pages 278–83):
- From fabric A, cut 18 small squares and 8 small triangles

- From fabric B, cut 2 octagons

Template piecing

With right sides together, pin and sew four different fabric A small triangles to the corners of each octagon to make two octagon squares; press seams over the octagon.

Make the block

Balance the colored patches Arrange the squares in two sets of 3 by 3 squares each, making sure you have a pleasing balance of color and pattern.

Sew two nine-patch squares Pin and sew nine squares together in three rows of three. Alternate the direction of seams and press open. Repeat to make another nine-patch square.

Make two rows Sew one nine-patch square to one octagon square, lining up the squares and the edge of the octagon; press seam open. Repeat.

Complete the square Pin and sew the two rows together along an edge, keeping the octagons at opposite corners; press seams open.

diamonds

The seam allowance is ¼ inch throughout.

Half-square triangles create elongated diamonds in this beautiful block. Use a variety of floral prints for maximum prettiness, but be careful to use only two tones of fabric—otherwise you may muddy the effect.

A
A
A
A
A
A
A
B
B
C

Fabric quantities

- At least 6 different orange solid and print fabrics A: 10 x 10 inches in total

- At least 2 different light and medium purple solid and print fabrics B: 10 x 10 inches in total

- White fabric C: 10 x 20 inches

Prepare the patches

Rotary method
- From fabrics A and C, make twelve 3½-inch half-square triangles (see page 12)

- From fabrics B and C, make four 3½-inch half-square triangles

or

Template cutting
Using the 4 x 4 templates (pages 269–73):
- From fabric A, cut 12 small triangles

- From fabric B, cut 4 small triangles

- From fabric C, cut 16 small triangles

Template piecing

With right sides together, sew a fabric C small triangle to each of the fabric A and fabric B small triangles to make 16 half-square triangles; press seam over the dark fabric.

Make the block

Sew four rows Lay out the half-square triangles in four rows of four, alternating the print and white triangles, as shown above.

Rearrange as necessary to get a good balance of colors. One row at a time, pin and sew the half-square triangles together; press seams over fabrics A and B.

Complete the square With right sides together, pin and sew the rows, matching the points carefully; press seams open.

four patch

The seam allowance is ¼ inch throughout.

Patchwork doesn't come much simpler than this: just two fabrics and four large squares. If joining several blocks edge to edge, use a directional print and solid or textured fabric to create extra visual interest with a woven look. A precut charm package of 5-inch squares will save time and provide a more random selection of fabric, but the finished block will be smaller.

A
B

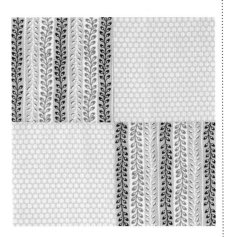

Fabric quantities

- Medium yellow print fabric A: 7 x 14 inches
- Medium coordinating striped or directional print B: 7 x 14 inches

Prepare the patches

Rotary method
- From fabrics A and B, cut two 6½-inch squares each

or

Template cutting
Using the 4 x 4 templates (pages 269–73):
- From fabrics A and B, cut 2 large squares each

Make the block

Join two rows With right sides together, pin and sew a fabric A large square to a fabric B large square, with the stripes running vertically; press seam over the striped fabric. Repeat with the two remaining squares.

Complete the square With right sides together, pin and sew the two rows together so that the print and solid fabrics are opposite one another. Press seams open.

---

white diamond

The seam allowance is ¼ inch throughout.

A square set at 45 degrees is known as an on-point square, or a diamond square. Here, a White Diamond is made up of four boat-shape patches. Set multiple White Diamond blocks edge to edge for a simple but effective checkerboard pattern overlaid by open white diamonds.

A
B
C

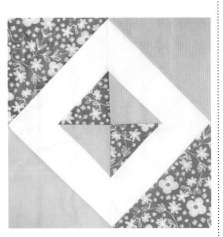

Fabric quantities

- Medium gray print fabric A: 8 x 13 inches
- Light yellow fabric B: 8 x 13 inches
- White fabric C: 8 x 12 inches

Prepare the patches

Rotary method
- From fabrics A and C and fabrics B and C, make two 6½-inch boat squares (see page 13) each

or

Template cutting
Using the 4 x 4 templates (pages 269–73):
- From fabrics A and B, cut 2 large triangles and 2 small triangles each
- From fabric C, cut 4 diagonal boats

Template piecing

With right sides together, pin and sew the fabric A small triangles to the short edges of the two fabric C diagonal boats; press seams open. Join the fabric A large triangles to the long sides of each diagonal boat to complete the boat squares. Repeat with the fabric B triangles and the remaining fabric C diagonal boats.

Make the block

Join the rows With right sides together, pin and sew a fabric A boat square to a fabric B boat square, with the small triangles facing inward; press seams open. Repeat to form the second row.

Complete the square With right sides together, pin and sew the two rows along a long edge, with the small triangles in the center and lining up the seams; press seams open.

color wheel

An adaptation of Card Trick on page 235, this block features a plain center square. Overlapping triangles create movement, while bright citrus solids give it a fresh look.

The seam allowance is ¼ inch throughout.

A
B
C
D
E

Fabric quantities

- Medium yellow fabric A: 6 x 12 inches
- Medium orange fabric B: 6 x 12 inches
- Medium lime fabric C: 6 x 12 inches
- Medium turquoise fabric D: 6 x 12 inches
- White fabric E: 11 x 15 inches

Prepare the patches

Rotary method
- From fabrics A, B, and E; fabrics B, C, and E; fabrics C, D, and E; and fabrics D, A, and E; make one 4½-inch three-quarter square triangle (see page 13) each

- From fabrics A and E; fabrics B and E; fabrics C and E; and fabrics D and E; make one 4½-inch half-square triangle (see page 12) each

- From fabric E, cut one 4½-inch square

or

Template cutting
Using the 6 x 6 templates (pages 278–83):
- From fabrics A, B, C, and D, cut 2 large triangles and 1 medium triangle each
- From fabric E, cut 1 large square, 4 large triangles, and 4 medium triangles

Template piecing

With right sides together, sew a fabric B medium triangle and a fabric E medium triangle together along a short side to make a larger triangle; press seam open. Join a fabric A large triangle along the diagonal to complete one three-quarter square triangle; press seam over large triangle. Repeat using fabrics C, E, and B; D, E, and C; and A, E, and D.

With right sides together, sew a fabric A large triangle and a fabric E large triangle along the diagonal edges to make one half-square triangle; press seams toward darker fabric. Repeat with fabrics B and E; C and E; and D and E.

Make the block

Sew three rows Lay out three rows of three squares, as shown above. For the top row, join the yellow half-square triangle to the matching edge of the yellow and orange three-quarter square triangle; press seam open. Match the orange half-square triangle to the right side of the strip; press seam open.

For the center row, join the yellow and turquoise three-quarter square triangle to the large white square along a turquoise edge, with the yellow small triangle on top; press seam open. Add the orange and lime three-quarter square triangle to the right edge of the strip along an orange edge with the lime small triangle on the bottom; press seam open.

For the third row, join the turquoise half-square triangle to the matching edge of the turquoise and lime three-quarter square triangle; press seam open. Match the lime half-square triangle to the right edge of the strip; press seam open.

Complete the square With right sides facing, pin and sew the rows together; press seams open.

calico puzzle

Calico Puzzle presents a subtle optical illusion, which you can make more or less apparent with your choice of fabrics.

Fabric quantities

- Medium mustard print fabric A: 12 x 12 inches
- Medium mustard fabric B: 10 x 10 inches
- White fabric C: 6 x 12 inches

Prepare the patches

Rotary method
- From fabrics A and C, make four 4½-inch half-square triangles (see page 12)
- From fabric A, cut one 4½-inch square
- From fabric B, cut four 4½-inch squares

or

Template cutting
Using the 6 x 6 templates (pages 278–83):
- From fabric A, cut 1 large square and 4 large triangles
- From fabric B, cut 4 large squares
- From fabric C, cut 4 large triangles

Template piecing

With right sides together, sew a fabric A large triangle to each of the fabric C large triangles to make four half-square triangles; press seams open.

Make the block

Sew three rows For the top row, pin and sew a fabrics A and C half-square triangle to the left side of a fabric B large square, with the print triangle pointing down and left. Join a second fabrics A and C half-square triangle to the right side, with the print triangle pointing up and left; press seams open. Repeat to make the third row.

For the center row, pin and sew a fabric B large square to each side of the fabric A large square. Press seams open.

Complete the square With right sides together and carefully matching seams, pin and sew the first and third rows to the center row, making sure the print triangles appear to rotate around the center of the block clockwise; press seams open.

---

shadow cross

A variation of the Windmill Square on page 249, the sails in Shadow Cross have a strong outline to make them stand out against the print background. Each quarter square is pieced in the same way, but with the print changing direction as the squares are rotated before being sewn together. Creating a block with the print running from top to bottom looks more static; see Calico Puzzle above for comparison. This geometric block is easily made using the rotary method.

Fabric quantities

- Light gray print fabric A: 8 x 12 inches
- Black print fabric B: 8 x 12 inches
- Medium yellow fabric C: 76 x 14 inches

Prepare the patches

Rotary method
- From fabric A, cut four 5½ x 3½-inch rectangles
- From fabric B, cut four 5½ x 1½-inch rectangles and four 4½ x 1½-inch rectangles
- From fabric C, cut four 6½ x 2½-inch rectangles

Make the block

Piece four squares With right sides together, pin and sew a long fabric B rectangle to the top long edge of a fabric A rectangle; press seam over fabric B. Sew a short fabric B rectangle to the left edge of the patch, pressing the seam over fabric B. Sew a fabric C rectangle to the top long edge of the rectangle, pressing seam upward. Repeat to make four squares.

Make two rows Lay one square with fabric A at the top, then rotate the second square so fabric A is at the right. With right sides together, pin and sew. Repeat to make the second row.

Complete the square Flip the second row so fabric A is at each outside corner of the block. With right sides together, pin and sew the rows together, matching the seams; press seams open.

balancing blocks

Rectangular blocks seem precariously balanced and on the point of collapse in this easy block. To add a feeling of height, grade colors from light to dark. Sew blocks on top of each other and separate by plain vertical strips for a quilt top. This block is easily made using the rotary method for a 12-inch block.

The seam allowance is ¼ inch throughout.

Fabric quantities

- Medium yellow print fabric A: 3 x 9 inches
- Light orange print fabric B: 3 x 9 inches
- Light gray print fabric C: 3 x 9 inches
- Medium orange fabric D: 3 x 9 inches
- Medium gray print fabric E: 3 x 9 inches
- Medium purple print fabric F: 3 x 9 inches
- White fabric G: 9 x 12 inches

Prepare the patches

Rotary method
- From fabrics A, B, C, D, E, and F cut one 8½ x 2½-inch rectangle each
- From fabric G, cut four 4½ x 2½-inch rectangles and four 2½-inch squares

Make the block

Join six rows With right sides together, pin and sew a fabric G rectangle to the right end of the fabric A rectangle, pressing seam over fabric A. Repeat with the fabrics C, D, and E rectangles.

With right sides together, pin and sew a fabric G square to each end of the fabric B rectangle; press seam over fabric B. Repeat with the fabric F rectangle.

Complete the square Lay the strips out in their final positions. Starting with the top row, pin and sew the strips in pairs at the long edges and press seams open, continuing until all six strips have been joined.

---

monkey wrench

This design resembles the jaws of an adjustable wrench. Like many quilt blocks, it has other names, including Dragon's Head, The Broad Ax, and Pioneer Patch. For a directional print, as here orient the pattern in the same direction throughout. This block is most accurately made using templates.

The seam allowance is ¼ inch throughout.

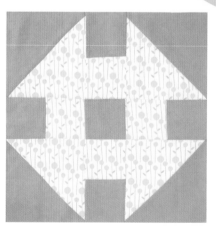

Fabric quantities

- Light yellow print fabric A: 10 x 14 inches
- Medium green fabric B: 10 x 15 inches

Prepare the patches

Template cutting
Using the 5 x 5 templates (pages 274–7):
- From fabric A, cut 4 large triangles and 4 small squares
- From fabric B, cut 4 large triangles and 5 small squares

Template piecing

With right sides together, sew a fabric A large triangle to a fabric B large triangle along the diagonal edge to make one half-square triangle (see page 12); press seams toward the darker fabric. Repeat to make another three half-square triangles.

Make the block

Join the small squares Pin and sew together a pair of fabrics A and B small squares along one side; press seam over fabric B. Make another three pairs.

Sew three rows For the top row, sew a half-square triangle to each side of a fabrics A and B strip, keeping fabric B at the top and the fabric B triangles pointing up and outward. Repeat to make the bottom row; press all seams outward. For the center row, sew a fabrics A and B rectangle, with fabric B at the outer edges, to each side of the fabric B square; press seams open.

Complete the square Join the three rows, lining up seams and pressing open.

corn and beans

The seam allowance is ¼ inch throughout.

A
B
C

This historic block is shown here in its original color palette: golden yellow for sweet corn and green for beans on a white background. Although the piecing is intricate, it follows a logical order. Start with a center square motif of four flying geese squares, then add a border of four flying geese rectangles with triangles at the sides, before completing the square with a large triangle at each corner.

Fabric quantities

- Medium green fabric A: 9 x 12 inches
- Medium yellow fabric B: 8 x 12 inches
- White fabric C: 12 x 12 inches

Prepare the patches

Template cutting
Using the 6 x 6 templates (pages 278–83):
- From fabric A, cut 2 large triangles and 4 medium triangles
- From fabric B, cut 12 small triangles
- From fabric C, cut 6 large triangles and 20 small triangles

Template piecing

With right sides together, join a fabric B and a fabric C small triangle along the diagonal edge. Sew a fabric C small triangle to each straight edge of the B small triangle; press all seams toward fabric B. Join the fabrics B and C triangle to the fabric A large triangle along the diagonal edges to complete one flying geese square; press seams toward fabric A. Repeat to make another fabrics A, B, and C flying geese square.

To make two flying geese squares with fabrics B and C, pin and sew fabric B and fabric C small triangles along the diagonal edge. Sew the straight edge of a fabric C small triangle to each straight edge of the B triangle, then press all seams toward fabric B. Join the fabrics B and C triangle to a fabric C large triangle along the diagonal edge, pressing the seam toward the large C triangle. Repeat to make another fabrics B and C flying geese square.

With right sides together, sew a fabric C small triangle to each diagonal edge of a fabric A medium triangle; press seams over the fabric A triangle. Repeat to make another three flying geese rectangles.

Make the block

Piece the center square With right sides together, pin and sew the four flying geese squares to make a center square. Fabrics A and C should form an hourglass motif at the center.

Add the flying geese border Pin and sew a fabric B triangle to both side edges of each flying geese rectangle, straight edges together, with the fabric B triangle pointing down and inward. Sew a flying geese strip to each side of the center square, with the fabric A triangle pointing outward.

Complete the square Sew the large fabric C triangles to the diagonal corners, pressing seams open.

flying out

Orange flying geese form an on-point square at the center of this block, while the yellow flying geese extend the motif outward.

The seam allowance is ¼ inch throughout.

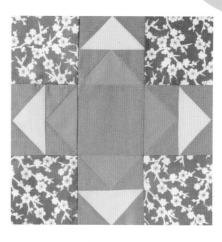

Fabric quantities

- Medium yellow fabric A: 6 x 10 inches
- Medium orange fabric B: 6 x 10 inches
- Medium gray fabric C: 9 x 12 inches
- Medium gray print fabric D: 10 x 10 inches

Prepare the patches

Rotary method
- From fabrics A and C and fabrics B and C, make four 4½ x 2½-inch flying geese rectangles (see page 17) each
- From fabric C, cut one 4½-inch square
- From fabric D, cut four 4½-inch squares

or

Template cutting
Using the 6 x 6 templates (pages 278–83):
- From fabrics A and B, cut 4 medium triangles each
- From fabric C, cut 1 large square and 16 small triangles
- From fabric D, cut 4 large squares

Template piecing

With right sides together, sew a fabric C small triangle to each diagonal edge of a fabric A or B medium triangle; press seams over the small triangle. Repeat to make four flying geese each from fabrics A and C, and fabrics B and C.

Make the block

Join three rows For the top row, with triangles pointing upward, sew a fabric D large square to each side edge of a flying geese patch, pressing seams outward over fabric D. Repeat to make the bottom row.

For the center row, with triangles pointing outward, sew the remaining two flying geese patches to the side edges of the fabric C large square, pressing seams inward over fabric C.

Complete the square With right sides together, pin and sew the second row to the first row, then the third row to the second row, lining up the seams and pressing open.

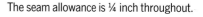

north star

This historic block is named after the North Star, which was for centuries a vital reference point for navigators and travelers.

The seam allowance is ¼ inch throughout.

Fabric quantities

- Medium yellow fabric A: 6 x 6 inches
- Medium yellow print fabric B: 6 x 10 inches
- Dark yellow print fabric C: 5 x 5 inches
- White fabric D: 10 x 16 inches

Prepare the patches

Rotary method
- From fabrics A and D, make four 4½ x 2½-inch flying geese rectangles (see page 17)
- From fabric B, cut four 4½ x 2½-inch rectangles
- From fabric C, cut one 4½-inch square
- From fabric D, cut four 4½-inch squares

or

Template cutting
Using the 6 x 6 templates (pages 278–83):
- From fabric A, cut 8 small triangles
- From fabric B, cut 4 short rectangles
- From fabric C, cut 1 large square
- From fabric D, cut 4 large squares and 4 medium triangles

Template piecing

With right sides together, sew a fabric A small triangle to each diagonal edge of a fabric D medium triangle; press seams over fabric A. Repeat to make another three flying geese rectangles.

Make the block

Sew three rows Sew a flying geese rectangle to a long edge of each fabric B short rectangle, with the white triangle pointing to the rectangle; press seams over fabric B. Repeat to make another three patches.

For the top row, sew a fabric D large square to each side of a flying geese patch, with the white triangle pointing inward; press seams outward. Repeat for the bottom row. For the center row, sew a flying geese patch to each side of the fabric C large square, with the white triangles pointing inward; press seams inward.

Complete the square Join the rows together; press seams open.

brick wall

You can use striped fabrics to emphasize the horizontal lines of the "bricks," but feel free to break the rules with the occasional vertically cut patch. The sample here is a random assortment of fabrics within a narrow color palette of gray, chartreuse, and turquoise. Every interpretation will be different, so experiment with various color combinations.

The seam allowance is ¼ inch throughout.

Fabric quantities

- At least 9 different fabrics A: 12 x 21 inches in total

Prepare the patches

Rotary method
- From fabrics A, cut fifteen 4½ x 2½-inch rectangles and six 2½-inch squares

or

Template cutting
Using the 6 x 6 templates (pages 278–83):
- From fabrics A, cut 15 short rectangles and 6 small squares

Make the block

Arrange the patches Lay out the fabric pieces, alternating three rows of three short rectangles with three rows of two short rectangles with a small square at each end. Arrange the patches to get a balance of color and pattern.

With right sides together, pin and sew the patches in each row, pressing all seams to the left.

Complete the square With right sides together, pin and sew the rows together, pressing all seams downward.

---

windmill box

Two rounds of patches create a double frame around a pinwheel. The white stands out against three adjacent color wheel hues: yellow, orange, and green.

The seam allowance is ¼ inch throughout.

Fabric quantities

- Medium yellow print fabric A: 4 x 8 inches
- White fabric B: 4 x 8 inches
- Medium orange fabric C: 6 x 8 inches
- Medium yellow fabric D: 6 x 8 inches
- Medium green fabric E: 12 x 13 inches

Prepare the patches

Rotary method
- From fabrics A and B, make one 4½-inch pinwheel square (see page 13)
- From fabrics C and D, cut two 4½ x 2½-inch rectangles and two 2½-inch squares each
- From fabric E, cut two 8½ x 2½-inch rectangles and two 12½ x 2½-inch rectangles

or

Template cutting
Using the 6 x 6 templates (pages 278–83):
- From fabrics A and B, cut 4 small triangles each
- From fabrics C and D, cut 2 short rectangles and 2 small squares each
- From fabric E, cut 2 full-length rectangles and two long rectangles

Template piecing

With right sides together, sew a fabric A small triangle and a fabric B small triangle along the long edges to make a half-square triangle (see page 12); press seam over fabric A. Repeat to make another three half-square triangles. Sew two half-square triangles along a light and dark edge; press seam over fabric A. Repeat. To complete the pinwheel square, join the rows along the long edge, with the light fabric touching the dark fabric and lining up seams; press seams open.

Make the block

Piece the center Join two pairs of fabric C and D small squares and press seams open; sew to the top and bottom of the pinwheel square, with fabric C above and below fabric B; press seams open. Join the fabric C and D short rectangles at their short edge; sew to the sides of the square, with fabric C adjacent; press seams open.

Complete the square Join the short fabric E strips to the top and bottom, then the long fabric E strips to the sides; press seams open.

seaside

A cheerful block, Seaside presents two rows of beach huts under a blue summer sky, with solid and striped prints juxtaposed to create a relaxed, vacation mood. You could make the block from all single "house" patches, like the bottom right two houses, or mix and match fabrics for house and roof. This block is specially designed as a companion to Beach Huts on page 167.

The seam allowance is ¼ inch throughout.

Fabric quantities

- Medium orange print fabric A: 3 x 5 inches
- Medium red print fabric B: 5 x 8 inches
- Medium red fabric C: 5 x 6 inches
- Dark turquoise fabric D: 3 x 5 inches
- Medium blue print fabric E: 3 x 5 inches
- Light green print fabric F: 3 x 5 inches
- Light orange print fabric G: 3 x 5 inches
- Dark blue fabric H: 5 x 5 inches
- Light blue fabric I: 6 x 13 inches
- Light yellow fabric J: 6 x 13 inches

Prepare the patches

Rotary method
- From fabrics A and I; fabrics B and I; fabrics C and I; and fabrics C and J, make one 4½ x 2½-inch flying geese rectangle (see page 17) each
- From fabrics B and J and fabrics H and J, make one house square (see page 14) each
- From fabrics D, E, F, and G, cut one 4½ x 2½-inch rectangle each
- From fabrics I and J, cut one 12½ x 2½-inch strip each

or

Template cutting
Using the 6 x 6 templates (pages 278–83):
- From fabric A, cut 1 medium triangle
- From fabric B, cut 1 house and 1 medium triangle
- From fabric C, cut 2 medium triangles
- From fabrics D, E, F, and G, cut 1 short rectangle each

- From fabric H, cut 1 house
- From fabrics I and J, cut 6 small triangles and one full-length rectangle each

Template piecing

With right sides together, sew a fabric I small triangle to both diagonal edges of the fabrics A, B, and C medium triangles to make three flying geese rectangles; press seams over the small triangles. Repeat to make one flying geese rectangle with fabrics C and J.

With right sides together, join a fabric J small triangle to each diagonal edge on the fabrics B and H houses to make two house squares; press seams open.

Make the block

Piece the houses With right sides together, pin and sew a flying geese rectangle to the long edge of a short rectangle; press seams open. Make houses from the following fabric combinations: A and D; B and E; C and F; and C and G.

Make the rows Lay the completed beach huts out in two rows of three. With right sides together, pin and sew the patches to make two rows; press seams open.

Make the center With right sides together, pin and sew the two house rows, making sure the roofs point in the same direction and matching the seams; press seams open.

Complete the square With right sides together, pin and sew the fabric I full-length rectangle to the top edge of the top row; press seam over the strip. Sew the fabric J full-length rectangle to the bottom row; press seam open.

cake stand

The seam allowance is ¼ inch throughout.

Here is just one of many "basket" blocks, all perennial favorites with quilters. This particular version was recorded in the 1930s, when it was described as having been "popular for generations," which takes its origins back to the nineteenth century. The name suggests a cut-glass cake stand, piled high with dainty cakes. Made from half-square triangles, squares, and rectangles, it's surprisingly easy to piece, avoiding diagonal seams. This block is most accurately made using templates when making a 12-inch square block.

A
B
C
D
E
F
G

Fabric quantities

- Light orange print fabric A: 3 x 3 inches
- Medium orange print fabric B: 3 x 3 inches
- Medium yellow fabric C: 3 x 3 inches
- Dark orange print fabric D: 3 x 3 inches
- Medium orange print fabric E: 3 x 3 inches
- Medium orange fabric F: 8 x 8 inches
- White fabric G: 16 x 20 inches

Prepare the patches

Template cutting
Using the 5 x 5 templates (pages 274–7):
- From fabrics A, B, C, D, E, and F, cut 2 small triangles each
- From fabric F, cut 1 large triangle
- From fabric G, cut 1 large triangle, 3 small squares, 12 small triangles, and 2 medium rectangles

Template piecing

With right sides together, sew a white small triangle to each diagonal edge of every orange and yellow small triangle to make 12 half-square triangles (see page 12); press seam toward the darker fabric.

Repeat to make one half-square triangle from the fabrics F and G large triangles.

Make the block

Arrange the patches Lay out the squares and patches, as shown above, in the following order: top row, fabric G small square, fabrics A and G half-square triangle, fabrics B and G half-square triangle, fabrics C and G half-square triangle; second row, fabrics C and G half-square triangle, fabric G small square, fabrics D and G half-square triangle, fabrics E and G half-square triangle. Sew these two rows together and press seams open.

For the third row, join a fabrics D and G half-square triangle and fabrics B and G half-square triangle as shown. Repeat for the fourth row, joining a fabrics E and G half-square triangle and fabrics A and G half-square triangle. Sew these two rows together to make a square, pressing seams open. Sew to the white side of the large fabrics F and G half-square triangle, with the G triangle pointing up and left.

With right sides facing, sew the top and bottom rows together, then press seams open.

Piece the square Sew a fabric G medium rectangle and the small fabrics F and G half-square triangle together along the orange edge; press seam upward. Sew to the right edge of the patch and press seams open.

Complete the square Join the remaining fabric G medium rectangle to the orange side of the remaining half-square small triangle; sew the fabric G small square to the other side of the half-square triangle. Sew the strip to the bottom edge of the square and press seams open.

plaid check

116

The seam allowance is ¼ inch throughout.

Joined edge to edge, the squares in many Plaid Check blocks create an allover modernist checkered pattern. Use different fabrics for each large square or make them all the same for a minimal look. The geometric grid pattern makes a good foil for swirling quilted designs with plenty of curves.

A
B
C
D
E
F

Fabric quantities

- Medium turquoise fabric A: 5 x 5 inches
- Medium green fabric B: 5 x 5 inches
- Medium yellow fabric C: 5 x 5 inches
- Medium orange fabric D: 5 x 5 inches
- Dark green fabric E: 6 x 6 inches
- White fabric F: 10 x 12 inches

Prepare the patches

Rotary method
- From fabrics A, B, C, and D, cut one 4½-inch square each
- From fabric E, cut four 2½-inch squares
- From fabric F, cut eight 4½ x 2½-inch rectangles

or

Template cutting
Using the 6 x 6 templates (pages 278–83):
- From fabrics A, B, C, and D, cut 1 large square each
- From fabric E, cut 4 small squares
- From fabric F, cut 8 short rectangles

Make the block

Join rectangles and squares With right sides together, sew a fabric F short rectangle to the left edge of each colored large square; press seams over the squares. With right sides facing, pin and sew the fabrics A and F patch to the left edge of the fabrics B and F patch.

With right sides together, sew a fabric E small square to one short end of each remaining fabric F short rectangle. Sew together in pairs to make the second and fourth rows; press seams over squares. Join to the bottom edges of the colored rows, pressing seams open.

Complete the square Pin and sew the two halves together at the long edge; press seam open.

---

thrift stripes

117

The seam allowance is ¼ inch throughout.

Another totally random scrappy block, this time made out of the narrowest scrap strips. Keep a box or other container on hand when you are making your blocks and save every scrap that's more than one inch wide. There are no precise colors specified, because every block will be different. This improvisational block is easily made using the rotary method.

Fabric quantities

- Mixed prints, all colors, of scrap fabrics A: at least 1½ inches wide each and of various lengths
- White fabric B: 10 x 13 inches

Prepare the patches

Rotary method
- From fabrics A, cut scraps into 1-inch-wide strips of varying lengths
- From fabric B, cut one 12½ x 2½-inch rectangle, one 12½ x 2-inch rectangle, and two 12½ x 1½-inch rectangles

Make the block

Piece the scraps Sew the fabric A strips into a continuous length using the chain piece technique (see page 19). Chain piece pairs of scraps together and snip the pairs apart; chain piece sets of pairs together and snip apart. Continue doing this until you have a single joined strip; press all seams to one side. Cut the long strip into thirteen 12½-inch lengths (you may need to make more strips). Pin and sew the strips together to make three rows, two of five strips and one of three strips. Press the seams open.

Complete the square Sew a narrow fabric B strip to one long edge of each row. Sew the wide fabric B strip to the other long edge of one row. With right sides together, pin and sew the patches in rows, making sure to alternate scraps and the white fabric. Press seams over the colored fabrics.

spectrum stripe

The seam allowance is ¼ inch throughout.

This beginner block highlights a narrow range of the color spectrum, but it would be stunning in any color. Try hues of blue or red, or make a rainbow block. Its simplicity is a perfect setting for intricate quilting patterns. This striped block is easily made using the rotary method.

A
B
C
D
E
F
G

Fabric quantities

- Medium green fabric A: 2 x 9 inches
- Light green fabric B: 2 x 9 inches
- Light yellow fabric C: 2 x 9 inches
- Light orange fabric D: 2 x 9 inches
- Medium orange fabric E: 2 x 9 inches
- Dark orange fabric F: 2 x 9 inches
- White fabric G: 13 x 24 inches

Prepare the patches

Rotary method
- From fabrics A, B, C, D, E, and F, cut one 8½ x 1½-inch rectangle each

- From fabric G, cut six 8½ x 1½-inch rectangles and two 12½ x 2½-inch rectangles

Make the block

Join the stripes With right sides together, pin and sew one of the shorter fabric G rectangles to each of the colored rectangles; press seams open.

With right sides together, pin and sew the strips in the correct color order; press seams over the colored fabrics.

Complete the square With right sides together, pin and sew the longer fabric G rectangles to each long edge of the striped block; press seams outward.

midsummer

The seam allowance is ¼ inch throughout.

Make this block in warm yellows and oranges in keeping with its name. While solids work, here the chevron stripe fabric adds movement and counterpoint to the white triangles. Consider combining it with the Sunburst block on page 102.

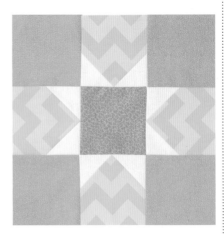

A
B
C
D

Fabric quantities

- Medium yellow print fabric A: 10 x 10 inches
- Light orange print fabric B: 10 x 10 inches
- Medium orange print fabric C: 5 x 5 inches
- White fabric D: 6 x 6 inches

Prepare the patches

Rotary method
- From fabrics A and D, make four 4½-inch house squares (see page 14)
- From fabric B, cut four 4½-inch squares
- From fabric C, cut one 4½-inch square

or

Template cutting
Using the 6 x 6 templates (pages 278–83):
- From fabric A, cut 4 houses

- From fabric B, cut 4 large squares
- From fabric C, cut 1 large square
- From fabric D, cut 8 small triangles

Template piecing

With right sides together, sew a fabric D triangle to each diagonal edge of the fabric A houses; press seams over fabric D.

Make the block

Join the rows For the top row, pin and sew a fabric B large square to each side of a house square with the "roof" pointing downward; press seams over the darker fabric. Repeat to make the bottom row. For the center row, pin and sew two house squares, with the roofs pointing inward, to the sides of the fabric C large square; press seams over the darker fabric.

Complete the square Arrange the rows with the roofs pointing to the center square. With right sides together, pin and sew the three rows together; press seams open.

octagons

Four identically pieced blocks combine into a light and dark counterchange pattern. Joining multiple octagon blocks edge to edge creates an Op Art effect, while the sophisticated gray background fabric keeps it contemporary looking.

The seam allowance is ¼ inch throughout.

A
B
C
D
E

Fabric quantities

- Medium orange print fabric A: 10 x 16 inches
- Light yellow print fabric B: 8 x 10 inches
- Dark yellow print fabric C: 8 x 10 inches
- Light gray fabric D: 8 x 12 inches
- Medium gray print fabric E: 8 x 12 inches

Prepare the patches

Rotary method
- From fabrics A and D, make eight 2½-inch half-square triangles (see page 12)
- From fabrics B and E and fabrics C and E, make four 2½-inch half-square triangles each
- From fabric A, cut eight 2½-inch squares
- From fabrics B and C, cut four 2½-inch squares each
- From fabrics D and E, cut two 2½-inch squares each

or

Template cutting
Using the 6 x 6 templates (pages 278–83):
- From fabric A, cut 8 small squares and 8 small triangles
- From fabrics B and C, cut 4 small squares and 4 small triangles each
- From fabrics D and E, cut 2 small squares and 8 small triangles each

Template piecing

With right sides together, sew one fabric A small triangle to one fabric D small triangle to make one half-square triangle; press seam over dark fabric. Repeat to make another seven fabrics A and D half-square triangles. Repeat to make four half-square triangles from fabrics B and E and four half-square triangles from fabrics C and E.

Make the block

Piece four patches For the top left patch, join a medium orange half-square triangle to each side of a fabric A small square, making sure the orange triangles point inward; press seams inward. Repeat. Join a fabric A small square to each side of a fabric D small square; press seams outward. Join the three rows; press seams open. Repeat for the bottom right patch. For the top right patch, repeat using the light yellow and gray units. For the bottom left patch, repeat for the dark yellow and gray units.

Complete the square Join the light yellow patch to a medium orange patch; press seam open. Join the dark yellow patch to the second medium orange patch; press seam open. Join the rows; press seam open.

sunburst

Here, a round of triangles frames the Puss in the Corner block on page 170. Use oranges and yellow to create a warm, glowing sun. This block would work well with Midsummer on page 100.

A
B
C
D

The seam allowance is ¼ inch throughout.

Fabric quantities

- Medium yellow fabric A: 6 x 15 inches
- Light orange print fabric B: 3 x 6 inches
- Medium orange print fabric C: 5 x 5 inches
- White fabric D: 12 x 19 inches

Prepare the patches

Rotary method
- From fabrics A and D, make four 4½ x 2½-inch flying geese rectangles (see page 17) and eight 2½-inch half-square triangles (see page 12)
- From fabrics B and D, make four 2½-inch half-square triangles
- From fabric C, cut one 4½-inch square
- From fabric D, cut four 4½ x 2½-inch rectangles and four 2½-inch squares

or

Template cutting
Using the 6 x 6 templates (pages 278–83):
- From fabric A, cut 16 small triangles
- From fabric B, cut 4 small triangles
- From fabric C, cut 1 large square
- From fabric D, cut 4 short rectangles, 4 medium triangles, 4 small squares, and 12 small triangles

Template piecing

With right sides together, sew a fabric A small triangle to each diagonal edge of a fabric D medium triangle; press seam over the small triangles. Repeat to make another three flying geese rectangles.

With right sides together, sew one fabric D small triangle to the diagonal edge of each fabric A and fabric B small triangle to make twelve half-square triangles; press seams over the darker fabric.

Make the block

Sew the center panel With right sides together, pin and sew two fabric D short rectangles to the side edges of the fabric C large square; press seams outward.

Sew a yellow half-square triangle to each end of the remaining two fabric D short rectangles, with the orange triangles pointing inward; press seams open. Sew the strips along the top and bottom edges of the center panel, with the orange triangles pointing inward; press seams inward.

Make the border Sew a yellow half-square triangle to each side of a flying geese rectangle, with the yellow triangles pointing outward; press seams open.

Sew a flying geese half-square triangle strip to each side of the center panel, with the white triangles pointing inward; press seams open.

Sew a fabric D small square to each end of the remaining two flying geese strips. Join to the top and bottom of the center panel, with the white triangles pointing inward; press seams open.

bauhaus

The seam allowance is ¼ inch throughout.

True to its name, the geometric Bauhaus block has a 1930s look, inspired by the woven rug designs of distinguished textile artist and printmaker Anni Albers. Here, a bold combination of subtle yellow textured fabric and black meets a mid-century style print in muted hues. This geometric block is easily made using the rotary method.

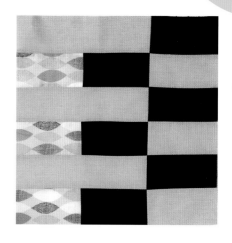

A
B
C

Fabric quantities

- Medium yellow print fabric A: 12 x 12 inches
- Black fabric B: 9 x 10 inches
- Light gray print fabric C: 5 x 9 inches

Prepare the patches

Rotary method
- From fabric A, cut three 8½ x 2½-inch rectangles and three 4½ x 2½-inch rectangles
- From fabric B, cut six 4½ x 2½-inch rectangles
- From fabric C, cut three 4½ x 2½-inch rectangles

Make the block

Sew six rows With right sides together, pin and sew the long fabric A rectangles to three short fabric B rectangles along the short edges; press seams over fabric B.

With right sides together, pin and sew the remaining fabric B short rectangles to the fabric A short rectangles at the short edge. Join the fabric C short rectangles to the other side of the fabric B rectangles; press seams over fabric B.

Complete the square With the black and yellow fabrics on the right, join the long edges of the fabric A and B strips to the long edges of the fabrics C, B, and A strips; press seams open.

Sew the pairs together, matching the seams; press all seams open.

the dandy

The seam allowance is ¼ inch throughout.

"Dandy" is a dapper name for a block that first appeared in print at the turn of the nineteenth century. As a variation, this is sometime made with the half-square triangles reversed, so the patterned triangles point inward.

A
B
C

Fabric quantities

- Medium green fabric A: 6 x 6 inches
- Light yellow print fabric B: 6 x 12 inches
- White fabric C: 11 x 17 inches

Prepare the patches

Rotary method
- From fabrics A and C, make four 4½-inch house squares (see page 14)
- From fabrics B and C, make four 4½-inch half-square triangles (see page 12)
- From fabric C, cut one 4½-inch square

or

Template cutting
Using the 6 x 6 templates (pages 278–83):
- From fabric A, cut 8 small triangles

- From fabric B, cut 4 large triangles
- From fabric C, cut 1 large square, 4 houses, and 4 large triangles

Template piecing

With right sides together, sew a fabric A small triangle to each diagonal edge of a fabric D house; press seams over fabric A. Repeat to make another three house squares.

With right sides together, sew a fabric B large triangle to a fabric C large triangle along the diagonal edges; press seams toward the darker fabric. Repeat to make another three half-square triangles.

Make the block

Sew three rows For the top row, sew a large half-square triangle to each side of a house square, with the "roof" pointing inward and triangles pointing outward; press seams over

the half-square triangles. Repeat for the bottom row.

For the center row, sew a house square to each side edge of the fabric C large square, with the roofs pointing inward; press seams over fabric C.

Complete the square Arrange the rows with the roofs pointing toward the center square. Pin and sew the center row to the top row, then sew the bottom row to the center row; press seams open.

bordered checkerboard

The Checkerboard block can be used edge to edge as a horizontal border, or set together at alternate angles to create an interwoven look. Using more than one shade of a solid color creates an extra feeling of depth in a block. Here, three subtly graded yellows give warmth to the cool gray.

The seam allowance is ¼ inch throughout.

Fabric quantities

- Dark gray print fabric A: 9 x 12 inches
- Light yellow fabric B: 3 x 6 inches
- Medium yellow fabric C: 6 x 12 inches
- Dark yellow fabric D: 6 x 13 inches
- Light green fabric E: 3 x 6 inches

Prepare the patches

Rotary method
- From fabric A, cut twelve 2½-inch squares
- From fabrics B and E, cut two 2½-inch squares each
- From fabric C, cut eight 2½-inch squares
- From fabric D, cut two 12½ x 2½-inch strips

or

Template cutting
Using the 6 x 6 templates (pages 278–83):
- From fabric A, cut 12 small squares
- From fabrics B and E, cut 2 small squares each
- From fabric C, cut 8 small squares
- From fabric D, cut 2 full-length rectangles

Make the block

Sew four rows Lay out the patches in their final positions, alternating the gray fabric squares with the various yellow fabric squares as follows: top row, C, A, E, A, B, A; second row, A, C, A, C, A, C; third row, C, A, E, A, B, A; bottom row, A, C, A, C, A, C. Using the chain piecing technique (see page 19), chain piece pairs of yellow and gray squares; press seams over the gray fabric. Join three pairs to make each row; press seams over the gray fabric. Sew the rows together, making sure the colors alternate and the seams match; press seams open.

Complete the square Sew the fabric D full-length rectangles to the top and bottom of the block; press seams outward.

mosaic

Soft lemon with ditsy blue and gray floral prints give an old pattern a new springlike feel, although you could also use strong solids against a white background for a bolder look. This version is made from right diamond patches, but you could easily use left diamonds so that the motif appears to rotate in the opposite direction.

The seam allowance is ¼ inch throughout.

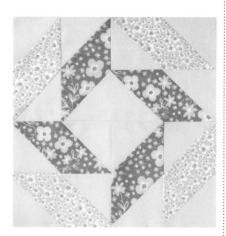

Fabric quantities

- Light gray print fabric A: 8 x 14 inches
- Light blue print fabric B: 8 x 140 inches
- Light yellow fabric C: 6 x 12 inches

Prepare the patches

Rotary method
- From fabrics A and C and fabrics B and C, make four 4½ x 2½-inch right diamond rectangles (see page 16) each

or

Template cutting
Using the 4 x 4 templates (pages 269–73):
- From fabrics A and B, cut 4 right diamonds each
- From fabric C, cut 16 small triangles

Template piecing
With right sides together, sew a fabric C small triangle to the diagonal edges of each diamond; press seams over fabric C. Repeat to make another eight diamond rectangles.

Make the block

Sew the squares With right sides together, join the long edge of a fabric A diamond rectangle to a long edge of a fabric B diamond rectangle, making sure fabric B is on the left. Repeat to make another three squares; press seams open.

Make the rows Lay out the four squares as shown above, so that the gray diamonds are innermost. Join in two pairs, matching the points; press seams open. Repeat to make the bottom row.

Complete the square Pin and sew the top and bottom rows together so the yellow triangles make a center diamond, making sure all points match; press seams open.

flying geese

This basic flying geese rectangle is used in stars and other geometric blocks to make a variety of patterns. Here, the Flying Geese block alternates the direction of the patches to emphasize movement in an allover design.

The seam allowance is ¼ inch throughout.

A
B
C
D
E

Fabric quantities

- Dark yellow print fabric A: 7 x 8 inch
- Medium yellow print fabric B: 7 x 8 inches
- Medium yellow fabric C: 7 x 8 inches
- Medium yellow print D: 7 x 8 inches
- White fabric E: 8 x 16 inches

Prepare the patches

Rotary method
- From fabrics A and E; fabrics B and E; fabrics C and E; and fabrics D and E, make two 6½ x 3½-inch flying geese rectangles (see page 12) each

or

Template cutting
Using the 4 x 4 templates (pages 269–73):
- From fabrics A, B, C, and D, cut 2 medium triangles each
- From fabric E, cut 16 small triangles

Template piecing

With right sides together, pin and sew a fabric E small triangle to each diagonal edge of the fabric A medium triangles to make two flying geese rectangles; press seams open. Repeat with the fabrics B, C and D medium triangles.

Make the block

Arrange the flying geese rectangles
Arrange the flying geese rectangles in two columns of four patches, balancing the colors and the prints.

Sew four rows With right sides together, pin and sew a fabric C flying geese rectangle to a fabric D flying geese rectangle, making sure they point in opposite directions; press seam open.

Repeat to make three more rows, making sure the first flying geese rectangle points up and the second one points down. First, join a fabric B flying geese rectangle to a fabric A flying geese rectangle. Second, join a fabric A flying geese rectangle to a fabric C flying geese rectangle. Last, join a fabric D flying geese rectangle to a fabric B flying geese rectangle.

Complete the square With right sides together, pin and sew the first row to the second row; press seam open. Repeat to join the remaining three rows.

offset squares

The seam allowance is ¼ inch throughout.

Here is another good way to use up scraps for a random patchwork feel. A simple pattern with no seams to match, this is also a great way for beginners to practice piecing. You can use tonal bands of color, as shown here, or mix patterns and colors in the same way that quilters once did when new fabrics were scarce. This scrappy block is easily made using the rotary method.

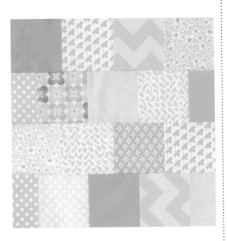

Fabric quantities

- Up to 18 different solid and print fabrics A: 16 x 19 inches in total

Prepare the patches

Rotary method
- From your mix of fabrics A, cut fourteen 3½-inch squares and four 3½ x 2-inch rectangles

Make the block

Join the rows Sew together two rows of four squares and two rows of three squares, pressing seams to one side. Add the rectangles to each end of the short rows.

Complete the square With right sides together, join all the rows along the long edges, making sure each row is offset from the rows above and below. If necessary, trim two offset rows; press all seams downward.

Note: These patches are 3½-inch square, but you can make this design on any scale and to any size.

rocky mountain puzzle

The seam allowance is ¼ inch throughout.

The sawtooth borders in this block suggest the jagged peaks of the Rocky Mountains in Colorado. The block is also effective turned on point.

A
B
C

Fabric quantities

- Light yellow print fabric A: 7 x 7 inches
- Medium yellow fabric B: 10 x 15 inches
- White fabric C: 10 x 19 inches

Prepare the patches

Rotary method
- From fabrics B and C, make ten 3½-inch half-square triangles (see page 12)
- From fabric A, cut one 6½-inch square
- From fabric C, cut two 3½-inch squares

or

Template cutting
Using the 4 x 4 templates (pages 269–73):
- From fabric A, cut 1 large square
- From fabric B, cut 10 small triangles
- From fabric C, cut 2 small squares and 10 small triangles

Template piecing

With right sides together, pin and sew one fabric C small triangle to each of the fabric B small triangles to make 10 half-square triangles.

Make the block

Join the rows For the top row, with right sides together, pin and sew three half-square triangles in a row, making sure the yellow triangles point down and right. Join a fabric C small square to the right edge of the strip; press seams open. Repeat to make the bottom row.

With right sides together, join one half-square triangle to the top of another so that the yellow triangles point down and to the left; press seam open. Repeat with two more half-square triangles. With right sides together, pin and sew one strip to the left edge of the fabric A large square so that the

yellow triangles point down and right. Join the other strip to the right edge of the fabric A square so that the yellow triangles point up and left; press seams open.

Complete the square With right sides together and carefully matching the seams, pin and sew the top row to the center row, making sure the yellow triangles adjoin the center square. Flip the bottom row, then join it to the center square. Press seams open.

jeweled crown

A fairy tale block for a child's room, Jeweled Crown could make a cute cushion cover or curtain edging. If using it for a quilt, consider having just one row in an otherwise plain quilt, which will highlight the bright colors. Choose vivid jewel colors for squares and two shades of yellow for the golden crown, and feel free to alternate jewels for repeats so that you have a mixture of rubies, diamonds, sapphires, and emeralds.

The seam allowance is ¼ inch throughout.

A
B
C
D
E
F
G

Fabric quantities

- Dark yellow fabric A: 8 x 9 inches
- Medium yellow fabric B: 8 x 9 inches
- Medium pink print fabric C: 3 x 6 inches
- Medium turquoise fabric D: 3 x 3 inches
- Medium purple fabric E: 3 x 6 inches
- Dark turquoise fabric F: 3 x 3 inches
- White fabric G: 9 x 16 inches

Prepare the patches

Rotary method
- From fabrics A and G, make three 4½ x 2½-inch left-tapered rectangles (see page 16)
- From fabrics B and G, make three 4½ x 2½-inch right-tapered rectangles (see page 16)
- From fabrics A and B, cut three 2½-inch squares each
- From fabrics C and E, cut two 2½-inch squares each
- From fabrics D and F, cut one 2½-inch square each
- From fabric G, cut two 12½ x 2½-inch strips

or

Template cutting
Using the 6 x 6 templates (pages 278–83):
- From fabric A, cut 3 left-tapered rectangles and 3 small squares
- From fabric B, cut 3 right-tapered rectangles and 3 small squares
- From fabrics C and E, cut 2 small squares each
- From fabrics D and F, cut 1 small square each
- From fabric G, cut 6 small triangles and 2 full-length rectangles

Template piecing

With right sides together, sew a fabric G small triangle to the diagonal edge of each tapered rectangle; press seams inward.

Make the block

Piece the crown With right sides together, sew a fabric A tapered rectangle to a fabric B tapered rectangle, with the fabric G triangles in the center and pointing downward; repeat to make three pairs, and press seams open. Sew the pairs together, making sure the colors alternate; press seams open. Sew the fabric G full-length rectangle to the top edge; press seam upward.

For the checkerboard rows, lay out the small squares, in the following order: top row, A, D, A, C, A, and E; bottom row, C, B, E, B, F, and B. Join the squares together in the top row; press all seams to the right. Join the squares in the bottom row; press seams to the left. With right sides together, pin and sew these two strips together; press seam open.

Complete the square With right sides together, pin and sew the top crown patch to the jewel patch, lining up seams, then pin and sew the fabric G full-length rectangle to the bottom of the block; press seams open.

pineapple

This tropical fruit traditionally symbolizes hospitality. It works with other fruit blocks, such as the Pear (see page 144), Plum (see page 229), and Strawberry (see page 28) blocks, but the Pineapple can stand on its own as a cushion cover.

The seam allowance is ¼ inch throughout.

A
B
C
D
E
F
G
H
I

Fabric quantities

- Medium green print fabric A: 6 x 9 inches
- Medium orange print fabric B: 3 x 6 inches
- Light orange print fabric C: 6 x 6 inches
- Medium orange print fabric D: 6 x 6 inches
- Light yellow print fabric E: 3 x 6 inches
- Medium orange fabric F: 3 x 3 inches
- Dark orange fabric G: 6 x 6 inches
- Dark orange print fabric H: 3 x 3 inches
- White fabric I: 13 x 13 inches

Prepare the patches

Template cutting

Using the 6 x 6 templates (pages 278–83):
- From fabric A, cut 1 medium triangle and 1 long boat
- From fabrics B and E, cut 2 small squares each
- From fabrics C and G, cut 1 small square and 2 small triangles
- From fabric D, cut 4 small squares
- From fabrics F and H, cut 1 small square each
- From fabric I, cut 1 right tapered rectangle, 1 left tapered rectangle, 6 small triangles, and two full-length rectangles

Template piecing

With right sides facing, pin and sew the fabric I tapered rectangles to each diagonal edge of the fabric A medium triangle; press seams open.

With right sides facing, pin and sew a fabric I small triangle to each diagonal edge of the fabric A long boat; press seams open.

With right sides facing, pin and sew a fabric I small triangle to each of the fabric C small triangles and fabric G small triangles to make four half-square triangles; press seams open.

Make the block

Piece the stem With right sides facing, pin and sew the stem strips together; press seams open.

Make the pineapple Arrange the orange and yellow squares to balance the colors and prints in four rows. Pin and sew together two small squares in the top and bottom rows and four small squares in the two middle rows. Add a dark and light half-square triangle to the ends of the top and bottom rows, as shown above; press seams open.

With right sides facing and carefully matching seams, pin and sew the two center rows together; press seam open. Add the first and fourth rows, then press seams open.

Complete the square With right sides facing, pin and sew the stem to the top of the pineapple, carefully matching seams; press seam open. Join the fabric I full-length rectangles to the sides of the block, then press seams out.

friendship square

The seam allowance is ¼ inch throughout.

The Friendship Square design can be found on ancient tiled walls and floors as well as in traditional country quilts. Honor this timeless pattern with retro floral prints or make it modern with crisp solid fabrics.

A
B
C

Fabric quantities

- Light yellow print fabric A: 7 x 7 inches
- Light yellow print fabric B: 8 x 14 inches
- Light green fabric C: 8 x 12 inches

Prepare the patches

Rotary method
- From fabrics A and C, make one 6½-inch diamond square (see page 15)
- From fabric B, cut four 6½ x 3½-inch rectangles
- From fabric C, cut four 3½-inch squares

or

Template cutting
Using the 4 x 4 templates (pages 269–73):

- From fabric A, cut 1 diamond square
- From fabric B, cut 4 short rectangles
- From fabric C, cut 4 small squares and 4 small triangles

Template piecing

With right sides together, pin and sew the fabric C small triangles to the diagonal edges of the fabric A diamond square; press seams open.

Make the block

Sew three rows With right sides together, pin and sew a fabric B short rectangle to each side of the fabrics A and C diamond square; press seams open.

With right sides together, pin and sew one fabric C small square to each side of the remaining fabric B rectangles; press seams open.

Complete the square With right sides together and carefully matching seams, join the top and bottom rows to the center row; press seams open.

split nine patch

The seam allowance is ¼ inch throughout.

This block splits the classic Nine-Patch Square (on page 34) with four patch squares in the corners and the center. Play with darker and lighter shades of fabric to emphasize different secondary patterns within the block.

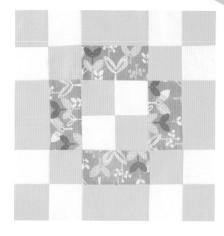

A
B
C

Fabric quantities

- Medium yellow fabric A: 9 x 18 inches
- Dark yellow print fabric B: 6 x 10 inches
- White fabric C: 9 x 15 inches

Prepare the patches

Rotary method
- From fabrics A and B, make four 4½-inch rectangle squares (see page 11)
- From fabrics A and C, make five 4½-inch four-patch squares (see page 11)

or

Template cutting
Using the 6 x 6 templates (pages 278–83):
- From fabric A, cut 4 short rectangles and 10 small squares
- From fabric B, cut 4 short rectangles

- From fabric C, cut 10 small squares

Template piecing

With right sides together, pin and sew one fabric A short rectangle to each of the fabric B short rectangles to make four rectangle squares; press seams open.

With right sides together, pin and sew one fabric A small square to each of the fabric C small squares. Make five four-patch squares by joining two fabrics A and C strips, alternating colors; press seams open.

Make the block

Join three rows With right sides together and carefully matching seams, pin and sew one four-patch square to each side of a rectangle square. Make sure the fabric A small squares adjoin the fabric B rectangles; press seams open. Repeat to make the bottom row.

With right sides together, pin and sew two rectangle squares along the fabric B rectangles to each side of a four-patch square, making sure a fabric A small square is in the bottom right corner; press seams open.

Complete the square With right sides together and carefully matching seams, pin and sew the first and third rows to the second row, making sure the print fabric abuts the center four-patch square; press seams open.

diagonal triangles

A
A
A
A
B
B
B
B
C
C
C
C

This block uses half-square triangles effectively, yet is different from Harlequin Triangles (see page 60). To make these stripes really stand out, make sure that the background provides a lot of contrast with the colored triangles, whether you decide to choose a specific color palette or try a scrappy approach.

Fabric quantities

- 4 different medium yellow solid and print fabrics A: 8 x 8 inches in total

- 4 different medium orange solid and print fabrics B: 8 x 8 inches in total

- 4 different white, light yellow, and light gray sold and print fabrics C: 8 x 16 inches in total

Prepare the patches

Rotary method
- From fabrics A and C, make eight 3½-inch half-square triangles (see page 12)

- From fabrics B and C, make eight 3½-inch half-square triangles

or

Template cutting
Using the 4 x 4 templates (pages 269–73):
- From fabric A, cut 8 small triangles

- From fabric B, cut 8 small triangles

- From fabric C, cut 16 small triangles

Template piecing

With right sides together, pin and sew a fabric C small triangle to each of the fabric A small triangles and fabric B small triangles to make 16 half-square triangles; press seams open.

Make the block

Assemble the stripes Arrange the half-square triangles to form alternating yellow and orange stripes, being careful to balance the prints with the solids.

Join the rows With right sides together, pin and sew the first row of half-square triangles, making sure the first yellow triangle points down and right and the last orange triangle points up and left; press seams open.

Repeat to sew the remaining three rows. In the second row, make sure the first yellow triangle points up and left and the last yellow triangle points down and right. In the third row, make sure the first orange triangle points down and right and the last yellow triangle points up and left. In the fourth row, make sure the first orange triangle points up and left and the last orange triangle points down and right.

Complete the square With right sides together, pin and sew the first and third rows to the second row; press seams open. Join the fourth row to the third row; press seam open.

cross patch

The seam allowance is ¼ inch throughout.

Muted gold, black, and a black or gray print combine into a sophisticated color palette in this block. Join multiple blocks edge to edge for an allover design.

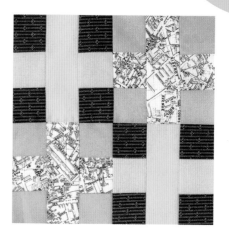

Fabric quantities

- Black print fabric A: 6 x 12 inches
- Light gold fabric B: 6 x 14 inches
- Black-and-white print fabric C: 6 x 14 inches
- Dark gold fabric D: 6 x 12 inches

Prepare the patches

Rotary method
- From fabrics A and D, cut eight 2½-inch squares each
- From fabrics B and C, cut two 6½ x 2½-inch rectangles and four 2½-inch squares each

or

Template cutting
Using the 6 x 6 templates (pages 278–83):

- From fabrics A and D, cut 8 small squares each
- From fabrics B and C, cut 2 medium rectangles and 4 small squares each

Make the block

Sew the squares With right sides together, pin and sew two fabric A small squares to the top and bottom edges of each fabric B small square, making four strips; press seams over fabric B. Sew each strip to a long edge of a fabric B medium rectangle, making two patches; press seams inward.

With right sides together, pin and sew two fabric D small squares to the top and bottom edges of each fabric C small square, making four strips; press seams over fabric C. Sew each strip to a long edge of a fabric C medium rectangle, making two patches; press seams inward.

Complete the square With right sides together, sew a fabrics A and B patch to a fabrics C and D patch; press seams open. Repeat with the remaining two patches.

With right sides together, pin and sew the rows together, making sure the fabric A and B blocks are diagonal to one another; press seams open.

---

butterfly block

The seam allowance is ¼ inch throughout.

Sewing each hourglass in a different color gives animation to this block, with the motifs looking like butterflies wheeling through the air.

Fabric quantities

- Medium orange fabric A: 5 x 5 inches
- Medium red fabric B: 5 x 5 inches
- Medium yellow fabric C: 5 x 5 inches
- Medium purple fabric D: 5 x 5 inches
- White fabric E: 14 x 17 inches

Prepare the patches

Rotary method
- From fabrics A and E; fabrics B and E; fabrics C and E; and fabrics D and E, make two 3½-inch half-square triangles (see page 17) each
- From fabric E, cut four 6½ x 2½-inch rectangles

or

Template cutting
Using the 4 x 4 templates (pages 269–73):

- From fabrics A, B, C, and D, cut 2 small triangles each
- From fabric E, cut 8 small triangles and 4 short rectangles

Template piecing

With right sides facing, sew a fabric E small triangle to each of the colored small triangles along the diagonal edge to make four half-square triangles; press seams toward the darker fabric.

Make the block

Piece the center panel Lay out four half-square triangles, one color each, with the fabric E triangles in the center. Pin and sew together the orange and red pair along one white edge; press seams open. Repeat with the purple and yellow pair. Join the two patches, creating a white square in the center; press seams open.

Complete the square Join a fabric E short rectangle to each side of the center panel; press seams outward. For the top row, sew the fabrics A and B half-square triangles to the ends of another fabric E short rectangle, with the color triangles pointing inward and down. Repeat with the fabrics C and D half-square triangles and the final rectangle for the bottom row. Sew the top and bottom rows to the center panel. Press seams open.

shoofly star

A sawtooth star motif and half-square triangles form a multilayered pattern. Use a medium-scale print or fussy-cut fabric (see page 10) to highlight the center square.

The seam allowance is ¼ inch throughout.

Fabric quantities

- Medium yellow fabric A: 11 x 17 inches
- Medium blue print fabric B: 10 x 12 inches
- White fabric C: 8 x 8 inches

Prepare the patches

Rotary method
- From fabrics A and B, make four 3½-inch half-square triangles (see page 12)
- From fabrics A and C, make four 6½ x 3½-inch flying geese rectangles (see page 17)
- From fabric B, cut one 6½-inch square

or

Template cutting
Using the 4 x 4 templates (pages 269–73):
- From fabric A, cut 4 medium triangles and 4 small triangles
- From fabric B, cut 1 large square and 4 small triangles
- From fabric C, cut 8 small triangles

Template piecing

With right sides together, pin and sew a fabric C small triangle to each diagonal edge of the fabric A medium triangles to make four flying-geese units; press seams open.

With right sides together, pin and sew one fabric A small triangle to each of the fabric B small triangles to make four half-square triangles; press seams open.

Make the block

Join three rows With right sides together, pin and sew two flying geese rectangles to the fabric B large square so that they point toward the center of the block; press seams open.

With right sides together, pin and sew two half-square triangles to each of the remaining flying geese rectangles, making sure the fabric B triangles point toward the center of the block; press seams open.

Complete the square With right sides together, pin and sew the two strips to the top and bottom edges of the middle row, making sure the flying geese rectangles point toward the center of the block; press seams open.

---

variable star

This block is known by many names: the Ohio Star, the Texas Star, and the Eastern Star. Whatever you call it, it's always made from pointed hourglass stars. Join the Variable Star with the Butterfly Star (see page 237), the Open Star (see page 63), and Aunt Eliza's Star (see page 59) to make a twinkly sampler quilt.

The seam allowance is ¼ inch throughout.

Fabric quantities

- Medium yellow fabric A: 12 x 12 inches
- Medium yellow print fabric B: 5 x 5 inches
- White fabric C: 12 x 22 inches

Prepare the patches

Rotary method
- From fabrics A and C, make four 4½-inch hourglass squares (see page 13)
- From fabric B, cut one 4½-inch square
- From fabric C, cut four 4½-inch squares

or

Template cutting
Using the 6 x 6 templates (pages 278–83):
- From fabric A, cut 8 medium triangles
- From fabric B, cut 1 large square
- From fabric C, cut 4 large squares and 8 medium triangles

Template piecing

With right sides together, pin and sew one fabric C medium triangle to each of the fabric A medium triangles; press seams open. Join them in pairs, alternating colors, to make four hourglass squares; press seams open.

Make the block

Join three rows With right sides together, pin and sew a fabric C large square to each side of an hourglass square along the yellow triangles; press seams open. Repeat to make the bottom row.

With right sides together, pin and sew two hourglass squares to each side of the fabric B large square, adjoining them along the white triangle edges.

Complete the square With right sides together and carefully matching seams, pin and sew the top and bottom rows to the center row; press seams open.

floating square

This simple geometric block is begging for novelty print centers. Use it to frame favorite prints in analogous colors, such as green and yellow.

The seam allowance is ¼ inch throughout.

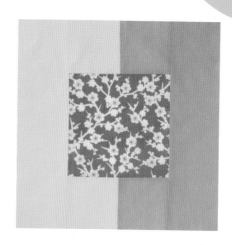

A
B
C

Fabric quantities

- Medium yellow fabric A: 8 x 13 inches
- Medium green fabric B: 8 x 13 inches
- Medium gray print fabric C: 7 x 7 inches

Prepare the patches

Rotary method
- From fabrics A and B, cut one 12½ x 3½-inch rectangle and two 3½-inch squares each
- From fabric C, cut one 6½-inch square

or

Template cutting
Using the 4 x 4 templates (pages 269–73):
- From fabrics A and B, cut 2 small squares and 1 full-length rectangle each
- From fabric C, cut 1 large square

Make the block

Join the center panel With right sides together, pin and sew one fabric A small square to each of the fabric B small squares; press seams open.

With right sides together, pin and sew the fabrics A and B strips to the top and bottom edges of the fabric C large square, making sure the fabric A squares are on the left side.

Complete the square With right sides together, pin and sew the fabric A full-length rectangle to the left side of the block and the fabric B full-length rectangle to the right side; press seams open.

---

overlap

The Overlap block creates the illusion of a translucent overlay in the center square that looks like you blended two colors to get the third. You could try using red, blue, and purple, or yellow, blue, and green on a crisp white background.

The seam allowance is ¼ inch throughout.

A
B
C
D

Fabric quantities

- Light orange fabric A: 5 x 5 inches
- Medium orange fabric B: 6 x 7 inches
- Medium yellow fabric C: 6 x 7 inches
- White fabric D: 12 x 13 inches

Prepare the patches

Rotary method
- From fabric A, cut one 4½-inch square
- From fabrics B and C, cut one 4½ x 2½-inch rectangle and one 6½ x 2½-inch rectangle each
- From fabric D, cut two 2½-inch squares, two 8½ x 2½-inch rectangles, and two 12½ x 2½-inch rectangles

or

Template cutting
Using the 6 x 6 templates (pages 278–83):
- From fabric A, cut 1 large square
- From fabrics B and C, cut 1 short rectangle and 1 medium rectangle each
- From fabric D, cut 2 small squares, 2 long rectangles, and 2 full-length rectangles

Make the block

Join three rows With right sides together, pin and sew the fabric B short rectangle to the top edge of the fabric A large square; join the fabric C short rectangle to the bottom edge; press seams open.

With right sides together, pin and sew a fabric D small square to one end of the fabric B medium rectangle and the fabric C medium rectangle; press seams open.

With right sides together, pin and sew the fabrics B and D strip to the left edge of the light orange square with the white square at the bottom. Join the fabric C and D strip to the right edge with the white square at the top; press seams open.

Complete the square With right sides together, pin and sew a fabric D long rectangle to the top and bottom edges of the square; press seams open. Join the fabric D full-length rectangles to each side; press seams open.

single pinwheel

This simple pinwheel is a popular motif which is ideally suited to baby quilts. Setting triangles on their points give this block its sense of movement. The Single Pinwheel works well in solid colors or small scale prints, as long as the background is in strong contrast to the sails.

A

B

The seam allowance is ¼ inch throughout.

Fabric quantities

- Medium yellow print fabric A: 10 x 10 inches
- White fabric B: 13 x 16 inches

Prepare the patches

Rotary method
- From fabric A and B, make four 6½-inch three-quarter square triangles (see page 13)

or

Template cutting
Using the 4 x 4 templates (pages 269–73):
- From fabric A, cut 4 large triangles and 4 medium triangles
- From fabric B, cut 4 medium triangles

Template piecing

With right sides together, pin and sew a fabric A medium triangle to a fabric B medium triangle along their short sides, making sure that the yellow triangles are on the right; press seams open. Repeat to make three more large triangles.

With right sides together, pin and sew a fabric A large triangle to each long edge of the triangles to make four three-quarter square triangles.

Make the block

Join two rows Arrange the four three-quarter square triangles so that the fabric A triangles meet at the center and all point in the same direction. With right sides together, pin and

sew the top two three-quarter square triangles; press seams open. Repeat to join the remaining two three-quarter square triangles.

Complete the square With right sides together and matching seams carefully, pin and sew the two rows together; press seam open.

corner cross

Using different colored fabrics can totally transform a basic block design. This simple cross is made in exactly the same way as Cross Weave (page 42)

A

B

C

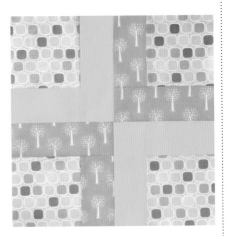

The seam allowance is ¼ inch throughout.

Fabric quantities

- Medium yellow fabric A: 6 x 12 inches
- Medium green print fabric B: 6 x 12 inches
- Medium gray print fabric C: 10 x 10 inches

Prepare the patches

Rotary method
- From fabrics A and B, cut two 6½ x 2½-inch rectangles and two 4½ x 2½-inch rectangles each
- From fabric C, cut four 4½-inch squares

or

Template cutting
Using the 6 x 6 templates (pages 278–83):
- From fabrics A and B, cut 2 short rectangles and 2 medium rectangles each
- From fabric C, cut 4 large squares

Make the block

Piece the top left patch With right sides together, pin and sew a fabric A short rectangle to the bottom edge of a fabric C large square; press seam open. Join a fabric A medium rectangle to the right edge; press seam open.

Piece the top right patch With right sides together, pin and sew a fabric B short rectangle to the left edge of a fabric C large square; press seam open. Join a fabric B medium rectangle to the bottom edge; press seam open.

Piece the bottom right patch With right sides together, pin and sew a fabric A short rectangle to the top edge of a fabric C large square; press seam open. Join a fabric A medium rectangle to the left edge.

Piece the bottom left patch With right sides together, pin and sew a short fabric B rectangle to the right edge of the fabric C

large square; press seam open. Join a fabric B medium rectangle to the top edge; press seam open.

Complete the square With right sides together, pin and sew the two top patches along the colored edges; press seam open. Repeat with the bottom two patches. With right sides together and carefully matching seams, pin and sew the two rows together; press seam open.

chain and hourglass

The seam allowance is ¼ inch throughout.

The allover pattern of this block includes hourglass squares. Depending on choice of background fabric, the secondary arrow pattern will be more or less obvious. This geometric block is easily made using the rotary method.

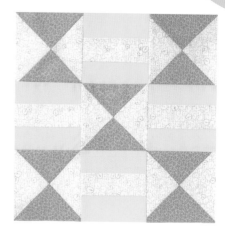

A
B
C

Fabric quantities

- Medium orange print fabric A: 12 x 18 inches

- Medium yellow fabric B: 10 x 10 inches

- Light gray print fabric C: 15 x 18 inches

Prepare the patches

Rotary method

- From fabrics A and C, make five 4½-inch hourglass squares (see page 13)

- From fabrics B and C, make four 4½-inch three-stripe squares (see page 11)

Make the block

Piece three rows With right sides together, pin and sew an hourglass square to each side of one striped square, keeping the stripes horizontal; press seams away from the stripes. Repeat to make the bottom row. For the center row, with right sides together, pin and sew a striped square to each side of the remaining hourglass square along the gray sides. Keep the stripes horizontal; press seams away from the stripes.

Complete the square With right sides together, join the top and bottom rows to the center row, matching seams; press seams open.

---

octagon check

The seam allowance is ¼ inch throughout.

143

When these large octagonal units are made up in plain white with dark triangles at the corners, they are called "snowballs"—see Nine-Patch Snowballs on page 89. They look very different when the colors are reversed, as here. The two 6½-inch squares are a good showcase for large-scale print.

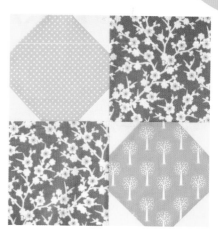

A
B
C
D

Fabric quantities

- Light yellow fabric A: 6 x 6 inches

- Light green print fabric B: 7 x 7 inches

- Medium green print fabric C: 7 x 7 inches

- Medium gray print fabric D: 7 x 14 inches

Prepare the patches

Rotary method

- From fabrics A and B and fabrics A and C, make one 6½-inch octagon square (see page 18) each

- From fabric D, cut two 6½-inch squares

or

Template cutting
Using the 6 x 6 templates (pages 278–83):

- From fabric A, cut 8 small triangles

- From fabrics B and C, cut 1 octagon each

- From fabric D, cut 2 very large squares

Template piecing

With right sides together, pin and sew one small fabric A triangle to each diagonal edge on both octagons; press seams open.

Make the block

Sew two rows With right sides together, pin and sew one fabric D very large square to one side of an octagon square, making sure the print is oriented in the correct direction; press seam open. Repeat to make the second row.

Complete the square With right sides together, join the two rows, making sure the octagon squares are placed diagonally; press seam open.

shoofly

This block is often found in traditional Amish quilts. Its simple structure works well with prints and solids, and it scales up and down easily.

The seam allowance is ¼ inch throughout.

A
B
C

Fabric quantities

- Medium yellow print fabric A: 5 x 5 inches
- Medium yellow print fabric B: 6 x 12 inches
- White fabric C: 12 x 16 inches

Prepare the patches

Rotary method
- From fabrics B and C, make four 4½-inch half-square triangles (see page 12) each
- From fabric A, cut one 4½-inch square
- From fabric C, cut four 4½-inch squares

or

Template cutting
Using the 6 x 6 templates (pages 278–83):
- From fabric A, cut 1 large square
- From fabric B, cut 4 large triangles
- From fabric C, cut 4 large squares and 4 large triangles

Template piecing

With right sides together, pin and sew a fabric B large triangle to each of the fabric C large triangles along the diagonal edges to make four half-square triangles; press seams open.

Make the block

Join three rows With right sides together, pin and sew a half-square triangle to each side of a fabric C large square, making sure the yellow triangles point toward the center of the block; press seams open. Repeat to make the bottom row.

With right sides together, pin and sew a fabric C large square to each side of the fabric A large square; press seams open.

Complete the square With right sides together, pin and sew the top and bottom rows to the center row, making sure all of the yellow triangles point to the center square; press seams open.

---

sunrise

This block is a variation on the Log Cabin Square on page 65, and it's also widely known as Courthouse Steps. The strips are sewn in pairs instead of rounds.

The seam allowance is ¼ inch throughout.

A
B
C
D
E
F
G

Fabric quantities

- Light blue fabric A: 4 x 4 inches
- Light blue fabric B: 5 x 4 inches
- Light yellow fabric C: 5 x 7 inches
- Medium blue fabric D: 5 x 7 inches
- Dark yellow fabric E: 5 x 10 inches
- Medium turquoise fabric F: 5 x 10 inches
- Medium orange fabric G: 5 x 13 inches

Prepare the patches

Rotary method
- From fabric A, cut one 3½-inch square
- From fabric B, cut two 3½ x 2-inch rectangles
- From fabrics C and D, cut two 6½ x 2-inch rectangles each
- From fabrics E and F, cut two 9½ x 2-inch rectangles each
- From fabric G, cut two 12½ x 2-inch rectangles

Make the block

Join the first round With right sides together, pin and sew the two fabric B rectangles to the side edges of the fabric A square; press seams out.

Join the second round With right sides together, pin and sew the fabric C rectangles to the top and bottom edges of the center patch; press seams out.

Join the third round With right sides together, pin and sew the fabric D rectangles to the side edges of the center patch; press seams out.

Join the fourth round With right sides together, pin and sew the fabric E rectangles to the top and bottom edges of the center patch; press seams out.

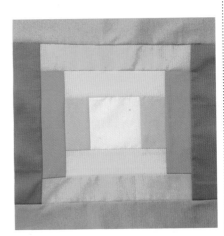

Join the fifth round With right sides together, pin and sew the fabric F rectangles to the side edges of the center patch; press seams out.

Complete the square With right sides together, pin and sew the fabric G rectangles to the top and bottom edges of the center patch; press seams out.

weather vane

The seam allowance is ¼ inch throughout.

Weather Vane was described in 1930 as an "old-time block," and it was first used sometime in the nineteenth century. The four floral house patches suggest the points of the compass on a weathervane spinning above a barn.

Fabric quantities

- Light yellow fabric A: 8 x 16 inches
- Dark yellow fabric B: 8 x 9 inches
- Medium blue print fabric C: 10 x 10 inches
- White fabric D: 14 x 16 inches

Prepare the patches

Rotary method
- From fabrics A and D, make eight 2½-inch half-square triangles (see page 12)
- From fabrics C and D, make four 4½-inch house squares (see page 14)
- From fabric B, cut one 4½-inch square and four 2½-inch squares
- From fabric D, cut four 2½-inch squares

or

Template cutting
Using the 6 x 6 templates (pages 278–83):
- From fabric A, cut 8 small triangles
- From fabric B, cut 1 large square and 4 small squares
- From fabric C, cut 4 house squares
- From fabric D, cut 4 small squares and 16 small triangles

Template piecing

With right sides together, pin and sew a fabric D small triangle to each of the fabric A small triangles to make eight half-square triangles; press seams open.

With right sides together, pin and sew a fabric D small triangle to each of the diagonal edges of the fabric C house squares; press seams open.

Make the block

Piece the corner patches With right sides together, pin and sew a white small square to the left edge of four of the half-square triangles, making sure the yellow triangles point down and left; press seams open.

With right sides together, pin and sew a dark yellow small square to the right edge of the four remaining half-square triangles, making sure the yellow triangles point up and right; press seams open.

With right sides together, pin and sew a pair of strips together to make a square, with both fabric A triangles adjacent to the fabric B square and carefully matching the seams to create an arrow shape; press seam open. Join the remaining strips to make another three corner patches.

Sew three rows With right sides together, pin and sew a fabrics A, B, and D patch to each side of a house square, making sure the house points out and the arrows point in; press seams open. Repeat to make the third row.

To make the center row, join a house square to each side of the fabric B large square, making sure the arrows point out; press seams open.

Complete the square With right sides together, pin and sew the first and third rows to the center row, carefully matching the seams; press seams open.

the anvil

Like its variation, Rocky Mountain Puzzle (page 106), this block works equally well set on point. Contrasting a light, solid fabric for the triangles with a dark print background emphasizes the sawtooth edge of the geometric anvil.

The seam allowance is ¼ inch throughout.

Fabric quantities

- Dark gray print fabric A: 10 x 18 inches
- Light yellow fabric B: 10 x 10 inches
- Light gray print fabric C: 7 x 7 inches

Prepare the patches

Rotary method
- From fabrics A and B, make eight 3½-inch half-square triangles (see page 12)
- From fabric A, cut four 3½-inch squares
- From fabric C, cut one 6½-inch square

or

Template cutting
Using the 4 x 4 templates (pages 269–73):
- From fabric A, cut 4 small squares and 8 small triangles
- From fabric B, cut 8 small triangles
- From fabric C, cut 1 large square

Template piecing

With right sides together, pin and sew one fabric A small triangle to each of the fabric B small triangles to make eight half-square triangles; press seams open.

Make the block

Sew three rows With right sides together, pin and sew two half-square triangles together, making sure the yellow triangles point down and right. Join a fabric A small square on each side of the strip; press seams open. Repeat to make the bottom row, then flip it.

With right sides together, pin and sew two pairs of half-square triangles, making sure the yellow triangles point down and left; press seams open. Join these strips to the side edges of the fabric C large square; press seams open.

Complete the square With right sides together, pin and sew the top and bottom rows to the center row, carefully matching seams; press seams open.

checks

This basic checkerboard pattern gives you plenty of practice in matching seams. Add a wide strip to the side to enliven this block with a fresh floral pattern. Use Checks to make a baby quilt or a single cushion cover, choosing either a tonal color palette or raiding your scraps for a random design. This scrappy block is easily made using the rotary method.

The seam allowance is ¼ inch throughout.

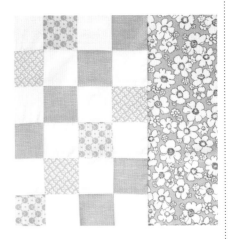

Fabric quantities

- Medium yellow print fabric A: 3 x 9 inches
- Medium yellow print fabric B: 6 x 9 inches
- Medium yellow print fabric C: 3 x 9 inches
- White fabric D: 9 x 12 inches
- Medium blue print fabric E: 5 x 13 inches

Prepare the patches

Rotary method
- From fabrics A and C, cut three 2½-inch squares each
- From fabric B, cut six 2½-inch squares
- From fabric D, cut twelve 2½-inch squares
- From fabric E, cut one 12½ x 4½-inch rectangle

Make the block

Piece the checkerboard Arrange the squares in six rows of four squares, alternating white and colored patches and making sure that four fabric B squares make a diagonal line from the top right of the block and that two fabric B squares are at the bottom right corner.

With right sides together, pin and sew the squares in the first row; press seams to the right. Join the squares in the second row; press seams to the left. Repeat to make another four rows, alternating the direction you press the seams.

Complete the square With right sides together, pin and sew the first row to the second row; press seam open. Repeat to join the remaining rows.

With right sides together, pin and sew the fabric E rectangle to the right side of the block; press seam open.

rectangles

This simple one-patch design gives you room to experiment with fabrics and play with colors or practice your improvization skills with a totally random layout.

The seam allowance is ¼ inch throughout.

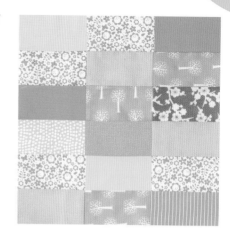

Fabric quantities

- Medium gray print fabric A: 3 x 5 inches
- Light gray print fabric B: 6 x 10 inches
- Medium green print fabric C: 5 x 9 inches
- Light green fabric D: 5 x 9 inches
- Medium orange print fabric E: 3 x 5 inches
- Medium orange fabric F: 5 x 6 inches
- Light yellow fabric G: 5 x 6 inches
- Light yellow print fabric H: 3 x 5 inches
- Medium orange print fabric I: 3 x 5 inches

Prepare the patches

Rotary method
- From fabrics A, E, H, and I, cut one 4½ x 2½-inch rectangle each
- From fabric B, cut four 4½ x 2½-inch rectangles

- From fabrics C and D, cut three 4½ x 2½-inch rectangles each
- From fabrics F and G, cut two 4½ x 2½-inch rectangles each

or

Template cutting
Using the 6 x 6 templates (pages 278–83):
- From fabrics A, E, H, and I, cut 1 short rectangle each
- From fabric B, cut 4 short rectangles
- From fabrics C and D, cut 3 short rectangles each
- From fabrics F and G, cut 2 short rectangles each

Make the block

Sew six rows Arrange the rectangles in six rows of three, balancing pattern and color.

With right sides together, sew the first three rectangles in a row, joining the short sides; press seams to the right. Repeat to make the second row, but press seams to the left. Join the remaining rows of patches in the same way, alternating the direction you press the seams.

Complete the square Pin and sew the rows together; press seams open.

---

octagon frame

This simple geometric block is perfect for highlighting a fussy-cut square or playing with large-scale prints in a quilt. Try partnering a neutral print for the octagon with a pictorial fabric for the center square.

The seam allowance is ¼ inch throughout.

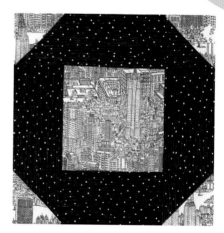

Fabric quantities

- Medium black-and-white print fabric A: 12 x 13 inches
- Dark black-and-yellow print fabric B: 10 x 15 inches

Prepare the patches

Rotary method
- From fabrics A and B, make four 3½-inch half-square triangles (see page 12)
- From fabric A, cut one 6½-inch square
- From fabric B, cut four 6½ x 2½-inch rectangles

or

Template cutting
Using the 4 x 4 templates (pages 269–73):

- From fabric A, cut 1 large square and 4 small triangles
- From fabric B, cut 4 short rectangles and 4 small triangles

Template piecing

With right sides together, pin and sew a fabric A small triangle to each fabric B small triangle to make four half-square triangles.

Make the block

Sew two rows With right sides together, pin and sew a half-square triangle to each end of one fabric B short rectangle, making sure the fabric A triangles are pointing away from the center square; press seams open. Repeat to make the bottom row.

Piece the center panel With right sides together, pin and sew a fabric B short rectangle to each side of the fabric A large square; press seams open.

Complete the square With right sides together, pin and sew the top and bottom rows to the center row, carefully matching the seams; press seams open.

turbo prop

The seam allowance is ¼ inch throughout.

This dynamic take on a star motif radiates a strong sense of movement. Here, the light blue background provides contrast for the mustard-colored fabrics.

A
B
C

Fabric quantities

- Medium yellow print fabric A: 8 x 14 inches

- Dark yellow print fabric B: 9 x 14 inches

- Light blue fabric C: 9 x 14 inches

Prepare the patches

Rotary method

- From fabrics A and C, make four 6½ x 3½-inch right diamond rectangles (see page 16)

- From fabrics B and C, make four 6½ x 3½-inch right tapered rectangles (see page 16)

or

Template cutting

Using the 4 x 4 templates (pages 269–73):
- From fabric A, cut 4 right diamonds

- From fabric B, cut 4 right tapered rectangles

- From fabric C, cut 12 small triangles

Template piecing

With right sides together, pin and sew the fabric C small triangles to the diagonal edge of each fabric A right diamond and fabric B right tapered rectangle.

Make the block

Piece four patches With right sides together, pin and sew one right diamond to one right tapered rectangle to make a corner patch, making sure they both point up to the top right corner of the patch; press seam open. Repeat to make another three corner patches.

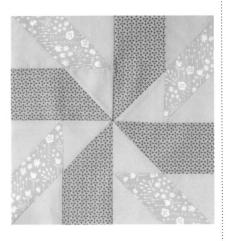

Sew two rows With right sides together, pin and sew the patches into pairs, carefully matching the right tapered rectangle points where they meet in the center; press seams toward the right tapered rectangles.

Complete the square With right sides together, pin and sew the top row to the bottom row, carefully matching the right tapered rectangle points in the center of the block; press seam open.

---

diagonal cross

The seam allowance is ¼ inch throughout.

Made from four hexagon squares, the Diagonal Cross is a good way to use charm squares or show off medium-scale prints—and it is a simple block for beginners.

A
B
C
D
E
F

Fabric quantities

- Medium yellow print fabric A: 7 x 7 inches

- Medium orange print fabric B: 7 x 7 inches

- Light green print fabric C: 7 x 7 inches

- Medium green print fabric D: 7 x 7 inches

- Light blue fabric E: 6 x 6 inches

- Light yellow fabric F: 6 x 6 inches

Prepare the patches

Rotary method

- From fabrics A and E; fabrics B and E; fabrics C and F; and fabrics D and F, make one 6½-inch hexagon square (see page 15) each

or

Template cutting

Using the 4 x 4 templates (pages 269–73):
- From fabrics A, B, C, and D, cut 1 hexagon each

- From fabrics E and F, cut 4 small triangles each

Template piecing

With right sides together, pin and sew the fabric E small triangles to the diagonal edges of the fabric A and fabric B hexagons to make two hexagon squares; press seams open.

Repeat to make two hexagons using fabric F small triangles and fabrics C and D hexagons.

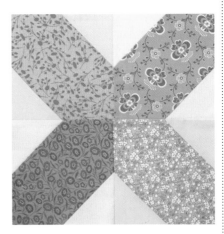

Make the block

Sew two rows With right sides together, pin and sew the fabric A and fabric C hexagon squares together; press seam open. Join the fabric B and fabric D hexagon squares together; press seam open.

Complete the square With right sides together, pin and sew the top row to the bottom row, making sure the colors match on the diagonal; press seam open.

eight-point star

This classic star is made up of eight diamond-shape patches combined with squares and triangles. Pieced in the traditional way, with set-in seams, this block takes longer to make, but it is worth the effort. For a speedier, rotary-pieced version (with no difficult Y seams), see the Eight-Point Triangle Star on page 240.

The seam allowance is ¼ inch throughout.

A
B
C
D
E

Fabric quantities

- Medium pink print fabric A: 6 x 8 inches
- Medium yellow print fabric B: 6 x 8 inches
- Medium orange fabric C: 6 x 8 inches
- Medium purple print fabric D: 6 x 8 inches
- White fabric E: 12 x 16 inches

Prepare the patches

Template cutting
Using the 4 x 4 templates (pages 269–73):
- From fabrics A and C, cut 2 right diamonds each
- From fabrics B and D, cut 2 left diamonds each
- From fabric E, cut 4 medium triangles and 4 small squares

Make the block

Prepare the patches Using a fading pen, mark the ¼-inch seam allowance around each edge of each patch.

Position the patches in their final positions, as shown above. With right sides together and starting at the top left corner, join the fabric A right diamond to the adjacent fabric B left diamond along the diagonal edge, leaving the seam allowance unstitched at both ends.

With right sides together, sew the bottom edge of a fabric E small square to the top edge of the fabric A diamond, from the point where the seam allowances meet at the inside corners to the outside edge. Join the fabric B diamond to the fabric E small square along the marked seam allowance from the inside corner to the outside edge; press seams over the square. Repeat with the other diamonds to make another three patches as shown above.

Join the rows For the top row, with right sides together, pin and sew the two pairs of diamonds along the straight edges of the yellow and orange fabrics, leaving the seam allowance unstitched at both ends. Sew a fabric E medium triangle to the diagonal edge of fabric B, from where the seam allowance lines meet at the inside corner to the outside edge. Now sew the other diagonal edge of the fabric E triangle along the fabric C diamond, from the inside corner to the outside edge, using the seam allowance lines; press the diagonal seams over the diamonds.

Join the remaining two squares in the same way for the bottom row.

Complete the square With right sides together, pin and sew the top and bottom rows along the straight edges of the yellow and purple fabrics. Add the fabric E triangles as above; press center seam open.

whirligig

The seam allowance is ¼ inch throughout.

A
B
C

The Whirligig block offers one more way to join half-square triangles in an interesting, lively pattern. Use your favorite scraps for the center square, but maintain the same colors for the half-square triangles. Be careful to match seams carefully, especially where six individual seams meet.

Fabric quantities

- Light green fabric A: 12 x 12 inches
- Medium green print fabric B: 5 x 5 inches
- White fabric C: 12 x 12 inches

Prepare the patches

Rotary method
- From fabrics A and C, make eight 4½-inch half-square triangles (see page 12)
- From fabric B, cut one 4½-inch square

or

Template cutting
Using the 6 x 6 templates (pages 278–83):
- From fabrics A and C, cut 8 large triangles each
- From fabric B, cut 1 large square

Template piecing

With right sides together, pin and sew a fabric C large triangle to each of the fabric A large triangles along the long diagonal edges to make eight half-square triangles; press seams open.

Make the block

Sew three rows With right sides together, pin and sew one half-square triangle to a second half-square triangle, joining the white triangles and making sure the green triangles meet at a point at the bottom. Add a third half-square triangle to the right side of the strip, aligning the edges of the green triangles; press seams open. Repeat to make the third row.

With right sides together, pin and sew a half-square triangle to each side of the fabric B square, aligning the green triangles with the square, with the left one pointing up and right and the right one pointing down and left.

Complete the square Lay out the rows with the top row having the green fabric A on the left side and the bottom row having the green fabric A on the right side, as shown above.

With right sides together, pin and sew the first row to the second row, making sure the green triangles form the top of the pinwheel; press seam open.

With right sides together, pin and sew the third row to the second row, making sure the green triangles form the bottom of the pinwheel; press seam open.

grandmother's cross

The seam allowance is ¼ inch throughout.

Grandmother's Cross is a traditional design steeped in history. Dating back to the mid-nineteenth century, it's also called Memory Quilt or T-Quilt, because of the secondary letter shapes formed by the background fabric. This block is most accurately made from templates when making a 12-inch square.

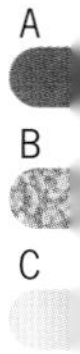

A
B
C

Fabric quantities

- Dark green fabric A: 6 x 9 inches
- Medium green print fabric B: 14 x 14 inches
- Light blue fabric C: 12 x 15 inches

Prepare the patches

Template cutting
Using the 5 x 5 templates (pages 274–7):
- From fabric A, cut 5 small squares
- From fabric B, cut 4 large triangles
- From fabric C, cut 4 short rectangles and 8 small triangles

Template piecing

With right sides together, pin and sew two fabric C small triangles to adjacent sides of four of the fabric A small squares; press seams open. Join one fabrics A and C unit to each fabric B large triangle along the long diagonal edges to complete four triangle-and-square patches; press seams open.

Make the block

Make three rows With right sides together, pin and sew one triangle-and-square patch to each long edge of the fabric C rectangles, making sure the fabric B triangles point to the center of the block; press seams open. Repeat to make the bottom row.

With right sides together, pin and sew the remaining fabric C short rectangles to each side of the last fabric A small square; press seams open.

Complete the square With right sides together, pin and sew the top and bottom rows to the center row, carefully matching seams; press seams open.

- -

watermill

The seam allowance is ¼ inch throughout.

156

Watermill is similar to the Single Pinwheel block (see page 114), but with an even greater sense of movement. Emphasize the whirling motion by combining a dark solid with white for the background and a small floral or even a stripe.

A
B
C

Fabric quantities

- Dark green fabric A: 5 x 10 inches
- Medium green print fabric B: 8 x 16 inches
- Light green fabric C: 5 x 10 inches

Prepare the patches

Rotary method
- From fabrics A, B, and C, make four 6½-inch three-quarter square triangles (see page 13)

or

Template cutting
Using the 4 x 4 templates (pages 269–73):
- From fabrics A and C, cut 4 medium triangles each
- From fabric B, cut 4 large triangles

Template piecing

With right sides together, pin and sew a fabric A medium triangle to each fabric C medium triangle along a short diagonal edge; press seams open. Join the fabrics A and C units to each of the fabric B large triangles along a long diagonal edge to make four three-quarter squares; press seams open.

Make the block

Sew two rows With right sides together, pin and sew two three-quarter square triangles together, making sure the green print triangles are on the outside edge and an end point meets in the center; press seam open. Repeat to make the bottom row.

Complete the square With right sides together, pin and sew the two rows together, carefully matching the points at the center of the block and making sure the white triangles stay on the outside edges; press seam open.

cotton reel

Use a striped fabric for the large center square of this graphic block, so that it looks as if the reel is wound with brightly colored thread. Cotton Reel is sewn with set-in seams at the corners, which is a technical challenge for advanced quilters.

A
B
C

The seam allowance is ¼ inch throughout.

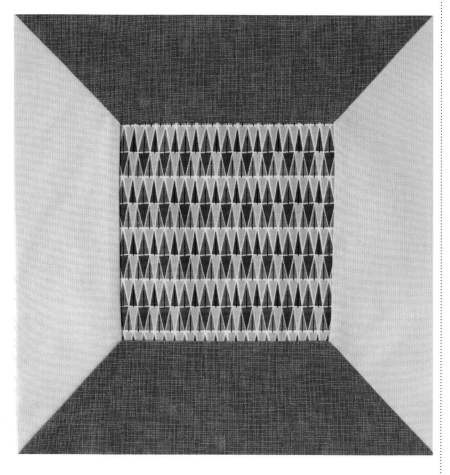

Fabric quantities

- Dark green print fabric A: 13 x 8 inches
- Light green fabric B: 13 x 8 inches
- Dark green print fabric C: 7 x 7 inches

Prepare the patches

Rotary method
- From fabrics A and B, cut two 12½ x 3½-inch rectangles each
- From fabric C, cut one 6½-inch square
- or
- Template cutting
- Using the 4 x 4 templates (pages 269–73):
- From fabrics A and B, cut 2 long boats each
- From fabric C, cut 1 large square

Rotary piecing

Mark a diagonal line that slopes up from each bottom corner on the fabric A and fabric B rectangles. Measure and mark the center of each of the shorter long edges.

Mark the seam allowance on the upper edge of the fabric A and fabric B rectangles. Mark the seam allowance on all four edges of the fabric C square. Measure and mark the centers along all four edges.

The set-in seams are stitched in the same way as for the Perspective Square units on page 18. Pin the shorter marked long edge of a fabric A rectangle centrally to the bottom edge of the C fabric square and stitch along the seam allowance, leaving the last ¼ inch open at each end. Sew the other fabric A rectangle to the bottom edge in the same way. Add the B fabric rectangles to the two side edges, again leaving the seam allowance unstitched at the ends of the seam. Pin the corners of the fabric A and B rectangles together and sew along each of the marked diagonal lines. Trim the seam allowance to ¼ inch. Press the diagonal seams over fabric A and the straight seams outwards.

Make the block

Join set-in seams Measure and mark the centers along all four edges of the fabric C large square. Using the center marks as a guide, center the top edge of a fabric A long boat on the top edge of the fabric C large square, pin, and then sew along the seam allowance, leaving the last ¼ inch open at each end. Repeat to join the second fabric A long boat to the bottom edge.

Repeat to sew both fabric B long boats to the fabric C large square.

Complete the square Pin the corners of the long boats together and sew along each diagonal line. Trim the seams to ¼ inch.

Press the diagonal seams over fabric A and the straight seams outward.

end of the day

The seam allowance is ¼ inch throughout.

The shift from light to dark fabrics, mirroring day turning into night, gives this block its evocative name. It is made from two contrasting prints with allover designs. Multiple blocks joined edge to edge create an interesting mosaic pattern, especially if each block is made from different fabrics. This block is most accurately made from templates when making a 12-inch block.

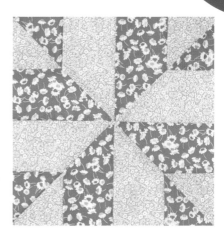

A
B

Fabric quantities

- Medium blue print fabric A: 13 x 14 inches
- Light green print fabric B: 13 x 14 inches

Prepare the patches

Template cutting
Using the 4 x 4 templates (pages 269–73):
- From fabric A, cut 4 right tapered rectangles and 4 small triangles
- From fabric B, cut 4 left tapered rectangles and 4 small triangles

Make the block

Sew eight triangles With right sides together, pin and sew a fabric A small triangle to the diagonal edge of each fabric B left tapered rectangle; press seams over fabric A. Repeat to attach a fabric B small triangle to each fabric A right tapered rectangle.

Make two rows With right sides together, pin and sew pairs of opposite triangles together to make four quarter squares; press seams open. With right sides together, pin and sew two opposite quarter squares together, making sure the tapered rectangles point to the center of the block; press seams over fabric A. Repeat to make the bottom row.

Complete the square With right sides together, pin and sew the top row to the bottom row; press seam open.

158

---

freewheeling star

The seam allowance is ¼ inch throughout.

Like other pinwheel blocks, the Freewheeling Star has a feeling of movement. If you are using a striped pattern for the background squares, set all of the patches in the same direction to avoid the block looking too busy.

A
B
C

Fabric quantities

- Dark turquoise fabric A: 12 x 12 inches
- Medium blue print fabric B: 10 x 15 inches
- White fabric C: 12 x 12 inches

Prepare the patches

Rotary method
- From fabrics A and C, make four 4½-inch half-square triangles (see page 12)
- From fabric B, cut five 4½-inch squares

or

Template cutting
Using the 6 x 6 templates (pages 278–83):
- From fabrics A and C, cut 4 large triangles each
- From fabric B, cut 5 large squares

Template piecing

With right sides together, pin and sew one fabric A large triangle to each fabric C large triangle to make four half-square triangles; press seams open.

Make the block

Sew three rows With right sides together, pin and sew a fabric B large square to each side of a half-square triangle, making sure the turquoise triangle points down and to the right; press seam open. Repeat to make the bottom row.

With right sides together, pin and sew a half-square triangle to each side of the remaining fabric B large square, making sure the turquoise triangles are adjacent to the center square, and the right one points down and the left points up; press seam open.

Complete the square Flip the bottom row. With right sides together and carefully matching seams, pin and sew the top and bottom rows to the center row, making sure the long edges of the fabric A triangles adjoin the center square; press seams open.

159

square blocks

The green and teal fabrics, punctuated by white patches, give a clean, modern look to this block. The staggered rows of alternating squares and rectangles are quick to make, offering beginner quilters a fun patchwork design.

A
B
C
D
E
F

The seam allowance is ¼ inch throughout.

Fabric quantities

- Medium green fabric A: 5 x 10 inches
- Medium green print fabric B: 5 x 10 inches
- Medium green print fabric C: 5 x 10 inches
- Medium teal fabric D: 7 x 8 inches
- Medium teal print fabric E: 7 x 8 inches
- White fabric F: 8 x 12 inches

Prepare the patches

Rotary method
- From fabrics A, B, and C, cut two 3½-inch squares each
- From fabrics D and E, cut two 3½-inch squares, one 3½ x 1½-inch rectangle, and one 3½ x 2½-inch rectangle each

- From fabric F, cut twelve 3½ x 1½-inch rectangles

Make the block

Add the white rectangles With right sides together, pin and sew one white rectangle to one side of each of the fabrics A, B, C, D, and E squares. Join one white rectangle to one side of the fabrics D and E smallest rectangles; press seams open.

Join the columns With right sides together, pin and sew a column of three green patches starting with the white rectangle; press seams open. Repeat to make another column, making sure you arrange the green prints in a different order.

With right sides together, pin and sew a column of four teal patches, starting with the fabric D rectangle without a white patch;

press seams open. Repeat to make the fourth column, starting with the fabric E rectangle without a white patch.

Complete the square Arrange the columns, alternating colors. With right sides together, pin and sew the first column and the third column to the second column, and the fourth column to the third column; press seams open.

steps

Mix prints and solids in gradient tones to create depth in the Steps block. Join multiple blocks edge to edge to create diagonal lines across the surface of a quilt.

A
B
C
D
E
F
G

The seam allowance is ¼ inch throughout.

Fabric quantities

- Light teal fabric A: 3 x 5 inches
- Light teal print fabric B: 3 x 7 inches
- Medium teal fabric C: 3 x 7 inches
- Medium teal print fabric D: 3 x 7 inches
- Dark green fabric E: 3 x 7 inches
- Dark teal fabric F: 3 x 5 inches
- White fabric G: 10 x 18 inches

Prepare the patches

Rotary method
- From fabric A, cut one 4½ x 2½-inch rectangle
- From fabrics B, C, D, and E, cut one 6½ x 2½-inch rectangle each
- From fabric F, cut one 4½ x 2½-inch rectangle

- From fabric G, cut two 8½ x 2½-inch rectangles, two 6½ x 2½-inch rectangles, two 4½ x 2½-inch rectangles, and two 2½-inch squares

Make the block

Sew six rows With right sides together, pin and sew the longest white rectangles to the left edge of the fabric A rectangle and the right edge of the fabric E rectangle; press seams over the colored fabric.

With right sides together, pin and sew the medium length white rectangles to the left edge of the fabric B rectangle and the right edge of the fabric E rectangle; press seams over the colored fabric.

With right sides together, pin and sew the shortest white rectangles to the left edge of the fabric C rectangle and the right edge of the fabric D rectangle; press seams over the colored fabric.

With right sides together, pin and sew the white squares to the right edge of the fabric C rectangle and the left edge of the fabric D rectangle; press seams over the colored fabric.

Complete the square With right sides together, pin and sew the strips in descending order, making sure the colored patches form steps; press seams open.

faceted diamond

The seam allowance is ¼ inch throughout.

Using light, medium, and dark fabrics creates an optical illusion in this geometric design. Joining multiple Faceted Diamond blocks edge to edge only deepens the feeling of depth in each block.

Fabric quantities

- Medium teal fabric A: 8 x 8 inches
- Light green fabric B: 8 x 8 inches
- White fabric C: 16 x 16 inches

Prepare the patches

Rotary method
- From fabrics A and C and fabrics B and C, make two 6½-inch half-square triangles (see page 12) each
- From fabrics A and B, cut two 3½-inch squares each
- From fabric C, cut four 3½-inch squares

or

Template cutting
Using the 4 x 4 templates (pages 269–73):
- From fabrics A and B, cut 2 diagonal boats and 2 small triangles each
- From fabric C, cut 4 diagonal boats and 4 small triangles

A
B
C

Rotary piecing

Mark a diagonal line between the opposite corners of each fabric A, fabric B, and fabric C square. Matching colors on the half-square triangles, pin a white square to the colored corner of a half-square triangle; pin a colored square to the opposite corner, on the white half of the half-square triangle. Using the stitch-and-flip method (see page 14), stitch on the diagonal lines and trim the excess square; press seam toward the darker fabric.

Template piecing

With right sides together, pin and sew the fabric C small triangles to the short diagonal edges of the fabric A and fabric B diagonal boats to make patchwork triangles; press seams open. Repeat using the fabrics A and B small triangles and fabric C diagonal boats.

Matching colors, join the patchwork triangles in pairs to make two teal-and-white striped squares and two green-and-white striped squares; press seams open.

Make the block

Sew two rows With right sides together and carefully matching seams, pin and sew a fabric A striped patch to a fabric B striped patch, making sure the colored stripes adjoin the white stripes; press seam open. Repeat to make the bottom row, making sure the fabric A triangles point to the center of the block.

Complete the square With right sides facing, pin and sew the two rows together, carefully matching the points of the triangles in the center of the block; press seam open.

shoofly square

A half-hidden, bottle green shoofly motif, like the one that lies within Shoofly Star (see page 112), sits at the center of this nine-patch block.

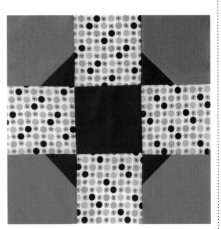

The seam allowance is ¼ inch throughout.

Fabric quantities

- Medium green fabric A: 10 x 10 inches
- Dark green fabric B: 5 x 10 inches
- Medium green print fabric C: 10 x 10 inches

Prepare the patches

Rotary method
- From fabrics A and B, make four 4½-inch corner squares (see page 14)
- From fabric B, cut one 4½-inch square
- From fabric C, cut four 4½-inch squares

or

Template cutting
Using the 6 x 6 templates (pages 278–83):
- From fabric A, cut 4 corner squares
- From fabric B, cut 1 large square and 4 small triangles
- From fabric C, cut 4 large squares

Template piecing

With right sides together, pin and sew one fabric B small triangle to the diagonal edge of each fabric A corner square; press seams open.

Make the block

Sew three rows With right sides together, pin and sew a corner square to each side of a fabric C large square, making sure the B fabric triangles point inward; press seams open. Repeat to make the bottom row.

With right sides together, pin and sew the remaining two fabric C large squares to the fabric B large square; press seams open.

Complete the square With right sides together, pin and sew the top and the bottom rows to the center row, being careful to match the seams and making sure all of the dark green triangles point to the center of the block; press seams open.

road to california

Dramatic and easy to make, this traditional block has acquired many names, including Wagon Tracks, Stepping Stones, and Jacob's Ladder.

The seam allowance is ¼ inch throughout.

Fabric quantities

- Dark blue fabric A: 6 x 12 inches
- Light blue print fabric B: 6 x 12 inches
- Medium teal fabric C: 6 x 15 inches
- White fabric D: 6 x 15 inches

Prepare the patches

Rotary method
- From fabrics A and B, make four 4½-inch half-square triangles (see page 12)
- From fabrics C and D, make five 4½-inch four-patch squares (see page 11)

or

Template cutting
Using the 6 x 6 templates (pages 278–83):
- From fabrics A and B, cut 4 large triangles each
- From fabrics C and D, cut 10 small squares each

Template piecing

With right sides together, pin and sew one fabric A large triangle to each of the fabric B large triangles to make four half-square triangles; press seams open.

With right sides together, pin and sew one fabric C small square to each fabric D small square; press seams open. Join these strips in pairs, alternating colors, to create five four-patch squares; press seams open.

Make the block

Sew three rows For the top row, with right sides together, pin and sew one four-patch square to each side of a half-square triangle, with the dark blue triangle pointing down and left; press seams open. Repeat to make the bottom row.

With right sides together, pin and sew one half-square triangle to each side of the remaining four-patch square; the dark blue triangle on the left should point up and right, and the dark blue triangle on the right should point down and left.

Complete the square Flip the bottom row. With right sides together, pin and sew the top and bottom rows to the center row, carefully matching seams and making sure the fabric A triangles make two diagonal lines; press seams open.

through the square window

The seam allowance is ¼ inch throughout.

Like the Shaded Squares block on page 152, Through the Square Window uses carefully chosen fabrics of the same color to create an optical illusion. The block is pieced similarly to the Log Cabin Square on page 65. This geometric block is easily made using the rotary method.

Fabric quantities

- Dark green fabric A: 10 x 13 inches
- Medium green fabric B: 10 x 10 inches
- Light green fabric C: 8 x 10 inches
- Light green print fabric D: 6 x 6 inches

Prepare the patches

Rotary method
- From fabric A, cut four 6½ x 2-inch rectangles and four 5 x 2-inch rectangles
- From fabric B, cut four 5 x 2-inch rectangles and four 3½ x 2-inch rectangles
- From fabric C, cut four 3½ x 2-inch rectangles and four 2-inch squares
- From fabric D, cut four 2-inch squares

Make the block

Piece four squares With right sides together, pin and sew a fabric D square to the left edge of a fabric C square; press seam open. Join a short fabric C rectangle to the top edge; press seam open.

With right sides together, pin and sew a short fabric B rectangle to the left edge of the fabrics C and D square; press seam open. Join a long fabric B rectangle to the top edge; press seam open.

With right sides together, pin and sew a short fabric A rectangle to the left edge of the fabrics B, C, and D square; press seam open. Join a long fabric A rectangle to the top edge; press seam open.

Make three more squares in the same way.

Sew two rows With right sides together, pin and sew two squares together, making sure the dark green rectangles align on top; press seam open. Repeat to make the bottom row.

Complete the square With right sides together, pin and sew the top and the bottom rows together, carefully matching the seams in the center of the block; press seams open.

---

quick susanna

The seam allowance is ¼ inch throughout.

This is a simplified version of a nineteenth-century block known as Oh! Susanna, in honor of the popular song of the day. The original had a diamond square center patch and set-in seams, but this quick version is made of four identical squares.

Fabric quantities

- Dark gray print fabric A: 8 x 14 inches
- Medium green print fabric B: 5 x 10 inches
- Light gray print fabric C: 8 x 14 inches

Prepare the patches

Rotary method
- From fabrics A and C, make four 6½ x 3½-inch right tapered rectangles (see page 16)
- From fabric B, cut four 6½ x 3½-inch rectangles

or

Template cutting
Using the 4 x 4 templates (pages 269–73):
- From fabric A, cut 4 right tapered rectangles
- From fabric B, cut 4 short rectangles
- From fabric C, cut 4 small triangles

Template piecing

With right sides together, pin and sew one fabric C small triangle to the diagonal edge of each fabric A right tapered rectangle to form a complete rectangle; press seams over the triangles.

Make the block

Make four squares With right sides together, pin and sew a fabric B short rectangle to each of the fabrics A and C right tapered rectangles to make four squares; press seams open.

Sew two rows With right sides together, pin and sew two squares together, adjoining the fabric C small triangles; press seams open. Repeat to make the bottom row.

Complete the square With right sides together, pin and sew the two rows together, matching the light gray triangles in the middle; press seams open.

woven cross

The seam allowance is ¼ inch throughout.

This block is made in the same way as Cross Weave on page 42, but the smaller white corner squares in Woven Cross give this variation a more compact look. Use it in a sampler quilt or sew multiple blocks edge to edge so that the four different colors join to form continuous interwoven stripes.

A
B
C
D
E

Fabric quantities

- Medium green fabric A: 4 x 11 inches
- Dark teal fabric B: 4 x 11 inches
- Medium turquoise fabric C: 4 x 11 inches
- Light green fabric D: 4 x 11 inches
- White fabric E: 8 x 8 inches

Prepare the patches

Rotary method
- From fabrics A, B, and E; fabrics A, C, and E; fabrics C, D, and E; and fabrics B, D, and E, make one 6½-inch three-patch square (see page 11) each

or

Template cutting
Using the 4 x 4 templates (pages 269–73):
- From fabrics A, B, C, and D, cut 1 small square and 1 short rectangle
- From fabric E, cut 4 small squares

Template piecing

With right sides together, pin and sew a fabric E small square to the fabric A small square; press seam over fabric A. With the green square at the bottom left, join the fabric B rectangle to the right edge of the strip to make the first three-patch square; press seam open. Repeat to make one three-patch square each from fabrics A, C, and E; fabrics C, D, and E; and fabrics B, D, and E.

Make the block

Sew two rows With right sides together, pin and sew the top two three-patch squares, as shown above, making sure the green fabrics form a stripe at the bottom of the strip; press seam open.

With right sides together, pin and sew the bottom two three-patch squares together, making sure the light green fabrics form a stripe at the top of the strip; press seam open.

Complete the square With right sides together, pin and sew the two rows together, carefully matching the seams in the center of the block; press seam open.

oregon

The seam allowance is ¼ inch throughout.

This traditional block is given a fresh appeal with a bright new color palette. The center motif seems to balance on the triangles at the corners of the nine-patch block. This block is more accurately made from templates for a 12-inch square.

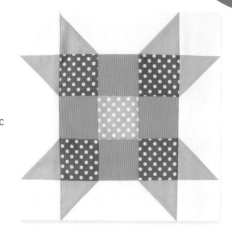

Fabric quantities

- Medium green fabric A: 10 x 10 inches
- Dark green print fabric B: 8 x 8 inches
- Medium orange fabric C: 8 x 8 inches
- Light green print fabric D: 4 x 4 inches
- White fabric E: 12 x 16 inches

Prepare the patches

Template cutting
Using the 5 x 5 templates (pages 274–7):
- From fabric A, cut 8 small triangles
- From fabrics B and C, cut 4 small squares each
- From fabric D, cut 1 small square
- From fabric E, cut 4 short boats and 4 small squares

Template piecing

With right sides together, pin and sew a fabric A small triangle to each diagonal edge of the four fabric E short boats; press seams open.

Make the block

Piece the nine-patch square For the top row, with right sides together, pin and sew a fabric B small square to each side of a fabric C small square; press seams open. Repeat for the bottom row.

With right sides together, pin and sew a fabric C small square to each side of the fabric D small square; press seams open.

Flip the bottom row. With right sides together, pin and sew the top and bottom rows of the nine-patch square to the center row, carefully matching the seams; press seams open.

Complete the square With right sides together, pin and sew a fabrics A and E short boat to each side edge of the nine-patch square; press seams open.

With right sides together, pin and sew a fabric E small square to each end of the remaining short boats; press seams open. Join these strips to the top and bottom edge of the block; press seams open.

twist

The seam allowance is ¼ inch throughout.

This graphic block is simple to stitch, but delivers a high impact. The patches are straightforward to piece, and you don't have to worry about matching seams. It's especially dramatic with a dark background. This geometric block is easily made using the rotary method.

Fabric quantities

- Light green fabric A: 6 x 9 inches
- Medium green fabric B: 6 x 9 inches
- Charcoal fabric C: 11 x 13 inches

Prepare the patches

Rotary method
- From fabrics A and B, cut one 4½ x 2½-inch rectangle and one 8½ x 2½-inch rectangle each
- From fabric C, cut two 4½-inch squares, two 4½ x 2½-inch rectangles, and two 6½ x 4½-inch rectangles.

Make the block

Piece three columns With right sides together, pin and sew a fabric C square to the long edge of the short fabric B rectangle; press seam open. For the right column, pin and sew a long fabric C rectangle to the other side of the short fabric B rectangle; press seam open. For the right column, repeat with the short fabric A rectangle.

For the middle column, with right sides together, pin and sew a short fabric C rectangle to the short end of the long fabric A rectangle; press seam open. Repeat with the long fabric B rectangle. Pin and sew the strips together lengthwise, with fabric A on the upper left and fabric B on the lower right; press seam open.

Complete the square With right sides together, pin and sew the left and right columns to the middle column, making sure the fabric B rectangles appear to weave through the fabric A rectangles; press seams open.

churn dash quarters

The seam allowance is ¼ inch throughout.

A
B
C
D
E

This is a modern interpretation of the traditional Churn Dash block on page 152. It's divided into quarters, each made from different, bold solid color. The dark background makes the center motif pop luminously.

Fabric quantities

- Medium green fabric A: 6 x 9 inches
- Light turquoise fabric B: 6 x 9 inches
- Medium lime green fabric C: 6 x 9 inches
- Dark turquoise fabric D: 6 x 9 inches
- Charcoal fabric E: 11 x 12 inches

Prepare the patches

Rotary method
- From fabrics A and E; fabrics B and E; fabrics C and E; fabrics D and E, make one 4½-inch half-square triangle (see page 12) each
- From each of fabrics A, B, C, and D, cut two 2½-inch squares
- From fabric E, cut one 4½-inch square and four 4½ x 2½-inch rectangles

or

Template cutting
Using the 6 x 6 templates (pages 278–83):
- From each of fabrics A, B, C, and D, cut 1 large triangle and 2 small squares
- From fabric E, cut 1 large square, 4 large triangles, and 4 short rectangles

Template piecing

With right sides together, pin and sew a fabric E large triangle to each of the colored large triangles along the long diagonal edge to make four half-square triangles; press seams open.

Make the block

Piece four squares With right sides together, pin and sew a fabric A small square to a fabric B small square; press seam open. Join a fabric E rectangle to the top edge with the green square on the left; press seam open.

With right sides together, pin and sew a fabric B small square to a fabric C small square; press seam open. Join a fabric E rectangle to the right edge with the light turquoise square on the top; press seam open.

With right sides together, pin and sew a fabric C small square to a fabric D small square; press seam open. Join a fabric E rectangle to the bottom edge with the dark turquoise square on the left; press seam open.

With right sides together, pin and sew a fabric D small square to a fabric A small square; press seam open. Join a fabric E rectangle to the left edge with the green square on the top; press seam open.

Sew three rows For the top row, with right sides together, pin and sew the green half-square triangle to the left edge of the green and turquoise square; press seam open. Join the light turquoise half-square triangle on the right edge; press seam open.

For the middle row, with right sides together, pin and sew the fabrics A, D, and E square to the left edge of the fabric E large square; press seam open. Join the fabrics B, C, and E square to the right side; press seam open.

For the bottom row, with right sides together, pin and sew the dark turquoise half-square triangle to the left edge of the fabrics D, C, and E square; press seam open. Join the lime green half-square triangle on the right edge; press seam open.

Complete the square With right sides together, pin and sew the top and bottom rows to the center row, carefully matching seams; press seams open.

forest paths

The seam allowance is ¼ inch throughout.

Make this pinwheel block with a mixture of green fabrics in keeping with its traditional name. Try sneaking in a subtle tree print in the corners.

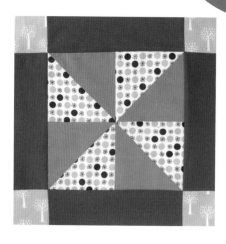

A
B
C
D

Fabric quantities

- Medium green fabric A: 6 x 12 inches
- Light green print fabric B: 6 x 12 inches
- Light green print fabric C: 6 x 6 inches
- Dark green fabric D: 9 x 12 inches

Prepare the patches

Rotary method
- From fabrics A and B, make one 8½-inch pinwheel square (see page 13)
- From fabric C, cut four 2½-inch squares
- From fabric D, cut four 8½ x 2½-inch rectangles

or

Template cutting
Using the 6 x 6 templates (pages 278–83):
- From fabrics A and B, cut 4 large triangles each
- From fabric C, cut 4 small squares
- From fabric D, cut 4 long rectangles

Template piecing

With right sides together, pin and sew one fabric A large triangle to one fabric B large triangle along the diagonal edges; press seam open. Repeat to make another three half-square triangles.

With right sides together, pin and sew two half-square triangles together, making sure the fabric B triangles are pointing clockwise; press seam open. Repeat with the second set of half-square triangles.

Join the two strips to complete the pinwheel square; press seam open.

Make the block

Make the frame With right sides together, pin and sew a fabric D rectangle to each side of the pinwheel; press seams open.

Complete the square With right sides together, pin and sew a fabric C square to each short end of two fabric D rectangles; press seams open. Join the two strips to the top and bottom edges of the pinwheel; press seams open.

matching triangles

The seam allowance is ¼ inch throughout.

Using only triangles, you can make an entire quilt top of matching half-square triangles. Choose a graphic print for one half and a coordinating solid fabric for the other half—match the color of the solid triangles to one of the colors in the print. You will need to take time to carefully match the seams in each block for a crisp look. The 4½-inch half-square triangles are a good size to work with—neither too small or too big—when using them to make up an allover quilt.

A
B

Fabric quantities

- Medium green fabric A: 12 x 18 inches
- Light green print fabric B: 12 x 18 inches

Prepare the patches

Rotary method
- From fabrics A and B, make nine 4½-inch half-square triangles (see page 12)

or

Template cutting
Using the 6 x 6 templates (pages 278–83):
- From fabrics A and B, cut 9 large triangles each

Template piecing

With right sides together, pin and sew a fabric A large triangle to each of the fabric B large triangles along the diagonal edges to make nine half-square triangles; press seams open.

Make the block

Arrange the square Lay out the half-square triangles in three rows of three, making sure all of the fabric A triangles point up to the top left corner of the block.

Sew three rows With right sides together, pin and sew the three half-square triangles in each row together. Press the seams open.

Complete the square With right sides together, pin and sew the top and bottom rows to the center row, carefully matching the seams; press seams open.

pinwheel square

The seam allowance is ¼ inch throughout.

A vibrant, contrasting background print helps to define the diamond pinwheel in the center panel of this block. Set stripes so that they run in alternate directions to add to the feeling of movement.

A
B
C

Fabric quantities

- Light green fabric A: 5 x 10 inches
- Light green print fabric B: 5 x 10 inches
- Medium red print fabric C: 8 x 16 inches

Prepare the patches

Rotary method
- From fabrics A, B, and C, make four 6½-inch three-quarter square triangles (see page 13)

or

Template cutting
Using the 4 x 4 templates (pages 269–73):
- From fabrics A and B, cut 4 medium triangles each
- From fabric C, cut 4 large triangles

Template piecing

With right sides together, pin and sew a fabric A medium triangle to each of the fabric B medium triangles along one short edge, keeping fabric A to the left; press seams open.

Join a fabric C large triangle to each of the fabrics A and B units along the diagonal edge, making four identical three-quarter squares; press seams open.

Make the block

Sew two rows With right sides together, pin and sew two three-quarter squares together, carefully matching a fabric A triangle with a fabric B triangle and making sure the background pattern runs in alternate directions; press seam open. Repeat with the second pair of three-quarter squares.

Complete the square With right sides together, pin and sew the two rows together, carefully matching the seams and making sure to create a pinwheel in the center of the block; press seam open.

striped rectangle

The seam allowance is ¼ inch throughout.

Similar to Paint Swatches on page 136, this block demonstrates that a white border adds vibrancy to your fabrics. Experiment by varying the size of the rectangles and the width of the border. This geometric block works perfectly with jellyrolls or charm packs, and is easily made using the rotary method.

A
B
C
D
E

Fabric quantities

- Medium green print fabric A: 7 x 3 inches
- Light green print fabric B: 7 x 3 inches
- Dark green fabric C: 7 x 3 inches
- Dark green print fabric D: 7 x 3 inches
- White fabric E: 13 x 14 inches

Prepare the patches

Rotary method
- From fabrics A, B, C, and D, cut one 6½ x 2½-inch rectangle each
- From fabric E, cut two 6½ x 2½-inch rectangles and two 12½ x 3½-inch rectangles

Make the block

Join the stripes With right sides together, pin and sew the four colored rectangles in a row, joining them at the long sides; press seams open.

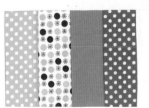

Make the border Add a short fabric E rectangle to each side edge of the striped panel; press seams away from fabric E.

With right sides together, pin and sew the long fabric E rectangles to the top and bottom edges; press seams away from fabric E.

arrowheads

This modern, versatile block works will with shades of neon solids and a monotone small-scale print background fabric.

The seam allowance is ¼ inch throughout.

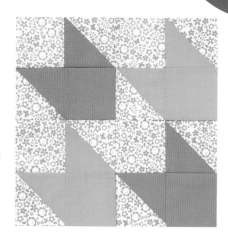

Fabric quantities

- Dark green fabric A: 10 x 10 inches
- Light green fabric B: 10 x 10 inches
- Light gray print fabric C: 20 x 20 inches

Prepare the patches

Rotary method
- From fabrics A and C and fabrics B and C, make four 3½-inch half-square triangles (see page 12) each
- From fabrics A and B, cut two 3½-inch squares each
- From fabric C, cut four 3½-inch squares

or

Template cutting
Using the 4 x 4 templates (pages 269–73):
- From fabrics A and B, cut 2 small squares and 4 small triangles each
- From fabric C, cut 4 small squares and 8 small triangles

Template piecing

With right sides together, pin and sew a fabric C triangle to each fabric A small triangle and fabric B small triangle to make eight half-square triangles; press seams open.

Make the block

Piece the squares With right sides together, pin and sew a fabric C square to a dark green half-square triangle, with the green fabric pointing down and left; press seam open. Join a dark green half-square triangle to a dark green small square, with the green fabric pointing up and right; press seam open. Join strips, with green fabric abutting, to make one patch; press seam open. Repeat another three times to make one more dark green patch and two light green patches.

Complete the square With right sides together, sew a light green patch to the right side of a dark green patch, with the arrows pointing in the same direction; press seam open. Repeat, but with the light green arrow to the left side of the dark green arrow.

Join the two strips, carefully matching the seams and with all four arrows pointing in the same direction; press seam open.

squares and crosses

By alternating the hourglasses and squares within squares, you create secondary patterns when you join several of these blocks together.

The seam allowance is ¼ inch throughout.

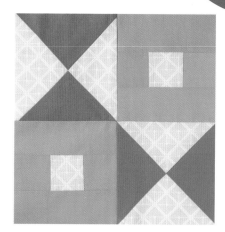

Fabric quantities

- Medium turquoise fabric A: 8 x 16 inches
- Light blue print fabric B: 16 x 16 inches
- Light turquoise fabric C: 10 x 12 inches

Prepare the patches

Rotary method
- From fabrics A and B, make two 6½-inch hourglass squares (see page 13)
- From fabric B, cut two 2½-inch squares
- From fabric C, cut four 6½ x 2½-inch rectangles and four 2½-inch squares

or

Template cutting
Using the 6 x 6 templates (pages 278–83):
- From fabric A, cut 4 medium triangles
- From fabric B, cut 4 medium triangles and 2 small squares
- From fabric C, cut 4 medium rectangles and 4 small squares

Template piecing

With right sides together, pin and sew a fabric A medium triangle to each of the fabric B medium triangles on a short side, making sure fabric A is on the left; press seams open. Join them in pairs to create the two hourglass units; press seams open.

Make the block

Piece the squares With right sides together, pin and sew a fabric C small square to each side of the two fabric B small squares; press seams over fabric C. Join a fabric C medium rectangle to the top and bottom edges of each fabrics B and C strip; press seams over fabric C.

Sew two rows With right sides together, pin and sew a square patch to an hourglass square along a fabric B edge; press seam open.

With right sides together, pin and sew a square patch to an hourglass square along a fabric A edge; press seam open.

Complete the square With right sides together, pin and sew the two rows together, making sure the points of each patch meet in the center of the block; press seam open.

paint swatches

This simple block is a perfect way to highlight favorite fabrics. Set solid squares against a white background for a minimalist, modern look. Choose closely related colors to resemble a paint swatch card and make an entire quilt with rows of squares in spectrum progression.

A
B
C
D
E

Fabric quantities

- Light turquoise fabric A: 4 x 4 inches
- Medium green fabric B: 4 x 4 inches
- Light green fabric C: 4 x 4 inches
- Dark turquoise fabric D: 4 x 4 inches
- White fabric E: 13 x 18 inches

Prepare the patches

Rotary cutting
- From fabrics A, B, C, and D, cut one 4-inch square each
- From fabric E, cut six 4 x 2¼-inch rectangles and three 12½ x 2¼-inch rectangles

or

Template cutting
Using the 7 x 7 templates (pages 284–5)
- From fabrics A, B, C, and D, cut 1 large square each
- From fabric E, cut 6 short rectangles and three full-length rectangles

Make the block

Piece the colored patches With right sides together, pin and sew a white short rectangle to the top and bottom edges of the fabric A large square and the fabric B large square; press seams away from the white fabric. Sew a white short rectangle to the bottom edges of the fabric C large square and the fabric D large square; press seams away from the white fabric.

Make two columns With right sides together, pin and sew the light turquoise patch to the dark turquoise patch; press seams away from the white fabric. Repeat with the medium green and light green patches.

With right sides together, pin and sew a white long rectangle to each long side of the turquoise column; press seams over the squares. Join the remaining white rectangle to the long side of the green column; press seam over the squares.

Complete the square With right sides together, pin and sew the two columns together; press seam over the squares.

flower basket

The seam allowance is ¼ inch throughout.

Give this old-fashioned block a modern look by using crisp colors on a white background. Like many traditional patterns, Flower Basket has several variations: reverse the colors to give a green plant in a pink container, and it becomes Cactus Basket. This block is most accurately made from templates for a finished 12-inch square.

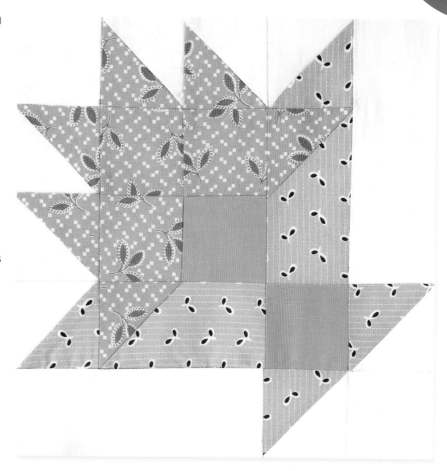

A
B
C
D

Fabric quantities

- Medium pink print fabric A: 8 x 15 inches
- Medium green print fabric B: 8 x 12 inches
- Medium green fabric C: 3 x 6 inches
- White fabric D: 8 x 21 inches

Prepare the patches

Template cutting
Using the 5 x 5 templates (pages 274–7):

- From fabric A, cut 3 small squares and 6 small triangles

- From fabric B, cut 1 right tapered rectangle, 1 left tapered rectangle, and 4 small triangles

- From fabric C, cut 2 small squares

- From fabric D, cut 2 medium rectangles, 2 small squares, and 8 small triangles.

Template piecing

With right sides together, pin and sew a fabric D small triangle to four of the fabric A small triangles and all of the fabric B small triangles along the long diagonal edge to make eight half-square triangles (see page 12); press seams open.

With right sides together, pin and sew the remaining two fabric A small triangles to the fabric B tapered rectangles along the diagonal edges; press seams open.

Make the block

Make the first row With right sides together, pin and sew two pink half-square triangles so that fabric A is pointing down and to the left. Join a white square to the left side of the strip. Join a green print half-square triangle to the right side of the strip, making sure fabric B is pointing down and right; press seams open to complete the first row.

Make the second row With right sides together, pin and sew a pink half-square triangle to one side of a pink small square, making sure that the fabric A triangle is pointing up and right. Join another pink small square to the right side of the strip; press seams open.

Make the third row With right sides together, pin and sew a pink half-square triangle to one side of the remaining pink small square, making sure the fabric A triangle points up and right. Join a medium green small square to the right edge; press seam open.

Make the fourth row With right sides together, pin and sew these two strips together, carefully matching seams; press seam open. Join the green right-tapered rectangle to the right side of this unit, carefully matching the pink triangle to the pink square; press seam open.

With right sides together, pin and sew a green half-square triangle to the green left-tapered rectangle, aligning the green triangle with the pink triangle. Join the remaining medium green small square to the right side of the strip; press seams open. With right sides together, pin and sew the fourth row to the third row, carefully matching seams; press seam open.

Make the basket With right sides together, pin and sew a green half-square triangle to a short end of a white medium rectangle, making sure the green triangle points up and left; press seam open. Join strip to the fourth row; press seam open.

With right sides together, pin and sew the first row to the top of the second row, carefully matching seams and making sure the green triangle points down and right; press seam open.

Complete the square With right sides together, pin and sew the remaining green half-square triangle to a short end of the remaining white medium rectangle, making sure the green triangle points up and left. Join the remaining white small square to the bottom side of the strip; press seam open. With right sides together, pin and sew the strip to the right side of the block, carefully matching seams and completing the basket; press seam open.

single wedding ring

The seam allowance is ¼ inch throughout.

A
B
C
D

The **Single Wedding Ring** block gives the illusion of a circle, but it has only straight seams. It's easier to cut and piece than other, more traditional wedding ring designs. This block is more accurately made with templates for a 12-inch finished block.

Fabric quantities

- Dark turquoise fabric A: 8 x 12 inches
- Light turquoise fabric B: 9 x 12 inches
- Medium turquoise fabric C: 5 x 10 inches
- White fabric D: 10 x 16 inches

Prepare the patches

Template cutting
Using the 5 x 5 templates (pages 274–7):
- From fabric A, cut 4 small squares and 4 small triangles
- From fabric B, cut 4 short boats
- From fabric C, cut 4 small triangles
- From fabric D, cut 1 small square and 16 small triangles

Template piecing

With right sides together, pin and sew a fabric D small triangle to each of the fabric A small triangles to make four half-square triangles (see page 12); press seams open. Repeat, joining fabric D and fabric C small triangles to make four more half-square triangles.

With right sides together, pin and sew a fabric D small triangle to each diagonal edge of the fabric B short boats; press seams open.

Make the block

Piece the center patch With right sides together, pin and sew a fabric A small square to each side of the fabric D small square; press seams open. With right sides together, pin and sew a dark turquoise half-square triangle to each side of a fabric A small square, making sure the turquoise triangles point down and to the center of the block; press seams open. Repeat to make the third row of the center octagon.

Flip the third strip. With right sides together, pin and sew the first and third strip to the middle strip, carefully matching seams, to make the center patch; press seams open.

Make the border With right sides together, pin and sew a light turquoise short boat to each side of the center patch; press seams open.

Complete the square Join a medium turquoise half-square triangle to each end of the remaining two short boats; press seams open. With right sides together, pin and sew the strips to the top and bottom of the center patch; press seams open.

pine trees

These stylized trees have a folksy charm, like a child's drawing. The Pine Trees block is made from four flying geese rectangles and appliquéd trunks. Pine Trees is a good place to start when making a story quilt for a baby.

The seam allowance is ¼ inch throughout.

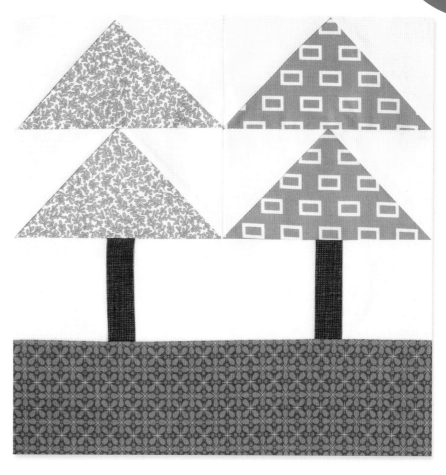

Fabric quantities

- Light green print fabric A: 8 x 7 inches
- Medium green print fabric B: 8 x 7 inches
- Dark green print fabric C: 4 x 13 inches
- Dark green print fabric D: 3 x 4 inches
- White fabric E: 11 x 13 inches

Prepare the patches

Rotary method
- From fabrics A and E and fabrics B and E, make two 6½ x 3½-inch flying geese rectangles (see page 17) each
- From fabrics C and E, cut one 12½ x 3½-inch rectangle each
- From fabric D, cut two 3½ x 1¼-inch rectangles

or

Template cutting
Using the 4 x 4 templates (pages 269–73):
- From fabrics A and B, cut 2 medium triangles each
- From fabric C, cut 1 full-length rectangle
- From fabric D, cut 2 narrow very small rectangles
- From fabric E, cut 1 full-length rectangle and 8 small triangles

Template piecing

With right sides together, pin and sew a fabric E small triangle to the short edges of each of the fabric A medium triangles to make two flying geese rectangles; press seams over the medium triangles. Repeat using the remaining fabric E small triangles and the fabric B medium triangles to make another two flying geese rectangles.

Make the block

Make the trees With right sides together, pin and sew the flying geese rectangles in matching pairs, making sure they each point up. Join the patches together, along a short edge with fabric A on the left side and making sure the trees retain their points; press seam open.

Sew the trunks Press under a ¼ inch turning at the long edges of each fabric D narrow very small rectangle. Appliqué (see page 20) the fabric D rectangles to the fabric E rectangle, making sure each trunk is centered directly below the points of the trees.

Complete the square With right sides together, pin and sew the fabric E full-length rectangle to the bottom of the patch, then press seam open. Join the fabric C full-length rectangle to the bottom edge, then press seam open.

oh! susanna framed

The seam allowance is ¼ inch throughout.

The Oh! Susanna panel in the center acquired its name in the mid-nineteenth century from the popular song. This is the classic way of piecing it, with set-in seams. The instructions are for using templates, but you can speed things up if you prefer rotary piecing; use the method given in Quick Susanna (see page 129).

A
B
C
D

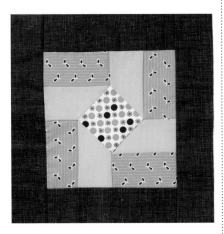

Fabric quantities

- Medium green print fabric A: 6 x 10 inches
- Light green fabric B: 6 x 10 inches
- Light green print fabric C: 3 x 3 inches
- Dark green print fabric D: 12 x 13 inches

Prepare the patches

Template cutting
Using the 6 x 6 templates (pages 278–83):
- From fabric A, cut 4 short rectangles
- From fabric B, cut 4 left tapered rectangles
- From fabric C, cut 1 diamond square
- From fabric D, cut 2 long rectangles and two full-length rectangles

Make the block

Piece four patches With right sides together, pin and sew a fabric A rectangle to each of the fabric B left tapered rectangles along the longest edge; press seams open.

Mark the set-in seams Mark a ¼-inch seam allowance on the short diagonal edge of each tapered rectangle. Mark a ¼-inch seam allowance also on all four edges of the fabric C diamond square.

Complete the center square With right sides together, pin one edge of the diamond square to the marked diagonal edge of a tapered rectangle. Stitch along the marked line between the points where the other two lines intersect. Refold so that the short edges of a fabric A rectangle and a fabric B left

tapered rectangle are aligned. Stitch along the marked line. Repeat another three times; press seams over fabric A.

Make the frame With right sides together, pin and sew the fabric D long rectangles to the top and bottom edges of the patch; press seams outward. Add the fabric D full-length rectangles to the side edges in the same way.

---

winter pines

The seam allowance is ¼ inch throughout.

Winter Pines stands well on its own but is designed as a companion for Pine Trees on page 139. Combine the two to make a forest-themed quilt.

A
B
C

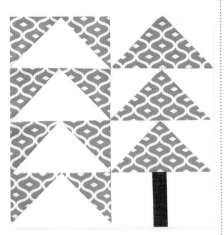

Fabric quantities

- Medium green print fabric A: 10 x 12 inches
- Dark green print fabric B: 2 x 4 inches
- White fabric C: 12 x 13 inches

Prepare the patches

Rotary method
- From fabrics A and C, make four 6½ x 3½-inch flying geese rectangles (see page 17) with fabric C in the center and three 6½ x 3½-inch flying geese rectangles with fabric A in the center
- From fabric B, cut one 3½ x 1¼-inch rectangle
- From fabric C, cut one 6½ x 3½-inch rectangle

or

Template cutting
Using the 4 x 4 templates (pages 269–73):

- From fabric A, cut 3 medium triangles and 8 small triangles
- From fabric B, cut 1 narrow very small rectangle
- From fabric C, cut 1 short rectangle, 4 medium triangles, and 6 small triangles

Template piecing

With right sides together, pin and sew the eight fabric A small triangles to the short edges of the four fabric C medium triangles to make four flying geese rectangles; press seams open.

With right sides together, join the six fabric C small triangles to the short edges of the three fabric A medium triangles to make three flying geese rectangles; press seams open.

Make the block

Join the columns With right sides together, pin and sew the four white flying geese

rectangles in a column, making sure the triangles point up; press seams up. Repeat to join the three green flying geese rectangles.

Make the trunk Appliqué (see page 20) the fabric B narrow very small rectangle in the center of the fabric C rectangle. With right sides together, pin and sew the rectangle to the bottom of the three green flying geese column.

Complete the square With right sides together, join the columns, matching the seams and maintaining the triangle points; press open.

summer tree

The seam allowance is ¼ inch throughout.

Bright green prints give this tree block a summery, sunny look. You could also use browns and oranges to create a tree in fall. To make a quilt for all seasons, add one in pinks for a blossoming fruit tree and one in grays for a wintery, snowy look.

Fabric quantities

- 5 different light green print fabrics A: 4 x 4 inches each

- Gray print fabric B: 7 x 9 inches

- White fabric C: 10 x 20 inches

Prepare the patches

Rotary method
- From fabrics A and C, make twelve 2½-inch half-square triangles (see page 12)

- From fabrics B and C, make three 2½-inch half-square triangles

- From fabric B, cut one 8½ x 2½-inch rectangle

- From fabric C, cut one 4½-inch square, two 4½ x 2½-inch rectangles, three 2½-inch squares, and one 6½ x 4½-inch rectangle

or

Template cutting
Using the 6 x 6 templates (pages 278–83):
- From fabric A, cut 12 small triangles

- From fabric B, cut 3 small triangles and 1 long rectangle

- From fabric C, cut 1 large square, 2 short rectangles, 3 small squares, 15 small triangles, and 1 wide medium rectangle

Template piecing

With right sides together, pin and sew a fabric C small triangle to each of the fabrics A and B small triangles to make 15 half-square triangles; press seams open.

Make the block

Arrange the half-square triangles Lay out all of the patches in their final positions, as shown above, being careful to balance the green fabrics around the trunk.

A
A
A
A
A
B
C

Join the top two rows To make the first row and the top of the tree, join fabric A half-square triangles, a fabric C small square, and a fabric A half-square triangle; press seams open.

To make the second row, with right sides together, join a fabric C small square and a fabric A half-square triangle, then sew a fabric B half-square triangle to the right edge, with the gray triangle pointing down and right. Add another two fabric A half-square triangles.

With right sides together, pin and sew these two rows, carefully matching the seams; press seam open. Join a fabric C short rectangle to the right side; press seam open.

Make the bottom left unit Join a fabric A half-square triangle and a fabric C small square; press seam open. Join a fabric A half-square triangle and a fabric B half-square triangle, aligning the white triangles and with the gray triangle pointing up and right; press seam open. Join these two strips, making sure the gray triangle is on the bottom right; press seam open.

With right sides together, pin and sew the fabric C large square to the bottom edge; press seam open.

With right sides together, pin and sew the fabric B long rectangle to the right edge of the square; press seam open.

Make the bottom right unit Join a fabric B half-square triangle to a fabric A half-square triangle, making sure the gray triangle points up and left. Add another fabric A half-square triangle to the right edge of the strip; press seams open.

Join the remaining fabric A half-square triangle to the short end of the fabric C short rectangle; press seam open.

With right sides together, pin and sew these two strips, making sure the gray triangle is on the top left; press seam open.

With right sides together, pin and sew the fabric C wide medium rectangle to the bottom edge; press seam open.

Complete the square With right sides together, pin and sew the bottom right unit to the right side of the trunk; press seam open.

With right sides together, pin and sew the top of the block to the bottom of the block, carefully matching seams and aligning the gray pieces; press seam open.

checker star

The seam allowance is ¼ inch throughout.

This block has a four-patch square centered in a sawtooth star that works well as part of a sampler quilt along with the Sawtooth Star (see page 55) and other stars.

A
B
C
D
E

Fabric quantities

- Medium pink print fabric A: 8 x 8 inches
- Light green print fabric B: 4 x 8 inches
- Light green print fabric C: 4 x 4 inches
- Light green print fabric D: 4 x 4 inches
- White fabric E: 12 x 16 inches

Prepare the patches

Rotary method
- From fabrics A, B, and E, make four 6½ x 3½-inch flying geese rectangles (see page 17): 2 with A on the left and 2 with B on the left
- From fabrics A, C, and D, make one 6½-inch four-patch square (see page 11)
- From fabric E, cut four 3½-inch squares

or

Template cutting
Using the 4 x 4 templates (pages 269–73):
- From fabric A, cut 2 small squares and 4 small triangles
- From fabric B, cut 4 small triangles
- From fabrics C and D, cut 1 small square each
- From fabric E, cut 4 medium triangles and 4 small squares

Template piecing

With right sides together, sew a fabric A small triangle to the left short edge of a fabric E triangle. Join a fabric B triangle to the right edge; press seams open. Repeat to make a second flying geese rectangle. Repeat twice more, but with a fabric B triangle on the left and a fabric A triangle on the right.

With right sides together, sew a fabric C small square to a fabric A small square; press seam open. Repeat using a fabric D small square and a fabric A small square. Join the two strips, alternating colors, to make a four-patch square; press seam open.

Make the block

Sew three rows Join a flying geese rectangle to each side of the four-patch square, with orange triangles abutting green squares and white triangles pointing to the center; press seams open.

Join a white small square to each end of the remaining flying geese rectangles; press seams open.

Complete the square Join the strips to the top and bottom of the patch, with flying geese rectangles pointing to the center; press seams open.

framed nine patch

The seam allowance is ¼ inch throughout.

Combine this block with the Nine-Patch Square on page 34 for a subtle twist on a traditional theme. Match the frame fabric to a color in the floral fabric in the middle to enhance the nine-patch motif. This block is best made using templates.

Fabric quantities

- Medium orange print fabric A: 6 x 9 inches
- Dark teal print fabric B: 9 x 12 inches
- Light blue fabric C: 6 x 6 inches
- White fabric D: 6 x 6 inches

Prepare the patches

Template cutting
Using the 5 x 5 templates (pages 274–7):
- From fabric A, cut 5 small squares
- From fabric B, cut 4 medium rectangles
- From fabrics C and D, cut 4 small squares each

Make the block

Piece the nine-patch For the top row, with right sides together, pin and sew a fabric A small square to each side of a fabric D small square; press seams over fabric A. Repeat to make the bottom row.

For the center row, with right sides together, pin and sew a fabric D small square to each side of the remaining fabric A small square; press seams over fabric A.

With right sides together, pin and sew the top and bottom rows to the center row of the nine-patch square, carefully matching the seams; press seams over fabric A.

Join the frame With right sides together, pin and sew a fabric B medium rectangle to the top and bottom of the nine-patch square; press seams out.

With right sides together, pin and sew a fabric C small square to each short end of the remaining fabric B medium rectangles; press seams in.

Complete the square Join the strips to each side of the nine-patch square; press seams out.

village square

The seam allowance is ¼ inch throughout.

Village Square is similar in structure to Old Maid's Puzzle (see page 179), but the different balance of color and shade gives much more emphasis to the rectangular patches and the corner triangles.

Fabric quantities

- Medium orange print fabric A: 5 x 10 inches
- Medium green fabric B: 10 x 10 inches
- Light green print fabric C: 8 x 14 inches
- Dark orange print fabric D: 7 x 7 inches

Prepare the patches

Rotary method
- From fabrics A and B, make four 3½-inch half-square triangles (see page 12)
- From fabrics B and D, make one 6½-inch diamond square (see page 15)
- From fabric C, cut four 6½ x 2½-inch rectangles

or

Template cutting

Using the 4 x 4 templates (pages 269–73):
- From fabric A, cut 4 small triangles
- From fabric B, cut 8 small triangles
- From fabric C, cut 4 short rectangles
- From fabric D, cut 1 diamond square

Template piecing

With right sides together, pin and sew a fabric B small triangle to each of the fabric A small triangles to make four half-square triangles; press seams open.

With right sides together, pin and sew a fabric B small triangle to each diagonal edge of the fabric D diamond square; press seams out.

Make the block

Sew three rows With right sides together, pin and sew a fabric C short rectangle to each side edge of the diamond square; press seams open.

With right sides together, pin and sew a fabrics A and B half-square triangle to each side of the remaining fabric C short rectangles, making sure the green triangles point to the center of the block; press seams open.

Complete the square With right sides together, pin and sew strips to the top and bottom of the diamond square; press seams open.

pear

Combining light and dark green prints will make your pear appear three dimensional. Consider adding a single red print for a pop of color and some added realism. The stem is appliquéd.

Fabric quantities

- 8 different dark green print fabrics A: 12 x 12 inches in total

- Dark blue fabric B: 3 x 2 inches

- White fabric C: 10 x 18 inches

Prepare the patches

Rotary method

- From fabrics A and C, make six 2½-inch half-square triangles (see page 12) each

- From fabrics A, cut ten 2½-inch squares

- From fabric B, cut 1 stem using the template on page 286

- From fabric C, cut one 4½ x 2½-inch rectangle, two 6½ x 2½-inch rectangles, and two 6½ x 4½-inch rectangles

or

Template cutting

Using the 6 x 6 templates (pages 278–83):

- From fabrics A, cut 10 small squares and 6 small triangles

- From fabric B, cut 1 stem using the template on page 286

- From fabric C, cut 1 short rectangle, 2 medium rectangles, 6 small triangles, and 2 wide medium rectangles

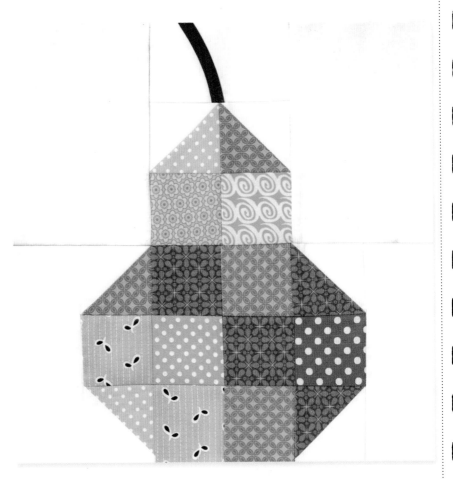

The seam allowance is ¼ inch throughout.

Template piecing

With right sides together, pin and sew a fabric A small triangle to each of the fabrics C small triangles to make six half-square triangles; press seams open.

Make the block

Arrange the patches Lay out the green squares and half-square triangles in the pear shape, balancing the dark and light tones, as shown above.

Make the top of the pear With right sides together, pin and sew the top two green and white half-square triangles along a short green side; press seam open. Appliqué (see page 20) the stem to the white short rectangle, making sure it will meet the top of the pear. With right sides together, pin and sew the strips together; press seam open.

Join two green small squares; press seam open. Add the strip to the bottom of the patch; press seam open.

With right sides together, pin and sew a white wide medium rectangle to each side of the top of the pear; press seams out.

Make the bottom of the pear With right sides together, pin and sew two green small squares together; press seam open. Join a green half-square triangle to each side of the strip, matching the seams and making sure the green triangles point down and in; press seams open.

With right sides together, pin and sew four small green squares in a row; press seams open. With right sides together, pin and sew the strips together; press seam open.

With right sides together, pin and sew two green small squares together; press seam open. Join a green half-square triangle to each side of the strip, carefully matching the seams and making sure the green triangles point up and in; press seams open. Join the strip to the bottom of the patch; press seam open.

With right sides together, pin and sew a white medium rectangle to each side of the patch; press seams open.

Complete the square With right sides together, pin and sew the two halves of the pear together, carefully matching the seams; press seam open.

patience corner

The seam allowance is ¼ inch throughout.

Patience Corner is made from four three-patch squares pieced in alternating directions to form a blocky figure-eight. Make it scrappy so each block is cut from a different fabric, as shown, or combine the white background with a single print.

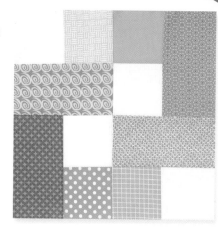

Fabric quantities

- 4 different medium and dark green print fabrics A: 8 x 15 inches in total
- 4 different light and medium green solid and print fabrics B: 8 x 8 inches in total
- White fabric C: 8 x 8 inches

Prepare the patches

Rotary method
- From fabrics A, B, and C, make four 6½-inch three-patch squares (see page 11)

or

Template cutting
Using the 4 x 4 templates (pages 269–73):
- From fabrics A, cut 4 short rectangle
- From fabrics B and C, cut 4 small squares each

Template piecing

With right sides together, sew a fabric B small square to a fabric C small square; press seam open. Join the strip to a fabric A short rectangle to make a three-patch square; press seam open. Repeat to make three more half-square triangles.

Make the block

Sew two rows Arrange the four three-patch squares in two rows of two patches, making sure two white small squares meet in the middle and the other two are in the top left and bottom right corners.

Complete the square With right sides together, pin and sew the patches in rows; press seams open. Join the rows; press seam open.

- -

roman tees

The seam allowance is ¼ inch throughout.

This geometric arrangement of four interlocked "T" shapes is derived from an ancient Roman mosaic floor design. Vibrant greens and soothing grays give it a modern feel. Roman Tees works equally well in complementary solid colors.

Fabric quantities

- Light gray print fabric A: 8 x 8 inches
- Light green print fabric B: 8 x 8 inches
- Dark gray print fabric C: 8 x 8 inches
- Dark green print fabric D: 8 x 8 inches

Prepare the patches

Rotary method
- From fabrics A, B, C, and D, cut two 3½-inch squares and one 6½ x 3½-inch rectangle each

or

Template cutting
Using the 4 x 4 templates (pages 269–73):
- From fabrics A, B, C, and D cut 1 short rectangle and 2 small squares each

Make the block

Piece the center patch With right sides together, pin and sew one fabric B small square to the right edge of a fabric A small square; press seam open.

With right sides together, pin and sew one fabric C small square to the right edge of a fabric D small square; press seam open. Join the strips together, with the light and dark greens at opposite corners, to make the center square; press seam open.

Sew three rows With right sides together, join the fabric D short rectangle to the left edge of the center patch, then join the fabric B short rectangle to the right edge; press seams open.

With right sides together, pin and sew the remaining fabric A small square to the left end of the fabric A short rectangle. Join the remaining fabric B small square to the right end; press seams open.

With right sides together, pin and sew the strip to the top of the center patch, carefully matching the seams. With right sides together, pin and sew the remaining fabric D small square to the left end of the fabric C short rectangle. Join the remaining fabric C small square to the right edge; press seams open.

Complete the square With right sides together, pin and sew the strip to the bottom edge of the center panel, matching seams. Press seam open.

patchwork dog

The seam allowance is ¼ inch throughout.

To make this a true patchwork dog, you need a random selection of coordinating scraps for the squares. Reverse the order of the patches to make a dog that faces left. You can join several of these blocks—facing both directions—with white sashing and corner squares to make a puppy quilt.

Fabric quantities

- 10 different medium tones of coordinating scrap fabrics A : 12 x 15 inches in total
- Dark blue fabric B: 4 x 4 inches
- White fabric C: 8 x 14 inches

Prepare the patches

Rotary method
- From fabrics A, cut twenty 2½-inch squares
- From fabrics B and C, make two 2½-inch half-square triangles (see page 12)
- From fabric C, cut one 6½ x 4½-inch rectangle, one 6½ x 2½-inch rectangle, two 4½ x 2½-inch rectangles, and one 2½-inch square

or

Template cutting
Using the 6 x 6 templates (pages 278–83):
- From fabrics A, cut 20 small squares
- From fabric B, cut 2 small triangles
- From fabric C, cut 1 medium rectangle, 2 short rectangles, 1 small square, 2 small triangles, and one wide medium rectangle

Template piecing

With right sides together, pin and sew a fabric C small triangle to both fabric B small triangles to make two half-square triangles; press seams open.

Make the block

Arrange the patches Lay out the small squares in the dog pattern, balancing the light and dark colors as well as the different shades, as shown above. Use a half-square triangle for the ear and one for the tail. Join in sections.

Make the top left corner With the dark blue triangle pointing down and left, pin and sew the dark blue half-square triangle to the left short edge of a white short rectangle; press seam open. Join the strip to the bottom edge of the white wide medium rectangle; press seam open.

Make the top right corner With the dark blue triangle pointing down and left, pin and sew the dark blue half-square triangle to the left short edge of the remaining white short rectangle; press seam open.

With right sides together, pin and sew two rows of three fabric A small squares; press seams open. Join the rows; press seam open. Join this patch to the bottom edge of the first strip, carefully matching the seams so the ear lines up with the dog's head.

Make the bottom left corner With right sides together, pin and sew two rows of three fabric A small squares; press seams open. Join the rows; press seam open. Join two fabric A squares to the left edge of the white small square; press seams open. Join the strip to the bottom of the patch, making sure the white square is at the bottom right; press seam open.

Make the bottom right corner With right sides together, pin and sew three rows of two fabric A small squares; press seams open. Join the rows; press seam open. Join the white medium rectangle to the right edge of the patch; press seam open.

Complete the square With right sides together, pin and sew the top left corner to the top right corner, carefully matching the seams, making sure the tail is in the bottom left corner and the ear is in the top row, toward the center; press seam open. Repeat to join the bottom left corner to the bottom right corner, making sure the "legs" are at the bottom.

Being careful to match the seams, with right sides together pin and sew the two halves of the block together; press seam open.

brave new world

The seam allowance is ¼ inch throughout.

The optimistic name of this block is a quote from Shakespeare's play "The Tempest." This pinwheel block is straightforward to piece, but be careful when matching the seams in the center to keep the sharp points of the triangles.

A
B
C

Fabric quantities

- Medium green print fabric A: 10 x 10 inches
- Light blue fabric B: 8 x 8 inches
- Dark green fabric C: 8 x 16 inches

Prepare the patches

Rotary method
- From fabrics A, B, and C, make four 6½-inch triangle-and-square blocks (see page 15)

or

Template cutting
Using the 4 x 4 templates (pages 269–73):
- From fabric A, cut 8 small triangles
- From fabric B, cut 4 small squares
- From fabric C, cut 4 large triangles

Template piecing

With right sides together, pin and sew a fabric A small triangle to the top edge of a fabric B small square, making sure it points down and left. Sew a second fabric A small triangle to the right edge, so it also points down and left. With right sides together, pin and sew a fabric C large triangle to the diagonal edge of the joined patches. Repeat to make three more triangle-and-square blocks.

Make the block

Sew two rows With right sides together, pin and sew two patches together, joining a fabric B small square to a short side of a fabric C large triangle and making sure the fabric C triangles point clockwise in each patch; press seam open. Repeat with the second set of patches.

Complete the square With right sides together, pin and sew the two rows together, carefully matching the seams to maintain the sharp points in the center of the block; press seam open.

- -

rail fence

The seam allowance is ¼ inch throughout.

Join several of these blocks edge to edge for an allover basket-weave pattern. Choose similar tones for a subtle pattern, or experiment with low-volume prints for a more modern spin on this traditional design.

A
B
C
D

Fabric quantities

- Medium orange print fabric A: 7 x 12 inches
- Light green fabric B: 7 x 6 inches
- Medium green fabric C: 7 x 12 inches
- Light yellow print fabric D: 7 x 6 inches

Prepare the patches

Rotary method
- From fabrics A and B, make two 6½-inch three-stripe squares (see page 11) with fabric B in the center
- From fabrics C and D, make two 6½-inch three-stripe squares with fabric D in the center

or

Template cutting

Using the 6 x 6 templates (pages 278–83):
- From fabrics A and C, cut 4 medium rectangles each
- From fabrics B and D, cut 2 medium rectangles each

Template piecing

With right sides together, pin and sew a fabric A medium rectangle to each long side of the fabric B medium rectangles to make two three-strip squares; press seams open.

With right sides together, pin and sew a fabric C medium rectangle to each long side of the fabric D medium rectangles to make two three-strip squares; press seams open.

Make the block

Sew two rows With right sides together, pin and sew a fabric A and B three-stripe square to a fabric C and D three-stripe square, making sure the fabric A stripes are horizontal and the fabric C stripes are vertical; press seams open. Repeat with the second pair of three-strip squares.

Complete the square Right sides together, pin and sew the two rows together, with the corners of the fabric A rectangles meeting at the center of the block; press seam open.

country lanes

The seam allowance is ¼ inch throughout.

A
B
C
D
E

This simple folk-style chain-pieced block is traditionally made in a variety of green prints to evoke the countryside. When several Country Lane blocks are joined together, an overall landscape pattern of meandering paths and cultivated fields is created. This block is most accurately made using templates.

Fabric quantities

- Dark green fabric A: 6 x 6 inches
- Light green print fabric B: 6 x 12 inches
- Medium green print fabric C: 6 x 6 inches
- Dark green print fabric D: 3 x 3 inches
- White fabric E: 6 x 12 inches

Prepare the patches

Template cutting
Using the 5 x 5 templates (pages 274–7):
- From fabrics A and C, cut 4 small squares each
- From fabric B, cut 8 small squares
- From fabric D, cut 1 small square
- From fabric E, cut 4 short rectangles

Template piecing

With right sides together, sew a fabric B small square to each fabric A and fabric C small square; press seams over the darker fabric. Join the strips in pairs so each four-patch square contains one fabric A square, two fabric B squares, and one fabric C square, with the fabric B squares in opposite corners.

Make the block

Sew three rows With right sides together, pin and sew a four-patch square to each long edge of a fabric E rectangle, making sure the fabric A squares are in the top outside corners; press seams over the rectangles.

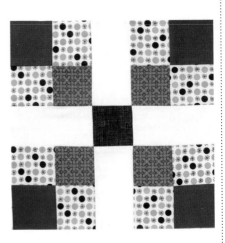

Repeat for the bottom row, with the fabric A squares in the bottom outside corners.

With right sides together, pin and sew a fabric E rectangle to each side of the fabric D square; press seams over the square.

Complete the square With right sides together, pin and sew the top and bottom rows to the center row, carefully matching the seams; press seams open.

---

broken dishes diamond

The seam allowance is ¼ inch throughout.

A
A
A
A
B
B
B
B

A basic division of a square into eight triangles, the Broken Dishes Diamond looks dramatic at any size. Here, it's made as a scrappy block with each triangle cut from a different fabric. When you choose two analogous colors, one warm and one cool, you create a vibrant, modern block from simple geometric shapes.

Fabric quantities

- 4 different medium green solid and print fabrics A: 16 x 16 inches in total
- 4 different medium yellow and orange solid and print fabrics B: 16 x 16 inches in total

Prepare the patches

Rotary method
- From fabrics A and B, make four 6½-inch half-square triangles (see page 12)

or

Template cutting
Using the 4 x 4 templates (pages 269–73):
- From fabrics A and B, cut 4 large triangles each

Template piecing

With right sides together, pin and sew a fabric A large triangle to the long diagonal edge of each of the fabric B large triangles to make four half-square triangles.

Make the block

Sew two rows With right sides together, pin and sew two half-square triangles together, joining a yellow triangle to a green triangle; press seam open. Repeat with the other pair of half-square triangles.

Complete the square With right sides together, pin and sew the two rows together, carefully matching the seams and maintaining the sharp triangle points; press seam open.

the lost ship

This stylized nautical motif, made up of large and small triangles, suggests a ship in full sail. You could use four variations of the same color, such as four different greens, or go with a variety of solids with the same intensity of color. The 'lost' white ship of the title can be seen in reverse, in the negative space between the motifs.

The seam allowance is ¼ inch throughout.

A
B
C
D
E

Fabric quantities

- Light green fabric A: 8 x 14 inches
- Medium yellow fabric B: 8 x 14 inches
- Medium green fabric C: 8 x 14 inches
- Medium turquoise fabric D: 8 x 14 inches
- White fabric E: 17 x 32 inches

Prepare the patches

Rotary method
- From fabrics A and E; fabrics B and E; fabrics C and E; and fabrics D and E, make one 4½-inch half-square triangle (see page 12) and five 2½-inch half-square triangles each

or

Template cutting
Using the 6 x 6 templates (pages 278–83):
- From fabrics A, B, C, and D, cut 1 large triangle and 5 small triangles each
- From fabric E, cut 4 large triangles and 20 small triangles

Template piecing

With right sides together, pin and sew a white small triangle to each of the colored small triangles to make 20 half-square triangles; press seams open. Repeat with the large white and colored triangles to make another four half-square triangles.

Make the block

Piece four patches Group the half-square triangles by color. Working with one color at a time, with right sides together, pin and sew a small half-square triangle to the side edge of another small half-square triangle, making sure the colored triangles point down and right; press seams open. Repeat with the remaining three small half-square triangles.

With right sides together, pin and sew the strip of two half-square triangles to the top of the large half-square triangle of the same color, making sure the large colored triangle points up and left and the small triangles point down and right; press seam open. Now, join the strip of three small half-square triangles to the left edge of the patch, making sure the small colored triangles point down and right; press seam open.

Repeat with the remaining three sets of half-square triangles.

Sew two rows For the first row, with right sides together, pin and sew the light green patch to the left edge of the medium yellow patch, carefully matching the seams; press seam open.

For the second row, with right sides together, pin and sew the medium green patch to the left edge of the turquoise patch, carefully matching seams; press seam open.

Complete the square With right sides together, pin and sew the two rows together; press seam open.

fields of green

The seam allowance is ¼ inch throughout.

Like Country Lanes on page 148, this simple one-patch block is made from a selection of green fabrics for a rural look. Joined together—in the same direction or at alternate right angles—several blocks create a shaded ombré effect.

A
B
C
D
E

Fabric quantities

- Dark green fabric A: 8 x 8 inches
- Medium green fabric B: 8 x 8 inches
- Light green fabric C: 8 x 8 inches
- Medium green print fabric D: 8 x 8 inches
- Light green print fabric E: 4 x 8 inches

Prepare the patches

Rotary method
- From fabrics A and D, cut four 3½-inch squares each
- From fabrics B and C, cut three 3½-inch squares each
- From fabric E, cut two 3½-inch squares

or

Template cutting
Using the 4 x 4 templates (pages 269–73):
- From fabrics A and D, cut 4 small squares each
- From fabrics B and C, cut 3 small squares each
- From fabric E, cut 2 small squares

Make the block

Make four rows With right sides together, pin and sew a fabric A small square to the left side of a fabric B small square. Join a fabric D small square to the right side of the strip, followed by a fabric E small square; press seams left.

Repeat for the second row, starting with a fabric C small square, followed by fabrics A, B, and D small squares; press seams right.

Repeat for the third row, starting with a fabric D small square, followed by fabrics C, A, and B small squares; press seams left.

Repeat for the fourth row, starting with a fabric E small square, followed by fabrics D, C, and A small squares; press seams right.

Complete the square Join the first and third rows to the second row, matching seams. Join the fourth row to the third row. Press seams open.

diagonal squares

The seam allowance is ¼ inch throughout.

Diagonal Squares is the Double Four Patch (see page 74) reinterpreted for the modern quilter. Its narrow range of clear solid colors pop against a white background. This minimalist block would fit into any contemporary interior plan.

A
B
C
D
E

Fabric quantities

- Medium turquoise fabric A: 4 x 4 inches
- Light turquoise fabric B: 4 x 4 inches
- Light green fabric C: 4 x 4 inches
- Dark green fabric D: 4 x 4 inches
- White fabric E: 14 x 15 inches

Prepare the patches

Rotary method
- From fabrics A, B, and E and fabrics C, D, and E, make one 6½-inch four-patch square (see page 11) each
- From fabric E, cut two 6½-inch squares

or

Template cutting
Using the 4 x 4 templates (pages 269–73):
- From fabrics A, B, C, and D, cut 1 small square each
- From fabric E, cut 4 small squares and 2 large squares

Template piecing

With right sides together, pin and sew a fabric E small square to the fabric A small square; press seam open. Repeat to join a fabric E small square to the fabric B small square; press seams open. Join the strips, alternating the fabric E squares to create a small checkerboard, completing the first four-patch square; press seam open.

Repeat, combining the remaining fabric E small squares with the fabrics C and D small squares to make another four-patch square.

Make the block

Sew two rows With right sides together, pin and sew a large white square to the left side of the fabrics A, B, and E four-patch square; press seams open. Join the other large square to the right side of the second four-patch square in the same way; press seam open.

Complete the square Carefully matching the seams, join the strips to create a diagonal line of colored squares; press seam open.

random roads

The seam allowance is ¼ inch throughout.

Avid quilters hoard their every scrap of leftover fabric, and this is a good way to incorporate them into an interesting modern, improv block. The street map fabric is a good background for the bright colored columns, but other dense, small-scale black-and-white prints work just as well. Because the size of the patches depends on scraps in random sizes, measurements cannot be precise, and it is easiest to rotary cut the strips. Each block will be unique.

Fabric quantities

- 10 different random scraps of fabrics A: 2 inches wide by 1 to 3 inches long each

- Black-and-white print fabric B: 13 x 15 inches

Prepare the patches

Rotary method
- From fabrics A, cut the 10 scraps into 1½ to 3½-inch-long by 2-inch-wide rectangles

- From fabric B, cut four 12½-inch-long by 2-inch to 3-inch-wide strips

Make the block

Piece a scrappy patch With right sides together, pin and sew the scraps horizontally, along their 2-inch width, grading the colors from light to dark and then back to dark; press seams to one side. Cut the patch into strips 2 to 3 inches wide and 12½ inches long.

Complete the square Starting with a fabric B strip, alternate background and patchwork strips. With right sides together, pin and sew along the long sides; press seams over fabric B. Trim the finished block to a 12½-inch square.

practical orchard

The seam allowance is ¼ inch throughout.

A traditional block with a quirky name, this nine-patch variation dates back to at least the 1890s, when it first appeared in print. The usual center square is replaced with an hourglass square. The directional print gives it a horizontal emphasis, but cutting each corner square and the dark triangles from different fabrics would alter the look completely.

Fabric quantities

- Medium green print fabric A: 10 x 16 inches

- White fabric B: 6 x 6 inches

- Light yellow fabric C: 10 x 10 inches

Prepare the patches

Rotary method
- From fabrics A and B, make one 4½-inch hourglass square (see page 13)

- From fabrics A and C, cut four 4½-inch squares each

or

Template cutting
Using the 6 x 6 templates (pages 278–83):
- From fabric A, cut 4 large squares and 2 medium triangles

- From fabric B, cut 2 medium triangles

- From fabric C, cut 4 large squares

Template piecing

With right sides together, pin and sew a fabric A medium triangle along a short edge of a fabric B medium triangle; press seam open. Repeat with the remaining fabrics A and B medium triangles. Sew the two patches together along the long diagonal seam to make the hourglass square.

Make the block

Sew three rows For the center row, with right sides together, pin and sew a fabric C square to each fabric B edge of the hourglass square. For the top and bottom rows, join a fabric A square to each side edge of the remaining two fabric C squares.

Complete the square With right sides together, join the top and bottom rows to the center row; press seams open.

200

shaded squares

Narrow rectangles in four shades of green combine to create a sophisticated graphic look to this block. Join several Shaded Squares blocks edge to edge to create a woven look. This geometric block is easily made using the rotary method.

A
B
C
D

Fabric quantities

- Dark green fabric A: 7 x 10 inches
- Medium green fabric B: 7 x 10 inches
- Light green fabric C: 7 x 10 inches
- Light green fabric D: 7 x 10 inches

Prepare the patches

Rotary method
- From fabrics A, B, C, and D, cut four 6½ x 2-inch rectangles each

Make the block

Piece four squares With right sides together, pin and sew four rectangles, one of each color in descending order from the darkest to lightest green; press seams open. Repeat to make another three patches.

Join two rows With right sides together, pin and sew two squares together, adjoining the fabric A rectangle along the side edge of the other square; press seam open. Repeat to make the bottom row.

Complete the square With right sides together, pin and sew the top and bottom rows together, carefully matching the seams and making sure the dark green rectangles meet in the center of the block; press seam open.

201

churn dash

This traditional block is given a contemporary look with a mid-century modern print and a crisp background. The name comes from its resemblance to the wooden tool that was once used to churn milk into butter by hand.

A
B

Fabric quantities

- Medium green print fabric A: 12 x 12 inches
- Light blue fabric B: 12 x 14 inches

Prepare the patches

Rotary method
- From fabrics A and B, make four 4½-inch half-square triangles (see page 12) and four 4½ x 2½-inch rectangle squares (see page 11)
- From fabric B, cut one 4½-inch square

or

Template cutting
Using the 6 x 6 templates (pages 278–83):
- From fabric A, cut 4 large triangles and 4 short rectangles
- From fabric B, cut 1 large square, 4 large triangles, and 4 short rectangles.

Template piecing

With right sides together, pin and sew a fabric A large triangle to each of the fabric B large triangles to make four half-square triangles; press seams open.

With right sides together, pin and sew a fabric A short rectangle to a long edge of each of the fabric B short rectangles to make four rectangle squares; press seams open.

Make the block

Sew three rows With right sides together, pin and sew a half-square triangle to each side of one rectangle square, making sure the print fabric triangles will point to the center of the block and the print fabric rectangle will adjoin the center square; press seams open. Repeat to make the bottom row.

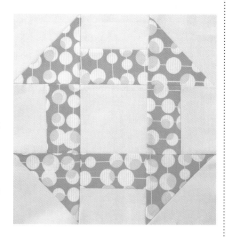

With right sides together, pin and sew the print fabric side of the remaining rectangle squares to each side of the fabric B large square; press seams open.

Complete the square Flip the bottom row. With right sides together, pin and sew the top and bottom rows to the center row, carefully matching the seams; press seams open.

christmas forest

The seam allowance is ¼ inch throughout.

Mix in a variety of subtle prints to enhance the look of the forest in the Christmas Forest block. A single red tree adds a touch of festivity, and white polka dots suggest snow. To make an entire quilt top, you can simply add triangles to make longer rows, then increase the number of rows you make. You will need to use templates to cut these isosceles triangles.

Fabric quantities

- Medium green print fabric A: 10 x 10 inches
- Medium green print fabric B: 5 x 15 inches
- Medium green fabric C: 5 x 5 inches
- Dark green fabric D: 5 x 5 inches
- Dark red print fabric E: 5 x 5 inches
- Light blue fabric F: 10 x 20 inches

Prepare the patches

Template cutting
Using the 6 x 6 templates (pages 278–83):

- From fabric A, cut 2 isosceles triangles, 2 right half triangles, and 1 left half triangle
- From fabric B, cut 2 isosceles triangles and 1 left half triangle
- From fabrics C, D, and E, cut 1 isosceles triangle each
- From fabric F, cut 8 isosceles triangles, 1 right half triangle, and 1 left half triangle

Make the block

Arrange the triangles Lay out the triangles in three rows, with the green triangles pointing up and the blue triangles pointing down, balancing the light and dark fabrics, and mixing up the prints. Position the half triangles at the end of each row and offset the red triangle.

Sew three rows Starting at the left side of the first row, with right sides together, pin and sew the triangles together, carefully matching the points; press seams open. Repeat to make three rows.

Complete the square With right sides together and carefully matching the seams, pin and sew the first and third rows to the second row; press seams open.

A
B
C
D
E
F

circle

The octagonal shape, which suggests the circle of the block's name, makes the perfect frame for a fussy-cut (see page 10) square of your favorite print. Here, the green and yellow fabrics complement the patterned fabric in the center.

A
B
C
D

The seam allowance is ¼ inch throughout.

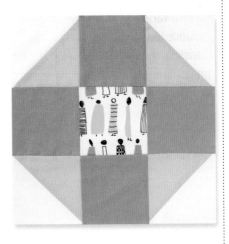

Fabric quantities

- Medium yellow fabric A: 12 x 12 inches
- Medium green fabric B: 10 x 10 inches
- Light green print fabric C: 5 x 5 inches
- White fabric D: 10 x 10 inches

Prepare the patches

Rotary method
- From fabrics A and D, make four 4½-inch half-square triangles (see page 12)
- From fabric B, cut four 4½-inch squares
- From fabric C, cut one 4½-inch square

or

Template cutting
Using the 6 x 6 templates (pages 278–83):

- From fabrics A and D, cut 4 large triangles each
- From fabric B, cut 4 large squares
- From fabric C, cut 1 large square

Template piecing

With right sides together, pin and sew a fabric D large triangle to each of the fabric A large triangles to make four half-square triangles; press seams open.

Make the block

Sew three rows With right sides together, pin and sew a half-square triangle to each side of a fabric B large square, making sure the yellow triangles point toward the center of the square; press seams over fabric B. Repeat to make the third row.

With right sides together, pin and sew a fabric B large square to each side of the fabric C large square; press seams over fabric B.

Complete the square Flip the third row. With right sides together and carefully matching the seams, pin and sew the first row and the third row to the second row; press seams open.

maltese cross

A dark background, such as this dark blue, always makes plain solid colors sing out. Each arm of this cross motif is made from a different color, with the same tonal value. The orange square at the center pulls together the citrus and blue hues. Like the other blocks made up of isosceles triangles, the patches are cut from templates.

A
B
C
D
E
F

The seam allowance is ¼ inch throughout.

Fabric quantities

- Light yellow fabric A: 5 x 10 inches
- Light blue fabric B: 5 x 10 inches
- Light green fabric C: 5 x 10 inches
- Light turquoise fabric D: 5 x 10 inches
- Light orange fabric E: 5 x 5 inches
- Dark blue fabric F: 10 x 20 inches

Prepare the patches

Template cutting
Using the 6 x 6 templates (pages 278–83):
- From fabrics A, B, C, and D, cut 1 right half triangle and 1 left half triangle each
- From fabric E, cut 1 large square

- From fabric F, cut 4 large squares and 4 isosceles triangles

Make the block

Piece four patches With right sides together, pin and sew the half triangles of each fabric color to the diagonal edges of the fabric F isosceles triangles; press seams over fabric F.

Sew three rows With right sides together, pin and sew a dark blue large square to each side of the yellow patch, making sure the triangles point out; press seams over fabric F. Repeat with the green patch.

To make the center row, join the light blue patch and the turquoise patch to each side of the orange large square, making sure the triangles point out; press seams over fabric F.

Complete the square With right sides together and carefully matching the seams, pin and sew the first and third rows to the center row; press seams open.

single irish chain

The seam allowance is ¼ inch throughout.

Single Irish Chain is usually made from green and white fabrics in tribute to the Emerald Isle. This version includes a little blue, reminiscent of the Irish Sea. This block is more accurately made with templates for a finished 12-inch square.

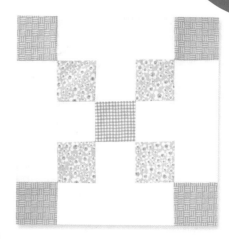

A
B
C
D

Fabric quantities

- Light blue print fabric A: 6 x 6 inches
- Medium blue print fabric B: 3 x 3 inches
- Light green print fabric C: 6 x 6 inches
- White fabric D: 9 x 12in

Prepare the patches

Template cutting
Using the 5 x 5 templates (pages 274–7):
- From fabrics A and C, cut 4 small squares each
- From fabric B, cut 1 small square
- From fabric D, cut 4 medium rectangles and 4 small squares

Make the block

Piece the nine-patch square With right sides facing, pin and sew a fabric A small square to each side of a fabric D small square; press over fabric A. Repeat to make the third row.

With right sides facing, pin and sew a fabric D small square to each side of the fabric B small square; press seams over fabric B. Join the first two rows of the nine-patch square to this strip. Press seams away from fabric D.

Complete the square With right sides facing, pin and sew a fabric D medium rectangle to each side of the nine-patch square; press seams open.

With right sides facing, pin and sew a fabric C small square to each short end of the remaining fabric D medium rectangles; press seams over fabric C. Join strips to the top and bottom of the nine-patch square; press seams open.

- -

easy four patch

The seam allowance is ¼ inch throughout.

This variation on the Single Irish Chain (see above) forms a pattern of diagonal rows of squares when several blocks are joined edge to edge. This example has extra seams on the rectangles at top and bottom, born of necessity when the white fabric ran out. Such small details add character to your patchwork.

A
B
C
D
E

Fabric quantities

- Medium green fabric A: 5 x 5 inches
- Medium yellow print fabric B: 5 x 12 inches
- Light green fabric C: 6 x 6 inches
- Dark yellow print fabric D: 6 x 6 inches
- Light yellow fabric E: 6 x 18 inches

Prepare the patches

Rotary method
- From fabric A, cut one 4½-inch square
- From fabric B, cut four 4½ x 2½-inch rectangles
- From fabrics C and D, cut four 2½-inch squares each
- From fabric E, cut four 8½ x 2½-inch rectangles

Make the block

Piece the center patch With right sides together, pin and sew a fabric B short rectangle to each side of the fabric A large square; press seams open.

With right sides together, pin and sew a fabric C small square to each end of the remaining fabric B rectangles; press seams open. Join a strip to the top and bottom of the center patch; press seams open.

Complete the square With right sides together, pin and sew a fabric E rectangle to each side of the center patch; press seams open.

With right sides together, pin and sew a fabric D small square to each short end of the remaining fabric E rectangles. Join a strip to the top and bottom of the center patch; press seams open.

triangle tree

The seam allowance is ¼ inch throughout.

A
B
C
D
E
F

This stylized pine tree is large enough to cover the entire block. Made of half-square triangles, Triangle Tree is a good way to practice matching your seams accurately. Combine this block with Country Lanes (see page 148), Fields of Green (see page 150), or any other block featuring trees.

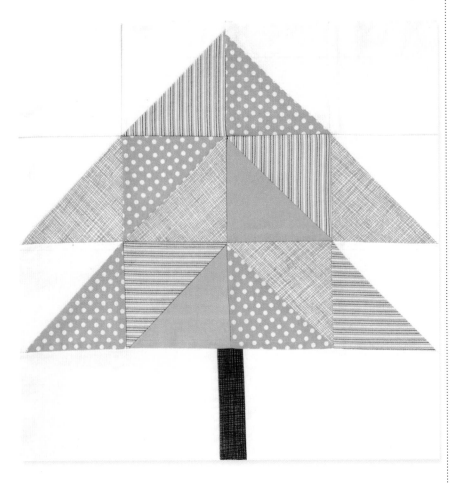

Fabric quantities

- Light green print fabric A: 10 x 10 inches
- Light green fabric B: 10 x 10 inches
- Medium green print fabric C: 10 x 10 inches
- Medium green print fabric D: 10 x 10 inches
- Dark green print fabric E: 2 x 4 inches
- White fabric F: 14 x 18 inches

Prepare the patches

Rotary method
- From fabrics A and D; fabrics A and F; fabrics B and C; fabrics C and F; and fabrics D and F, make two 3½-inch half-square triangles (see page 12) each
- From fabric E, cut one 3½ x 1¼-inch rectangle
- From fabric F, cut one 12½ x 3½-inch rectangle and two 3½-inch squares

or

Template cutting
Using the 4 x 4 templates (pages 269–73):
- From fabrics A, C, and D, cut 4 small triangles each
- From fabric B, cut 2 small triangles
- From fabric E, cut 1 narrow very small rectangle
- From fabric F, cut 2 small squares, 6 small triangles, and one full-length rectangle

Template piecing

With right sides together, pin and sew a fabric A small triangle to a fabric D small triangle to make a half-square triangle; press seams open. Repeat to make a second half-square triangle from fabrics A and D and two half-square triangles from fabrics B and C.

With right sides together, pin and sew the remaining fabric F small triangles to the remaining fabrics A, C, D small triangles to make six half-square triangles; press seams open.

Make the block

Join the first row With right sides together, pin and sew a white small square to a fabrics C and F half-square triangle, making sure the green triangle points down and right. Join a fabrics A and F half-square triangle to the right side of the strip, making sure the green triangle points down and left. Join another white small square to the right side of the strip; press seams open.

Join the second row Pin and sew a fabrics D and F half-square triangle, with the green triangle pointing down and right, to a fabrics A and D half-square triangle. Join a fabrics B and C half-square triangle to the right side of the strip. Join another fabrics D and F half-square triangle to the right side of the strip, making sure the green triangle points down and left; press seams open.

Join the third row Pin and sew a fabrics A and F half-square triangle, with the green triangle pointing down and right, to a fabrics B and C half-square triangle. Join a fabrics A and D half-square triangle to the right side of the strip. Join a fabrics C and F half-square triangle to the right side of the strip, making sure the green triangle points down and left; press seams open.

Join the fourth row Turn the ends of the fabric E rectangle under ¼ inch. Making sure it is centered on the fabric F full-length rectangle, appliqué (see page 20) the fabric E strip to the white strip.

Complete the square With right sides together and carefully matching the seams, pin and sew the first row to the second row, the third row to the second row, and then the fourth row to the third row; press seams open.

the faraway tree

Pine tree blocks that are made up of half-square triangles have a perennial appeal, and they can be found on quilts dating back to the mid-1800s. This block is more accurately made from templates for a finished 12-inch square.

The seam allowance is ¼ inch throughout.

A
B
C
D

Fabric quantities

- Dark green fabric A: 10 x 18 inches
- Dark green print fabric B: 10 x 10 inches
- Medium green print fabric C: 10 x 10 inches
- White fabric D: 14 x 24 inches

Prepare the patches

Template cutting
Using the 5 x 5 templates (pages 274–7):
- From fabric A, cut 12 small triangles and one 6 x 2-inch bias rectangle
- From fabric B, cut 4 small triangles
- From fabric C, cut 1 small square and 5 small triangles
- From fabric D, cut 1 large square, 2 small squares, and 16 small triangles

Template piecing

With right sides together, pin and sew a white small triangle to 10 of the fabric A small triangles and each of the fabric B small triangles to make 14 green half-square triangles (see page 12); press seams open.

Repeat with the remaining two fabric A small triangles and fabric C small triangles to make two more half-square triangles.

Repeat with the remaining fabric C small triangles and fabric D small triangles to make another two half-square triangles.

Make the block

Piece the trunk patch Press under a ¼-inch seam along each side edge of the green bias rectangle. Appliqué (see page 20) it to the fabric D large square diagonally, from the top right corner to the bottom left corner.

Using the stitch and flip method (see page 14), draw a diagonal line across the wrong side of a C square and, with right sides together, pin it to the top right corner of the appliquéd square. Sew along the line and

trim the seam allowance back to ¼ inch; press the seam toward the triangle.

Piece the first row With right sides together, pin and sew four fabrics A and D half-square triangles in a row, making sure the green triangles point down and right. Join a white small square to the right side of the strip; press seams open.

Piece the second row With right sides together, pin and sew a fabrics A and D half-square triangle to a fabrics B and D half-square triangle. Add another fabrics B and D half-square triangle to the right edge of the strip, making sure all of the green triangles point down and right. Join a white small square to the right edge of the strip. With the green triangle pointing up and left, add a fabrics D and D half-square triangle to the right side of the strip; press seams open.

Piece the third row With right sides together, pin and sew a fabrics C and D half-square triangle to a fabrics A and C half-square triangle, joining along the fabric C edge to create a medium triangle pointing down. Join a fabric C small square to the right edge of the strip. Add a fabrics B and D half-square triangle to the right edge of the strip, then join a fabrics A and D half-square

triangle, with the green triangles pointing up and left; press seams open.

Piece the fourth row With right sides together, pin and sew a fabrics A and C half-square triangle to a fabrics B and D half-square triangle, making sure both darker green triangles point up and left. Add a fabrics A and D half-square triangle, also with the green triangle pointing up and left; press seams open.

Piece the fifth row With right sides together, pin and sew a fabrics C and D half-square triangle to a fabrics A and D half-square triangle, joining them along the green edge to create a two-color medium triangle pointing down. Add another fabrics A and D half-square triangle, making sure the green triangle points up and left; press seams open.

Complete the square With right sides together, pin and sew the fourth and fifth rows together, carefully matching the seams; press seam open. Join the trunk patch to the left edge of the patch; press seams open.

With right sides together, pin and sew the first and third rows to the second row; press seams open. Carefully matching the seams, join together the two halves of the block; press seams open.

nine-patch chain

The seam allowance is ¼ inch throughout.

In this block, the traditional nine-patch motif is alternated with plain squares to create a checkerboard pattern. Perfect for a scrappy quilt, use it to showcase the last scraps of your favorite prints on a white background. To make this block with the templates, you'll use both 6 x 6 and 4 x 4 templates.

Fabric quantities

- Up to 10 different medium print fabrics A: 9 x 12 inches in total
- Light green print fabric B: 7 x 14 inches
- White fabric C: 6 x 12 inches

Prepare the patches

Rotary method
- From fabrics A, cut ten 2½-inch squares
- From fabric B, cut two 6½-inch squares
- From fabric C, cut eight 2½-inch squares

or

Template cutting

Using the 6 x 6 templates (pages 278–83):
- From fabric A, cut 10 small squares
- From fabric C, cut 8 small squares

Using the 4 x 4 templates (pages 269–73):
- From fabric B, cut 2 large squares

Make the block

Piece the nine-patch squares With right sides together, pin and sew two fabric A small squares to each side of a fabric C small square; press seams open. Repeat to make the third row. With right sides together, pin and sew a fabric C small square to each side of a fabric A small square; press seams open. Join the three rows, carefully matching seams; press seams open. Repeat to make the second nine-patch block.

Complete the square With right sides together, pin and sew a fabric B large square to the left side of one nine-patch block; press seam open. Repeat to join the second fabric B large square to the right side of the remaining nine-patch block.

With right sides together, pin and sew the two rows together, carefully matching the seams; press seam open.

A
A
A
A
A
A
A
A
A
A
B
C

---

the old windmill

The seam allowance is ¼ inch throughout.

With a pinwheel at the center, this block has a sense of movement that makes it ideal for a child's quilt. Join the patches with plain sashing and colored corner squares to emphasize the geometric shape of four sails rotating in the wind.

A
B
C
D

Fabric quantities

- Medium green fabric A: 10 x 10 inches
- Dark orange print fabric B: 10 x 10 inches
- Light green print fabric C: 8 x 8 inches
- Light green fabric D: 8 x 14 inches

Prepare the patches

Rotary method
- From fabrics A and B, make four 3½-inch half-square triangles (see page 12)
- From fabric C, cut four 3½-inch squares
- From fabric D, cut four 6½ x 3½-inch rectangles

or

Template cutting

Using the 4 x 4 templates (pages 269–73):
- From fabrics A and B, cut 4 small triangles each
- From fabric C, cut 4 small squares
- From fabric D, cut 4 short rectangles

Template piecing

With right sides together, pin and sew a fabric A small triangle to each of the fabric B small triangles to make four half-square triangles.

Make the block

Piece four patches With right sides together, pin and sew a fabric C small square to the green bottom edge of each half-square triangle, making sure the orange triangle points up and left; press seams open. With right sides together, pin and sew a fabric D short rectangle to the left edge of each square patch; press seams open.

Complete the square Arrange the patches so that the orange triangles form a pinwheel in the center. With right sides together, pin and sew the top two patches, joining the half-square triangles; press seams open. Repeat with the bottom two patches.

With right sides together, pin and sew the two rows together, carefully matching the seams and maintaining the triangle points in the center; press seam open.

goose tracks

Maybe the original maker of this block was inspired by the random footprints left by the webbed feet of a goose in her muddy farmyard. The footprint squares at the corners can be made in two colors, such as shown here, or in a single fabric, as seen in the block's variation Tulip Ladyfingers (see page 266). This block is most accurately made from templates to make a finished 12-inch square.

The seam allowance is ¼ inch throughout.

A

B

C

Fabric quantities

- Medium green fabric A: 10 x 10 inches
- Medium green print fabric B: 6 x 9 inches
- White fabric C: 13 x 18 inches

Prepare the patches

Template cutting
Using the 5 x 5 templates (pages 274–7):
- From fabric A, cut 8 small triangles
- From fabric B, cut 5 small squares
- From fabric C, cut 4 short rectangles, 4 small squares, and 8 small triangles

Template piecing

With right sides together, pin and sew a fabric C small triangle to each of the fabric A small triangles to make eight half-square triangles (see page 12).

Make the block

Piece four patches With right sides together, pin and sew a fabric C small square to the green edge of a half-square triangle, making sure the green triangle points down and left; press seams over the darker fabric.

With right sides together, pin and sew a half-square triangle to a fabric B small square, making sure the green triangle points up and right; press seams over the darker fabric.

Carefully matching the seams, join the strips to make a patch, making sure the green triangles meet in the middle. Press seams over fabric C.

Repeat to make another three green and white corner patches.

Make three rows With right sides facing, pin and sew a fabric C short rectangle to the right edge of a green and white corner patch, making sure the fabric B square is in the bottom right corner; press seam open. Join a second green and white corner patch to the right edge of the strip, making sure the fabric B square is the bottom left corner. Press seam over fabric C. Repeat to make the third row.

For the middle row, with right sides facing, pin and sew a fabric C short rectangle to each side of the remaining fabric B small square. Press seams over fabric C.

Complete the square With right sides facing, pin and sew the first and third rows to the second row, making sure the green print squares meet in the center of the block; press seams over fabric C.

leaves

The seam allowance is ¼ inch throughout.

Hexagonal leaves, set on each side of a center stem, create a bold graphic design. Use a single square to make a contemporary cushion cover or join several blocks vertically to make tall plants. Finish off at the top with a large flower-shape block, such as Big Flower on page 187 or Violet on page 262. Three or four plants of different heights would make a stunning quilt.

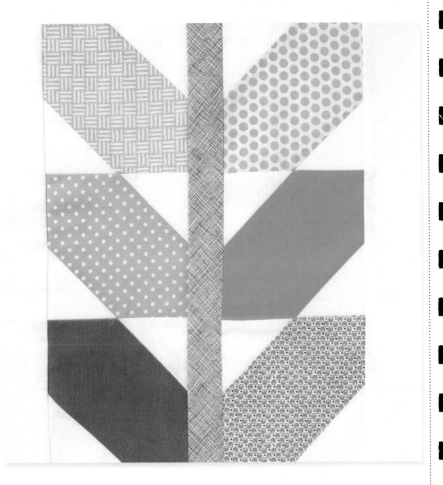

Fabric quantities

- Light green print fabric A: 5 x 5 inches
- Light green print fabric B: 5 x 5 inches
- Medium green print fabric C: 5 x 5 inches
- Medium green fabric D: 5 x 5 inches
- Dark green fabric E: 5 x 5 inches
- Dark green print fabric F: 5 x 5 inches
- Medium green print fabric G: 2 x 13 inches
- White fabric H: 9 x 16 inches

Prepare the patches

Rotary method
- From fabrics A and H; fabrics B and H; fabrics C and H; fabrics D and H; fabrics E and H; and fabrics F and H, make one 4½-inch hexagon square (see page 15) each
- From fabric G, cut one 12½ x 1½-inch rectangle
- From fabric H, cut two 12½ x 2-inch rectangles

Make the block

Sew two columns Arrange the hexagon squares in two columns of three patches, balancing the light and dark shades. With right sides together, pin and sew the top and bottom hexagon squares to the center hexagon squares; press seams open.

Complete the square With right sides together, pin and sew one column to each long side of the fabric G rectangle; press seams open. Join the fabric H long rectangles to each side of the block; press seams out.

plain blue check

The seam allowance is ¼ inch throughout.

The medium blue squares where the light and dark stripes intersect create the illusion of transparency, in imitation of woven checkered fabrics.

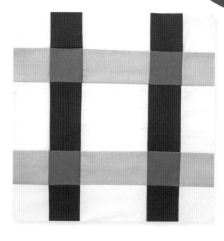

Fabric quantities

- Light blue fabric A: 8 x 9 inches
- Medium blue fabric B: 6 x 6 inches
- Dark blue fabric C: 8 x 9 inches
- White fabric D: 11 x 13 inches

Prepare the patches

Rotary method

- From fabrics A and C, cut two 4½ x 2½-inch rectangles and four 2½-inch squares each
- From fabric B, cut four 2½-inch squares
- From fabric D, cut one 4½-inch square, four 4½ x 2½-inch rectangles, and four 2½-inch squares

or

Template cutting

Using the 6 x 6 templates (pages 278–83):

- From fabrics A and C, cut 2 short rectangles and 4 small squares each
- From fabric B, cut 4 small squares
- From fabric D, cut 1 large square, 4 short rectangles, and 4 small squares

Make the block

Sew five rows For the first row, with right sides together, sew a fabric A small square to each short end of a fabric D short rectangle. Join a fabric D small square to each end of the strip; press seams over the darker fabric. Repeat for the fifth row. For the second row, with right sides together, sew a fabric B small square to each short end of a fabric C short rectangle. Join a fabric C small square to each end of the strip; press seams over the darker fabric. Repeat to make the fourth row.

For the middle row, with right sides together, pin and sew a fabric A short rectangle to each side of the fabric D large square. Join the remaining fabric D short rectangles to each side of the strip; press seams over the darker fabric.

Complete the square With right sides together, pin and sew the first and third rows to the second row, matching the seams. Join the fourth and fifth rows, matching seams. Press seams open.

---

bow tie

The seam allowance is ¼ inch throughout.

A nineteenth-century quilt design recalling the neckwear of fashionable gentlemen, the Bow Tie block has resurged in popularity in recent years. This small-scale blue print is similar to silk tie fabric—look for similar designs to add a touch of sartorial elegance to your quilt. Rows of Bow Ties (see page 161) is a smaller-scale variation of this block, and combined in a quilt, would make a fun sampler.

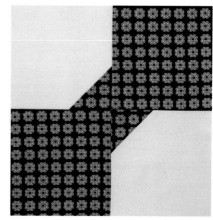

Fabric quantities

- Dark blue print fabric A: 10 x 14 inches
- Light blue fabric B: 7 x 14 inches

Prepare the patches

Rotary method

- From fabrics A and B, make two 6½-inch corner squares (see page 14)
- From fabric A, cut two 6½-inch squares

or

Template cutting
Using the 4 x 4 templates (pages 269–73):

- From fabric A, cut 2 large squares and 2 small triangles
- From fabric B, cut 2 corner squares

Template piecing

With right sides together, pin and sew a fabric A small triangle to the diagonal edge on each fabric B corner square; press seams open.

Make the block

Sew two rows With right sides together, pin and sew a corner square to one fabric A large square, making sure the dark blue triangle is at the center of the block; press seam open. Repeat with the remaining corner square and fabric A large square.

Complete the square With right sides together, pin and sew the strips together, carefully matching the seams; press seam open.

215

figure eight

The seam allowance is ¼ inch throughout.

This asymmetric design, also known as Patience Corner, is a variation of the green block on page 145. Using two color palettes of the same print gives cohesion to the arrangement, while the solid white rectangles add a fresh, modern look to a traditional block.

A
B
C

Fabric quantities

- Light green print fabric A: 5 x 10 inches
- Medium blue print fabric B: 5 x 10 inches
- White fabric C: 10 x 15 inches

Prepare the patches

Rotary method
- From fabrics A and B, cut two 4½-inch squares each
- From fabric C, four 6½ x 2½-inch rectangles and four 4½ x 2½-inch rectangles

or

Template cutting
Using the 6 x 6 templates (pages 278–83):

- From fabrics A and B, cut 2 large squares each
- From fabric C, cut 4 medium rectangles and 4 short rectangles

Make the block

Sew two rows With right sides together, pin and sew a white short rectangle to each of the fabrics A and B squares; press seams open. With right sides together, pin and sew a white medium rectangle to an adjoining side of each of the squares; press seams open.

With right sides together, pin and sew a fabrics A and C square to a fabrics B and C square, making sure the green patch is in the center of the strip and the blue patch is in the top right corner; press seams open.

With right sides together, pin and sew a fabrics B and C square to a fabrics A and C square, making sure the green patch is in the center of the strip and the blue patch is in the bottom left corner; press seams open.

Complete the square With right sides together and carefully matching seams, join the strips, making sure the green squares meet at the center to form a figure eight; press seams open.

216

frame

The seam allowance is ¼ inch throughout.

This block, a variation of the basic Stretched Nine Patch on page 39, makes a perfect frame for an illustrative square patch. The rectangles are made from two narrow strips—pick a solid fabric that contrasts with the featured print for the inner frame square. This geometric block is easily made using the rotary method.

A
B
C
D

Fabric quantities

- Dark blue print fabric A: 7 x 7 inches
- Light green fabric B: 7 x 8 inches
- Medium blue fabric C: 8 x 8 inches
- White fabric D: 7 x 12 inches

Prepare the patches

Rotary method
- From fabric A, cut one 6½-inch square
- From fabric B, cut four 6½ x 1½-inch rectangles
- From fabric C, cut four 3½-inch squares
- From fabric D, cut four 6½ x 2½-inch rectangles

Make the block

Sew the center row With right sides together, pin and sew a light green rectangle to each of the white rectangles; press seams over the darker fabric. Join a strip to each side of the fabric A large square, aligning the green edge; press seams over fabric A.

Sew the top and bottom rows With right sides together, pin and sew each turquoise small square to a short end of the remaining fabrics B and D strips.

Complete the square Join the strips to the top and bottom of the square; press seams open.

banded stripes

The seam allowance is ¼ inch throughout.

A simple striped design takes on a bright new look when colorful printed fabrics are separated by narrow bands of plain white. The palette here includes strong, contrasting colors in simple patterns, but you could create a more subtle look by picking a narrow range of blue or green hues. This block is easily made using the rotary method.

Fabric quantities

- Dark orange print fabric A: 13 x 3 inches
- Medium yellow print fabric B: 13 x 3 inches
- Medium green dot fabric C: 13 x 3 inches
- Medium blue print fabric D: 13 x 3 inches
- Gray fabric E: 13 x 10 inches

Prepare the patches

Rotary method
- From fabrics A, B, C, and D, cut one 12½ x 2½-inch rectangle each
- From fabric E, cut four 12½ x 1½-inch rectangles

Make the block

Sew four strips With right sides together, pin and sew a gray rectangle to the top edge of each colored rectangle; press seams away from fabric E.

Complete the square Arrange the strips in your preferred color order. With right sides together, pin and sew the first and third strips to the second strip then add the fourth strip. Press seams away from fabric E.

- -

ribbon tail star

The seam allowance is ¼ inch throughout.

Ribbon Tail Star is made like Two-Way Star on page 62, but using a single, different solid color for each of the ribbon tails gives it a more modern look.

Fabric quantities

- Light green fabric A: 5 x 10 inches
- Medium green fabric B: 5 x 10 inches
- Medium blue fabric C: 5 x 10 inches
- Medium turquoise fabric D: 5 x 10 inches
- White fabric E: 10 x 20 inches

Prepare the patches

Rotary method
- From fabrics A and E; fabrics B and E; fabrics C and E; and fabrics D and E, make one 4½-inch three-quarter square triangle (see page 13) each
- From fabric E, cut five 4½-inch squares

or

Template cutting
Using the 6 x 6 templates (pages 278–83):
- From fabrics A, B, C, and D, cut 1 large triangle and 1 medium triangle each

- From fabric E, cut 5 large squares and 4 medium triangles

Template piecing

With right sides together, pin and sew a fabric E medium triangle to a left short side of each of the colored medium triangles; press seams over the colored fabric. With right sides together, pin and sew each of the triangle patches along the long diagonal edge of the large triangle in the same color to complete the four quarter-square triangles; press seams over the colored fabric.

Make the block

Sew three rows For the top row, with right sides together, pin and sew a white large square to each side of the light green quarter-square triangles, with the triangles pointing up; press seams open. Repeat with the medium blue quarter-square triangle, with the triangles pointing down, to make the bottom row.

For the middle row, with right sides together, pin and sew the fabric D quarter-square triangle to the left edge of the remaining white large square and the medium green quarter-square triangle to the right edge, with the triangles pointing outward; press seams open.

Complete the square With right sides together, pin and sew the first and third rows to the middle row, carefully matching the seams; press seams open.

219

windmill sails

A careful choice of fabrics lifts this simple block out of the ordinary. Neutral textures, such as the wood-grain fabric used for the "sails" in this block, make a good foil for busy, ditsy florals. The two whimsical flower prints are part of a charming nature-inspired designer collection; look for similar complementary fabrics online or at your local quilting store.

A
B
C

The seam allowance is ¼ inch throughout.

Fabric quantities

- Light blue print fabric A: 7 x 10 inches
- Light green print fabric B: 7 x 10 inches
- Light gray print fabric C: 7 x 12 inches

Prepare the patches

Rotary method
- From fabrics A and B, cut two 6½ x 4½-inch rectangles each
- From fabric C, cut two 6½ x 2½-inch rectangles

or

Template cutting

Using the 6 x 6 templates (pages 278–83):
- From fabrics A and B, cut 2 wide medium rectangles each
- From fabric C, cut 4 medium rectangles

Make the block

Piece four patches With right sides together, pin and sew a fabric C rectangle to the bottom edge of each of the fabrics A and B rectangles; press seams over fabric C.

Sew two rows With right sides together, pin and sew a fabrics A and C square to a fabrics B and C square, with the blue print square in the top left corner and the green print square in the top right corner, making sure the gray

rectangles meet perpendicularly in the center; press seam over fabric C. Repeat to make another row.

Complete the square Flip the bottom row. With right sides together, pin and sew the rows together, making sure the gray rectangles meet in the center to form sails; press seam open.

220

southern belle

Some quilt blocks have been around for so many years that they have acquired different names, with individual makers having interpreted them in different ways. Other blocks share the same name, although they look slightly different. This is just one of the blocks that share the evocative name of Southern Belle.

A
B
C
D
E

The seam allowance is ¼ inch throughout.

Fabric quantities

- Light blue fabric A: 7 x 14 inches
- Medium blue print fabric B: 7 x 14 inches
- Light green fabric C: 7 x 14 inches
- Medium turquoise fabric D: 7 x 14 inches
- White fabric E: 8 x 16 inches

Prepare the patches

Rotary method
- From fabrics A and E; fabrics B and E; fabrics C and E; and fabrics D and E, make two 6½-inch three-quarter square triangles (see page 13) each

or

Template cutting

Using the 4 x 4 templates (pages 269–73):
- From fabrics A, B, C, and D, cut 1 large triangle and 1 small triangle each
- From fabric E, cut 4 small triangles

Template piecing

With right sides together, join a fabric A small triangle to a fabric E small triangle along the short edge, with the colored triangle on the left; press seams open. Join this patchwork triangle to the fabric A large triangle along the diagonal edges, being sure to match colors to complete the three-quarter square triangle; press seams open. Repeat to make three more three-quarter square triangles using fabrics B and E, fabrics C and E, and fabrics D and E.

Make the block

Sew two rows Lay out the squares, making sure the white triangles are at the outside edges, as shown above. With right sides together, sew the top pair together, pressing seam left. Repeat with the bottom pair.

Complete the square Pin and sew the top and bottom rows together; press seam open.

sailboat

The seam allowance is ¼ inch throughout.

Pictorial blocks were popular in the 1920s, and this bright and breezy boat has the angular look of the Art Deco era. It's a good choice for a seaside home, sunny green room, or a child's bedroom. Choose a pale blue for the sky and a blue-green for the sea, with a contrasting colored print for the boat. Tall Ship on page 195 is an ideal companion block for Sailboat. Frame the individual blocks with sashing or sew them together edge to edge to make a whole flotilla.

A
B
C
D

Fabric quantities

- Light blue fabric A: 10 x 18 inches
- Medium yellow print fabric B: 4 x 13 inches
- Dark blue print fabric C: 4 x 16 inches
- White fabric D: 5 x 10 inches

Prepare the patches

Rotary method
- From fabrics A and D, make four 3½-inch half-square triangles (see page 12)
- From fabrics B and C, make one 12½ x 3½-inch long boat (see page 17)
- From fabric A, cut two 6½ x 3½-inch rectangles
- From fabric C, cut one 12½ x 3½-inch rectangle

or

Template cutting
Using the 4 x 4 templates (pages 269–73):
- From fabric A, cut 2 short rectangles and 4 small triangles
- From fabric B, cut 1 long boat
- From fabric C, cut 2 small triangles and one full-length rectangle
- From fabric D, cut 4 small triangles

Template piecing

With right sides together, pin and sew a fabric D small triangle to each of the fabric A small triangles to make four half-square triangles; press seams open.

With right sides together, pin and sew the fabric C small triangles to the diagonal edges of the fabric B long boat; press seams open.

Make the block

Piece the sails With right sides together, pin and sew the fabrics A and D half-square triangles in two rows of two squares, making sure all of the white triangles point down and right; press seams over fabric A. Join a fabric A short rectangle to each side of the square, then press seams open.

Complete the square With right sides together, pin and sew the fabric C full-length rectangle to the bottom edge of the long boat; press seam over fabric C.

With right sides together, pin and sew the two strips; press seam over the boat.

zigzag

A
B
C
D

This block offers an easy way to create a zigzag design with no diamond patches to cut or sharp angles to match up. This is a quick-and-easy block that's made up of a single repeated patch: a rectangle square. Set the block on point and extend the number of squares in each row to make a quilt top with horizontal zigzags. You can then square off the edges with 4½-inch right triangles.

Fabric quantities

- Light turquoise fabric A: 3 x 9 inches
- Medium blue fabric B: 6 x 9 inches
- Lime green fabric C: 3 x 5 inches
- Medium gray print fabric D: 9 x 9 inches

Prepare the patches

Rotary method
- From fabrics A and D, make three 4½-inch rectangle squares (see page 11)
- From fabrics B and D, make five 4½-inch rectangle squares
- From fabrics C and D, make one 4½-inch rectangle square

or

Template cutting
Using the 6 x 6 templates (pages 278–83):
- From fabric A, cut 3 short rectangles
- From fabric B, cut 5 short rectangles
- From fabric C, cut 1 short rectangle
- From fabric D, cut 9 short rectangles

Template piecing

With right sides together, pin and sew a fabric D short rectangle to each of the fabrics A, B, and C short rectangles, making nine rectangle squares; press seams open.

Make the block

Sew three rows For the top row, with right sides together, pin and sew together two fabrics A and D rectangle squares, making sure the turquoise rectangles are perpendicular and one is horizontal along the bottom. Join a fabrics B and D rectangle square to the right side of the strip so that the blue rectangle is also horizontal; press seams open.

For the second row, with right sides together, pin and sew together two fabrics B and D rectangle squares, making sure the blue rectangles are perpendicular and the center one is along the bottom. Join a fabrics A and D rectangle square to the left side of the strip so that the fabric A rectangle is vertical and on the outside; press seams open.

For the third row, with right sides together, pin and sew together two fabrics B and D rectangle squares, making sure the blue rectangles are perpendicular and one is horizontal along the bottom. Join the fabrics C and D rectangle square to the right side of the strip so that the green rectangle is horizontal and at the bottom; press seams open.

Complete the square With right sides together, pin and sew the first row and the third row to the second row, carefully matching seams to create the zigzag; press seams open.

beach huts

While a whimsical block all on its own, Beach Huts is designed to be used alongside Seaside on page 97, which features two rows of smaller huts. The beach in the foreground is pieced from several different yellow fabrics, but it could alternatively be cut from a single 12½ x 4½-inch rectangle.

The seam allowance is ¼ inch throughout.

Fabric quantities

- Dark blue fabric A: 7 x 9 inches
- Dark red fabric B: 7 x 9 inches
- Light blue striped fabric C: 5 x 6 inches
- Medium red striped fabric D: 3 x 4 inches
- Light blue fabric E: 7 x 13 inches
- Up to 6 different medium yellow print fabrics F: 9 x 10 inches in total

Prepare the patches

Rotary method
- From fabrics A and E, make one 4½-inch house square (see page 14)
- From fabrics B and E, make two 4½ x 2½-inch flying geese rectangles (see page 17)
- From fabric A, cut one 4½ x 2½-inch rectangle and four 2½ x 2-inch rectangles
- From fabric B, cut one 2½ x 1½-inch rectangle
- From fabric C, cut one 4½ x 2½-inch rectangle and two 2½ x 2-inch rectangles
- From fabric D, cut two 2½ x 1½-inch rectangles
- From fabric E, cut one 12 x 2½-inch rectangle
- From fabrics F, cut six 4½ x 2½-inch rectangles

Make the block

Piece the doors Sew two fabric A 2½ x 2-inch rectangles to the long edges of each of the fabric D 2½ x 1½-inch rectangles, and two fabric C 2½ x 2-inch rectangles to the long edges of the fabric B 2½ x 1½-inch rectangle; press seams outward.

Make the houses Sew the house square to the top edge of the fabrics A and D door rectangle; press seam open. Sew the flying geese rectangles to the top edges of the fabric A and fabric C short rectangles; join these to the matching door rectangles; then press seams open.

Sew the three huts together, matching the seams, and add the fabric E full-length rectangle to the top edge.

Complete the square Sew the fabric F rectangles together in two rows of three and join to the bottom edge of the house patch. Press all seams open.

ocean wave

The seam allowance is ¼ inch throughout.

The blue and white triangles that give this block its title evoke the patterns made by foaming waves, but its alternative title is equally descriptive. In the 1930s, it was recorded as Cut Glass Dish, because the texture is similar to the pattern of the glass fruit and sugar bowls that were an essential part of the polite dining table. Patches in four shades of light blue are used to make this version, but because their placement is random, the instructions are for only one light blue fabric.

A
A
A
A
B

Fabric quantities

- Light blue fabrics A: 11 x 18 inches in total
- White fabric B: 9 x 12 inches

Prepare the patches

Rotary method
- From each of fabrics A and B, make twenty-four 2½ inch half-square triangles (see page 12)
- From fabric A, cut three 4½-inch squares

or

Template cutting
Using the 6 x 6 templates (pages 278–83):
- From fabric A, cut 3 large squares and 24 small triangles
- From fabric B, cut 24 small triangles

Template piecing

With right sides together, pin and sew a fabric A triangle along the diagonal edge of a fabric B triangle to make a half-square triangle; press seam over fabric A. Repeat to make another 23 half-square triangles.

Make the block

Piece six patches With right sides together, pin and sew the half-square triangles in six patches of four, with the white triangles all pointing down and right and balancing the various light blue triangles; press seams open.

Make three rows Lay out the patches in three rows of three, as shown above, with the three solid squares forming a diagonal line from the bottom left to top right.

For the top row, with right sides together, pin and sew two half-square triangle patches together, then join a solid fabric A square to the right end of the strip; press seams open. Repeat to make the bottom row, but add the fabric A large square to the left end of the strip.

For the middle row, sew a half-square triangle patch to each end of a solid fabric A square.

Complete the square With right sides together, pin and sew the top and bottom rows to the middle row, carefully matching the seams and points; press seams open.

domino

The seam allowance is ¼ inch throughout.

"Domino" is the geometric name given to two equal squares joined together to make a rectangle—so it's clear where this block got its name. Domino is divided into a series of concentric squares, counterchanged in light and dark.

Fabric quantities

- Dark blue fabric A: 8 x 18 inches
- Light blue print fabric B: 8 x 18 inches

Prepare the patches

Rotary method
- From fabrics A and B, cut two 6½ x 2½-inch rectangles, four 4½ x 2½-inch rectangles, and four 2½-inch squares each

or

Template cutting
Using the 6 x 6 templates (pages 278–83):
- From fabrics A and B, cut 2 medium rectangles, 4 short rectangles, and 4 small squares each

Make the block

Piece four patches For the top left patch, with right sides together, pin and sew a fabric A small square to the top edge of a fabric B small square; press seam out. Join a fabric A short rectangle to the left edge; press seam out. Add a fabric B short rectangle to the top of the square and a fabric B medium rectangle to the left edge; press seams out.

Repeat to make the bottom right patch.

For the top right patch, with right sides together, pin and sew a fabric B small square to the top edge of a fabric A small square; press seam out. Join a fabric B small rectangle to the right edge; press seam out. Add a fabric A short rectangle to the top of the square and a fabric A medium rectangle to the right edge; press seams out.

Repeat to make the bottom left patch.

Complete the square With right sides together, pin and sew the top left patch to the top right patch; press seam open.

With right sides together, pin and sew the bottom left patch to the bottom right patch; press seam open.

Carefully matching the seams, join the two halves of the block, making sure the small squares meet in the middle; press seam open.

little yacht

The seam allowance is ¼ inch throughout.

This block is made from up-cycled shirts in true patchwork tradition. Striped fabrics work well together, or you can mix them with checks, ginghams, and chambray. Here, the stripes run in opposing directions to give the sails animation.

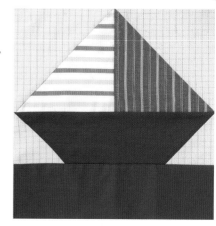

Fabric quantities

- Light blue print fabric A: 8 x 8 inches
- Dark blue print fabric B: 8 x 8 inches
- Dark pink fabric C: 4 x 13 inches
- Dark blue fabric D: 4 x 13 inches
- Light blue print fabric E: 8 x 12 inches

Prepare the patches

Rotary method
- From fabrics A and E and fabrics B and E, make one 6½-inch half-square triangle (see page 12) each
- From fabrics C and E, make one 12½ x 3½-inch long boat (see page 17)
- From fabric D, cut one 12½ x 3½-inch rectangle

or

Template cutting
Using the 4 x 4 templates (pages 269–73):
- From fabrics A and B, cut 1 large triangle each
- From fabric C, cut 1 long boat
- From fabric D, cut 1 full-length rectangle
- From fabric E, cut 2 large triangles and 2 small triangles

Template piecing

With right sides together, pin and sew a fabric E large triangle to the fabric A and fabric B large triangles to make two half-square triangles; press seams open.

With right sides together, pin and sew the fabric E small triangles to the diagonal edges of the fabric C long boat; press seams open.

Make the block

Piece the boat With right sides together, pin and sew the two half-square triangles together, with the stripes running perpendicularly; press seam open. Join the sails to the top edge of the long boat; press seam down.

Complete the square With right sides together, pin and sew the fabric D full-length rectangle to the bottom edge of the long boat; press seam down.

225

226

A
B

A
B
C
D
E

227

alaska homestead

The seam allowance is ¼ inch throughout.

This enduring design, also known as **Pioneer Patch**, is a variation on **Monkey Wrench** (see page 93)—they are pieced in the same way, but look different because of their color palettes. The block is named for the homesteaders who lived in the northern state. The triangular patches echo the pitched roofs of their wooden cabins, and the white background suggests the snow-covered landscape.

A
B
C
D

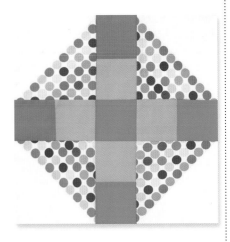

Fabric quantities

- Blue print fabric A: 8 x 16 inches
- White fabric B: 8 x 16 inches
- Light turquoise fabric C: 6 x 6 inches
- Dark turquoise fabric D: 6 x 9 inches

Prepare the patches

Template cutting
Using the 5 x 5 templates (pages 274–7):
- From fabrics A and B, cut 4 large triangles each
- From fabric C, cut 4 small squares
- From fabric D, cut 5 small squares

Template piecing

Right sides together, sew a fabric A large triangle to a fabric B large triangle along the long diagonal edge; press seam over the darker fabric. Repeat to make another three half-square triangles (see page 12).

Make the block

Sew two rows Right sides together, sew a fabric C small square to four of the fabric D small squares; press seams over fabric D. Join the half-square triangles to the long edges of two of these blocks, so the fabric A triangles point down and inward and the fabric C squares are on the outside edge; press seams over the triangles. Repeat to make the bottom row.

Make the center row Join the other two pairs of fabric C and D squares to the side edges of the remaining fabric D square, with the fabric D squares outermost; press seams over the fabric C squares.

Complete the square With right sides together, pin and sew the three rows together, matching the seams; press seams open.

228

puss in the corner

The seam allowance is ¼ inch throughout.

The block dates back at least to the 1900s. Like many old quilt patterns, it is known by several names, including the equally feline **Kitty Corner**. It shares one of its other names with **Shoofly** (see page 116), but has a larger center patch than the alternative version.

A
B
C

Fabric quantities

- Dark blue fabric A: 5 x 10 inches
- Dark blue print fabric B: 7 x 7 inches
- Light blue print fabric C: 13 x 14 inches

Prepare the patches

Rotary method
- From fabrics A and C, make four 3½-inch half-square triangles (see page 12)
- From fabric B, cut one 6½-inch square
- From fabric C, cut four 6½ x 3½-inch rectangles

or

Template cutting
Using the 4 x 4 templates (pages 269–73):

- From fabric A, cut 4 small triangles
- From fabric B, cut 1 large square
- From fabric C, cut 4 short rectangles and 4 small triangles

Template piecing

With right sides together, sew a fabric A small triangle to a fabric C small triangle along the long diagonal edge; press seam over fabric A. Repeat to make another three half-square triangles.

Make the block

Make the top and bottom rows Sew a half-square triangle to each short edge of two fabric C rectangles, so the fabric A triangles point inward and down. Repeat to make the bottom row.

Make the center row With right sides together, sew a fabric C rectangle to each side edge of the fabric B large square.

Complete the square Flip the bottom row. Pin and sew the top and bottom rows to the center row, matching the seams; press seams open.

seated cat

The seam allowance is ¼ inch throughout.

This block has been designed especially for the many dedicated feline-loving quilters. Piecing it together requires extra attention and time, but the patches fit together in a logical way. The gray, black, and white color palette suggests a slinky Siamese, but you could change the fabrics to match your own favorite cat.

Fabric quantities

- Medium gray print fabric A: 12 x 16 inches
- Black print fabric B: 8 x 7 inches
- Medium turquoise fabric C: 8 x 11 inches
- White fabric D: 4 x 10 inches

Prepare the patches

Rotary method
- From fabrics A and B, make two 2½-inch half-square triangles for the tip of the tail (see page 12)
- From fabrics A and C, make one 4½-inch corner square for the chest (see page 14)
- From fabrics A and D, make one 6½ x 4½-inch cat head (see page 17) for the face and one 6½ x 2½-inch short boat (see page 17) for the bib
- From fabrics B and C, make one 6½ x 2½-inch short boat for the ears and one 2½-inch half-square triangle for the bottom of the tail
- From fabric A, cut one 6½-inch square for the body
- From fabric B, cut one 4½ x 2½-inch rectangle for the tail
- From fabric C, cut one 2½-inch square for the main body and one 6½ x 4½-inch rectangle

or

Template cutting
Using the 6 x 6 templates (pages 278–83):
- From fabric A, cut 1 cat head, 1 corner square, and 4 small triangles
- From fabric B, cut 1 short rectangle and 5 small triangles
- From fabric C, cut 1 short boat, 1 small square, 2 small triangles, and one wide medium rectangle

- From fabric D, cut 1 short boat and 2 small triangles

Using the 4 x 4 templates (pages 269–73):
- From fabric A, cut 1 large square for the main body

Template piecing

To make the ears, with right sides together, sew a fabric B small triangle to each diagonal edge of the fabric C short boat; press seam over fabric B.

To make the face, sew a fabric D small triangle to each diagonal edge of the fabric A cat head; press seams over fabric A.

To make the bib, sew a fabric A small triangle to each diagonal edge of a fabric D short boat; press seams over fabric A.

To make the chest, sew a fabric C small triangle to the fabric A corner square along the diagonal edge; press seam open.

To make the tail tip, join a fabric A small triangle to the long diagonal edge of a fabric B small triangle; press seam over fabric B. Repeat to make another half-square triangle. Repeat using fabric B and fabric C small triangles to make a third half-square triangle.

Make the block

Piece the cat To complete the body, use the stitch-and-flip method (see page 14). Draw a diagonal line across the fabric C small square; with right sides together, pin it to the top right corner of the fabric A large square. Stitch across the line, trim the seam allowance to ¼ inch, and press seam inward.

Lay out the patches, as shown above, then sew the blocks together in two halves.

Sew the left half Join the ears to the top edge of the head and the bib to the bottom edge of the head; press seams open.

Sew the fabrics A and B half-square triangles together, with the black print forming a diamond. Sew the tail tip to the right side of the chest, then join the patch to the bottom edge of the bib.

Sew the right half Sew the fabric C rectangle to the top edge of the body; press seam over fabric C. Join the fabrics B and C half-square triangle to the right short edge of the fabric B short rectangle, then sew the strip to the bottom edge of the body.

Complete the square With right sides together, pin and sew the two halves together; press seam open.

A

B

C

D

hexagon path

The seam allowance is ¼ inch throughout.

This block looks good on its own, but it works best when repeated over a quilt. Joined edge to edge it makes diagonal rows, or paths, of hexagons and squares.

A
B
C
D

Fabric quantities

- Dark blue fabric A: 8 x 8 inches
- Light blue print fabric B: 8 x 8 inches
- Light blue print fabric C: 7 x 14 inches
- Dark orange print fabric D: 4 x 8 inches

Prepare the patches

Rotary method
- From fabrics A and B, make two 6½-inch four-patch squares (see page 11)
- From fabrics C and D, make two 6½-inch hexagon squares (see page 15)

or

Template cutting
Using the 4 x 4 templates (pages 269–73):
- From fabrics A and B, cut 4 small squares each

- From fabric C, cut 2 hexagons
- From fabric D, cut 4 small triangles

Template piecing

With right sides together, pin and sew a fabric A small square to each of the fabric B small squares; press seams open. Join two strips, alternating the squares, to make a four-patch square; press seam open. Repeat to make the second four-patch square.

With right sides together, pin and sew the fabric D small triangles to the diagonal edges of the fabric C hexagons to make two hexagon squares; press seams open.

Make the block

Sew two rows Join a four-patch square to the left edge of a hexagon square, making sure the blue square is in the center and the

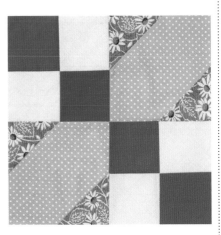

hexagon points up and right; press seam open. Repeat, with the four-patch square to the right edge of the hexagon; press seam open.

Complete the square Carefully matching the seams, join the rows, making sure the hexagons and blue squares meet in the center of the block.

---

mississippi spin

The seam allowance is ¼ inch throughout.

An asymmetric design with a great sense of rotary movement, this block works particularly well when made from just two contrasting fabrics. In this interpretation, the plain white motif stands out against a floral background. Reversing the light and dark patches will create a different look.

A
B

Fabric quantities

- Medium gray print fabric A: 12 x 13 inches
- White fabric B: 10 x 15 inches

Prepare the patches

Rotary method
- From fabrics A and B, make four 4½-inch hexagon squares (see page 15)
- From fabric A, cut four 4½-inch squares
- From fabric B, cut one 4½-inch square

or

Template cutting
Using the 6 x 6 templates (pages 278–83):
- From fabric A, cut 4 large squares and 8 small triangles

- From fabric B, cut 1 large square and 4 hexagons

Template piecing

To make the four hexagon blocks, join the fabric A small triangles along the diagonal edges of the hexagons; press seams inward.

Make the block

Arrange the patches Lay the hexagon squares out in three rows of three, creating a pinwheel shape in the center of the block, as shown above.

For the top row, with right sides together, pin and sew a fabric A large square to each side of a hexagon square; press seams over fabric A. Repeat to make the bottom row.

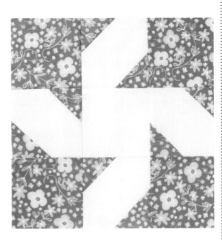

For the center row, join a hexagon square to each side of a fabric B large square; press seams over fabric B.

Complete the square With right sides together, pin and sew the top and bottom rows to the center row, matching the seams; press seams open.

chinese coin stacks

The seam allowance is ¼ inch throughout.

This block is a great stash buster for scrap hoarders. Because there are no seams to match, it is quick to make. It is also adaptable: The columns of "coins" and the plain stripes that divide them can be made to any length or width you want. This scrappy block is easily made using the rotary method.

Fabric quantities

- Up to 24 different light and medium blue solid and print fabrics A: 12 x 16 inches in total
- Dark blue fabric B: 7 x 13 inches

Prepare the patches

Rotary method
- From fabrics A, cut twenty-four 3½ x 1½-inch rectangles
- From fabric B, cut three 12½ x 2½-inch rectangles

Make the block

Piece two columns Lay out the fabric A narrow short rectangles in two columns of 12, rearranging them until you have a good balance of color and pattern. With right sides together, pin and sew the rectangles together; press seams downward.

Complete the square With right sides together, pin and sew a fabric B full-length rectangle to the left edge of each column, then join the third full-length rectangle to the right edge of one column. Join the two columns; press seams over the long rectangles.

---

square upon square

The seam allowance is ¼ inch throughout.

A dramatic new block, this design looks like three overlapping squares laid out in a diagonal row. It is easy to put together from square and rectangular patches.

Fabric quantities

- Light green fabric A: 8 x 7 inches
- Light turquoise fabric B: 8 x 7 inches
- Dark turquoise fabric C: 7 x 7 inches
- White fabric D: 11 x 8 inches

Prepare the patches

Rotary method
- From fabrics A and B, cut one 6½ x 3½-inch rectangle and one 3½-inch square each
- From fabric C, cut one 6½-inch square
- From fabric D, cut two 6½ x 3½-inch rectangles and two 3½-inch squares

or

Template cutting
Using the 4 x 4 templates (pages 269–73):
- From fabrics A and B, cut 1 short rectangle and 1 small square each

- From fabric C, cut 1 large square
- From fabric D, cut 2 short rectangles and 2 small squares

Make the block

Piece the top row Lay out all the patches in their final positions, and start piecing from the top right corner. Join the light green small square to the left edge of the white short rectangle; press seam away from fabric D.

Join the small white square to the left edge of the light turquoise short rectangle; press seam away from fabric B. Sew these two strips together, making sure the small light green square is at top left, and press the seam open. Join the light green rectangle to the left edge; press the seam over fabric A.

Piece the bottom row Starting at the bottom left corner, join the light turquoise small square to the white small square and press the seam away from fabric D. Join the strip to the right edge of the short white rectangle, making sure the turquoise square is in the top right corner; press seam open. Sew the completed unit to the left edge of the large dark turquoise square and press seam over fabric C.

Complete the square With right sides facing, pin and sew the top row to the bottom row, carefully matching the seam. Press seam open.

merry kite

The seam allowance is ¼ inch throughout.

This is a simplified version of a block that appeared in Nancy Cabot's *Chicago Daily Tribune* column in 1933, which has been adapted for machine stitching. It looks just the same as the original, but there are no inset seams to sew. Cabot wrote that the pattern was "inspired by the kites every boy flies with more or less skill," but the four arrow shapes are also reminiscent of the tails of a bird of prey called a red kite.

Fabric quantities

- Dark blue fabric A: 12 x 17 inches
- Light blue print fabric B: 12 x 15 inches

Prepare the patches

Rotary method
- From fabrics A and B, make four 4½-inch three-patch squares (see page 11), four 4½ x 2½-inch right diamond rectangles (see page 16), and four 4½ x 2½-inch left diamond rectangles
- From fabric A, cut one 4½-inch square

or

Template cutting
Using the 6 x 6 templates (pages 278–83):
- From fabric A, cut 1 large square, 4 right diamonds, 4 left diamonds, and 4 small squares
- From fabric B, cut 4 short rectangles, 4 small squares, and 16 small triangles

Template piecing

With right sides together, pin and sew a fabric A small square to a fabric B small square; press seam over fabric A. Sew this strip to the long edge of a fabric B short rectangle; press seam open. Repeat to make another three three-patch squares.

With right sides together, sew the fabric B small triangles to the diagonal edges of the diamonds, pressing seams inward, to make four left and four right diamond rectangles.

Make the block

Make the top and bottom rows Lay out all the patches, as shown above. With right sides together, join a left diamond rectangle to a right diamond rectangle along the long edges to make an arrow shape; press seam open. Repeat to make another three arrow patches.

With right sides together, pin and sew a three-patch square each side of an arrow patch, making sure the arrow points inward and the fabric A squares are in the top outside corners. Repeat to make the bottom row.

Make the center row With the arrows pointing inward, join the remaining arrow patches to each side of the fabric A large square; press seams over fabric A.

Complete the square With right sides together, pin and sew the top row to the center row, matching the seams. Join the bottom row. Press all seams open.

road to oklahoma

Join this block edge to edge to create a larger allover pattern. Try rotating alternate blocks by 90 degrees to create green stars within blue diamonds.

The seam allowance is ¼ inch throughout.

A
B
C
D
E
F

Fabric quantities

- Light green fabric A: 10 x 10 inches
- Light blue fabric B: 4 x 4 inches
- Light blue fabric C: 4 x 4 inches
- Medium blue fabric D: 4 x 4 inches
- Dark blue fabric E: 4 x 4 inches
- White fabric F: 13 x 15 inches

Prepare the patches

Rotary method
- From fabrics A and F, make four 3½-inch half-square triangles (see page 12)
- From fabrics B, C, and F and fabrics D, E, and F, make one 6½-inch four-patch square (see page 11) each
- From fabrics A and F, cut two 3½-inch squares each

or

Template cutting
Using the 4 x 4 templates (pages 269–73):
- From fabric A, cut 2 small squares and 4 small triangles
- From fabrics B, C, D, and E, cut 1 small square each
- From fabric F, cut 6 small squares and 4 small triangles

Template piecing

Sew a fabric A small triangle to a fabric F small triangle along the long diagonal edge; press seam over fabric A. Repeat to make another three half-square triangles.

To make two four-patch squares, sew each fabric B, C, D, and E small square to one side of a fabric F small square; press seam away from fabric F. With white squares in opposite corners, join the fabrics B and F strip to the fabrics C and F strip at the long edge; repeat to join the fabrics D and F strip to the fabrics E and F strip; press seams left.

Make the block

Piece two patches With right sides together, join a fabric A small square to two half-square triangles along a green edge, making sure the green triangles point down and left; press seams over the squares. Join two fabric F small squares to the remaining half-square triangles along a white edge, making sure the green triangles point down and right; press seams over the squares. Matching seams, join one of each strip to make a four-patch square with the green forming an arrow; press seams open. Repeat to make a second patch.

Complete the square With the green arrow pointing up and left, join the half-square triangle patch to the lighter blue four-patch square, making sure the fabric B square is in the upper right corner; press seam open. With the green arrow pointing down and right, join the half-square triangle patch to the right edge of the darker blue four-patch square, making sure the fabric E square is in the bottom left corner.

breezy bunting

The seam allowance is ¼ inch throughout.

This versatile new block resembles both a row of flags fluttering in the breeze, and the crenelated turret of an Italian Renaissance castle. Join edge to edge as a border or sew two blocks together for a long bolster cushion to add color to a plain sofa.

A
B
C
D
E

Fabric quantities

- Medium red fabric A: 4 x 9 inches
- Medium turquoise fabric B: 4 x 9 inches
- Dark turquoise fabric C: 4 x 9 inches
- Light blue print fabric D: 8 x 13 inches
- White fabric E: 10 x 13 inches

Prepare the patches

Rotary method
- From fabrics A and E, make two 3½-inch three-quarter square triangle (see page 13)
- From from fabrics B and E and fabrics C and E, make one 3½-inch three-quarter square triangle each
- From fabric D, cut two 12½ x 3½-inch rectangles
- From fabric E, cut four 3½-inch squares

or

Template cutting
Using the 4 x 4 templates (pages 269–73):
- From fabric A, cut 2 small triangles and 2 tiny triangles
- From fabrics B and C, cut 1 small triangle and 1 tiny triangle each
- From fabric D, cut 2 full-length rectangles
- From fabric E, cut 4 small squares and 4 tiny triangles

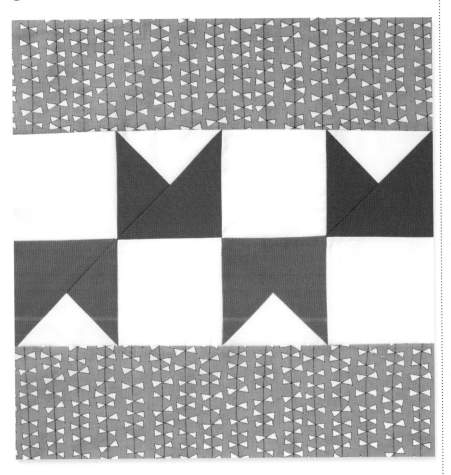

Template piecing

With right sides together, join a fabric A tiny triangle to a fabric E tiny triangle along the short edge, with the colored triangle on the left; press seams open. Join this half-square triangle (see page 12) to the long diagonal edge of a fabric A small triangle; press seams open. Repeat with fabric A, fabric B, and fabric C to make another three three-quarter square triangles.

Make the block

Sew two rows Sew a fabric E small square to the top edge of each three-quarter square triangle with the fabric E triangle pointing upward; press seams over the squares. Join these four units together at the long edges, alternating the direction of the patches, as shown above; press seams open.

Complete the square Join the fabric D full-length rectangles to the top and bottom edges; press seams open.

five square

This is one of six similar blocks that work well together as a sampler quilt. The others are Hen and Chicks (see page 83), Chinese Coin (see page 87), Monkey Wrench (see page 93), Alaska Homestead (see page 170), and Grandmother's Cross (see page 123). This block is most accurately made from templates.

Fabric quantities

- Medium turquoise fabric A: 10 x 10 inches
- Light turquoise fabric B: 6 x 6 inches
- Light blue print fabric C: 6 x 9 inches
- White fabric D: 12 x 16 inches

Prepare the patches

Template cutting
Using the 5 x 5 templates (pages 274–7):
- From fabric A, cut 8 small triangles
- From fabric B, cut 4 small squares
- From fabric C, cut 5 small squares
- From fabric D, cut 4 short rectangles and 8 small triangles

Template piecing

With right sides together, sew a fabric A small triangle to a fabric D small triangle along the diagonal edge; press seam over fabric A. Repeat to make another seven half-square triangles.

The seam allowance is ¼ inch throughout.

A
B
C
D

Make the block

Piece four corner squares Sew a fabrics A and D half-square triangle to the right edge of a fabric B square, with the white triangle pointing up and left; press seam over the square. Sew a fabrics A and D half-square triangle to the left edge of a fabric C square, with the white triangle pointing up and left; press seam over the square. Join the strips to make a four-patch square, matching the center seams with the fabric A triangles pointing in the same direction; press seam open. Repeat to make another three four-patch squares.

Make the rows For the top row, with right sides facing, pin and sew a four-patch square to each long side of a fabric D short rectangle, with the fabric A triangles pointing inward and down; press seams over fabric D. Repeat to make the bottom row.

Join fabric D short rectangles to each side of the remaining C square; press seams over fabric D.

Complete the square Flip the bottom row. With right sides together, pin and sew the top and bottom rows to the center row, matching the seams; press seams open.

broken dishes

Broken Dishes is a simple allover arrangement of half-square triangles that could be made in any size. In keeping with its name, the floral prints used here echo the patterns on vintage transfer-print ceramics.

The seam allowance is ¼ inch throughout.

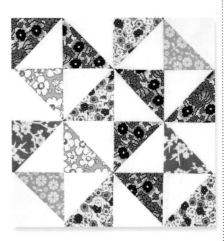

Fabric quantities

- 5 different medium gray and blue print fabrics A: 10 to 20 inches in total
- White fabric B: 10 x 20 inches

Prepare the patches

Rotary method
- From fabrics A and B, make sixteen 3½-inch half-square triangles (see page 12)

or

Template cutting
Using the 4 x 4 templates (pages 269–73):
- From fabrics A and B, cut 16 small triangles each

Template piecing

With right sides together, pin and sew a fabric B small triangle to each long diagonal edge of a fabric A small triangle to make 16 half-square triangles. Press seams over fabric A.

Complete the block

Arrange the patches Lay out the half-square triangles, alternating the white triangles to form pinwheels, as shown above, and balancing the colored triangles for colors and patterns.

Sew four rows For the first and third rows, with right sides together, pin and sew four half-square triangles, with the white triangles pointing down and right in the first and third squares, and up and right in the second and fourth squares; press seams open.

For the second and fourth rows, join four half-square triangles, with the white triangles pointing down and left in the first and third squares, and up and left in the second and fourth squares. Press seams open.

Complete the square With right sides together and carefully matching seams, pin and sew the first and third rows to the second row; press seams open. Join the fourth row to the third row; press seam open.

cross check

A classic geometric design sourced from an old reference book on Roman mosaic floors, this cross forms a stunning trompe l'oeil design when repeated edge to edge. Choose plain white fabric for the highlights, with two distinctive light and dark shades of another solid color for the other patches.

The seam allowance is ¼ inch throughout.

Fabric quantities

- Light blue fabric A: 7 x 12 inches
- White fabric B: 7 x 12 inches
- Dark blue fabric C: 8 x 8 inches

Prepare the patches

Rotary method
- From fabrics A and B, make four 6½-inch half-square triangles (see page 12)
- From fabric C, cut eight 3½-inch squares

or

Template cutting
Using the 4 x 4 templates (pages 269–73):
- From fabrics A and B, cut 4 diagonal boats each
- From fabric C, cut 8 small triangles

Rotary piecing

Following the instructions for making a hexagon square (see page 15), sew two fabric C squares to opposite corners of each half-square triangle, to make the four quarter squares.

Template piecing

With right sides together, pin and sew a fabric C small triangle to the short diagonal edge of each diagonal boat to make 8 triangles; press seams open. With right sides together, pin and sew the long edges of the fabric A diagonal boats to the long edges of the fabric B diagonal boats. Press seams over fabric A.

Make the block

Join two rows Lay out the four quarter squares so that the diagonal boats make a cross and fabrics A and B alternate. Matching the seams, join the top two blocks together and press the seam open. Join the bottom two together in the same way.

Complete the square With right sides together, pin and sew the top and bottom rows together, carefully matching the seams; press seam open.

old maid's puzzle

The seam allowance is ¼ inch throughout.

In the 1930s, Ruby McKim railed against the traditional name of this block, declaring that "there haven't been any 'old maids' in a generation, and 'bachelor girls' are not so easily puzzled!" More recently, certain feminist quilters have half-jokingly renamed it "Bachelorette." Whatever the story behind the block, it has a striking design, and it is far from puzzling to put together the pieces. McKim suggested making a quilt border by repeating the red hourglass square.

A
B
C
D

Fabric quantities

- Medium red fabric A: 5 x 10 inches
- Medium turquoise fabric B: 7 x 11 inches
- Medium blue fabric C: 7 x 11 inches
- White fabric D: 9 x 15 inches

Prepare the patches

Rotary method
- From fabrics A and D, make four 3½-inch half-square triangles (see page 12)
- From fabrics B and D and fabrics C and D, make one 6½-inch flying geese square (see page 15) each
- From fabric D, cut four 3½-inch squares

or

Template cutting
Using the 4 x 4 templates (pages 269–73):
- From fabric A, cut 4 small triangles
- From fabric B and C, cut 1 large triangle and 1 small triangle each
- From fabric D, cut 4 small squares and 10 small triangles

Template piecing

With right sides together, pin and sew a fabric A small triangle along the long diagonal edge of a fabric D small triangle to make a half-square triangle; press seam over fabric A. Repeat to make another three half-square triangles.

With right sides together, pin and sew a fabric B small triangle along the diagonal edge of a fabric D small triangle. Sew the straight edge of two fabric D small triangles to each straight edge of the fabric B small triangle in the square; press all seams toward fabric B. Join the fabrics B and D triangle to a fabric B large triangle along the diagonal edges to complete the flying geese square; press seam toward the fabric B large triangle. Repeat with fabrics C and D to make another flying geese square.

Make the block

Sew two patches With the red triangles pointing down and right, sew a fabric A half-square triangle to the left edge of each of the fabric D small squares. Sew these strips together in pairs, with the white squares in opposite corners, to make two hourglasses; press seams open.

Make two rows Arrange the four blocks so the large triangles meet at the center and the hourglasses lie at the top left and bottom right. With right sides together, pin and sew a half-square triangle patch to a flying geese square; press seam over the large triangle. Repeat with the second pair of patches.

Complete the square With right sides together, pin and sew the top and bottom rows together, making sure the red patches are placed diagonally; press seams open.

241

arkansas snowflake

A

B

C

The seam allowance is ¼ inch throughout

A gray-and-white star print, white linen salvaged from a vintage pillowcase, and a background the color of a wintry sky give a frosty, sparkling look to this block. Sometimes the center hourglass square is rotated by 90 degrees, turning the four points of the star into single-colored kite shapes. Because of the isosceles triangles, this block is most accurately pieced from templates.

Fabric quantities

- Medium gray print fabric A: 6 x 11 inches
- White fabric B: 6 x 11 inches
- Light blue fabric C: 10 x 20 inches

Prepare the patches

Template cutting
Using the 6 x 6 templates (pages 278–83):
- From fabrics A and B, cut 2 isosceles triangles and 2 medium triangles each
- From fabric C, cut 4 right half triangles, 4 left half triangles, and 4 large squares

Template piecing
With right sides together, join a fabric A medium triangle to each of the fabric B medium triangles to make two half-square triangles; press seams over fabric A.

Make the block

Piece the hourglass With right sides together, join the two half-square triangles along the long edge to make an hourglass square; press seams open.

Piece the triangles Sew the fabric C left and right half triangles to each of the diagonal edges of the fabric A and fabric B isosceles triangles, making sure they form square patches; press seams over fabric C.

Complete the square Lay out the squares in three rows of three, as shown above. With right sides together, pin and sew squares together to make each row; press seams away from fabric B. Join the three rows together, making sure the isosceles triangles point outward and matching the seams; press seams open.

242

crossbow

A

B

C

D

E

The seam allowance is ¼ inch throughout.

Using counterchange within a design—that is, alternating the arrangement of dark and light patches in a symmetrical pattern—gives a sophisticated look to this simple block.

Fabric quantities

- Dark turquoise fabric A: 8 x 8 inches
- Light turquoise fabric B: 7 x 7 inches
- Medium turquoise fabric C: 8 x 8 inches
- Dark blue fabric D: 7 x 7 inches
- Medium blue print fabric E: 11 x 16 inches

Prepare the patches

Rotary method
- From fabrics A and E and fabrics C and E, make one 6½-inch arrow square (see page 14) each
- From fabrics B and E, make one 6½-inch arrow square with a fabric B arrow
- From fabrics D and E, make one 6½-inch arrow square with a fabric D arrow

or

Template cutting
Using the 4 x 4 templates (pages 269–73):
- From fabrics A and C, cut 3 small triangles each
- From fabrics B and D, cut 1 arrow each
- From fabric E, cut 2 arrows and 6 small triangles

Template piecing

With right sides together, pin and sew a fabric A small triangle to each of the three straight edges of a fabric E arrow to make an arrow square; press seams over fabric A. Repeat to make another three arrow squares, joining three fabric C small triangles to the second fabric E arrow, and three fabric E triangles to the fabrics B and fabrics D arrows.

Make the block

Sew two rows Lay out the four squares with the points of the arrows meeting in the center and the blue print arrows in opposite corners. With right sides together, pin and sew the top two squares, then repeat with the bottom two squares; press seams open.

Complete the square With right sides together, pin and sew the top and bottom rows together; press seams open.

180

four ways

The seam allowance is ¼ inch throughout.

The arrows that make up this block give it a busy sense of continuous movement, emphasized by the windmill shape that appears in the negative space between the motifs. Four Ways will add animation to a sampler quilt, especially if the arrows are made from four different fabrics. It is a self-contained motif, so it makes a good cushion cover, especially on a larger scale.

A
B
C
D
E

Fabric quantities

- Dark blue fabric A: 4 x 11 inches

- Medium turquoise dot fabric B: 4 x 11 inches

- Medium lime green fabric C: 4 x 11 inches

- Medium turquoise fabric D: 4 x 11 inches

- White fabric E: 12 x 14 inches

Prepare the patches

Rotary method

- From fabrics A and E; fabrics B and E; fabrics C and E; and fabrics D and E, make one 6½ x 3½-inch flying geese rectangle (see page17) each

- From fabrics A, B, C, and D, cut one 3½-inch square each

- From fabric E, cut eight 3½ x 2-inch rectangles

Make the block

Complete the patches Sew a small fabric E rectangle to each side edge of the four small squares; press seams over the squares.

Sew the dark blue patch to a long edge of the fabric A matching flying geese rectangle, with the square adjacent to the long edge of the triangle to make an arrow, as shown above; press seams open. Repeat to make another three patches, matching the colors.

Make two rows Arrange the patches so the arrows point in a counterclockwise direction, as shown above. With right sides together, pin and sew the top and bottom pairs together; press seams left.

Complete the square With right sides together, pin and sew the top and bottom rows together, matching the seams; press seams open.

fireflies

The hourglass motifs here all lie in the same direction, and the plain yellow patches are set against a dusky blue background to suggest the darting movements of the fireflies that give the block its name.

A

B

Fabric quantities

- Medium yellow fabric A: 12 x 12 inches
- Medium blue print fabric B: 13 x 17 inches

Prepare the patches

Rotary method
- From fabrics A and B, make two 6½-inch flying geese squares (see page 15) and four 3½-inch half-square triangles (see page 12)

- From fabric B, cut four 3½-inch squares

or

Template cutting
Using the 4 x 4 templates (pages 269–73):
- From fabric A, cut 2 large triangles and 6 small triangles

- From fabric B, cut 4 small squares and 10 small triangles

Template piecing

With right sides together, sew a fabric A small triangle to the long diagonal edge of a fabric B small triangle to make a half-square triangle; press seam over fabric A. Repeat to make another three half-square triangles.

Sew a fabric A small triangle along the diagonal edge of a fabric B small triangle, then sew a fabric B small triangle to each side of the fabric A large triangle along the short edges; press seams toward fabric A. Join the fabrics A and B triangle to a fabric A large triangle along the diagonal edges to complete the flying geese square; press seams toward the large triangle. Repeat to make another flying geese square.

Make the block

Piece two patches Sew a fabric B small square to the right edge of each half-square triangle with the yellow triangles pointing down and right. Sew the units together in pairs to make hourglass squares; press seams over fabric A.

Complete the square Arrange all four blocks so the large triangles meet at the center and the hourglass squares lie at the top right and bottom left. Join the flying geese squares to the hourglass squares; press seams over fabric A. With right sides together, pin and sew the top and bottom rows, matching the seams; press seams open.

thrift four patch

The seam allowance is ¼ inch throughout.

The word "thrift" in a block name usually indicates that there's a scrappy element in its design, and that the patches are cut from random fabrics. The four large squares that form the center cross in this block are cut from four different greens.

Fabric quantities

- Medium blue print fabric A: 11 x 12 inches

- 4 different green fabrics B: 10 x 10 inches in total

- White fabric C: 6 x 12 inches

Prepare the patches

Rotary method
- From fabrics A and C, make four 4½-inch four-patch squares (see page 11)

- From fabric A, cut one 4½-inch square

- From fabrics B, cut four 4½-inch squares

or

Template cutting
Using the 6 x 6 templates (pages 278–83):
- From fabric A, cut 1 large square and 8 small squares

- From fabrics B, cut 4 large squares

- From fabric C, cut 8 small squares

Template piecing

With right sides together, sew each fabric A small square to a fabric C small square; press seams over fabric A. Pin and sew the long edge of each pair together, keeping colors opposite, to make one four-patch square; press seams open. Repeat to make another three four-patch squares.

Make the block

Sew the top and bottom rows With right sides together, join a four-patch square to each side of the darkest green large square; press seams inward. Repeat to make the bottom row, but using the lightest green large square.

Make the center row Join the remaining fabric B large squares to each side of the large fabric A square; press seams outward.

Complete the square With right sides together, pin and sew the three rows together, matching the seams; press seams open.

- -

dancing pinwheel

The seam allowance is ¼ inch throughout.

There is a lot going on in this traditional block, but using a dark fabric for the center triangles and neutral colors for the other patches keeps it looking contemporary.

Fabric quantities

- Light gray print fabric A: 11 x 16 inches

- Dark blue fabric B: 4 x 8 inches

- Medium gray print fabric C: 8 x 12 inches

Prepare the patches

Rotary method
- From fabrics A, B, and C, make four 6½ x 3½-inch flying geese rectangles (see page 17)

- From fabrics A and C, cut four 3½-inch squares each

or

Template cutting
Using the 4 x 4 templates (pages 269–73):
- From fabric A, cut 4 medium triangles and 4 small squares

- From fabric B, cut 4 small triangles

- From fabric C, cut 4 small squares and 4 small triangles

Template piecing

With right sides together, sew a fabric B small triangle to the left diagonal edge of a fabric A medium triangle. Sew a fabric C small triangle to the right edge of the medium triangle to complete the flying geese rectangle; press seams across the small triangles. Repeat to make another three flying geese rectangles, with the dark blue triangles on the left and the medium gray print triangles on the right.

Make the block

Piece four patches With right sides together, sew a fabric A small square to the right edge of each fabric C small square, keeping the pattern of the prints in the same direction; press seams open. Join these strips to the top edges of the flying geese rectangles, keeping the fabric A square on the right; press seams open.

Make two rows Lay out the four patches so the light gray print fabric triangles form a pinwheel in the center. With right sides together, pin and sew together in pairs to make the top and bottom rows.

Complete the square With right sides together, pin and sew the two rows together, being careful to match the points and seams; press seams open.

four square

This block is quick to make and an excellent way to reduce your stash. Choose four patches in different shades of the same color, or four completely different prints and hues. If you are using precut squares from a charm pack, you will need to adjust the proportions of the white rectangles to fit the size of your patches.

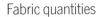

The seam allowance is ¼ inch throughout.

Fabric quantities

- Light blue print fabric A: 5 x 5 inches
- Medium blue print fabric B: 5 x 5 inches
- Dark blue print fabric C: 5 x 5 inches
- Dark blue fabric D: 5 x 5 inches
- White fabric E: 10 x 12 inches

Prepare the patches

Rotary method
- From fabrics A, B, C, and D, cut one 4½-inch square each
- From fabric E, cut four 6½ x 2½-inch rectangles and four 4½ x 2½-inch rectangles

or

Template cutting
Using the 6 x 6 templates (pages 278–83):
- From fabrics A, B, C, and D, cut 1 large square each
- From fabric E, cut 4 medium rectangles and 4 short rectangles

Make the block

Piece four patches With right sides together, pin and sew a fabric E short rectangle to the top edge of each blue large square; press seams outward. Sew a fabric E medium rectangle to the left edge of each unit; press seams outward.

Complete the square Lay out the four patches so the blue prints are all in the center, as shown above. With right sides together, pin and sew the top two patches together, then join the bottom two patches. Pin and sew the rows together to make the block; press seams open.

---

four-patch friendship star

Friendship Star is the traditional name for a motif made from four right triangles set around a square. Here, it is interpreted in dark blues and gold.

The seam allowance is ¼ inch throughout.

Fabric quantities

- Dark blue print fabric A: 6 x 12 inches
- Dark gold fabric B: 6 x 12 inches
- Dark blue fabric C: 5 x 5 inches
- Light yellow fabric D: 12 x 18 inches

Prepare the patches

Rotary method
- From fabrics A and D, make four 4½-inch half-square triangles (see page 12)
- From fabric B and D, make four 4½-inch four-patch squares (see page 11)
- From fabric C, cut one 4½-inch square

or

Template cutting
Using the 6 x 6 templates (pages 278–83):
- From fabric A, cut 4 large triangles
- From fabric B, cut 8 small squares

- From fabric C, cut 1 large square
- From fabric D, cut 4 large triangles and 8 small squares.

Template piecing

With right sides together, sew a fabric A large triangle along the long diagonal edge of a fabric D large triangle; press seam over fabric A to make a half-square triangle. Repeat to make another three half-square triangles.

With right sides together, sew each fabric B small square to a fabric D small square; press seam over fabric D. Join strips in pairs along a long edge with colors opposite; press seams open. Repeat to make another three four-patch squares.

Make the block

Sew three rows For the top row, join a four-patch square to each side of a half-square triangle, with the blue triangle

pointing down and left and the light yellow squares in the top outer corners; press seams outward. Repeat for the bottom row. For the center row, join a half-square triangle to each side of the dark blue square, with the blue triangles pointing toward the square; press seams over fabric C.

Complete the square Flip the bottom row. Join the top and bottom row to the center row, carefully matching seams; press seams open.

red, white, and blue

The seam allowance is ¼ inch throughout.

This historic block is traditionally made in a combination of red, white, and blue fabrics. Joined edge to edge in rows, the blocks create a red grid pattern on a blue background, reminiscent of tweed designs. This is best made from templates for a finished 12-inch square.

Fabric quantities

- Light blue print fabric A: 6 x 12 inches
- Dark blue fabric B: 6 x 6 inches
- Dark red fabric C: 6 x 12 inches
- White fabric D: 6 x 9 inches

Prepare the patches

Template cutting
Using the 5 x 5 templates (pages 274–7):
- From A, cut 8 small squares
- From B, cut 4 small squares
- From C, cut 4 short rectangles
- From D, cut 5 small squares

Template piecing

With right sides together, pin and sew a fabric D small square to a fabric A small square. Join a fabric A small square to a fabric B small square. Pin and sew the two strips together, with the fabric A squares in opposite corners to complete the four-patch square (see page 11). Repeat to make another three four-patch squares.

Make the block

Sew three rows With right sides together, pin and sew a red short rectangle to the right edge of a four-patch square, making sure the blue small square is in the bottom right corner; press seams over fabric C. Join a second four-patch square to the other side of the red short rectangle, with the blue small

square in the bottom left corner; press seams open. Repeat to make the bottom row.

For the center row, with right sides together, join the remaining red short rectangles to each side of a white small square; press seams over fabric C.

Complete the square Flip the bottom row. With right sides together, join the top and bottom four-patch rows to the center strip; press seams open.

---

bird's nest

The seam allowance is ¼ inch throughout.

The spotted prints used here are inspired by the textures found on birds' eggs and the clear blue skies of early spring.

Fabric quantities

- Medium gray print fabric A: 12 x 18 inches
- Medium turquoise print fabric B: 5 x 5 inches
- Light blue print fabric C: 5 x 5 inches
- Medium turquoise fabric D: 12 x 18 inches

Prepare the patches

Rotary method
- From fabrics A and D, make five 4½ -inch half-square triangles (see page 12)
- From fabrics B and C, cut one 4½-inch square each
- From fabric D, cut two 4½-inch squares

or

Template cutting
Using the 6 x 6 templates (pages 278–83):
- From fabric A, cut 5 large triangles
- From fabrics B and C, cut 1 large square each
- From fabric D, cut 2 large squares and 5 large triangles

Template piecing

With right sides together, sew a fabric A large triangle to a fabric D large triangle along the diagonal edges to make a half-square triangle; press seam over fabric D. Repeat to make another four half-square triangles.

Make the block

Sew three rows To make the first row, join three half-square triangles so the turquoise triangles point up and right; press seams open.

To make the second row, join a fabric D large square to the left edge of the fabric C large square; add a half-square triangle to the right edge. Press seams open.

To make the third row, join the fabric B large square to the left edge of a fabric D large square; join the remaining half-square triangle to the right edge. Press seams open.

Complete the square With right sides together, pin and sew the top and bottom rows to the middle row, carefully matching the points and seams; press seams open.

fruit basket

The seam allowance is ¼ inch throughout.

The handle of this basket block is made in three shades of turquoise flower print, but you could simplify the design by making all of the half-square triangles from the same dark green as the main basket. Alternatively, a selection of bright citrus solids would make the design live up to its name. This block is most accurately made from templates.

A
B
C
D
E

Fabric quantities

- Dark green print fabric A: 10 x 13 inches
- Dark turquoise print fabric B: 5 x 5 inches
- Medium turquoise print fabric C: 6 x 6 inches
- Light turquoise print fabric D: 5 x 5 inches
- White fabric E: 16 x 19 inches

Prepare the patches

Template cutting
Using the 5 x 5 templates (pages 274–7):
- From fabric A, cut 1 small square and 7 small triangles
- From fabric B, cut 2 small triangles
- From fabric C, cut 2 small squares and 2 small triangles
- From fabric D, cut 1 small triangle
- From fabric E, cut 1 very large triangle, 2 medium rectangles, 1 large triangle, and 7 small triangles

Template piecing

With right sides together, sew a fabric A small triangle to the long diagonal edge of a fabric E small triangle; press seam over the dark fabric. Repeat to make another six fabrics A and E half-square triangles. Repeat to make two half-square triangles each from fabrics A and E; fabrics B and C; and fabrics C and E. Make one half-square triangle from fabrics D and E.

Make the block

Piece the basket With right sides together, pin and sew a fabric A small triangle to the top edge of a fabric C small square, then join a fabric A small square to the bottom edge; press seams open.

Sew a fabric A small triangle to each of the top and left edges of the remaining fabric C small square; press seams open.

Sew the two strips to form the bowl of the basket, as shown above; press seams open. Join the patch along the diagonal edge of the fabric E very large triangle; press seam over fabric A.

Make the handle To form the right side of the handle, lay out the fabrics C and E, fabrics B and E, and fabrics A and E half-square triangles, as shown above. With right sides together, pin and sew the half-square triangles together; join this strip to the top edge of the basket.

Join the remaining four half-square triangles together, with the fabrics D and E half-square triangle at the top, followed by the fabrics C and E, B and E, and A and E half-square triangles. Join this strip to the left edge of the basket; press seams open.

Complete the square Sew the remaining two fabric A small triangles to the short ends of the fabric E medium rectangles, with the fabric A strips in opposite directions. Sew the strips to the right and bottom edges of the basket, making sure the fabric A triangles form the foot for the basket.

With right sides together, pin and sew the large fabric E triangle to the bottom right corner along the diagonal line formed by the fabric A triangles; press seam open.

big flower

A scaled-up version of Poppy on page 26, this splashy Pop Art flower is the perfect partner for Leaves on page 160. It's quick to piece from house patches.

The seam allowance is ¼ inch throughout.

Fabric quantities

- Medium turquoise fabric A: 7 x 14 inches
- Medium turquoise print fabric B: 7 x 7 inches
- Dark turquoise print fabric C: 7 x 7 inches
- Medium print fabric D: 3 x 3 inches
- Light yellow fabric E: 3 x 3 inches
- White fabric F: 6 x 6 inches

Prepare the patches

Rotary method

- From fabrics A, D, and F, make two 6½-inch house squares (see page 14) with fabric F on the left and fabric D on the right
- From fabrics B, E, and F, make one 6½-inch house square with fabric F on the left and fabric E on the right
- From fabrics C, E, and F, make one 6½-inch house square with fabric F on the left and fabric E on the right

or

Template cutting

Using the 4 x 4 templates (pages 269–73):
- From fabric A, cut 2 houses
- From fabrics B and C, cut 1 house each
- From fabrics D and E, cut 2 small triangles each
- From fabric F, cut 4 small triangles

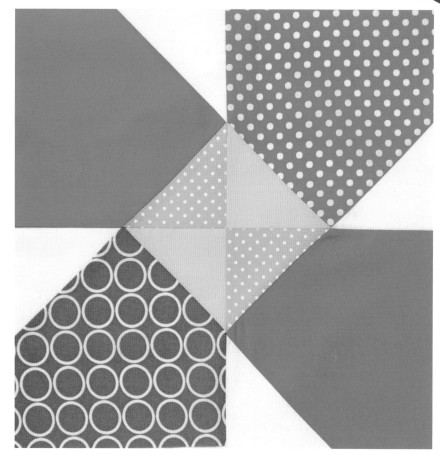

A
B
C
D
E
F

Template piecing

With right sides together, sew a fabric F small triangle to the left top edges of each house. Sew the fabric D small triangles to the top right edges of the fabric A house. Sew the fabric E small triangles to the top right edges of the fabric C house and the fabric B house; press seams over the houses.

Make the block

With right sides together, sew a medium turquoise house to the turquoise print house, joining the two yellow triangles at the center; press seam open. Repeat, joining the turquoise print house and a medium turquoise house.

Join the top and bottom rows, carefully matching the seams and points; press seam open.

little basket

The seam allowance is ¼ inch throughout.

Basket blocks always have a country feel, so emphasize the look by choosing feed-sack prints for the six half-square triangles on this small-scale version. The patterned yellow fabric echoes that of a woven wicker basket.

A
B
C
D

Fabric quantities

- Light blue print fabric A: 5 x 5 inches
- Medium blue print fabric B: 5 x 10 inches
- Dark yellow print fabric C: 7 x 12 inches
- White fabric D: 17 x 20 inches

Prepare the patches

Template cutting
Using the 4 x 4 templates (pages 269–73):
- From fabric A, cut 2 small triangles
- From fabric B, cut 4 small triangles
- From fabric C, cut 1 large triangle and 2 small triangles
- From fabric D, cut 2 short rectangles, 1 large triangle, and 8 small triangles

Template piecing

With right sides together, sew a fabric A s mall triangle to the long diagonal edge of a fabric D small triangle to make a half-square triangle; press seam away from fabric D. Repeat to make another half-square triangle with fabrics A and D and four half-square triangles with fabrics B and D.

To make the flying geese square, sew two fabric D small triangles to the bottom and right edges of a fabrics A and D half-square triangle; press seams over fabric A. Join this triangle to the fabric C large triangle along the diagonal edges; press seam over fabric C.

Make the block

Piece the basket With right sides together, pin and sew two fabrics B and D half-square triangles together, one on top of the other and making sure the blue print small triangles point down and right; join the strip to the left edge of the flying geese square making sure the fabric B small triangles point down and right; press seam open.

Join the remaining fabrics B and D half-square triangles side-by-side, making sure the fabric B small triangles point down and right; join the last fabrics A and D half-square triangle to the left edge of the strip. Press seams open, then sew the strip to the top edge of the flying geese square.

Join a fabric C small triangles to the ends of the fabric D short rectangles, with the two fabric C small triangles pointing in opposite directions; press seams open. Sew strips to the right and bottom edge of the block.

Complete the square Join the fabric D large triangle to the diagonal edge of the fabric C small triangles; press seam open.

sweet heart

A big blue patchwork heart is given added romance with a fabric featuring outline drawings of Parisian streets. You can add your own personal touch with a special print: a subway map, street plan, or patches cut from old garments. The four squares at the center of the heart could be replaced with a large single square cut from a figurative print.

A
A
A
A
A
B

Fabric quantities

- At least five different dark and medium blue solid and print fabrics A: 10 x 16 inches in total

- White fabric B: 10 x 13 inches

Prepare the patches

Rotary method
- From fabrics A and B, make eight 3½-inch half-square triangles (see page 12)

- From fabrics A, cut six 3½-inch squares

- From fabric B, cut two 3½-inch squares

or

Template cutting
Using the 4 x 4 templates (pages 269–73):
- From fabrics A, cut 6 small squares and 8 small triangles

- From fabric B, cut 2 small squares and 8 small triangles

Template piecing

With right sides together, pin and sew a fabric A small triangle to the long diagonal edge of a fabric B small triangle to make a half-square triangle; press seam over fabric A. Repeat to make another seven half-square triangles.

Make the block

Arrange the heart Lay out the patches in four rows of four squares, as shown above, with the white triangles on the outside; adjust the patches to balance the shades and patterns.

Sew four rows With right sides together, join two half-square triangles along the blue edges, creating a point at the top; press seam open. Repeat to make the second point of the heart. Join the strips along the white edges to make the top of the heart; press seams open.

For the second row, with right sides together, join four fabric A squares, alternating light and dark blues; press all seams open.

For the third row, join a half-square triangle to the right edge of a blue square, making sure the blue triangle points up and right; press seam open. Repeat, but making sure the blue triangle points up and left. Join the strips along the blue edges to form the middle of the heart; press seams open.

For the bottom row, join two half-square triangles along a blue edge. Join the remaining two fabric B white squares to the ends of the strip to make the bottom of the heart; press seams open.

Complete the square With right sides together, pin and sew the four rows together, carefully matching the seams; press seams open.

simple diamond pinwheel

The seam allowance is ¼ inch throughout.

A simple pinwheel resembling a child's toy is framed by four large triangles. Each "sail" is made from a different fabric for a colorful look. These patches could be cut from bright stripes to give an extra feeling of movement to the block.

A
B
C
D
E
F

Fabric quantities

- Medium orange fabric A: 4 x 7 inches
- Medium lime green fabric B: 4 x 7 inches
- Medium pink fabric C: 4 x 7 inches
- Light green fabric D: 4 x 7 inches
- Medium blue fabric E: 7 x 14 inches
- White fabric F: 4 x 8 inches

Prepare the patches

Rotary method
- From each of fabrics A, B, C, and D, cut one 6½ x 3½-inch rectangle
- From fabric E, cut four 6½-inch squares
- From fabric F, cut four 3½-inch squares

or

Template cutting
Using the 4 x 4 templates (pages 269–73):
- From each of fabrics A, B, C, and D, cut 1 right tapered rectangle
- From fabric E, cut 4 large triangles
- From fabric F, cut 4 small triangles

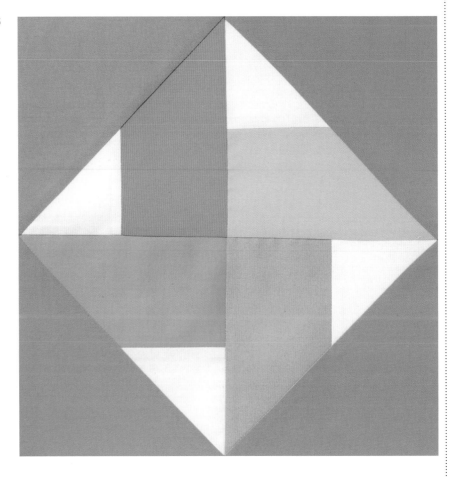

Rotary piecing

To make a patch, sew a fabric F square to the bottom left edge of the fabric A rectangle. Draw a diagonal line across the back of a fabric E square. With right sides together, pin the fabric E square to the fabrics F and A unit and stitch together along the line—there will be excess fabric. Cut the seam allowance to ¼ inch; press seam over the triangle. Repeat to make another three patches, using the fabrics B, C, and D rectangles.

Template piecing

Join the fabric F small triangles to the short left edges of each right tapered rectangle; press seam over the rectangle.

Make the block

Sew two rows With right sides together, sew the patches so the orange tapered rectangle is perpendicular to the lime green tapered rectangle; press seam open.

Repeat, joining the remaining patches so that the light green tapered rectangle is perpendicular to the pink tapered rectangle.

Complete the square With right sides together, pin and sew the rows together making sure the blue large triangles frame the pinwheel; press seams open.

faceted square

The seam allowance is ¼ inch throughout.

This trompe l'oeil geometric block shows its full potential when repeated edge to edge and made from three distinct light, medium, and dark fabrics.

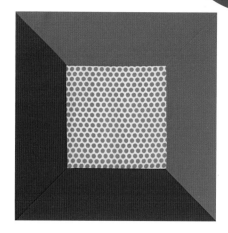

A
B
C

Fabric quantities

- Medium blue print fabric A: 7 x 7 inches
- Medium blue fabric B: 8 x 13 inches
- Dark blue fabric C: 8 x 13 inches

Prepare the patches

Template cutting
Using the 4 x 4 templates (pages 269–73):
- From fabric A, cut 1 large square
- From fabrics B and C, cut 2 long boats each

Make the block

Mark a seam allowance of ¼ inch around the short and diagonal edges of each long boat and the center square. Measure and mark the center of the seams.

With right sides together, pin and sew the short straight edge of a fabric B long boat centered on the top edge of the square, leaving the seam allowance open at each end. Join a fabric C long boat to the bottom edge in the same way. Repeat to join the second fabric B long boat to the right edge of the square and the other fabric C long boat to the left edge, leaving the ends unstitched.

Fold the block so the two diagonal edges at the top left corner line up. Sew along the marked line from the inner corner to the outer corner. Join the other three seams in the same way. Press the diagonal seams over fabric C and the straight seams over the boats.

big bow

The seam allowance is ¼ inch throughout.

Look at this bold block one way, and you'll see a blue bow on a white background. However, if you rotate it sideways, the motif turns into a white bow against a blue background. It can be scaled down using the small square and triangle templates.

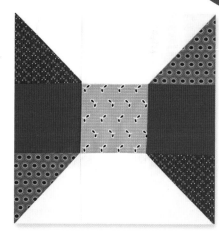

A
B
C
D
E

Fabric quantities

- Dark blue print fabric A: 6 x 6 inches
- Medium blue print fabric B: 6 x 6 inches
- Medium blue fabric C: 5 x 10 inches
- Medium gray print fabric D: 5 x 5 inches
- White fabric E: 11 x 11 inches

Prepare the patches

Rotary method
- From fabrics A and E and fabrics B and E, make two 4½-inch half-square triangles (see page 12) each
- From fabric C and E, cut two 4½-inch squares each
- From fabric D, cut one 4½-inch square

or

Template cutting
Using the 6 x 6 templates (pages 278–83):
- From fabrics A and B, cut 2 large triangles each
- From fabric C, cut 2 large squares
- From fabric D, cut 1 large square
- From fabric E, cut 2 large squares and 4 large triangles

Template piecing

With right sides together, sew a fabric A large triangle to the diagonal edge of a fabric E large triangle to make a half-square triangle; press seam over fabric A. Repeat to make a second half-square triangle. Repeat to make two half-square triangles from the fabric B and fabric E large triangles.

Make the block

Sew three rows For the top row, join a dark blue print half-square triangle to the left edge of a white large square; join a medium blue print half-square triangle to the right edge. Press seams away from fabric E. Repeat for the bottom row, then flip over. For the center row, sew a fabric C large square to both sides of the fabric D square; press seams over fabric C.

Complete the square Join the three rows together; press seams open.

richmond square

The seam allowance is ¼ inch throughout.

This simple arrangement of basic shapes makes a perfect frame for the center square of linen, which—like the white rectangles—was salvaged from an old hand-embroidered pillowcase. This block could be joined with white sashing and dark blue corner squares to create a showcase quilt for similar vintage fabrics.

Fabric quantities

- Dark blue fabric A: 6 x 10 inches
- Dark blue print fabric B: 10 x 10 inches
- White fabric C: 5 x 15 inches

Prepare the patches

Rotary method
- From fabrics A and C, make four 4½-inch rectangle squares (see page 11)
- From fabric B, cut four 4½-inch squares
- From fabric C, cut one 4½-inch square

or

Template cutting
Using the 6 x 6 templates (pages 278–83):

- From fabric A, cut 4 short rectangles
- From fabric B, cut 4 large squares
- From fabric C, cut 1 large square and 4 short rectangles

Template piecing

With right sides together, pin and sew each fabric A short rectangle to a fabric C short rectangle to make four rectangle squares; press seams away from fabric C.

Make the block

Sew three rows For the top row, sew a fabric B large square to each side of a rectangle square with fabric C uppermost; press seams over fabric B. Repeat to make the bottom row.

For the middle row, with fabric A on the inside, sew the remaining rectangle squares to the side edges of the fabric C square; press seams over fabric C.

Complete the square Flip the bottom row. With right sides together, pin and sew the three rows together; press seams open.

---

wild waves

The seam allowance is ¼ inch throughout.

This lively pattern of alternating triangles is made up of nine three-quarter square triangles. The block can easily be extended to make a full quilt top by adding more squares to the side and bottom edges. The negative space between the triangles forms a zigzag pattern, and the block can be set so that these run vertically, as here, or horizontally.

Fabric quantities

- At least 8 different solid and print fabrics A: 9 x 15 inches in total
- White fabric B: 17 x 18 inches

Prepare the patches

Rotary method
- From fabrics A and B, make nine 4½-inch three-quarter square triangles (see page 13)

or

Template cutting
Using the 6 x 6 templates (pages 278–83):
- From fabrics A, cut 9 medium triangles
- From fabric B, cut 9 large triangles and 9 medium triangles

Template piecing

To make a three-quarter square triangle, with right sides together, sew a fabric A medium triangle to a fabric B medium triangle, with fabric A on the right; press seam open. Sew a fabric B large triangle to the long edge of the fabrics A and B unit; press seam open. Repeat to make another eight three-quarter square triangles.

Make the block

Sew three rows Lay out the squares in three rows of three with the fabric A triangles pointing right in the top and bottom rows and left in the center row. Rearrange the squares until you have a well-balanced color arrangement.

With right sides together, pin and sew each row of three-quarter triangles together; press seams open.

Complete the square With right sides together, pin and sew the top and bottom rows to the center row; press seams open.

village

An album quilt is always a welcome gift for a small child. Search through these pages to find trees, forests, ships, seaside scenes, and assorted animals to combine with these little houses, which could act as the springboard for imaginative play or bedtime stories. You can use plain white sashing or join the blocks with squares of a solid color for a checkerboard effect.

The seam allowance is ¼ inch throughout.

A
B
C
D
E
F
G
H

Fabric quantities

- Medium red fabric A: 8 x 12 inches
- Medium red fabric B: 8 x 12 inches
- Dark red fabric C: 7 x 9 inches
- Dark blue print fabric D: 4 x 11 inches
- Dark blue fabric E: 4 x 6 inches
- Medium turquoise fabric F: 8 x 8 inches
- Light turquoise fabric G: 4 x 4 inches
- White fabric H: 9 x 12 inches

Prepare the patches

Template cutting
Using the 4 x 4 templates (pages 269–73):
- From fabric A, cut 1 small triangle
- From fabric B, cut 2 medium triangles
- From fabric C, cut 1 medium triangle, 1 small triangle, and one 2 x 1-inch rectangle
- From fabric D, cut 1 short rectangle and 1 small square
- From fabrics E, cut 1 small square and three 2 x 1-inch rectangles
- From fabric F, cut 3 small squares
- From fabric G, cut 1 small square
- From fabric H, cut 2 medium triangles and 4 small triangles

Make the block

Piece two rows of roofs Start by laying out the patches as shown. For the top row, sew a fabric A small triangle along the diagonal edge of a fabric H small triangle to make one half-square triangle; press seam open. Sew the small fabric C triangle to the left-hand edge of the fabric H medium triangle and press seam open. Sew the fabrics A and C small triangles together to complete the first roof; press seam open. Join the fabric B medium triangle to the right-hand edge of the fabric H medium triangle and press seam open. Sew the long edge of the small fabric H triangle to the right-hand edge of the fabric B medium triangle; press seam open.

For the bottom row, sew a fabric H small triangle to the left-hand edge of the fabric B medium triangle; press seam open. Join the left-hand edge of a fabric H medium rectangle to the right-hand edge; press seam open. Sew the left-hand edge of the fabric C medium triangle to the right hand edge of the fabric H medium triangle; press seam open. Complete by sewing the fabric H small triangle to the right-hand edge of the fabric C medium triangle; press seam open.

Make the houses For the top row of houses, join a fabric E square to the left edge of a fabric D square. Sew this strip to the right edge of the fabric D rectangle; press seams open.

For the second row of houses, with right sides together, pin and sew the remaining four blue and turquoise small squares together; press seams open.

Appliqué (see page 20) each of the 2 x 1-inch rectangles to the houses to make four doors, as shown above.

Complete the square With right sides together, pin and sew the top row of roofs to the top row of houses. Join the bottom row of roofs to the bottom row of houses. With right sides together, pin and sew the two panels together. Press all seams open.

snowballs and shooflies

The seam allowance is ¼ inch throughout.

Like its close cousins Nine-Patch Snowballs on page 89 and Hexagon Chain on page 215, Snowballs and Shooflies is seen at its best when repeated edge to edge as a quilt top. Interesting patterns are created between the squares. The hexagonal snowballs are cut from a busy printed fabric that picks up the colors from the solid and polka-dot patches.

A
B
C
D
E
F

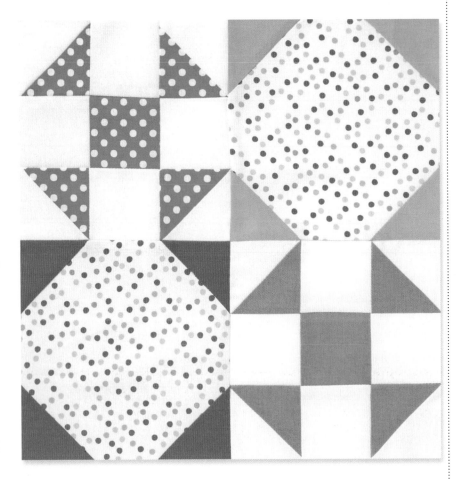

Fabric quantities

- Medium blue print fabric A: 8 x 11 inches
- Medium blue fabric B: 8 x 11 inches
- White print fabric C: 7 x 14 inches
- Light green fabric D: 3 x 6 inches
- Medium red fabric E: 3 x 6 inches
- White fabric F: 14 x 16 inches

Prepare the patches

Rotary method
- From fabrics A and F and fabrics B and F, make four 2½-inch half-square triangles (see page 12) each
- From fabrics C and D and fabrics C and E, make one 6½-inch hexagon square (see page 15)
- From fabrics A and B, cut one 2½-inch square each
- From fabric F, cut eight 2½-inch squares

or

Template cutting
Using the 6 x 6 templates (pages 278–83):
- From fabrics A and B, cut 1 small square and 4 small triangles each
- From fabric C, cut 2 hexagons
- From fabrics D and E, , cut 4 small triangles each
- From fabric F, cut 8 small squares and 8 small triangles

Template piecing

With right sides together, pin and sew a fabric F small triangle to each of the fabric A small triangles and fabric B small triangles, to make eight half-square triangles; press seams open.

With right sides together, pin and sew the fabric D small triangles to one fabric C hexagon to make a hexagon square; press seams over fabric D. Repeat with the fabric E small triangles to make the second hexagon square.

Make the block

Piece the shoofly patches With right sides together, pin and sew a fabrics A and F half-square triangle to each side of a fabric F small square, making sure the blue triangles point toward the center of the patch; press seams open. Repeat to make a second strip.

With right sides together, pin and sew a fabric F small square to each side of the fabric A small square; press seams open.

Flip the bottom strip. With right sides together, pin and sew the first and third strips to the second strip, carefully matching the seams; press seams open.

Repeat to make the second shoofly patch with fabrics B and F.

Complete the square With right sides together, pin and sew the fabrics A and F shoofly patch to the fabrics D and C hexagon square; press seams open.

With right sides together, pin and sew the fabrics B and F shoofly patch to the fabrics E and C hexagon square; press seams open.

Join the two halves of the block, with the shoofly patches in opposite corners and carefully matching the center seams; press seam open.

tall ship

The seam allowance is ¼ inch throughout.

Illustrative prints can add a light-hearted touch to a block. Paired with the fish on the green print for the sea, the blue seagull fabric is an ideal choice for the sky.

Fabric quantities

- Dark blue print fabric A: 11 x 15 inches
- White fabric B: 10 x 10 inches
- Medium brown fabric C: 4 x 13 inches
- Medium green print fabric D: 4 x 4 inches

Prepare the patches

Rotary method
- From fabrics A and B, make seven 3½-inch half-square triangles (see page 12)
- From fabrics C and D, make one 12½ x 3½-inch long boat (see page 17)
- From fabric A, cut one 6½ x 3½-inch rectangle and one 9½ x 3½-inch rectangle

or

Template cutting

Using the 4 x 4 templates (pages 269–73):
- From fabric A, cut 1 medium rectangle, 1 short rectangle, and 7 small triangles
- From fabric B, cut 7 small triangles
- From fabric C, cut 1 long boat
- From fabric D, cut 2 small triangles

Template piecing

With right sides together, pin and sew a fabric B triangle to each fabric A triangle to make seven half-square triangles; press seams open.

Sew the fabric D triangles to the diagonal edges of the fabric C long boat; press seams open.

Make the block

Piece the sails Join three pairs of half-square triangles with white triangles pointing down and right; press seams open. Join the strips into a column; press seams open.

With right sides together, sew the last half-square triangle to the bottom edge of the fabric A short rectangle, white triangle pointing down and right; press seam open. Matching seams, join the strip to the left side of the patch; press open. Add the fabric A medium rectangle to the right side of patch; press seam open.

Complete the square Join the long boat strip to the bottom of the patch; press seam over the long boat.

---

hole in the corner

The seam allowance is ¼ inch throughout.

A feedsack-style dress print gives an authentic period feel to this classic block. Reversing the balance of light and medium tones within the block, so that you have floral squares and white patches on the corner squares, gives an extra solidity to the design.

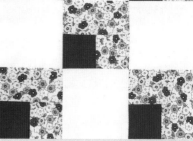

Fabric quantities

- Medium blue print fabric A: 12 x 14 inches
- Dark blue fabric B: 6 x 9 inches
- White fabric C: 10 x 10 inches

Prepare the patches

Rotary method
- From fabrics A and B, make five 4½-inch three-patch squares (see page 11)
- From fabric C, cut four 4½-inch squares

or

Template cutting
Using the 6 x 6 templates (pages 278–83):
- From fabric A, cut 5 short rectangles and 5 small squares

- From fabric B, cut 5 small squares
- From fabric C, cut 4 large squares

Template piecing

With right sides together, pin and sew a fabric A small square to the top edge of each fabric B small square; press seams open. Join a fabric A short rectangle to the right side of each strip, making five three-patch squares; press seams open.

Make the block

Sew three rows For the top row, with right sides together, pin and sew a three-patch square to each side of a white large square, making sure the dark blue squares are in the bottom left corner; press seams over the darker fabric. Repeat to make the bottom row.

For the middle row, with right sides together, pin and sew a white square to each side of the remaining three-patch square, making sure the dark blue square is in the bottom left corner; press seams over fabric C.

Complete the square With right sides together, pin and sew the first and third rows to the middle row, carefully matching the seams; press seams open.

crossroads

The seam allowance is ¼ inch throughout.

Like Windmill Sails (see page 164), this straightforward block has four rotating rectangles at its center. Long, thin patches are always a good way to display a striking print, such as this architectural fabric. The feeling of movement within the block is emphasized by the white patches that shadow the sails.

Fabric quantities

- Medium turquoise print fabric A: 10 x 10 inches
- White fabric B: 5 x 12 inches
- Medium blue print fabric C: 7 x 12 inches

Prepare the patches

Rotary method

- From fabric A, cut four 4½-inch squares
- From fabric B, cut four 4½ x 2½-inch rectangles
- From fabric C, cut four 6½ x 2½-inch rectangles

or

Template cutting

Using the 6 x 6 templates (pages 278–83):

- From fabric A, cut 4 large squares
- From fabric B, cut 4 short rectangles
- From fabric C, cut 4 medium rectangles

Make the block

Piece four patches With right sides together, pin and sew a fabric B short rectangle to the top of each fabric A large square; press seams open. Join a fabric C medium rectangle to the left side of each patch; press seams open. Repeat to make another three patches.

Make two rows For the top row, with right sides together, pin and sew a patch, with the white rectangle on the bottom, to another patch, with the white rectangle on the left and the blue rectangles perpendicular; press seam over fabric C. For the bottom row, join a patch with the white rectangle on the left to the last square, with the white rectangle on the top and blue rectangles perpendicular; press seam over fabric C.

Complete the square With right sides together and carefully matching seams, join the two strips with the blue rectangles meeting in the center of the block; press seams open.

---

crazy house

The seam allowance is ¼ inch throughout.

There is something unsettling about this block, as its name reflects—maybe it is the off-center blue patches. This block is most accurately made from templates.

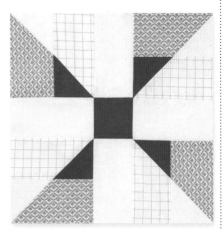

Fabric quantities

- Medium blue print fabric A: 6 x 12 inches
- Medium blue fabric B: 6 x 9 inches
- Light blue print fabric C: 6 x 12 inches
- White fabric D: 6 x 12 inches

Prepare the patches

Template cutting

Using the 5 x 5 templates (pages 274–7):

- From fabrics A and C, cut 4 left tapered rectangles
- From fabric B, cut 1 small square and 4 small triangles
- From fabric D, cut 4 short rectangles and 4 small triangles

Template piecing

With right sides together, pin and sew a fabric B small triangle to the short straight side of each fabric A left tapered rectangle to make four large patchwork triangles; press seams over fabric A.

With right sides together, pin and sew a fabric D small triangle to the short straight side edge of each fabric C left tapered rectangle to make four large patchwork triangles; press seams over fabric D.

Make the block

Piece the patches With right sides together, pin and sew a fabrics A and B patchwork triangle to each fabrics C and D patchwork triangle, aligning the blue triangle with the light blue left tapered rectangle, to make four large squares; press seams open.

Sew three rows For the top row, with right sides together, pin and sew a patch to each side of a fabric D short rectangle, with the blue triangles pointing outward; press seams open. Repeat to make the third row.

For the middle row, with right sides together, join a short edge of the remaining fabric D short rectangles to each side of the fabric B small square; press seams over fabric D.

Complete the square Flip the bottom row. With right sides together, pin and sew the top and bottom rows to the middle row, carefully matching the seams and maintaining the sharp points of the triangles; press seams open.

reels of cotton

Reels of Cotton is a smaller version of Cotton Reel on page 124, two blocks that make for an easy pairing. Inset or "Y" seams give a geometric precision to this design, which is also known as Bow Ties. The use of three distinct shades—light, medium, and dark—creates the illusion of three-dimensional space.

The seam allowance is ¼ inch throughout.

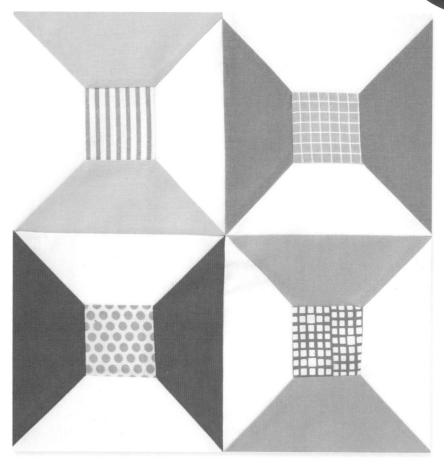

Fabric quantities

- Light green fabric A: 6 x 7 inches
- Light blue print fabric B: 3 x 3 inches
- Light blue fabric C: 6 x 7 inches
- Light turquoise print fabric D: 3 x 3 inches
- Medium green fabric E: 6 x 7 inches
- Medium green print fabric F: 3 x 3 inches
- Medium turquoise fabric G : 6 x 7 inches
- Medium turquoise print fabric H: 3 x 3 inches
- White fabric I: 12 x 14 inches

Prepare the patches

Rotary method
- From fabrics A, C, E, and G, cut two 6½ x 2½-inch rectangles each
- From fabrics B, D, F, and H, cut one 2½-inch square each
- From fabric I, cut eight 6½ x 2½-inch rectangles

or

Template cutting
Using the 6 x 6 templates (pages 278–83):
- From fabrics A, C, E, and G, cut 2 short boats each
- From fabrics B, D, F, and H, cut 1 small square each
- From fabric I, cut 8 short boats

Sewing set-in seams

To join the four cotton reel patches using set-in seams with rotary cut pieces, mark a diagonal line that slopes up from each bottom corner on all of the fabrics A, C, E, G, and I rectangles.

Mark a ¼ inch seam allowance on the upper edge of the rectangles, or short boats if template cutting, then mark the center of the edges.

Mark a ¼ inch seam allowance on all four edges of each of the fabrics B, D, F, and H small squares, then mark the center of the edges.

Center the top edge of a colored rectangle (or short boat) on the top edge of its corresponding small square. Pin and sew along the seam allowance, leaving the last ¼ inch open at each end. Repeat to join the matching medium rectangle or short boat to the bottom edge of the cotton reel patch. Repeat to sew the white medium rectangles to the patch.

Repeat with the remaining three pairs of colored medium rectangles and their corresponding small squares to make three more cotton reel patches.

For rotary cutting, pin the corners of the medium rectangles together and sew along each diagonal line. Trim the seams to ¼ inch.

Press the diagonal seams over the colored fabric and the straight seams outward.

Make the block

Sew two rows With right sides together, pin and sew the light green cotton reel patch to the light blue cotton reel patch, making sure they are perpendicular; press seam open.

With right sides together, pin and sew the turquoise cotton reel patch to the medium green cotton reel patch, making sure they are perpendicular; press seam open.

Complete the square With right sides together, pin and sew the two rows, alternating the green and blue cotton reel patches and carefully matching the seams; press seam open.

A
B
C
D
E
F
G
H
I

sunny hill

The green, blue, and white fabrics that make up Sunny Hill are inspired by the countryside in Wales, UK, in the peak of summer. The block is easy to piece, starting with the nine-patch square at the center. Join several blocks with narrow white sashing strips and small dark blue squares to produce an allover plaid pattern that resembles a Welsh woven blanket.

A
B
C
D

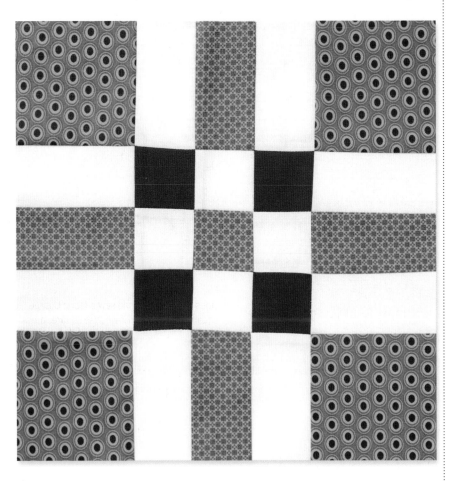

Fabric quantities

- Medium green print fabric A: 10 x 10 inches
- Medium blue print fabric B: 10 x 10 inches
- Navy blue fabric C: 7 x 7 inches
- White fabric D: 10 x 21 inches

Prepare the patches

Rotary method
- From fabric A, cut four 4 x 2¼-inch rectangles and one 2¼-inch square
- From fabric B, cut four 4-inch squares
- From fabric C, cut four 2¼-inch squares
- From fabric D, cut eight 4 x 2¼-inch rectangles and four 2¼-inch squares

or

Template cutting
Using the 7 x 7 templates (pages 284–5)
- From fabric A, cut 4 short rectangles and 1 small square
- From fabric B, cut 4 large squares
- From fabric C, cut 4 small squares
- From fabric D, cut 8 short rectangles and 4 small squares

Make the block

Piece the nine-patch square For the first row, with right sides together, pin and sew a fabric C small square to each side of a fabric D small square; press seams open. Repeat to make the bottom strip. For the middle row, with right sides together, pin and sew a fabric D small square to each side of the fabric A small square; press seams open.

With right sides together and carefully matching seams, pin and sew the first and third rows to the middle row to make a nine-patch square; press seams open.

Piece the striped patches With right sides together, pin and sew a fabric D short rectangle to each side of the fabric A short rectangles along the long edges to make four striped patches; press seams over fabric A.

Sew three rows For the middle row, with right sides together, pin and sew a striped patch to each side of the nine-patch square, carefully matching the seams and with the stripes horizontal; press seams open.

For the top and bottom rows, with right sides together, pin and sew a fabric B large square to each side of the remaining striped patches, making sure the stripes are vertical; press seams over fabric D.

Complete the square With right sides together and carefully matching the seams, pin and sew the first and third rows to the middle row; press seams open.

hidden star

The seam allowance is ¼ inch throughout.

Liberty of London's Tana lawn floral classics and seasonal special collections are a favorite source of inspiration to quilters worldwide. The fabrics blend together to create subtle drifts of color, and are thrown into relief against a white background. The two sweet pea fabrics seem to blend into each other, creating a hidden star.

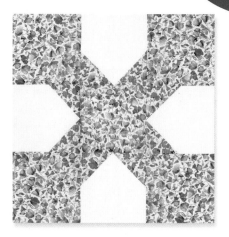

A
B
C

Fabric quantities

- Medium pink print fabric A: 6 x 6 inches
- White fabric B: 10 x 10 inches
- Medium blue print fabric C: 10 x 15 inches

Prepare the patches

Rotary method
- From fabrics A and B, make four 4½-inch house squares (see page 14)
- From fabric C, cut five 4½-inch squares

or

Template cutting
Using the 6 x 6 templates (pages 278–83):
- From fabric A, cut 8 small triangles

- From fabric B, cut 4 houses
- From fabric C, cut 5 large squares

Template piecing

With right sides together, pin and sew a fabric A small triangle to each diagonal edge of the fabric B houses; press seams open.

Make the block

Sew three rows For the top row, with right sides together, pin and sew a fabric C large square to each side of a house square; press seams over fabric C. Repeat for the third row.

For the middle row, with right sides together, pin and sew a house square to each side of the remaining fabric C large square, with the

pink triangles adjoining the white fabric; press seams over fabric C.

Complete the square Flip the bottom row. With right sides together and matching seams, join the first and third rows to the second row, with the houses pointing to the center; press seams open.

cogwheel

The seam allowance is ¼ inch throughout.

Also known as Prairie Queen, an historic name that recalls the American pioneer trail, this asymmetric block is a traditional pattern that is quick to assemble from four-patch squares and half-square triangles.

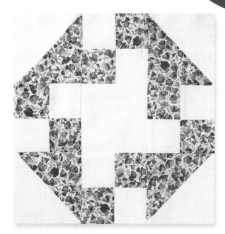

A
B

Fabric quantities

- Medium blue print fabric A: 12 x 12 inches
- White fabric B: 12 x 17 inches

Prepare the patches

Rotary method
- From fabrics A and B, make four 4½-inch half-square triangles (see page 12)
- From fabrics A and B, make four 4½-inch four-patch squares (see page 11)
- From fabric B, cut one 4½-inch square

or

Template cutting
Using the 6 x 6 templates (pages 278–83):
- From fabric A, cut 4 large triangles and 8 small squares
- From fabric B, cut 1 large square, 4 large triangles, and 8 small squares

Template piecing

With right sides together, pin and sew a fabric B large triangle along the long edge to each fabric A large triangle to make four half-square triangles; press seams over fabric A.

With right sides together, pin and sew a fabric A small square to each of the fabric B small squares; press seams over fabric A. Join two strips in pairs, alternating colors, to make four four-patch squares.

Make the block

Sew three rows For the top row, with right sides together, pin and sew a half-square triangle to each side of a four-patch square, making sure the blue triangles are pointing to the center of the block; press seams over fabric A. Repeat to make the bottom row. For the middle row, with right sides together,

join the remaining four-patch squares to each side of the fabric B large square; press seams open.

Complete the square Flip the bottom row. Join the top and bottom rows to the middle row; press seams open.

the go-between

Strong geometric designs, such as this square pinwheel superimposed on a diagonal cross, make good stand-alone blocks for cushion covers or for framing.

A
B
C
D

Fabric quantities

- Medium blue fabric A: 8 x 16 inches
- Medium turquoise print fabric B: 7 x 16 inches
- Light blue print fabric C: 5 x 10 inches
- White fabric D: 5 x 10 inches

Prepare the patches

Rotary method
- From fabrics A and B, make four 6½ x 3½-inch flying geese rectangles (see page 17)
- From fabrics C and D, make one 6½-inch pinwheel square (see page 13)
- From fabric A, cut four 3½-inch squares

or

Template cutting
Using the 4 x 4 templates (pages 269–73):
- From fabric A, cut 4 small squares and 8 small triangles
- From fabric B, cut 4 medium triangles
- From fabrics C and D, cut 4 small triangles each

Template piecing

With right sides together, join the fabrics C and D small triangles along the diagonal edges to make four half-square triangles; press seam over fabric C.

To make the pinwheel square, join two fabrics C and D half-square triangles along a light and dark edge; press seam toward the darker fabric. Repeat to make the second row, then join the rows along the long edge, with light fabric touching dark fabric and lining up seams; press seams open.

With right sides together, sew a fabric A small triangle to each diagonal edge of a fabric B medium triangle to make one flying geese rectangle; press seams across the small triangles. Repeat to make another three flying geese rectangles.

Make the block

Sew three rows With right sides together, sew a flying geese rectangle to each side of the pinwheel square, with triangles pointing inward. Sew a fabric A small square to each short edge of the remaining two flying geese rectangles for the top and bottom rows.

Complete the square With right sides together, join the top and bottom rows to the center row, with triangles pointing inward, matching seams and points; press seams open.

true blue

Three different shades of blue keep this patch true to its name. Rotate the center top and bottom four-patch squares 90 degrees to make Cogwheel on page 199.

The seam allowance is ¼ inch throughout.

A
B
C
D

Fabric quantities

- Light blue print fabric A: 11 x 12 inches
- Dark turquoise print fabric B: 6 x 12 inches
- Dark blue print fabric C: 6 x 12 inches
- White fabric D: 6 x 12 inches

Prepare the patches

Rotary method
- From fabrics A and B, make four 4½-inch four-patch squares (see page 11)
- From fabrics C and D, make four 4½-inch half-square triangles (see page 12)
- From fabric A, cut one 4½-inch square

or

Template cutting
Using the 6 x 6 templates (pages 278–83):
- From fabric A, cut 1 large square and 8 small squares
- From fabric B, cut 8 small squares
- From fabrics C and D, cut 4 large triangles each

Template piecing

With right sides together, pin and sew the fabric A small squares to the fabric B small squares; press seams over fabric B. With the fabric B small squares opposite one another, join two pairs together at the long edges to complete one four-patch square; press seams open. Repeat to make another three four-patch squares.

With right sides together, sew the fabric C large triangles along the diagonal edge of each fabric D triangle to make four half-square triangles; press seams over fabric C.

Make the block

Sew three rows With right sides together, pin and sew a half-square triangle to each side of a four-patch square so the dark blue print triangles point inward; press seam open. Repeat to make the bottom row.

With right sides together, join a four-patch square to each end of the fabric A large square, continuing the diagonal lines made by the turquoise print squares; press seams open

Complete the square Flip the bottom row. Carefully matching seams, join the top and bottom rows to the center row; press seams open.

autograph

The seam allowance is ¼ inch throughout.

Historically, this two-colored block was used to make presentation quilts. Each maker would write her name across the white rectangle patch in the center—hence, the name Autograph—then embroider over the writing to make a permanent record. Such quilts were made as a souvenir of friendship and community, often as a gift for a teacher or clergyman. Making it in a bright, modern solid color on a white background brings this block into the twenty-first century. This block is more accurately made with templates for a finished 12-inch square.

A

B

Fabric quantities

- Medium turquoise fabric A: 15 x 16 inches
- White fabric B: 15 x 21 inches

Prepare the patches

Template cutting
Using the 5 x 5 templates (pages 274–7):
- From fabric A, cut 8 small squares and 8 small triangles
- From fabric B, cut 1 medium rectangle, 6 small squares, and 8 small triangles

Template piecing

With right sides together, pin and sew a fabric B small triangle to each of the fabric A small triangles to make eight half-square triangles; press seams open.

Make the block

Piece four arrow patches With right sides together, pin and sew a half-square triangle to the right edge of a white small square, making sure the turquoise triangle points down and left; press seam open.

With right sides together, pin and sew a half-square triangle to the left edge of a turquoise small square, making sure the turquoise triangle points up and right; press seam open.

Join the strips to make an arrow, with the turquoise triangles adjacent to the turquoise square and carefully matching the seams; press seam open.

Repeat to make another three patches.

Sew five rows With right sides together, pin and sew a fabric A small square to the top edge of a fabric B small square; press seam open. Repeat, joining the fabric A small square to the bottom edge of the fabric B small square.

To make the first and third rows, join an arrow patch to each long side of each fabrics A and B strip, making sure the arrows will point toward the center of the block and the fabric A square is on the outside; press seams open.

To make the center row, pin and sew the remaining turquoise small squares to each short end of the white rectangle; press seams open.

Complete the square With right sides together and carefully matching the seams, pin and sew the first and third rows to the center row; press seams open.

square cross

The seam allowance is ¼ inch throughout.

A simple but effective block, Square Cross is ideal for making a quick quilt. The inner rectangles are cut randomly from a small piece of fabric, so the cross doesn't appear symmetrical.

Fabric quantities

- Medium blue print fabric A: 9 x 11 inches
- Medium gray print fabric B: 10 x 16 inches

Prepare the patches

Rotary method
- From fabrics A and B, make four 4½-inch rectangle squares (see page 11)
- From fabric A, cut one 4½-inch square
- From fabric B, cut four 4½-inch squares

or

Template cutting
Using the 6 x 6 templates (pages 278–83):
- From fabric A, cut 1 large square and 4 short rectangles
- From fabric B, cut 4 large squares and 4 short rectangles

Template piecing

With right sides together, pin and sew a fabric A short rectangle to a long edge of each of the fabric B short rectangles to make four rectangle squares; press seams over fabric A.

Make the block

Sew three rows For the first row, with right sides together, pin and sew a fabric B large square to each side of a fabrics A and B rectangle square, making sure the rectangles are horizontal and the blue edge abuts the center of the square; press seams over fabric A. Repeat to make the third row.

For the middle row, with right sides together, pin and sew a fabrics A and B rectangle square to each side of the fabric A large square, making sure the rectangles are vertical and the blue edges abut the center square; press seams over fabric B.

Complete the square With right sides together, pin and sew the first and third rows to the second row, carefully matching the seams and blue edges; press seams open.

- -

nine patch

The seam allowance is ¼ inch throughout.

One of the oldest and simplest blocks, Nine Patch can be found as an element within many other blocks, including Hexagon Chain on page 215 and Tic-Tac-Toe on page 250. By itself and on a larger scale, Nine Patch powerfully highlights small-scale prints and strong solid colors.

Fabric quantities

- Light blue print fabric A: 10 x 15 inches
- Dark blue fabric B: 10 x 10 inches

Prepare the patches

Rotary method
- From fabric A, cut five 4½-inch squares
- From fabric B, cut four 4½-inch squares

or

Template cutting
Using the 6 x 6 templates (pages 278–83):
- From fabric A, cut 5 large squares
- From fabric B, cut 4 large squares

Make the block

Sew three rows For the first row, with right sides together, pin and sew a fabric B large square to each side of a fabric A large square; press seams over fabric A. Repeat to make the third row.

With right sides together, pin and sew a fabric A large square to each side of a fabric B large square; press seams over B.

Complete the square With right sides together and carefully matching the seams, pin and sew the first and third rows to the second row; press seams open.

bricks and mortar

Quilt blocks are often associated with brightly colored and densely patterned fabrics, but working with a muted palette creates a sophisticated, pared-down look. These rows of neutral gray and putty shades are paired with indigo and duck egg blue, bordered with plain white strips. Bricks and Mortar is a toned-down patchwork block that stands well on its own as a cushion cover, or several can be combined to make an entire quilt.

A
A
A
A
A
A
A
B

The seam allowance is ¼ inch throughout.

Fabric quantities

- At least 6 different medium blue and gray solid and print fabrics A: 13 x 15 inches in total
- White fabric B: 13 x 8 inches

Prepare the patches

Rotary method

- From fabrics A, cut ten 4½ x 2½-inch rectangles and four 2½-inch squares
- From fabric B, cut four 12½ x 1½-inch rectangles

or

Template cutting

Using the 6 x 6 templates (pages 278–83):

- From fabrics A, cut 10 short rectangles and 4 small squares
- From fabric B, cut four narrow full-length rectangles

Make the block

Sew four rows Lay out the fabrics A patches in four rows, as shown above, arranging them with a good balance of colors and shades. The first and third row should have three colored rectangles. The second and fourth rows should have two colored rectangles and a colored square at each end.

With right sides together, pin and sew the patches in each row; press seams open. Join a fabric B rectangle to the top of each row; press seams open.

Complete the square With right sides together, pin and sew the first and second rows together; join the third and fourth rows, then press seams open. Join the two halves; press seam open.

---

alexander's star

Counterchange—where the colors of a motif and its background are reversed in an adjacent part of the same design—is especially effective in Alexander's Star.

A
B

The seam allowance is ¼ inch throughout.

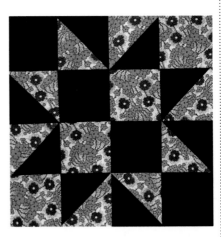

Fabric quantities

- Dark blue print fabric A: 12 x 20 inches
- Medium blue print fabric B: 12 x 20 inches

Prepare the patches

Rotary method

- From fabrics A and B, make eight 3½-inch half-square triangles (see page 12)
- From fabrics A and B, cut four 3½-inch squares each

or

Template cutting

Using the 4 x 4 templates (pages 269–73):

- From fabrics A and B, cut 4 small squares and 8 small triangles each

Template piecing

Sew each fabric A small triangle to a fabric B small triangle to make eight half-square triangles; press seams open.

Make the block

Piece four patches For the top left patch, with right sides together, pin and sew a dark blue small square to the blue print edge of a half-square triangle, with the dark blue triangle pointing up and right; press seam open.

With right sides together, join a blue print small square to the right edge of a half-square triangle along the blue print edge, with the dark blue triangle pointing down and left; press seam open.

Join the strips to make a path with a blue print hourglass in the center; press seams open. Repeat for the bottom right patch.

Repeat for the top right and bottom left patches using the fabric B small squares and paying attention to the directions of the blue triangles.

Complete the square Lay out the patches with solid squares meeting in the center and alternating, as shown above. With right sides together, pin and sew the top left and top right patches together, carefully matching seams; press seam open.

With right sides together, join the bottom left and bottom right patches together, carefully matching seams; press seam open.

Join the two halves, carefully matching seams; press seam open.

starry night

Making this detailed block will involve skill and patience, because it is composed of 41 individual patches. However, the results are worth the time invested. Starry Night was first published in the late nineteenth century, and the two-colored starburst design is as effective today as it was then. Before committing to making an entire quilt from this block, try making a single one for a cushion cover.

The seam allowance is ¼ inch throughout.

A

B

Fabric quantities

- Dark blue fabric A: 18 x 20 inches
- Light blue print fabric B: 12 x 16 inches

Prepare the patches

Rotary method
- From fabrics A and B, make eight 2½-inch half-square triangles (see page 12) and four 4½ x 2½-inch flying geese rectangles (see page 17)

- From fabric A, cut eight 2½-inch squares

- From fabric B, cut one 4½-inch square and four 4½ x 2½-inch rectangles

or

Template cutting
Using the 6 x 6 templates (pages 278–83):
- From fabric A, cut 4 medium triangles, 8 small squares, and 8 small triangles

- From fabric B, cut 1 large square, 4 short rectangles, and 16 small triangles

Template piecing

With right sides together, pin and sew a fabric A small triangle to each of the fabric B small triangles to make eight half-square triangles; press seams open.

With right sides together, pin and sew two fabric B small triangles to each of the fabric A medium triangles to make four flying geese rectangles; press seams open.

Make the block

Piece four hourglass patches With right sides together, pin and sew a fabric A small square to the right edge of a half-square triangle, making sure the light blue print triangle points up and right. Repeat to make another three strips; press seams open.

With right sides together, pin and sew a fabric A small square to the left edge of a half-square triangle, making sure the light blue print triangle points up and left. Repeat to make another three strips; press seams open.

Join the strips in sets of two to make four patches, each with a light blue print hourglass in the center; press seam open.

Make flying geese patches With the triangles pointing up, pin and sew a blue print short rectangle to the bottom edge of each flying geese rectangle; press seams open.

Sew three rows To make the top row, with right sides together and carefully matching seams, pin and sew a half-square triangle patch to each side of a flying geese patch, making sure the flying geese rectangles point to the center of the block. Repeat for the third row.

For the middle row, with right sides together, pin and sew a flying geese patch to each side of the fabric B large square, making sure the flying geese rectangles point toward the center of the block; press seams open.

Complete the square With right sides together and carefully matching seams, pin and sew the first and third rows to the second row; press seams open.

secret star

The seam allowance is ¼ inch throughout.

Secret Star is relatively straightforward, made from diamond squares and half-square triangles set around a plain center square. Stitch this block carefully to keep the triangle points looking sharp and crisp. The solid colors used here have an Amish-like plainness, but the block would look different if made from floral print triangles with pastel plains instead of white patches.

A
B
C

Fabric quantities

- Dark blue fabric A: 9 x 12 inches
- Medium purple fabric B: 6 x 6 inches
- White fabric C: 11 x 20 inches

Prepare the patches

Rotary method
- From fabrics A and B, make four 4½-inch half-square triangles (see page 12)
- From fabrics A, B, and C, make four 4½-inch diamond squares (see page 15)
- From fabric C, cut one 4½-inch square

or

Template cutting
Using the 6 x 6 templates (pages 278–83):
- From fabric A, cut 4 large triangles and 8 small triangles
- From fabric B, cut 8 small triangles
- From fabric C, cut 1 large square, 4 large triangles, and 4 diamond squares

Template piecing

With right sides together, pin and sew a fabric A large triangle to each of the fabric C large triangles to make four half-square triangles; press seams open.

With right sides together, pin and sew two fabric A small triangles to adjoining diagonal sides of each of the fabric C diamond squares. Join two fabric B small triangles to the other adjoining diagonal sides of the fabric C diamond squares; press seams open.

Make the block

Sew three rows For the top row, with right sides together, pin and sew two half-square triangles to each side of a diamond square with the large white triangles and the small blue triangles pointing to the center of the block; press seams open. Repeat for the third row.

For the middle row, with right sides together, pin and sew the remaining diamond squares to each side of the fabric C large square, with the small blue triangles pointing to the center of the block; press seams open.

Complete the square Flip the third row. With right sides together and carefully matching seams, pin and sew the first and third rows to the second row; press seams open.

at the window

The seam allowance is ¼ inch throughout.

A fat quarter bought from a New York quilt shop was the inspiration behind this graphic block. The outline illustration of clustered skyscrapers is seen through a window made up from four perspective square units.

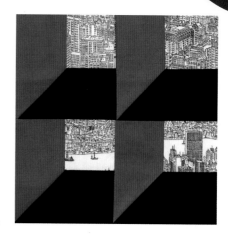

A
B
C

Fabric quantities

- White print fabric A: 8 x 8 inches
- Medium blue fabric B: 8 x 14 inches
- Dark blue fabric C: 8 x 14 inches

Prepare the patches

Rotary method

- From fabrics A, B, and C, make four 6½-inch perspective squares (see page 18)

or

Template cutting

Using the 4 x 4 templates (pages 269–73):

- From fabric A, cut 4 small squares
- From fabric B, cut 4 right tapered rectangles
- From fabric C, cut 4 left tapered rectangles

Mark the seams

Mark the ¼-inch seam allowances on the diagonal edges and the shorter of the long edges of the tapered rectangles. Then mark ¼-inch seam allowances around the squares.

Template piecing

With right sides together, pin and sew a fabric B right tapered rectangle to a fabric C left tapered rectangle, stopping ¼ inch from the ends, where the marked lines meet. Join a fabric A small square along each of the short edges; press seams open. Repeat to make another three perspective squares.

Make the block

Sew two rows With right sides together, pin and sew two perspective squares together, making sure the tapered rectangles point down and left; press seam open. Repeat with the second set of perspective squares.

Complete the square With right sides together, pin and sew the two halves of the block together, carefully matching seams in the middle; press seam open.

dutchman's puzzle

The seam allowance is ¼ inch throughout.

Maybe the traditional name of this block, which is also known as Flying Dutchman, comes from its resemblance to the whirling sails of a windmill. It's pieced from eight flying geese rectangles, all pointing in a clockwise direction.

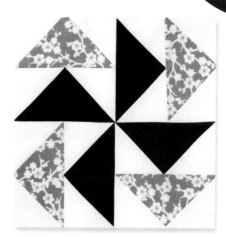

A
B
C

Fabric quantities

- Dark blue fabric A: 8 x 14 inches
- Medium gray print fabric B: 8 x 14 inches
- White fabric C: 8 x 16 inches

Prepare the patches

Rotary method

- From fabrics A and C and fabrics B and C, make four 6½ x 3½-inch flying geese rectangles (see page 17) each

or

Template cutting

Using the 4 x 4 templates (pages 269–73):

- From fabrics A and B, cut 4 medium triangles each
- From fabric C, cut 16 small triangles

Template piecing

With right sides together, pin and sew a fabric C small triangle to each of the diagonal edges of the fabric A medium triangles and the fabric B medium triangles to make eight flying geese rectangles; press seams open.

Make the block

Piece four patches With right sides together, pin and sew a gray print flying geese rectangle to the top edge of each of the dark blue flying geese rectangles, making sure all of them point up; press seams open.

Make two rows With right sides together, pin and sew two patches together, with the flying geese in the left patch pointing up and the flying geese in the right patch pointing right; press seam open.

With right sides together, pin and sew two patches together with the flying geese in the left patch pointing left and the flying geese in the right patch pointing down; press seam open.

Complete the square Join the two halves of the block, making sure the fabric B triangles meet in the middle, and being careful to maintain the sharp points of the flying geese rectangles; press seam open.

cross

The seam allowance is ¼ inch throughout.

The two diagonal lines between the patches give Cross its name. Try replacing the dark fabric with a lighter color and the green with floral prints for a softer look.

A
B
C
D

Fabric quantities

- Dark blue fabric A: 11 x 12 inches
- Light green fabric B: 11 x 12 inches
- Medium turquoise fabric C: 6 x 6 inches
- Dark blue fabric D: 6 x 6 inches

Prepare the patches

Rotary method
- From fabrics A and B, make four 4½-inch half-square triangles (see page 12)
- From fabrics C and D, make one 4½-inch hourglass square (see page 13)
- From fabrics A and B, cut two 4½-inch squares each

or

Template cutting
Using the 6 x 6 templates (pages 278–83):
- From fabrics A and B, cut 2 large squares and 4 large triangles each
- From fabrics C and D, cut 2 medium triangles each

Template piecing

With right sides together, join a fabric A large triangle to each fabric B large triangle to make four half-square triangles; press seams open.

With right sides together, pin and sew a fabric D medium triangle to the left short side of each fabric C medium triangle; press seams open. Join the strips along the long edge to make the hourglass square; press seam open.

Make the block

Sew three rows With right sides together, pin and sew a half-square triangle to each side of a fabric A square with the blue triangles pointing inward; press seams over fabric B. Repeat for the third row.

For the middle row, join the fabric B large squares to each turquoise side of the hourglass square; press seams over fabric A.

Complete the square With right sides together, join the first and third rows to the middle row, matching seams; press seam open.

lucky horseshoes

The seam allowance is ¼ inch throughout.

Although not exactly a horseshoe, this block should bring good fortune to the maker. Join several blocks edge to edge to create an angular allover pattern of alternate light and dark motifs, but keep them within a narrow color range.

Fabric quantities

- Medium blue print fabric A: 9 x 13 inches
- Dark blue print fabric B: 12 x 13 inches
- Light blue print fabric C: 5 x 6 inches

Prepare the patches

Rotary method
- From fabric A, cut two 6½ x 2½-inch rectangles and four 4½ x 2½-inch rectangles
- From fabric B, cut two 6½ x 2½-inch rectangles and six 4½in x 2½-inch rectangles
- From fabric C, cut two 4½ x 2½-inch rectangles

or

Template cutting
Using the 6 x 6 templates (pages 278–83):
- From fabric A, cut 2 medium rectangles and 4 short rectangles
- From fabric B, cut 2 medium rectangles and 6 short rectangles
- From fabric C, cut 2 short rectangles

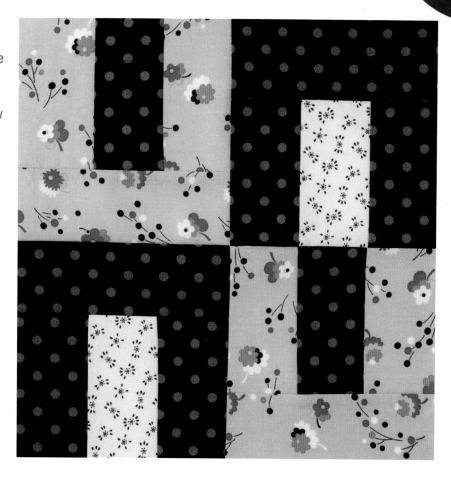

A

B

C

Make the block

Piece the horseshoe patches With right sides together, pin and sew a fabric A short rectangle to each side of two fabric B short rectangles; press seams open. Join a fabric A medium rectangle to a long edge of each patch; press seams open. Repeat to make a second patch.

With right sides together, pin and sew a fabric B short rectangle to each side of a fabric C short rectangle; press seams open. Join a fabric B medium rectangle to a long edge of each patch; press seams open. Repeat to make a second patch.

Make two rows With right sides together, pin and sew a light horseshoe patch, pointing up, to the left edge of a dark horseshoe patch, pointing down; press seam open.

With right sides together, join a light horseshoe patch, pointing up, to the right edge of a dark horseshoe patch, pointing down; press open.

Complete the square Join the two halves, matching seams; press seam open.

japanese lattice

The seam allowances are ¼ inch along the short edges and ⅕ inch along the long edges.

A Japanese indigo shibori fabric, with its scattering of small tie-dye motifs, is combined with plain white linen to produce this geometric block. Repeat the four square units in the top left corner for an allover lattice design of elongated "H" shapes interwoven with white lines. This geometric block is easily made using the rotary method. The rectangles should be joined with a slightly narrower seam allowance than usual—a fifth of an inch along the long edges to create a perfect 4½-inch square.

Fabric quantities

- Dark blue print fabric A: 10 x 20 inches
- White fabric B: 10 x 15 inches

Prepare the patches

Rotary method
- From fabric A, cut sixteen 4½ x 1¾-inch rectangles
- From fabric B, cut eleven 4½ x 1¾-inch rectangles

Template piecing

Piece nine squares With right sides together, pin and sew a fabric A rectangle to each long edge of seven fabric B rectangles; press seams over fabric A.

With right sides together, pin and sew a fabric B rectangle to each long edge of the remaining two fabric A rectangles; press seams over fabric A.

Make the block

Make three rows For the top row, with right sides together, pin and sew a patch with two blue stripes to each end of a patch with one blue stripe; make sure the stripe in the center patch is horizontal and the stripes in the side patches are vertical; press seams over fabric A. Repeat to make the third row.

For the middle row, with right sides together, pin and sew a patch with two blue stripes to each end of another patch with two blue stripes; make sure the stripes in the center patch are vertical and the stripes in the side patches are horizontal; press seams over fabric A.

Complete the square With right sides together, pin and sew the first and third rows to the second row, carefully matching seams; press seams open.

little boxes

Like the At the Window block on page 207, Little Boxes is an optical illusion. It creates the impression of four hollow boxes when you use a dark and a light shade of the same color for each box on a solid white background. This patch is most accurately made from templates.

The seam allowance is ¼ inch throughout.

Fabric quantities

- Medium red fabric A: 6 x 12 inches
- Light orange fabric B: 6 x 8 inches
- Dark purple fabric C: 6 x 12 inches
- Light purple fabric D: 6 x 8 inches
- White fabric E: 6 x 12 inches

Prepare the patches

Template cutting
Using the 6 x 6 templates (pages 278–83):
- From fabrics A and C, cut 2 long left tapered rectangles and 2 right tapered rectangles (see page 16) each
- From fabrics B and D, cut 2 short rectangles and 2 small squares each
- From fabric E, cut 4 small squares and 8 small triangles

Template piecing

With right sides together, pin and sew the fabric E small triangles to the diagonal edge of each fabric A and fabric C tapered rectangle; press seams away from fabric E.

With right sides together, pin and sew a small fabric E square to each of the fabric B and fabric D small squares; press seams away from fabric E. Join each strip to the matching short rectangle, with the fabric E square in the top right corner, to complete each three-patch square; press seams away from fabric E.

Make the block

Piece four patches With right sides together, pin and sew a medium red right tapered rectangle to the right edge of each light orange three-patch square, making sure the white triangles are in the bottom right corner; press seams open. Join the medium red long left tapered rectangle to the top edge of each patch; press seams open.

With right sides together, pin and sew a dark purple right tapered rectangle to the right edge of each light purple three-patch square, making sure the white triangles are in the bottom right corner; press seams open. Join the dark purple long left tapered rectangle to the top edge of each patch.

Complete the square With right sides together, pin and sew a purple patch to the right edge of an orange and red patch; press seams open. With right sides together, pin and sew an orange and red patch to the right edge of a purple patch; press seams open.

Carefully matching seams, join the two rows, making sure the white triangles meet in the center of the block; press seam open.

oh! susanna

The seam allowance is ¼ inch throughout.

Oh! Susanna is a new version of an old block, made in a simple way that avoids inset seams. Each colored square is cut from a different fabric for a scrappy look.

Fabric quantities

- 10 different medium and dark blue solid and print fabrics A: 8 x 20 inches in total
- 2 different dark purple fabrics B: 4 x 8 inches in total
- White fabric C: 7 x 18 inches

Prepare the patches

Rotary method
- From fabrics A, B, and C, make one 6½-inch diamond square (see page 15)
- From fabrics A, cut eight 3½-inch squares
- From fabric C, cut four 3½-inch squares

or

Template cutting
Using the 4 x 4 templates (pages 269–73):
- From fabric A, cut 8 small squares and 2 small triangles

- From fabric B, cut 2 small triangles
- From fabric C, cut 1 diamond square and 4 small squares.

Template piecing

With right sides together, pin and sew the fabric A triangles and fabric B triangles to the diagonal edges of the fabric C diamond square, alternating the colors; press seams open.

Make the block

Sew three rows Lay out the fabric A small squares around the diamond patch, balancing the colors, with the fabric C small squares in the four corners, as shown above. With right sides together, pin and sew the squares for the top row together; press seams open. Repeat for the bottom row.

For the center row, with right sides together, pin and sew the two small squares on each side of the diamond patch together to form two strips; press seams open. Join the strips to each side of the diamond square; press seams open.

Complete the square With right sides together, pin and sew the top row and the bottom row to the center row, carefully matching seams; press seams open.

. . . .

indigo windmill

The seam allowance is ¼ inch throughout.

Patchwork doesn't have to look like folk art. Dark colors, such as this Japanese print and the naturally dyed indigo solid, perfectly counterbalance the neutral colors in the print. Color combinations such as this yield edgy, urban quilts.

Fabric quantities

- Dark indigo print fabric A: 9 x 12 inches
- Dark indigo fabric B: 9 x 12 inches
- Light purple print fabric C: 7 x 12 inches

Prepare the patches

Rotary method
- From fabrics A and B, cut twelve 2½-inch squares each
- From fabric C, cut four 6½ x 2½-inch rectangles

or

Template cutting
Using the 6 x 6 templates (pages 278–83):
- From fabrics A and B, cut 12 small squares each
- From fabric C, cut 4 medium rectangles

Make the block

Piece four patches With right sides together, pin and sew the fabric A small squares and the fabric B small squares in pairs; press seams over fabric B. Join three pairs to make four patches, alternating the colors to look like a checkerboard; press seams open.

With right sides together, pin and sew a fabric C medium rectangle to the right edge of each checkerboard patch, with a fabric A square in the top left corner; press seams open.

Sew two rows With right sides together, pin and sew together two patches, making sure the fabric C medium rectangles are perpendicular and meet in the center of the block; press seam open. Repeat to make a second row.

Complete the square With right sides together, pin and sew the two rows together, making sure the fabric C medium rectangles meet in the center of the block; press seams open.

bubble and squeak

The seam allowance is ¼ inch throughout.

Although guidelines are given for fabric colors, every version of this block will be individual. The four rows of half-square triangles are upcycled leftovers from other rotary-pieced units. It's named, therefore, after a favorite British dish made from leftover vegetables.

A
B
C
D
E

Fabric quantities

- Light blue print fabric A: 8 x 12 inches
- Medium gray print fabric B: 8 x 8 inches
- Navy blue fabric C: 8 x 12 inches
- White fabric D: 8 x 16 inches
- Medium blue print fabric E: 6 x 13 inches

Prepare the patches

Rotary method
- From fabrics A and C, fabrics A and D, fabrics B and D, C and D, make six 2½-inch half-square triangles (see page 12) each
- From fabric E, cut two 12½ x 2½-inch rectangles

or

Template cutting
Using the 6 x 6 templates (pages 278–83):
- From fabrics A and C, cut 12 small triangles each
- From fabric B, cut 6 small triangles
- From fabric D, cut 18 small triangles
- From fabric E, cut 2 full-length rectangles

Template piecing

With right sides together, pin and sew a fabric D small triangle to six of the fabric A small triangles, all of the fabric B small triangles, and six of the fabric C small triangles to make 18 half-square triangles; press seams open.

With right sides together, pin and sew the remaining fabric A small triangles to the remaining fabric C small triangles to make another six half-square triangles; press seams open.

Make the block

Sew four columns For the left column, with right sides together, pin and sew a column of three fabrics A and C half-square triangles and three fabrics A and D half-square triangles, alternating colors and making sure the light blue triangles all point up and left, as shown above. Press seams open.

For the right column, repeat with the remaining fabrics A and C half-square triangles and fabrics A and D half-square triangles, but make sure the light blue triangles all point down and right; press seams open.

For the left middle column, pin and sew a column of three fabrics B and D half-square triangles and three fabrics C and D half-square triangles, alternating colors and making sure the white triangles all point up and left; press seams open.

For the right middle column, repeat with the remaining fabrics B and D half-square triangles and fabrics C and D half-square triangles, but make sure the white triangles all point down and right; press seams open.

Join the two middle columns, carefully matching seams; press seam open.

Complete the square With right sides together, pin and sew a fabric E full-length rectangle to the right edge of the first column; press seam open. Join the remaining fabric E full-length rectangle to the left edge of the last column; press seam open.

With right sides together, pin and sew the center column to the right edge of the left-hand column; press seam open. Join the left edge of the right-hand column to the right edge of the block; press seam open.

love-in-a-mist

The seam allowance is ¼ inch throughout.

A romantically named traditional block, Love in a Mist is made up in the colors of the elegant European flower that shares its name. Like Starry Night on page 205, the construction is far more straightforward than it first appears. It can be broken down into two repeating units set around a central plain square.

Fabric quantities

- Dark blue print fabric A: 8 x 13 inches
- Dark blue fabric B: 6 x 6 inches
- Medium purple print fabric C: 10 x 10 inches
- White fabric D: 12 x 17 inches

Prepare the patches

Rotary method
- From fabrics A and D, make eight 2½-inch half-square triangles (see page 12)
- From fabrics C and D, make four 4½-inch diamond squares (see page 15)
- From fabric A, cut one 4½-inch square
- From fabrics B and D, cut four 2½-inch squares each

or

Template cutting
Using the 6 x 6 templates (pages 278–83):
- From fabric A, cut 1 large square and 8 small triangles
- From fabric B, cut 4 small squares
- From fabric C, cut 4 diamond squares
- From fabric D, cut 4 small squares and 24 small triangles

Template piecing

With right sides together, pin and sew a fabric D small triangle to the long diagonal edge of each of the fabric A small triangles to make eight half-square triangles; press seams open.

With right sides together, pin and sew the remaining fabric D small triangles to the diagonal edges of each of the fabric C diamond squares; press seams open.

Make the block

Piece four arrow patches With right sides together, pin and sew a half-square triangle to the left edge of a fabric D small square, with the blue print triangle pointing down and left; press seams over fabric A. With right sides together, pin and sew a half-square triangle to the right edge of a fabric B small square with the blue print triangle pointing up and right; press seams over fabric A. Join the strips with the fabric A triangles in opposite corners. Repeat to make another three arrow patches.

Make three rows For the top row, with right sides together, pin and sew an arrow patch to each side of a diamond square, with the fabric B squares at the bottom and adjacent to the diamond square; press seams open. Repeat to make the bottom row.

For the middle row, with right sides together, pin and sew a diamond square to each side of the fabric A large square; press seams open.

Complete the square Flip the bottom row. With right sides together pin and sew the top and bottom rows to the middle row, with the arrows pointing toward the square in the center and carefully matching seams; press seams open.

hexagon chain

The seam allowance is ¼ inch throughout.

Hexagon Chain is a simple combination of octagonal snowballs and nine-patch squares, similar to Nine-Patch Snowballs on page 89.

Fabric quantities

- Dark navy fabric A: 6 x 6 inches
- Dark navy print fabric B: 6 x 12 inches
- Dark navy print fabric C: 3 x 6 inches
- White fabric D: 13 x 14 inches

Prepare the patches

Rotary method
- From fabrics A and D, make two 6½-inch octagon squares (see page 18)
- From fabrics B and D, cut eight 2½-inch squares each
- From fabric C, cut two 2½-inch squares

or

Template cutting
Using the 6 x 6 templates (pages 278–83):
- From fabric A, cut 8 small triangles

- From fabric B, cut 8 small squares
- From fabric C, cut 2 small squares
- From fabric D, cut 2 octagons and 8 small squares

Template piecing

With right sides together, pin and sew the fabric A small triangles to each diagonal edge of the fabric D octagons; press seams over fabric A.

Make the block

Piece two nine-patches With right sides together, pin and sew a fabric B small square to each side of a fabric D small square; press seams open. Repeat to make a second strip. Sew a fabric D small square to each side of a fabric C small square; press seams open. Join the strips in a nine-patch square to resemble a checkerboard, carefully matching seams. Repeat to make a second nine-patch square.

Complete the square With right sides together, join a nine-patch square to the right edge of an octagon square, then join a nine-patch square to the left edge of an octagon square; press seams open. Join the two halves of the block, carefully matching seams; press seam open.

stonemason's puzzle

The seam allowance is ¼ inch throughout.

When multiples of this historic puzzle block is repeated edge to edge, a dramatic design of concentric squares appears. You could use a fifth solid color for the center square. This geometric block can be easily made using the rotary method.

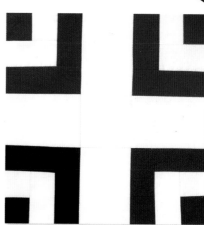

Fabric quantities

- Medium purple fabric A: 5 x 7 inches
- Medium blue fabric B: 5 x 7 inches
- Dark purple fabric C: 5 x 7 inches
- Dark blue fabric D: 5 x 7 inches
- White fabric E: 12 x 16 inches

Prepare the patches

Rotary method
- From fabrics A, B, C, and D, cut one 5 x 2-inch rectangle, one 3½ x 2-inch rectangle, and one 2-inch square each
- From fabric E, cut four 5 x 3½-inch rectangles, one 3½-inch square, four 3½ x 2-inch rectangles, and four 2-inch squares

Make the block

Piece four patches With right sides together, pin and sew a white small square to each of the colored squares; press seams open. With the white small square at the top, join a white short rectangle to the right edge of each strip; press seams open. Add the matching colored short rectangle to the top edge of each patch; press seams open. Add the matching colored long rectangle to the right edge of each patch; press seams open.

Sew three rows For the top row, with right sides together, pin and sew the medium purple patch and the medium blue patch to the long sides of a wide white rectangle, making sure the small colored squares are in the outside corners; press seams open. Repeat with the dark blue and dark purple patches to make the bottom row.

For the middle row, with right sides together, join the remaining wide white rectangles to each side of the large white square; press seams open.

Complete the square With right sides together, pin and sew the top and bottom rows to the center row, carefully matching seams; press seams open.

octagon star

The narrow triangles give the Octagon Star block an exuberant sense of movement. It almost twinkles against the dusky purple background. Cut and stitch the narrow points as accurately as you can to keep them looking sparkly. Because of the isosceles triangles, this block is best made from templates.

The seam allowance is ¼ inch throughout.

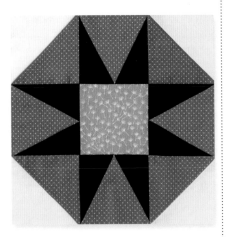

Fabric quantities

- Medium purple print fabric A: 12 x 16 inches
- Dark blue fabric B: 10 x 10 inches
- Light purple print fabric C: 5 x 5 inches
- White fabric E: 12 x 12 inches

Prepare the patches

Template cutting
Using the 6 x 6 templates (pages 278–83):
- From fabric A, cut 4 large triangles and 4 isosceles triangles
- From fabric B, cut 4 right half triangles and 4 left half triangles
- From fabric C, cut 1 large square

- From fabric D, cut 4 large triangles

Template piecing

With right sides together, pin and sew a fabric D large triangle to each of the fabric A large triangles to make four half-square triangles; press seams open.

Make the block

Piece four patches With right sides together, pin and sew a fabric B right half triangle and left half triangle to each of the long sides of the fabric A isosceles triangles to make four patches; press seams open.

Sew three rows With right sides together, pin and sew a half-square triangle to each side of an isosceles triangle patch, making

sure the purple print triangles all point inward; press seams open. Repeat to make the bottom row.

With right sides together, pin and sew the isosceles triangle patches to each side of the fabric C large square, with the fabric A triangles pointing inward; press seams open.

Complete the square Join the top and bottom rows to the center row, carefully matching seams; press seams open.

---

nelson's victory

In 1906, just over a century after Lord Nelson's navy defeated the French at Trafalgar, this block was featured in *Practical Needlework* magazine.

The seam allowance is ¼ inch throughout.

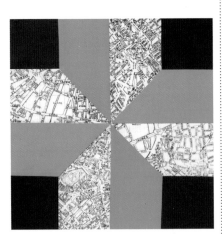

Fabric quantities

- Dark blue fabric A: 8 x 8 inches
- Medium turquoise fabric B: 7 x 16 inches
- Light gray print fabric C: 7 x 16 inches

Prepare the patches

Rotary method
- From fabrics A, B, and C, make four 6½-inch perspective squares (see page 18)

or

Template cutting
Using the 4 x 4 templates (pages 269–73):
- From fabric A, cut 4 small squares
- From fabric B, cut 4 left tapered rectangles
- From fabric C, cut 4 right tapered rectangles

To make set-in seams, mark the ¼-inch seam allowance around the short and diagonal edges of each tapered rectangle and all four edges of the fabric A small squares. Measure and mark the center of these seams.

With right sides together, pin and sew the short straight edge of a fabric B left tapered rectangle centered on the right edge of a fabric A small square, sewing up to where the marked lines meet at the end. Join a fabric C right tapered rectangle to the bottom edge of the fabric A small square in the same way, then pin and sew the rectangles together along their diagonal edges. Press the diagonal seams over fabric B and the straight seams over the rectangles. Repeat to make another three perspective squares.

Make the block

Sew two rows With right sides together, pin and sew two perspective squares together, making sure the fabric A small squares are at the outside top corners. Join the remaining two perspective squares together with the fabric A small squares at the outside bottom corners; press seams open.

Complete the square With right sides together, pin and sew the two rows together, carefully matching the seams; press seam open.

spinning star

The seam allowance is ¼ inch throughout.

The charcoal, brown, and turquoise palette used here gives this dynamic star a somewhat somber look, which would suit a large urban living space. You can choose brighter colors and bolder patterns to make a quilt for a bedroom or country kitchen. This block is easily made with templates.

A
B
C

Fabric quantities

- Dark charcoal fabric A: 8 x 16 inches
- Dark turquoise print fabric B: 8 x 9 inches
- White fabric C: 8 x 12 inches

Prepare the patches

Template cutting
Using the 4 x 4 templates (pages 269–73):
- From fabric A, cut 4 diagonal boats
- From fabric B, cut 4 left diamonds
- From fabric C, cut 12 small triangles

Make the block

Piece four patches With right sides together, pin and sew a fabric C small triangle to the short top edge of each diagonal boat to make four large patchwork triangles; press seams open.

With right sides together, pin and sew a fabric C small triangle to the left side and the top edge of each left diamond to make another four large patchwork triangles; press seams open.

Join a fabrics A and C patchwork triangle to a fabrics B and C patchwork triangle, along the long diagonal edge; press seam open. Repeat to make another three patches.

Complete the square With right sides together, pin and sew two patches together, making sure the colored fabrics abut in the

center and carefully matching seams and points. Repeat with the remaining patches.

With right sides together, pin and sew the two halves of the block together, making sure the colored fabrics meet in the center and carefully matching seams and points; press seams open.

kew gardens

The seam allowance is ¼ inch throughout.

Kew Gardens is a simple block elevated by the choice of fabrics. Stark white and solid lilac patches provide the perfect foil for the delicate patterning on this Japanese shibori indigo fabric.

A
B
C

Fabric quantities

- Dark blue print fabric A: 10 x 10 inches
- Medium lilac fabric B: 8 x 12 inches
- White fabric C: 10 x 12 inches

Prepare the patches

Rotary method
- From fabrics A and B, make four 4½-inch corner squares (see page 14)
- From fabrics B and C, make four 4½-inch rectangle squares (see page 11)
- From fabric C, cut one 4½-inch square

or

Template cutting
Using the 6 x 6 templates (pages 278–83):
- From fabric A, cut 4 corner squares

- From fabric B, cut 4 short rectangles and 4 small triangles
- From fabric C, cut 1 large square and 4 short rectangles

Template piecing

With right sides together, pin and sew a fabric B small triangle to each diagonal edge on the fabric A corner squares; press seams open.

With right sides together, pin and sew a fabric B short rectangle to each of the fabric C short rectangles to make four rectangle squares; press seams open.

Make the block

Sew three rows For the top row, with right sides together, pin and sew a corner square to each side of a rectangle square, aligning

the lilac pieces; press seams open. Repeat to make the bottom row.

For the middle row, with right sides together, pin and sew the remaining rectangle squares to each side of the fabric C large square, joining them along the lilac edge; press seams open.

Complete the square Flip the bottom row. With right sides together, pin and sew the top and bottom rows to the center row, carefully matching the lilac pieces; press seams open.

bookshelf

There are no templates or precise measurements for this fun pictorial block because it's intended as inspiration for your own personal interpretation of Bookshelf. If you are an embroiderer, you could stitch names or titles along the spines to personalize the books. This scrappy block is easily made using the rotary method.

Fabric quantities

- At least 5 different dark blue and purple solid and print fabrics A: 2½ inches wide and 6½ to 10 inches long each

- At least 2 different medium and dark red solid and print fabrics B: 2½ inches wide and 2 to 4 inches long each

- White fabric C: 6 x 10 inches

- Medium brown fabric D: 6 x 13 inches

Prepare the patches

Rotary cutting
- From fabrics A, cut eight 2-inch wide rectangles, between 6 and 9½ inches long*

- From fabrics B, cut at least four 2-inch wide rectangles, between 1½ and 3½ inches long*

- From fabric C, cut eight 2-inch wide rectangles, between 1 and 4½ inches long*

- From fabric D, cut two 12½-inch x 2-inch rectangles

*Note: The length of the rectangles you need for fabrics A, B, and C will depend on how you choose to piece them together; once pieced, each strip should be 9½ x 2-inches in size, including the seam allowance. You could use fabrics A to make additional labels depending on the contrast.

Make the block

Piece eight book patches Make the books in different heights. For a book with a plain spine, sew a fabric C rectangle to the top short edge of a fabric A rectangle; press seam over fabric A and trim the length to 9½ inches.

For a book with a label on the spine, cut across a fabric A rectangle 2 to 4 inches down from the top edge. Sew the two pieces to the 2-inch ends of a fabric B rectangle; press seams over fabric A. Join a fabric C rectangle to the top end of the strip; press seams over fabric A, then trim the length to 9½ inches. Repeat to make six more book patches.

Complete the square Lay out the rectangles for a balance of colors and prints, as shown above. With right sides together, pin and sew the patches together along the long edges; press seams open.

With right sides together, pin and sew the fabric D rectangles to the top and bottom edges; press seams over fabric D.

square lock

The seam allowance is ¼ inch throughout.

This block is much easier to piece than it first appears. Four identical squares are pieced log-cabin style and set at opposing angles to create a graphic motif. Keep to dark and neutral fabrics or experiment with a pop of color.

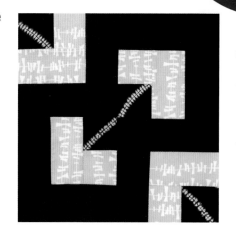

A
B
C

Fabric quantities

- Dark blue print fabric A: 6 x 6 inches
- Beige print fabric B: 9 x 12 inches
- Dark blue fabric C: 12 x 14 inches

Prepare the patches

Rotary method
- From fabric A, cut four 2½-inch squares
- From fabric B, cut four 2½-inch squares and four 4½ x 2½-inch rectangles
- From fabric C, cut four 4½ x 2½-inch rectangles and four 6½ x 2½-inch rectangles

or

Template cutting

Using the 6 x 6 templates (pages 278–83):
- From fabric A, cut 4 small squares
- From fabric B, cut 4 small squares and 4 short rectangles
- From fabric C, cut 4 short rectangles and 4 medium rectangles

Make the block

Piece four squares With right sides together, sew a fabric A small square to each fabric B small square; press seams over the darker fabric. With the blue print small squares on the left, sew a fabric B rectangle to the bottom edge; press seam over fabric B. Join a fabric C short rectangle to the right edge of the patch and a fabric C medium rectangle to the bottom edge; press seams over the darker fabric.

Complete the square Lay out the patches so that two blue print small squares are at the top left and bottom right corners and the other two meet at the center of the block. With right sides together, pin and sew the top pair of patches; press seam over the darker fabric. Repeat with the bottom pair of patches.

With right sides together, pin and sew the two rows together, matching the center points; press seam open.

---

trafalgar

The seam allowance is ¼ inch throughout.

This block is similar to Nelson's Victory (see page 216), so the two blocks would work together well on the same quilt if made in similar colors. This block is easily made using templates.

A
B
C
D

Fabric quantities

- Light blue print fabric A: 8 x 8 inches
- Dark blue print fabric B: 7 x 16 inches
- White fabric C: 8 x 8 inches
- Lilac print fabric D: 7 x 16 inches

Prepare the patches

Template cutting
Using the 4 x 4 templates (pages 269–73):
- From fabrics A and C, cut 4 small triangles each
- From fabric B, cut 4 right tapered rectangles
- From fabric D, cut 4 left tapered rectangles

Template piecing

Sew a fabric A small triangle to the top edge of the fabric B tapered rectangle. Join the fabric C triangle to the fabric D tapered rectangle. With right sides together, join these two patchwork large triangles along the diagonal edge; press seam open. Repeat to make another three patches.

Make the block

Sew two rows Lay out the four patches so the points of the tapered rectangles meet at the center. With right sides together, join the top pair; press seam over fabric B. Repeat with the bottom pair.

Complete the square With right sides together, pin and sew the top and bottom rows together, carefully matching the points in the center; press seam open.

linked squares

The seam allowance is ¼ inch throughout.

Although in appearance Linked Squares is similar to Square Lock on page 219, this block has to be made differently so that the two open squares look as if they are joined together. The indigo and duck egg blue color combination shown here creates a Japanese look. However, the block could also be made in two shades of plain gold to represent two linked wedding rings on a marriage quilt.

A

B

C

Fabric quantities

- Indigo fabric A: 8 x 12 inches

- Light blue print fabric B: 8 x 12 inches

- White fabric C: 10 x 11 inches

Prepare the patches

Rotary method
- From fabrics A and B, cut two 6½ x 2½-inch rectangles, two 4½ x 2½-inch rectangles, and one 2½-inch square each

- From fabric C, cut two 4½-inch squares, two 4½ x 2½-inch rectangles, and two 2½-inch squares

or

Template cutting
Using the 6 x 6 templates (pages 278–83):
- From fabrics A and B, cut 2 medium rectangles, 2 short rectangles, and 1 small square each

- From fabric C, cut 2 large squares, 2 short rectangles, and 2 small squares

Make the block

Piece four patches For the top left patch, with right sides together, sew a fabric A short rectangle to the bottom edge of a fabric C large square; join a fabric B medium rectangle to the right edge of the patch; press seam outward.

For the top right patch, sew the fabric A small square to a fabric C small square; press seam over fabric C. With fabric A on the left, sew a fabric C short rectangle to the top edge and a fabric B short rectangle to the right edge of the patch. Add a fabric B medium rectangle to the top edge; press seams outward.

For the bottom left patch, sew the remaining fabric C small square to the left edge of the fabric B small square; join a fabric C short rectangle to the bottom edge of the patch. Add the fabric A short rectangle to the left edge and a fabric A medium rectangle to the bottom edge of the patch; press seams outward.

For the bottom right patch, sew a fabric B short rectangle to the top of the remaining fabric C large square, then sew a fabric A long rectangle to the left edge of the patch; press all seams outward.

Complete the square With right sides together, pin and sew the top two squares together; press seams open. Repeat with the bottom two squares. Join the top and bottom rows together, carefully matching seams; press seams open.

little log cabin

The seam allowance is ¼ inch throughout.

This cross motif is made up of four quarter squares pieced using the log cabin method. It is the kind of block that would work well also if made from recycled shirting fabric, with the stripes running along the length of each patch.

Fabric quantities

- Light gray print fabric A: 5 x 6 inches
- Dark blue fabric B: 6 x 7 inches
- Light blue fabric C: 5 x 6 inches
- Medium blue print fabric D: 6 x 7 inches
- White fabric E: 6 x 6 inches

Prepare the patches

Rotary method
- From fabrics A and C, cut two 2½-inch squares and two 4½ x 2½-inch rectangles each
- From fabrics B and D, cut two 4½ x 2½-inch rectangles and two 6½ x 2½-inch rectangles each
- From fabric E, cut four 2½-inch squares

or

Template cutting
Using the 6 x 6 templates (pages 278–83):
- From fabrics A and C, cut 2 small squares and 2 short rectangles each
- From fabrics B and D, cut 2 short rectangles and 2 medium rectangles each
- From fabric E, cut 4 small squares

A
B
C
D
E

Make the block

Piece four patches For the top left patch, sew a fabric A small square to a fabric E small square; press seam over fabric A. With the fabric E small square uppermost, sew a fabric A short rectangle to the right edge of the strip; press seam over fabric A. Join a fabric B short rectangle to the bottom edge and a fabric B medium rectangle to the right edge of the patch; press seams over fabric B. Repeat to make the bottom right patch.

For the top right patch, sew a fabric C small square to a fabric E small square; press seam over fabric C. With the fabric E square uppermost, sew a fabric C short rectangle to the left edge of the strip. Join a fabric D short rectangle to the bottom edge and a fabric D medium rectangle to the right edge of the patch; press seams over fabric D. Repeat for the bottom left patch.

Complete the square With the fabric E squares in the outside corners, join a fabrics A, B, and E patch to a fabrics C, D, and E patch; press seams open. Repeat for the bottom row. Join the top and bottom rows together, matching center points; press seam open.

rolling stone

A freewheeling block that predates Mick Jagger by at least half a century, the name alone would make this a great quilt for any rock fan. Other titles that it has gathered over the years include Block Circle, Broken Wheel, Johnnie Round the Corner, and the delightfully obscure Squirrel in a Cage.

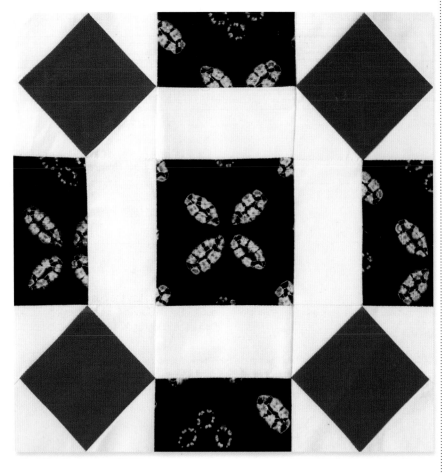

Fabric quantities

- Dark purple fabric A: 10 x 10 inches
- Dark blue print fabric B: 8 x 11 inches
- White fabric C: 11 x 12 inches

Prepare the patches

Rotary method
- From fabrics A and C, make four 4½-inch diamond squares (see page 15)
- From fabrics B and C, make four 4½-inch rectangle squares (see page 11)
- From fabric B, cut one 4½-inch square

or

Template cutting
Using the 6 x 6 templates (pages 278–83):
- From fabric A, cut 4 diamond squares
- From fabric B, cut 1 large square and 4 short rectangles
- From fabric C, cut 4 short rectangles and 16 small triangles

Template piecing

With right sides together, join a fabric C small triangle to the diagonal edge of each diamond square; press seams over fabric A.

Join a fabric B short rectangle to each fabric C short rectangle along a long edge to make four rectangle squares; press seam over fabric C.

Make the block

Sew three rows Arrange the patches in three rows of three. For the top row, pin and sew a diamond square to each side of a rectangle square, being careful to match the points; press seams open. Repeat to make the bottom row.

For the middle row, join a rectangle square to each end of the fabric B large square, being careful to match the points; press seams open.

Complete the square With right sides together, pin and sew the top and bottom row to the middle row, joining along the white edges and being careful to match the seams and points; press seams open.

double propeller

The seam allowance is ¼ inch throughout.

This square is also known as Beginner's Joy. Propeller blocks are traditionally made with blue and white backgrounds, to represent the sky and clouds. This block is easily made using templates.

Fabric quantities

- Light purple print fabric A: 10 x 10 inches
- Dark purple fabric B: 8 x 14 inches
- White fabric C: 10 x 10 inches
- Light blue print fabric D: 8 x 14 inches

Prepare the patches

Template cutting
Using the 4 x 4 templates (pages 269–73):
- From fabrics A and C, cut 4 small triangles each
- From fabric B, cut 4 left tapered rectangles
- From fabric D, cut 4 right tapered rectangles

Make the block

Piece four squares Sew a fabric A small triangle to the short straight edge of each fabric B tapered rectangle to make four dark patchwork triangles; press seams open. Join the fabric C small triangles to the fabric D tapered rectangles in the same way to make four light patchwork triangles.

Pin and stitch the light and dark triangles together in pairs along the diagonal edges, matching the seams carefully; press seams open.

Make two rows Lay the quarter squares out so that the fabric A small triangles form a pinwheel at the center.

With right sides facing, pin and stitch the top two squares together, matching the seams; press seam open. Sew the two bottom squares in the same way.

Complete the square Pin and stitch the two rows together, lining up the center seams; press seam open.

---

scrappy star

The seam allowance is ¼ inch throughout.

Scrappy blocks are always good for using the smallest fabric leftovers. You could make this open star design with a more random placement of colors and pattern.

Fabric quantities

- Dark blue print fabric A: 5 x 10 inches
- Dark blue fabric B: 5 x 10 inches
- Dark purple fabric C: 5 x 10 inches
- Dark brown print fabric D: 5 x 10 inches
- White fabric E: 8 x 16 inches

Prepare the patches

Rotary method
- From fabrics A and E, fabrics B and E, fabrics C and E, and fabrics D and E, make four 3½-inch half-square triangles (see page 12) each

or

Template cutting
Using the 4 x 4 templates (pages 269–73):
- From fabrics A, B, C, and D, cut 4 small triangles each
- From fabric E, cut 16 small triangles

Template piecing

With right sides together, pin and sew a fabric E small triangle to the long edge of each of the colored small triangles to make 16 half-square triangles; press seams open.

Make the block

Piece four patches For the top left patch, with right sides together, pin and sew a blue print half-square triangle to a blue half-square triangle, with the print triangle pointing up and left and the blue triangle pointing down and left; press seam open. Join a purple half-square triangle to a brown print half-square triangle, with the purple triangle pointing up and right and the print triangle pointing down and left; press seam open. Join the strips with the solid colors making an hourglass in the center; press seam open. Repeat for the bottom right patch.

Repeat for the top right patch, joining a purple half-square triangle to a blue print half-square triangle, with the purple triangle pointing down and right and the print triangle pointing up and right. Join a brown print half-square triangle to a blue half-square triangle, with both colored triangles pointing up and left. Join the strips as before. Repeat for the bottom left patch.

Complete the square With right sides together, sew the top two patches together, with the print triangles meeting in the center; press seam open. Repeat for the bottom two patches. Join the two rows, with the print triangles at the center; press seam open.

indigo flower basket

The seam allowance is ¼ inch throughout.

Before the development of chemical dyes in the nineteenth century, indigo blue and Turkey red (known as Rouge d'Andrinople in France), which were both derived from plants, were two of the only fabric dyes available. Their modern counterparts have been used for this basket block, which is inspired by an antique quilt. Multiple blocks can be joined edge to edge without sashing by adding 2½-inch borders to the bottom and right-hand edges to complete a quilt top. This block is easily made using the rotary method.

A
B
C

Fabric quantities

- Dark blue print fabric A: 11 x 16 inches
- Dark red fabric B: 8 x 15 inches
- White fabric C: 16 x 16 inches

Prepare the patches

Rotary method
- From fabrics A and C, make seven 2½-inch half-square triangles (see page 12)
- From fabrics B and C, make five 2½-inch half-square triangles
- From fabric A, cut two 2½-inch squares
- From fabric B, cut three 2½-inch squares
- From fabric C, cut one 12½ x 2½-inch rectangle, one 10½ x 2½-inch rectangle, two 6½ x 2½-inch rectangles, and one 2½-inch square

Make the block

Piece the basket With right sides together, lay out the 16 squares and half-square triangles that form the basket into four rows of four squares, as shown above.

For the top row, with right sides facing, pin and sew four blue half-square triangles together, with the fabric A triangles pointing down and right.

For the second row, join a blue half-square triangle to the left edge of a white small square with the blue triangle pointing down and right; press seam open. Join a blue small square to the right edge of the strip, then add a red half-square triangle with the red triangle pointing down and right; press seams open.

For the third row, join a blue half-square triangle to the left edge of a blue small square, with the blue triangle pointing down and left; press seam open. Add a red half-square triangle to the right edge of the strip with the red triangle pointing down and right; add a red small square. Press seams open.

For the fourth row, join a blue half-square triangle to a red half-square triangle, with both colored triangles pointing down and right; press seam open. Join two red small squares to the right edge of the strip; press seams open.

With right sides together, pin and sew the four rows together, matching seams and points; press seams open.

Complete the square Sew two red half-square triangles to the right short edges of the white short rectangles, with the fabric B triangle pointing down and left in one and up and left in the other. Sew the downward pointing strip to the right edge of the patchwork square. Sew the white small square to the right end of the remaining strip, then join to the bottom edge of the basket. Press seams open.

Join the shorter fabric C rectangle to the left edge of the block. Sew the final fabric C rectangle to the top edge. Press seams open.

hidden nine patch

The seam allowance is ¼ inch throughout.

Look hard at this seemingly random arrangement of multicolored fabrics and you'll see a camouflaged nine-patch square toward the bottom right corner. Hiding motifs such as this within a larger quilt top adds visual interest to the surface, making it a fun addition to a child's quilt.

Fabric quantities

- At least 9 different medium and dark blue solid and print fabrics A: 6 x 15 inches in total

- Dark orange print fabric B: 3 x 9 inches

- Blue print fabric C: 6 x 9 inches

- White fabric D: 6 x 6 inches

Prepare the patches

Rotary method
- From fabrics A, cut twenty-four 2½-inch squares

- From fabric B, cut three 2½-inch squares

- From fabric C, cut five 2½-inch squares

- From fabric D, cut four 2½-inch squares

or

Template cutting
Using the 6 x 6 templates (pages 278–83):
- From fabric A, cut 24 small squares

- From fabric B, cut 3 small squares

- From fabric C, cut 5 small squares

- From fabric D, cut 4 small squares

A
A
A
A
A
A
A
A
A
A
A
A
B
C
D

Make the block

Arrange the patches Make six rows of six squares each, starting with the nine-square patch. Join a fabric C small square to each side of a fabric D small square for both the top and bottom rows; join a fabric D small square to each side edge of a fabric C small square for the center row of the nine-patch square; press seams open. Join an orange small square and a blue small square to the left edge of the top nine-patch square row; press seams to the right. Add a blue small square to the right edge.

Join two blue small squares to the left edge of the center and bottom nine-patch square rows; add a blue small square to the right edges of both. Press seams on the center row to the left and seams on the bottom row to the right.

Arrange the remaining small squares to balance colors and patterns. Sew three rows of six small squares each; press seams in the first row to the right and seams in the second and last row to the left.

Complete the square With right sides together, pin and sew the first and third rows to the second row and the fourth and sixth row to the fifth row, then join the two halves of the block together; press seams open.

305 the knot block

The seam allowance is ¼ inch throughout.

Pretty monochrome blossom prints paired with hand-dyed shibori fabric give a Japanese feel to this simple block.

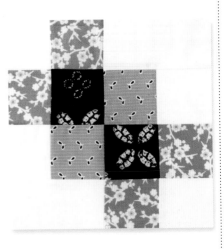

Fabric quantities

- Medium gray print fabric A: 8 x 8 inches
- Dark blue print fabric B: 4 x 8 inches
- Dark gray print fabric C: 4 x 8 inches
- White fabric D: 8 x 15 inches

Prepare the patches

Rotary method
- From fabrics A and C, make two 6½-inch three-patch squares (see page 11)
- From fabrics A, B, and D, make two 6½-inch four-patch squares (see page 11) with fabric A squares opposite each other

or

Template cutting
Using the 4 x 4 templates (pages 269–73):
- From fabric A, cut 4 small squares

- From fabrics B and C, cut 2 small squares each
- From fabric D, cut 2 short rectangles and 4 small squares

Template piecing

With right sides together, join a fabric C small square to a fabric D small square; press seam over fabric C. Sew the strip to the long side of a fabric D short rectangle to complete a three-patch square; press seam open. Repeat to make a second three-patch square.

With right sides together, sew a fabric B small square to a fabric A small square; press seam over fabric B. Repeat with a fabric A small square and a fabric D small square. Join the two strips along a long edge, keeping fabric A in opposite corners; press seams open. Repeat to make another four-patch square.

Make the block

Sew two rows Arrange the four patches with the fabric B and fabric C small squares opposite each other in the center. With right sides together, pin and sew the top pair together, matching seams. Repeat for the bottom pair.

Complete the square Join the halves together, matching seams; press open.

---

306 double hourglass

The seam allowance is ¼ inch throughout.

There are two hourglass shapes (sometimes called butterflies) at the center of this block, one plain and one patterned. Set multiple blocks edge to edge to make a quilt top, turning alternate blocks by 90 degrees to create a pattern of counterchanged squares. This block is most accurately made from templates.

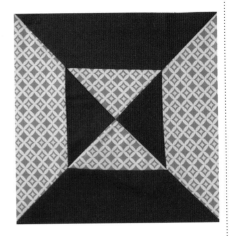

Fabric quantities

- Dark blue fabric A: 13 x 16 inches
- Medium blue print fabric B: 13 x 16 inches

Prepare the patches

Template cutting
Using the 4 x 4 templates (pages 269–73):
- From fabrics A and B, cut 2 long boats and 2 medium triangles each

Template piecing

With right sides together, join the fabric A medium triangles to the short straight edge of each fabric B long boat to make a large patchwork triangle; press seams open. Repeat to join the fabric B medium triangles to the shorter straight edge of each fabric A long boat.

Make the block

Join the triangles Sew two opposite pairs of large patchwork triangles along the short edges; press seams open. With right sides together, pin and sew the two halves together along the long edge, matching seams and points; press seams open.

squared star

A classic with a twist, this traditional block looks fresh and modern when made up in three colors, such as black, indigo blue, and white. Check your quilt shop or online suppliers for similar designer collections of monochrome fabrics.

The seam allowance is ¼ inch throughout.

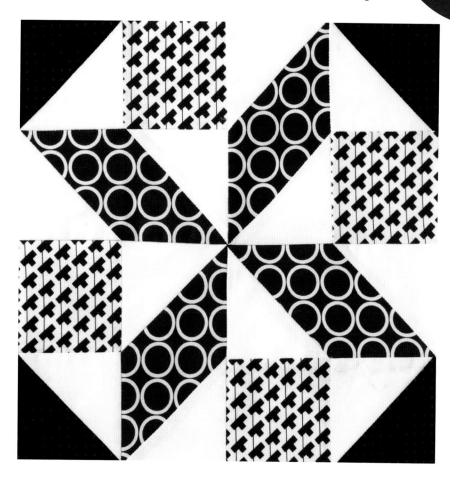

A
B
C

D

Fabric quantities

- Dark blue print fabric A: 6 x 14 inches
- Dark blue print fabric B: 8 x 8 inches
- Black print fabric C: 5 x 10 inches
- White fabric D: 14 x 18 inches

Prepare the patches

Rotary method
- From fabrics A and D, make four 6½ x 3½-inch right diamond rectangles (see page 16)
- From fabrics C and D, make four 3½-inch half-square triangles (see page 12)
- From fabric B, cut four 3½-inch squares

or

Template cutting
Using the 4 x 4 templates (pages 269–73):
- From fabric A, cut 4 right diamonds
- From fabric B, cut 4 small squares
- From fabric C, cut 4 small triangles
- From fabric D, cut 12 small triangles

Template piecing

With right sides together, sew a fabric D small triangle along each diagonal edge of the fabric A right diamonds to make four right diamond rectangles; press seams inward.

With right sides together, pin and sew a fabric D small triangle to each fabric C small triangle to make four half-square triangles; press seams away from fabric D.

Make the block

Piece four patches Sew a fabric B small square to the right edge of each half-square triangle with the black print triangles pointing up and left; press seams over fabric C. Sew a strip to the top edge of each right diamond rectangle; press seams over the right diamonds.

Complete the square Lay out the squares so all the right diamonds meet at the center and with the fabric C triangles in the corners, as shown above. With right sides together, pin and sew the top pairs together; press seam open. Repeat for the bottom pair.

With right sides together, pin and sew the top and bottom halves of the block together, carefully matching seams and points; press seams open.

garden path

This block has a symmetrical design reminiscent of the concentric patterns within an Elizabethan knot garden, and works well when made with small-scale floral fabrics.

A

B

C

D

E

Fabric quantities

- Light blue print fabric A: 7 x 7 inches
- Dark blue fabric B: 8 x 8 inches
- Light turquoise print fabric C: 8 x 14 inches
- Dark blue fabric D: 8 x 8 inches
- Dark pink fabric E: 8 x 8 inches

Prepare the patches

Rotary method
- From fabrics A and B, make one 6½-inch diamond square (see page 15)
- From fabrics C and D, make four 6½ x 3½-inch flying geese rectangles (see page 17)
- From fabric E, cut four 3½-inch squares

or

Template cutting
Using the 4 x 4 templates (pages 269–73):
- From fabric A, cut 1 diamond square
- From fabric B, cut 4 small triangles
- From fabric C, cut 4 medium triangles
- From fabric D, cut 8 small triangles
- From fabric E, cut 4 small squares

Template piecing

To make the diamond square, with right sides together, join the fabric B small triangles to the diagonal edges of the fabric A diamond square; press seams over fabric A.

With right sides together, sew a fabric D small triangle to each diagonal edge of a fabric C large triangle to make one flying geese rectangle; press seams across the small triangles. Repeat to make another three flying geese rectangles.

Make the block

Sew three rows With medium triangles pointing out, sew a flying geese rectangle to each side edge of the diamond square. Join a fabric E small square to each side edge of the remaining flying geese rectangles, with the triangles pointing up; press seams over fabric E.

Complete the square Flip the bottom row. Join the top and bottom rows to the middle row; press seams open.

plum

One of four specially designed fruit blocks, this luscious plum is stitched from five different purple fabrics, with an appliqué stem. If you want to extend the range, you can use four shades of green for a European-type green plum, or light orange for an apricot. This block is easily made using the rotary method.

The seam allowance is ¼ inch throughout.

Fabric quantities

- Dark purple fabric A: 8 x 11 inches
- Dark purple fabric B: 4 x 11 inches
- Medium purple fabric C: 4 x 4 inches
- Medium purple fabric D: 4 x 11 inches
- Light purple print fabric E: 3 x 3 inches
- Medium green print fabric F: 3 x 5 inches
- Medium brown fabric G: 1 x 4 inches
- White fabric H: 10 x 14 inches

Prepare the patches

Rotary method

- From fabrics A and B, fabrics A and D, fabrics A and H, fabrics B and H, fabrics C and H, and fabrics D and H, make one 2½-inch half-square triangle (see page 12) each
- From fabrics F and H, make one 4½ x 2½-inch left diamond rectangle (see page 16)
- From fabric A, cut three 2½-inch squares
- From fabrics B, D, and E, cut one 2½-inch square each
- From fabric G, cut 1 stem using the template on page 286
- From fabric H, cut one 12½ x 2½-inch rectangle, one 8½ x 4½-inch rectangle, one 4½-inch square, and two 4½ x 2½-inch rectangles

A B C D E F G H

Make the block

Prepare the stem Appliqué (see page 20) the stem to the large fabric G square 1 inch from the right edge.

Piece the plum Lay out the patches in their positions, as shown above. For the first row, with right sides together, pin and sew a fabrics B and H half-square triangle, with the B triangle pointing down and right, to the left edge of the fabrics A and B half-square triangle, with fabric B pointing up and right.

Add a fabrics C and H half-square triangle to the right edge, with the fabric C triangle pointing down and left. For the second row, join the fabric B small square to the left edge of a fabric A small square. Add the fabric E small square to the right edge of the strip. Press seams open.

For the third row, join two fabric A small squares, then add a fabric D square to the right edge.

For the bottom row join the fabrics A and H half-square triangle to the fabrics A and D half-square triangles along the fabric A edge, with the dark purple triangles pointing down; press seam open.

Add the fabrics D and H half-square triangle to the right edge of the strip, with the fabric D edges together and pointing in opposite directions; press seam open. Join the rows together; press seams open.

Complete the square Join the large fabric H rectangle to the right edge of the plum patch; press seams open. Sew a fabric H short rectangle to the top edge of the fabric F left diamond rectangle, then sew another fabric H short rectangle to the right edge of the patch; press seams open. Sew the stem square to the left edge of the leaf patch; press seams open. Sew this strip to the top edge of the plum patch; press seam open. Join the long rectangle to the left edge of the block; press seam open.

jacob's ladder

The seam allowance is ¼ inch throughout.

This historic block with a biblical name has been a favorite with generations of quilters. It is easily assembled from just two different units: half-square triangles and four-patch squares. When joined edge to edge at alternate angles, the purple "ladders" and rows of square patches meet up to create a double diagonal grid pattern.

A
B
C

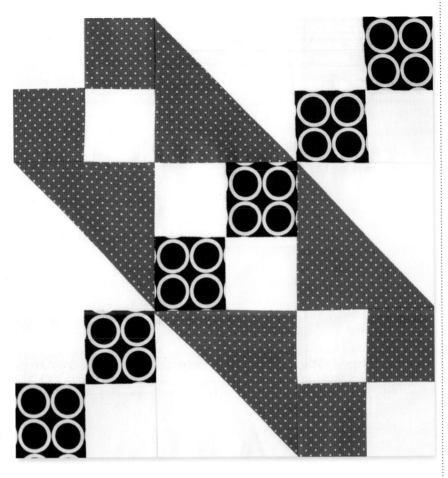

Fabric quantities

- Medium purple print fabric A: 6 x 18 inches
- Dark blue print fabric B: 6 x 9 inches
- White fabric C: 12 x 15 inches

Prepare the patches

Rotary method
- From fabrics A and C, make two 4½-inch four-patch squares (see page 11) and four 4½-inch half-square triangles (see page 12)
- From fabrics B and C, make three 4½-inch four-patch squares

or

Template cutting
Using the 6 x 6 templates (pages 278–83):
- From fabric A, cut 4 large triangles and 4 small squares
- From fabric B, cut 6 small squares
- From fabric C, cut 4 large triangles and 10 small squares

Template piecing

With right sides together, sew a fabric A large triangle to the diagonal edge of a fabric C large triangle; press seam over fabric A. Repeat to make another three half-square triangles.

With right sides together, sew a fabric A small square to a fabric C small square; press seam over fabric A. Repeat to make another pair, then join the pairs together along the long edge, keeping colors opposite, to complete a four-patch square; press seams open. Repeat to make another fabrics A and C four-patch square and to make two fabrics B and C four-patch squares.

Make the block

Arrange the patches Lay out the patches in three rows of three, with the dark blue small squares forming a line from the bottom left up to the top right.

Sew three rows For the top row, with right sides together, pin and sew a purple print four-patch square to the left edge of a half-square triangle, with the purple print triangle pointing down and left; press seam open. Join a blue print four-patch square to the right edge of the strip; press seam open. Repeat for the bottom row.

For the middle row, join a half-square triangle to the left edge of the remaining four-patch square, with the purple print triangle pointing up and right; press seam open. Add the remaining half-square triangle to the right edge of the strip, with the purple print triangle pointing down and left; press seam open.

Complete the square Flip bottom row over. With right sides together, pin and sew the top and bottom rows to the middle row; press seams open.

antique tile

The seam allowance is ¼ inch throughout.

This simple block, which first appeared in print in 1938, is made in a color palette that suggests blue-and-white Delftware and other antique ceramics.

Fabric quantities

- Dark blue fabric A: 6 x 6 inches
- Dark blue print fabric B: 6 x 10 inches
- Medium blue fabric C: 5 x 5 inches
- White fabric D: 9 x 20 inches

Prepare the patches

Rotary method
- From fabrics A and D, make four 4½-inch three-patch squares (see page 11)
- From fabrics B and D, make four 4½-inch rectangle squares (see page 11)
- From fabric C, cut one 4½-inch square

or

Template cutting
Using the 6 x 6 templates (pages 278–83):
- From fabric A, cut 4 small squares
- From fabric B, cut 4 short rectangles
- From fabric C, cut 1 large square
- From fabric D, cut 4 small squares and 8 short rectangles

A
B
C
D

Template piecing

With right sides together, pin and sew a fabric D small square to the top edge of the fabric A small squares; press seams over fabric D. Join a fabric D short rectangle to each left side of the strips to make four three-patch squares; press seams open.

With right sides together, pin and sew a fabric D short rectangle to the fabric B short rectangles to make four rectangle squares; press seams over fabric B.

Make the block

Sew three rows For the top row, with right sides together, pin and sew a three-patch square to each side of a rectangle square, with the blue squares in the center and the blue rectangle on the outside. Repeat for the bottom row.

For the middle row, with right sides together, join the remaining rectangle squares to each side of the fabric C large square, joining them along the white edge; press seams over fabric C.

Complete the square Sew the top and bottom rows to the middle row, with the blue rectangles on the outside; press seams open.

knot garden

Designed as a companion to Kew Gardens on page 217, Knot Garden is much easier to piece than might appear at first glance. It is made up of small squares and short rectangles set around the center square. Choose a mixture of florals, simple prints, and solid fabrics to emphasize the curious illusion of height and space within the design.

A
B
C
D
E

Fabric quantities

- Medium orange print fabric A: 8 x 11 inches
- Dark blue fabric B: 10 x 12 inches
- Medium pink print fabric C: 5 x 8 inches
- Medium blue print fabric D: 5 x 8 inches
- White fabric E: 6 x 10 inches

Prepare the patches

Rotary method
- From fabric A, cut one 4½-inch square, two 4½ x 2½-inch rectangles, and two 2½-inch squares
- From fabric B, cut four 4½ x 2½-inch rectangles and four 2½-inch squares
- From fabrics C and D, cut one 4½ x 2½-inch rectangle and one 2½-inch square each
- From fabric E, cut four 4½ x 2½-inch rectangles

or

Template cutting
Using the 6 x 6 templates (pages 278–83):
- From fabric A, cut 1 large square, 2 short rectangles, and 2 small squares
- From fabric B, cut 4 short rectangles and 4 small squares
- From fabrics C and D, cut 1 short rectangle and 1 small square each
- From fabric E, cut 4 short rectangles

Make the block

Sew the center patch With right sides together, pin and sew a fabric B small square to the fabric C small square; press seam over fabric B. Join the strip to the top edge of the fabric A large square, with the blue square on the left side; press seam over fabric B.

With right sides together, pin and sew a fabric B small square to the fabric D small square; press seam over fabric B. Join the strip to the bottom edge of the fabric A large square, with the blue square on the right side; press seam over fabric B.

With right sides together, pin and sew a fabric B short rectangle to the short end of the fabric D short rectangle; press seam open. Join the strip to the left edge of the center patch, matching the fabrics; press seam open.

With right sides together, pin and sew a fabric C short rectangle to the short end of the fabric B short rectangle; press seam open. Join the strip to the right edge of the center patch, matching the fabrics; press seam open.

Make the frame With right sides together, pin and sew a fabric A small square and a fabric B small square to each short end of two of the fabric E rectangles; press seams open. Join one strip to the left edge of the center patch, with the orange square on the top. Join the remaining strip to the right edge of the center patch, with the blue square on the top; press seams open.

Complete the square With right sides together, pin and sew a fabric A short rectangle and a fabric B short rectangle to each short end of the remaining fabric E rectangles; press seams open. Join the strips to the top and bottom edges of the center square, matching the fabrics; press seams open.

random squares

random squares

The seam allowance is ¼ inch throughout.

Make inroads into your stash with this completely random block. The challenge is to use a different fabric for every single square, so this is the perfect solution for the small-scale charm packs in your collection. Here, the squares are a manageable 3½ inches, but some antique examples feature tiny 1-inch patches.

Fabric quantities

- 16 different dark and medium print and solid fabrics A: 16 x 16 inches in total

Prepare the patches

Rotary method
- From fabrics A, cut sixteen 3½-inch squares

or

Template cutting
Using the 4 x 4 templates (pages 269–73):
- From fabrics A, cut 16 small squares

Make the block

Lay out the patches Arrange the small squares in four rows of four patches, balancing the colors and patterns in each row.

One row at a time, with right sides together, pin and sew together the squares in each row; press seams in alternate directions.

Complete the square With right sides together and carefully matching seams, pin and sew the first and third rows to the second row; press seams open. Add the fourth row; press seam open.

square propeller

The seam allowance is ¼ inch throughout.

Square Propeller is a new propeller design, but there are several historic variations on this theme. Most of them date back to the 1930s, an era when flying was a glamorous new way to travel, and quilt designers drew up new blocks featuring Art Deco-style airplanes.

A
B
C
D

Fabric quantities

- Dark blue print fabric A: 5 x 10 inches
- Dark blue fabric B: 8 x 8 inches
- Medium blue print fabric C: 8 x 14 inches
- White fabric D: 5 x 10 inches

Prepare the patches

Rotary method
- From fabric A and D, make four 3½-inch half-square triangles (see page 12)
- From fabric B, cut four 3½-inch squares
- From fabric C, cut four 6½ x 3½-inch rectangles

or

Template cutting
Using the 4 x 4 templates (pages 269–73):

- From fabrics A and D, cut 4 small triangles each
- From fabric B, cut 4 small squares
- From fabric C, cut 4 short rectangles

Template piecing

With right sides together, pin and sew a fabric A small triangle to each of the fabric D small triangles to make four half-square triangles; press seams open.

Make the block

Piece four patches With right sides together, pin and sew a half-square triangle to each of the fabric B small squares; press seams open. With the blue square at the top, join a blue print short rectangle to the left edge of each strip; press seams open.

Sew two rows With right sides together, pin and sew two patches together, making sure the half-square triangles meet in the center of the block; press seam open. Repeat with the second set of patches.

Complete the square With right sides together and carefully matching seams, join the two halves together, with the triangles forming a pinwheel in the center; press seam open.

315 pinwheels

This cheerful design can be extended to make a quilt top by repeating the block, either in the same colors or as a scrappy design, with each pinwheel in a different color. You will need to work carefully where the four triangle points converge.

The seam allowance is ¼ inch throughout.

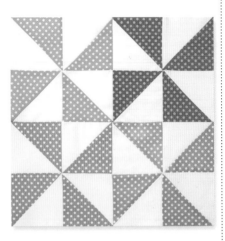

Fabric quantities

- Light purple print fabric A: 5 x 10 inches
- Medium pink print fabric B: 5 x 10 inches
- Medium red print fabric C: 5 x 10 inches
- Light green print fabric D: 5 x 10 inches
- White fabric E: 10 x 20 inches

Prepare the patches

Rotary method
- From fabrics A and E, fabrics B and E, fabrics C and E, and fabrics D and E, make one 6½-inch pinwheel square (see page 13) each

or

Template cutting
Using the 4 x 4 templates (pages 269–73):

- From fabrics A, B, C, and D, cut 4 small triangles each
- From fabric E, cut 16 small triangles

Template piecing

To make 16 half-square triangles, with right sides together, sew each of the fabric A small triangles to the long diagonal edge of a fabric E small triangle; press seams over fabric A. Repeat with the fabrics B, C, and D small triangles.

Join two purple print half-square triangles along a light and dark edge; press seam toward A. Repeat to make the second row. Join the two strips, alternating the purple triangles; press seams open. Repeat with the pink, green, and red half-square triangles to make another three pinwheel squares.

Make the block

Join the patches Join the green and red pinwheel squares; press seams open. Join the pink and purple pinwheel squares; press seams open.

Complete the square Join the pairs together at the long edge, matching the points; press seams open.

316 thrifty

Directional graphic prints, such as the outline leaf shown here, are ideally suited to larger patches. The print has also been used in the framelike Pig Pen on page 238. In keeping with the block's name, the smaller squares are cut from a mixture of different leftover fabrics.

The seam allowance is ¼ inch throughout.

Fabric quantities

- Light purple print fabric A: 6 x 6 inches
- Light purple print fabric B: 6 x 6 inches
- Dark purple print fabric C: 10 x 10 inches
- Medium purple print fabric D: 5 x 5 inches
- White fabric E: 6 x 12 inches

Prepare the patches

Rotary method
- From fabrics A, B, and E, make four 4½-inch four-patch squares (see page 11)
- From fabric C, cut four 4½-inch squares
- From fabric D, cut one 4½-inch square

or

Template cutting
Using the 6 x 6 templates (pages 278–83):
- From fabric A and B, cut 4 small squares each
- From fabric C, cut 4 large squares
- From fabric D, cut 1 large square
- From fabric E, cut 8 small squares

Template piecing

With right sides together, sew a fabric A small square to a fabric E small square; press seam over fabric E. Repeat with a fabric B small square and a fabric E small square. Join the two strips together along a long edge, keeping the fabric E squares diagonal to one another, to complete one four-patch square; press seams open. Repeat to make another three four-patch squares.

Make the block

Sew three rows For the top and bottom rows, with right sides together, pin and sew a four-patch square to each edge of a fabric C large square; press seams over fabric C. For the middle row, join two fabric C squares to the fabric D square; press seams over fabric C.

Complete the square Flip the bottom row. With right sides together, pin and sew the top and bottom rows to the middle row, carefully matching seams; press seams open.

card trick

The seam allowance is ¼ inch throughout.

Although this is sometimes categorized as a traditional block, Card Trick was actually designed in the early 1970s by Jeff Gutcheon. It first appeared in *The Perfect Patchwork Primer*, the seminal quilting book written by novelist Beth Gutcheon. Here, it's interpreted in four textured prints, but the ingenious optical illusion looks equally effective in solid citrus brights.

A
B
C
D
E

Fabric quantities

- Dark purple print fabric A: 6 x 12 inches
- Medium pink print fabric B: 6 x 12 inches
- Dark purple print fabric C: 6 x 12 inches
- Dark red print fabric D: 6 x 12 inches
- White fabric E: 12 x 17 inches

Prepare the patches

Rotary method
- From fabrics A and E, fabrics B and E, fabrics C and E, and fabrics D and E, make one 4½-inch half-square triangle (see page 12) each
- From fabrics A, B, and E, fabrics A, D, and E, fabrics B, C, and E, and fabrics C, D, and E, make one 4½-inch three-quarter square triangle (see page 13) each
- From fabrics A, B, C, and D, make one 4½-inch hourglass square (see page 13)

or

Template cutting
Using the 6 x 6 templates (pages 278–83):
- From fabrics A, B, C, and D, cut 2 large triangles and 2 medium triangles each
- From fabric E, cut 4 large triangles and 4 medium triangles

Template piecing

With right sides together, pin and sew a fabric A large triangle to the long diagonal edge of a fabric E large triangle to make one half-square triangle; press seam over fabric A. Repeat to make another three half-square triangles using fabrics B and E, fabrics C and E, and fabrics D and E.

With right sides together, pin and sew a fabric B medium triangle to a short side of a fabric E medium triangle with the fabric B triangle on the right; press seam open. Join a fabric A large triangle to the long edge of the patchwork triangle; press seam open. Repeat to make another three three-quarter square triangles with fabrics B, C, and E, fabrics C, D, and E, and fabrics A, D, and E.

To make an hourglass square, with right sides together, pin and sew a fabric A medium triangle to a short edge of a fabric B medium triangle. Join a fabric C medium triangle to a fabric D medium triangle along a short edge. Join the two patchwork triangles along the long edge, carefully matching seams and points, to make an hourglass square.

Make the block

Sew three rows For the top row, with right sides together and matching colored triangles, join the fabric A half-square triangle to the left edge of the fabrics A and B three-quarter square triangle; add the fabric B half-square triangle to the right edge of the strip. Press seams open.

For the middle row, matching colored triangles, join the fabrics A and D three-quarter square triangle to the left side of the hourglass square; add the fabrics B and C three-quarter square triangle to the right edge of the strip. Press seams open.

For the bottom row, matching colored triangles, join the fabric D half-square triangle to the left edge of the fabrics C and D three-quarter square triangle; add the fabric C half-square triangle to the right edge of the strip. Press seams open.

Complete the square With right sides together, pin and sew the top and bottom rows to the middle row, carefully matching seams and points; press seams open.

keyboard

The seam allowance is ¼ inch throughout.

This extremely simple block works best as an overall repeat joined edge to edge, which creates interesting negative space and a subtle ombre effect. It can be made in eight shades of any color. This geometric block is easily made using the rotary method.

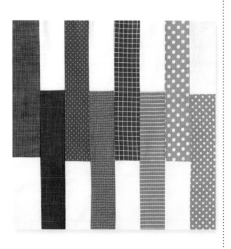

Fabric quantities

- 8 different light, medium, and dark purple print fabrics A: 9 x 20 inches in total
- White fabric B: 10 x 10 inches

Prepare the patches

Rotary method
- From fabrics A, cut one 8½ x 2-inch rectangle each
- From fabric B, cut eight 4½ x 2-inch rectangles

Make the block

Sew the keys Sew the fabric B rectangles to one short end of each fabric A rectangle; press seam over fabric A.

Complete the square Lay the long strips out vertically, arranging them with the darkest fabric on the left and the lightest fabric on the right, alternating fabric B at the top and bottom, as shown here.

With right sides together, pin and sew each strip together; press seams open.

---

checker square

The seam allowance is ¼ inch throughout.

Made up of squares and rectangles, this is a good block for a beginner to practice some basic quilting skills: cutting the patches on the grain of the fabric, matching seams accurately, and pressing the seam allowances correctly. Color opposites, such as the combination of orange and purple, add drama to a simple design.

Fabric quantities

- Medium purple fabric A: 4 x 8 inches
- Light purple fabric B: 4 x 8 inches
- Medium orange print fabric C: 8 x 14 inches
- Light orange print fabric D: 8 x 8 inches

Prepare the patches

Rotary method
- From fabrics A and B, make one 6½-inch four-patch square (see page 11)
- From fabric C, cut four 6½ x 3½-inch rectangles
- From fabric D, cut four 3½-inch squares

or

Template cutting

Using the 4 x 4 templates (pages 269–73):
- From fabrics A and B, cut 2 small squares each
- From fabric C, cut 4 short rectangles
- From fabric D, cut 4 small squares

Template piecing

With right sides together, sew a fabric A small square to a fabric B small square; press seam over fabric A. Repeat to make a second pair. Join the pairs together at the long edge, keeping colors diagonal to one another, to complete the four-patch square; press seams open.

Make the block

Sew three rows For the top and bottom rows, join a fabric D small square to each end of two fabric C short rectangles; press seams over fabric C. For the middle row, sew the remaining two fabric C short rectangles to each side edge of the four-patch square, with a fabric A small square at the top left; press seams over fabric C.

Complete the square With right sides together, join the top and bottom rows to the center row, matching seams; press seams open.

butterfly star

Another block in the nine-patch star family, this variation is set against a white octagon. The center hourglass motif lies within a diamond square, giving it a light and open feel. If multiple blocks are joined edge to edge, the star shape becomes less apparent and a diagonal grid of hourglasses separated by dark diamond squares appears.

The seam allowance is ¼ inch throughout.

A
B
C
D

Fabric quantities

- Dark purple fabric A: 6 x 12 inches
- Dark pink fabric B: 12 x 12 inches
- Medium purple fabric C: 6 x 12 inches
- White fabric D: 18 x 18 inches

Prepare the patches

Rotary method
- From fabrics A and D, make four 4½-inch half-square triangles (see page 12)
- From fabrics B and D, make four 4½-inch hourglass squares (see page 13)
- From fabrics C and D, make one 4½-inch hourglass square

or

Template cutting
Using the 6 x 6 templates (pages 278–83):
- From fabric A, cut 4 large triangles
- From fabric B, cut 8 medium triangles
- From fabric C, cut 2 medium triangles
- From fabric D, cut 4 large triangles and 10 medium triangles

Template piecing

With right sides together, pin a fabric D medium triangle to the right short side of each of the fabric B and C medium triangles; press seams away from fabric D. Join in matching pairs to make hourglass shapes, with the points of the triangles meeting in the center to make four dark pink hourglass squares and one medium purple hourglass square; press seams open.

With right sides together, sew a fabric A large triangle to the long diagonal edge of each fabric E large triangle to make four half-square triangles; press seam over fabric A.

Make the block

Sew three rows For the top row, with the dark purple triangles pointing up and outward, join a half-square triangle to each pink side of a fabrics B and D hourglass square; press seams open. Repeat to make the bottom row.

For the center row, join the white edge of a half-square triangle to each medium purple edge of the fabrics C and D hourglass square; press seams open.

Complete the square Flip the bottom row. With right sides together, pin and sew each row together, carefully matching points and seams; press seams open.

roman square

The seam allowance is ¼ inch throughout.

A

B

Many patchwork blocks are variations of others. Roman Square is an alternative version of Japanese Lattice on page 210; both are made up with repeated short rectangles in two colors. Joining multiple blocks edge to edge creates a pattern of horizontal blue chains on a white background. This geometric block is easily made using the rotary method.

Fabric quantities

- Dark purple print fabric A: 10 x 16 inches
- Light purple fabric B: 9 x 10 inches

Prepare the patches

Rotary method
- From fabrics A and B, make eight 4½-inch three-stripe squares (see page 11)
- From fabric B, cut one 4½-inch square

Make the block

Sew three rows Lay the nine squares out in three rows of three, with the light purple square at the center. The stripes on the four squares that lie at the corners should run vertically and the other four horizontally.

For the top row, sew a vertical stripe square to each side edge of a horizontal stripe square; press the seams over fabric A. For the center row, sew a horizontal stripe square to each side edge of the light purple square; press the seams over fabric B.

Complete the square With right sides facing, sew the top and bottom rows to the center row, carefully matching the seams; press seams open.

---

pig pen

The seam allowance is ¼ inch throughout.

A

B

C

D

Most symmetrical quilt blocks are based around a square, so this is unusual being based on a rectangle. The Pig Pen motif can be extended with long dark purple strips at the side edges and made larger by adding concentric rectangles of different fabric. There are several different blocks with this name; this particular construction method comes from the African-American quilting tradition and is found, in various forms, in many Gee's Bend quilts. This geometric block is easily made from the rotary method.

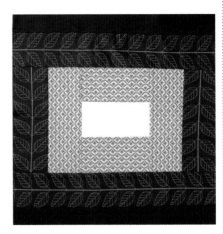

Fabric quantities

- White fabric A: 3 x 5 inches
- Medium purple print fabric B: 7 x 12 inches
- Dark purple print fabric C: 13 x 12 inches
- Dark purple fabric D: 4 x 13 inches

Prepare the patches

Rotary method
- From fabric A, cut one 4½ x 2½-inch rectangle
- From fabric B, cut two 6½ x 2½-inch rectangles and two 4½ x 2½-inch rectangles
- From fabric C, cut two 12½ x 2½-inch rectangles and two 6½ x 2½-inch rectangles
- From fabric D, cut two 12½ x 1½-inch rectangles

Make the block

Join the rectangles With right sides together, sew a fabric B short rectangle to the top and bottom edges of the fabric A rectangle; add the fabric B medium rectangles to the side edges of the patch. Press seams over fabric B. Join the fabric C shorter rectangles to the side edges of the patch and the fabric C longer rectangles to the top and bottom edges; press seams over fabric D.

Complete the square Finish by joining the fabric D narrow rectangles to the top and bottom edges of the patch; press seams open.

little cherry basket

The seam allowance is ¼ inch throughout.

A
B
C

This traditional design can be arranged in three ways to make a quilt: sashed in rows, so all the motifs lie in the same direction; in fours with the "cherries" at the corners and a white diamond at the center; or on point, separated by large squares. To change the look, the Little Cherry Basket block becomes a spiky cactus pot when it's made from green fabrics in a terracotta pot.

Fabric quantities

- Dark purple print fabric A: 5 x 15 inches
- Medium yellow print fabric B: 10 x 15 inches
- White fabric C: 14 x 20 inches

Prepare the patches

Rotary method
- From fabrics A and C, make five 3½-inch half-square triangles (see page 12)
- From fabrics B and C, make four 3½-inch half-square triangles
- From fabric B, cut one 3½-inch square
- From fabric C, cut two 6½ x 3½-inch rectangles and two 3½-inch squares

or

Template cutting
Using the 4 x 4 templates (pages 269–73):
- From fabric A, cut 5 small triangles
- From fabric B, cut 1 small square and 4 small triangles
- From fabric C, cut 2 short rectangles, 2 small squares, and 9 small triangles

Template piecing

With right sides together, sew a fabric A small triangle to the long diagonal edge of a fabric C small triangle to make one half-square triangle; press seam over A. Repeat to make another four half-square triangles with fabrics A and C and four half-square triangles with fabrics B and C.

Make the block

Piece the center panel For the first row, join a purple half-square triangle to a yellow half-square triangle, with both white triangles pointing up and left; press seam open. For the second row, join a yellow half-square triangle to the left edge of a yellow small square, with the white triangle pointing up and left; press seam open. Join the two rows together, carefully matching seams; press seam open.

Add the cherries With right sides together, join the two purple half-square triangles on the short end, with the purple triangles pointing down and left; join strip to the top edge of the center panel. Press seams over fabric A.

Join another two purple half-square triangles along the short edges with the purple triangles pointing down and right; add a white small square to the right edge of the strip. Press seams open. With the white square at the top, join the strip to the left edge of the center panel; press seams open.

Complete the square Join a yellow half-square triangle to a white short rectangle along the yellow edge, carefully matching seams, making sure the yellow triangle points up and right; press seams open. With the yellow half-square triangle on the bottom, join the strip to the right side of the center panel; press seam open.

Sew a yellow half-square triangle to a short end of a white short rectangle with the yellow triangle pointing up and left; add a white small square to the right edge of the strip. Press seams open. Join strip to the bottom edge of the center panel, carefully matching seams; press seams open.

eight-point triangle star

The seam allowance is ¼ inch throughout.

This is a simplified way to make the classic Eight-Point Star (see page 121) without having to tackle any complicated seams or, if you're rotary piecing, any diagonal edges. Each diamond is made of two half-square triangles, so use small-scale prints and the seams between the triangles will be hardly noticeable.

A
B
C
D
E

Fabric quantities

- Dark pink print fabric A: 5 x 10 inches
- Light purple print fabric B: 5 x 10 inches
- Medium pink print fabric C: 5 x 10 inches
- Medium purple print fabric D: 5 x 10 inches
- White fabric E: 14 x 20 inches

Prepare the patches

Rotary method
- From fabrics A and B, fabrics A and E, fabrics B and E, fabrics C and D, fabrics C and E, and fabrics D and E, make two 3½-inch half-square triangles (see page 12) each
- From fabric E, cut four 3½-inch squares

or

Template cutting
Using the 4 x 4 templates (pages 269–73):
- From fabrics A, B, C, and D, cut 4 small triangles each
- From fabric E, cut 4 small squares and 8 small triangles

Template piecing

With right sides together, sew a fabric A small triangle to the long diagonal edge of a fabric B triangle to make one half-square triangle; press seam over fabric A. Repeat to make a second half-square triangle. Repeat again to make two half-square triangles each from fabrics A and E, fabrics B and E, fabrics C and D, fabrics C and E, and fabrics D and E.

Make the block

Arrange the half-square triangles Lay out the patches in four rows of four half-square triangles, positioning them to form a star and making sure the star points in matching colors are at opposite corners, as shown above.

Sew the center panel With right sides together, pin and sew a fabrics A and B half-square triangle to the left edge of a fabrics C and D half-square triangle, with fabrics B and D meeting in the center. Repeat for the bottom pair, then join the two pairs together, with matching fabrics opposite.

Piece the star points With right sides together, pin and sew a fabrics A and E half-square triangle to the top edge of a fabrics D and E half-square triangle, with the white fabric meeting in the center; press seam open. Repeat to make a second pair. Join these strips to each side edge of the center patch, matching the colors and with the star points on the outside edge.

With right sides together, pin and sew a fabrics C and E half-square triangle to a fabrics B and E half-square triangle, with the white fabric meeting in the center. Join a fabric E square to each end of the pair; press seams open. Repeat to make a second strip.

Complete the square With right sides together, sew each strip to the top and bottom edges of the patch, matching the colors and with the star points on the outside edge; press seams open.

stacks

The seam allowance is ¼ inch throughout.

With a pattern that looks like a precariously balanced tower of wooden blocks, Stacks has a fresh, new look. Choose monochrome prints with simple graphic patterns to keep the contemporary feel. You could extend the pattern to make a larger square, or even a quilt top, by increasing the number of light and dark rectangles in each row.

A
B
C

Fabric quantities

- Light blue print fabric A: 13 x 15 inches
- Medium purple print fabric B: 10 x 12 inches
- Medium purple print fabric C: 3 x 9 inches

Prepare the patches

Rotary method
- From fabric A, cut nine 4½ x 2½-inch rectangles and three 2½-inch squares
- From fabric B, cut six 4½ x 2½-inch rectangles
- From fabric C, cut three 2½-inch squares

or

Template cutting

Using the 6 x 6 templates (pages 278–83):
- From fabric A, cut 9 short rectangles and 3 small squares
- From fabric B, cut 6 short rectangles
- From fabric C, cut 3 small squares

Make the block

Sew six rows For the first, third, and fifth rows, join a fabric A small square to the left edge of a fabric B short rectangle; press seam open. Join a fabric A short rectangle to the right edge of the strip, then add a fabric C small square; press seams open.

For the second, fourth, and sixth rows, join a fabric A short rectangle to both sides of a fabric B short rectangle; press seams open.

Complete the square With right sides together, pin and sew the rows together; press seams open.

. . . .

h squares

The seam allowance is ¼ inch throughout.

A quilt made up from several H Squares would be the perfect gift for anyone whose name begins with "H," much as the Tee Block (see page 38) suits anybody with the initial "T". Play with fabric colors and placements to experiment with secondary patterns created between multiple H Squares joined end to end.

A
B
C
D
E

Fabric quantities

- Dark pink print fabric A: 6 x 10 inches
- Medium blue print fabric B: 6 x 10 inches
- Medium pink print fabric C: 6 x 10 inches
- Dark purple print fabric D: 6 x 10 inches
- White fabric E: 6 x 12 inches

Prepare the patches

Rotary method
- From fabric A, B, C, and D, cut two 6½ x 2½-inch rectangles and one 2½-inch square each
- From fabric E, cut eight 2½-inch squares

or

Template cutting

Using the 6 x 6 templates (pages 278–83):
- From fabrics A, B, C, and D, cut 2 medium rectangles and 1 small square each
- From fabric E, cut 8 small squares

Make the block

Piece four patches To make four patches, with right sides together, sew a fabric E small square to both sides of each colored small square; press seams inward. Sew one matching medium rectangle to each long edge of the four strips; press seams over the rectangles.

Sew two rows With right sides together, pin and sew a dark pink H patch to the left side of the blue H patch, alternating the direction of the H patch; press seam open. Repeat with the purple H patch and the medium pink H patch.

Complete the square Carefully matching seams, join the first row to the second row, making sure the vertical H patches are in opposite corners; press seam open.

grid stripes

Like City Grid (see page 242), this is a new geometric design that works well in two analogous fabrics plus crisp white. The elongated purple checkerboard appears to be superimposed on a pattern of wide alternating purple and white stripes, creating an undeniably contemporary look.

The seam allowance is ¼ inch throughout.

Fabric quantities

- Light purple print fabric A: 9 x 12 inches
- Dark purple fabric B: 10 x 15 inches
- White fabric C: 9 x 12 inches

Prepare the patches

Rotary method
- From fabrics A and C, cut nine 2½-inch squares each
- From fabric B, cut nine 4½ x 2½-inch rectangles

or

Template cutting
Using the 6 x 6 templates (pages 278–83):
- From fabrics A and C, cut 9 small squares each
- From fabric B, cut 9 short rectangles

Make the block

Sew three columns With right sides together, sew the fabric A squares and the fabric C squares together in pairs; press seams over fabric A. With the fabric C square at the top right, sew a fabric B rectangle to the bottom edge of each pair; press seam open.

For the first and third columns, alternate three light purple and white strips with three dark purple rectangles; press seams open.

For the second column, alternate three purple rectangles with three light purple and white strips; press seams open.

Complete the square With right sides together, pin and sew the first and third columns to the second column, carefully matching seams to create the checkerboard grid; press seams open.

. . . .

city grid

If you want a block with a distinctly urban feel as a counterpoint to the traditional patterns in this book, look to this rectangular grid, which is reminiscent of an abstract version of a street plan of Manhattan. It works well in dark and neutral fabrics for a sophisticated effect.

The seam allowance is ¼ inch throughout.

Fabric quantities

- Dark purple fabric A: 9 x 10 inches
- Medium beige print fabric B: 9 x 10 inches
- White fabric C: 9 x 12 inches

Prepare the patches

Rotary method
- From fabrics A and B, cut three 6½ x 2½-inch rectangles and three 2½-inch squares each
- From fabric C, cut twelve 2½-inch squares

or

Template cutting
Using the 6 x 6 templates (pages 278–83):
- From fabrics A and B, cut 3 medium rectangles and 3 small squares each
- From fabric C, cut 12 small squares

Make the block

Sew two columns With right sides together, sew a fabric C small square to both sides of each fabric A small square; press seams over fabric A. Repeat to make two more fabrics A and C strips.

Sew a fabric A medium rectangle to the bottom edge of each strip; press seams open. Join three strips along the long edges to make a column; press seams open. Repeat with fabrics B and C to make the second column.

Complete the square Lay out the two halves of the block in opposite directions, alternating the colors and without the white small squares touching. With right side edges together, pin and sew the columns together, matching the seams; press seam open.

interlocked cross

The seam allowance is ¼ inch throughout.

Seemingly made up of four overlapping squares, this block resembles a rotated Card Trick on page 235, but because it is made up of squares and rectangles, it is quicker to put together.

Fabric quantities

- Dark purple fabric A: 7 x 8 inches
- Medium gray print fabric B: 7 x 8 inches
- Medium purple fabric C: 7 x 8 inches
- Medium gray print fabric D: 7 x 8 inches
- Light purple fabric E: 8 x 8 inches

Prepare the patches

Rotary method
- From fabrics B, E, and A, fabrics C, E, and B, fabrics D, E, and C, and fabrics A, E, and D, make one 6½-inch three-patch square (see page 11) each

or

Template cutting
Using the 4 x 4 templates (pages 269–73):
- From fabrics A, B, C, and D, cut 1 short rectangle and 1 small square each
- From fabric E, cut 4 small squares

Template piecing

To make a three-patch square, with right sides together, join a fabric B small square to a fabric E small square; press seam over fabric B. Sew the strip to the long side of the fabric A short rectangle; press seam open. Repeat using fabrics C, E, and B; fabrics D, E, and C; and fabrics A, E, and D.

Make the block

Sew two rows Arrange the three-patch squares in their final positions, with the light purple squares at each corner, as shown above.

Complete the square With right sides together, pin and sew a pair of patches together; press seams open. Repeat with the second pair of patches. Carefully matching seams, pin and sew the two rows together; press seams open.

---

double x

The seam allowance is ¼ inch throughout.

In this variation on the two-colored Fireflies on page 182, the two corner small squares subtly change the dynamic of the block, giving it more stability.

Fabric quantities

- Light orange fabric A: 5 x 10 inches
- Purple print fabric B: 8 x 11 inches
- Purple fabric C: 8 x 11 inches
- White fabric D: 9 x 18 inches

Prepare the patches

Rotary method
- From fabrics A and D, make two 6½-inch hourglass squares (see page 13)
- From fabrics B and D and fabrics C and D, make one 6½-inch triangle-and-square block (see page 15) each

or

Template cutting
Using the 4 x 4 templates (pages 269–73):
- From fabric A, cut 4 small triangles
- From fabrics B and C, cut 1 large triangle and 1 small square each

- From fabric D, cut 4 small squares and 8 small triangles

Template piecing

With right sides together, join the fabric A and D small triangles in pairs to make four half-square triangles; press seams open. With the orange triangles pointing down and left, sew a fabric D small square to the left edge of each half-square triangle.

Repeat, then join strips in pairs so that the orange triangles meet at the center to form an hourglass; press seams open. Repeat to make a second hourglass square.

Join the short edge of two fabric D small triangles to the bottom and left edges of a fabric B small square; press seams over fabric B. Join the patchwork triangle to a fabric B large triangle along the diagonal edge; press seams over fabric B. Repeat to make another triangle-and-square block using fabrics C and D.

Make the block

Sew two rows Lay out the four quarter squares so that the hourglasses lie in the same direction, and opposite corners and the large triangles point inwards. With right sides together, join the top two squares; press seam open. Join the bottom two squares in the same way.

Complete the square With right sides together, pin and stitch the two rows together, matching the center seams; press seams open.

flying dutchman

The seam allowance is ¼ inch throughout.

The Flying Dutchman of legend is the cursed captain of a phantom ship, who is doomed to sail the seas for eternity. His gripping story has inspired Richard Wagner's epic opera of the same name, the movie series *Pirates of the Caribbean* and this block. Perhaps the arrangement of the triangular patches originally evoked the sails and rigging of a merchant vessel.

A
B
C
D

Fabric quantities

- Medium purple print fabric A: 5 x 10 inches

- Dark purple fabric B: 10 x 10 inches

- Light purple print fabric C: 10 x 10 inches

- White fabric D: 9 x 14 inches

Prepare the patches

Rotary method
- From fabrics A and D, make four 3½-inch half-square triangles (see page 12)

- From fabrics B and C, make eight 3½-inch half-square triangles

- From fabric D, cut four 3½-inch squares

or

Template cutting
Using the 4 x 4 templates (pages 269–73):
- From fabric A, cut 4 small triangles

- From fabrics B and C, cut 8 small triangles each

- From fabric D, cut 4 small squares and 4 small triangles

Template piecing

With right sides together, pin and sew a fabric A small triangle to the long diagonal edge of a fabric D triangle to make one half-square triangle; press seam over fabric A. Repeat to make another three half-square triangles from fabrics A and D and to make eight half-square triangles from fabrics B and C.

Make the block

Piece two butterfly squares With right sides together, sew a fabric D small square to the right edge of each fabrics A and D half-square triangle, with the fabric A triangles pointing down and right. Join the pairs, with the purple triangles meeting at the center, to make two butterfly squares; press seams open.

Piece two triangle squares With right sides together, pin and sew the fabrics B and C half-square triangles in pairs, with the fabric B triangles all pointing down and left. Join in pairs to make two triangle squares; press seams open.

Sew two rows With right sides together, join a butterfly square to the left edge of a triangle square with the dark purple triangles pointing down and left; press seams open.

Join the second butterfly square to the right edge of the second triangle square with the dark purple triangles pointing up and right; press seams open.

Complete the square With right sides together, pin and sew the two rows together, matching seams and points; press seam open.

flying squares

The seam allowance is ¼ inch throughout.

Asymmetric designs can sometimes appear a little awkward, however Flying Squares has an energy of its own that will add liveliness to an album quilt. This block is most accurately made from templates for a finished 12-inch square.

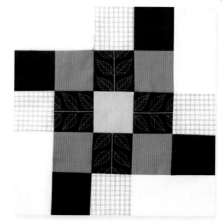

Fabric quantities

- Dark purple fabric A: 6 x 6 inches
- Medium purple fabric B: 6 x 6 inches
- Dark purple print fabric C: 6 x 6 inches
- Light purple print fabric D: 6 x 6 inches
- Light purple fabric E: 3 x 3 inches
- White fabric F: 6 x 12 inches

Prepare the patches

Template cutting
Using the 5 x 5 templates (pages 274–7):
- From fabrics A, B, C, and D, cut 4 small squares each
- From fabric E, cut 1 small square
- From fabric F, cut 4 short rectangles

Make the block

Piece two sections For the top row, with right sides together, pin and sew a fabric D small square to the right end of a fabric F short rectangle; join a fabric A small square. Press seams open. Repeat for the bottom row of the bottom section.

For the second row of the top section, join fabrics A, B, and C, small squares in a row; add another fabric B small square to the right edge of the strip. Press seams open. Repeat for the first row of the bottom section. With right sides together, join both rows of the top section; press seams open. Add a fabric F short rectangle to the right side of the patch; press seam open.

Flip both rows of the bottom section, then join them, carefully matching seams; press seam open. Add a fabric F short rectangle to the left side of the patch; press seam open.

Make the center row With right sides together, pin and sew a row of five small squares: fabrics D, C, E, C, and D; press seams open.

Complete the square Matching seams, join the top and bottom sections to the center row, making sure the dark purple squares are in opposite corners; press seams open.

- -

quarter cross

The seam allowance is ¼ inch throughout.

This cross is the same shape as the Greek Cross on page 267, but it's made up in a different way. Here, Four log cabin squares meet to form the cross in the center. Quarter Cross is quick to piece together, building out from a small center square, which could be cut from a sixth fabric to change the look of the block.

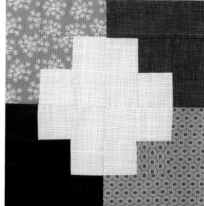

Fabric quantities

- Medium pink print fabric A: 6 x 8 inches
- Dark pink print fabric B: 6 x 8 inches
- Medium pink print fabric C: 6 x 8 inches
- Dark purple fabric D: 6 x 8 inches
- Light blue print fabric E: 9 x 12 inches

Prepare the patches

Rotary method
- From fabrics A, B, C, and D, cut one 6½ x 2½-inch rectangle, one 4½ x 2½-inch rectangle, and one 2½-inch square each
- From fabric E, cut four 4½ x 2½-inch rectangles and four 2½-inch squares

or

Template cutting

Using the 6 x 6 templates (pages 278–83):
- From fabrics A, B, C, and D, cut 1 medium rectangle, 1 short rectangle, and 1 small square each
- From fabric E, cut 4 short rectangles and 4 small squares

Make the block

Piece four quarter squares With right sides together, pin and sew the fabric A small square to the top edge of a fabric E small square; press seam over fabric A. Sew a fabric E rectangle to the right edge of the strip; press seam away from fabric E. Join the fabric A short rectangle to the top edge, pressing over fabric A, then add the fabric A medium rectangle to the left edge to complete the quarter square; press seam over fabric A. Repeat with fabrics B and E, C and E, and D and E to make another three quarter squares.

Sew two rows With the light blue pieces meeting in the center, join the fabric A patch to the fabric B patch; press seam open. Repeat to join the fabric D patch to the fabric C patch. The light blue patches should join at the center to create the cross.

Complete the square Sew the pairs together, matching seams. With right sides together, pin and sew the rows together, matching seams; press open.

birthday present

The seam allowance is ¼ inch throughout.

Specially designed to celebrate the birthday of your best friend or a close family member, this block could be converted into a Christmas gift by replacing the floral print with a seasonal fabric. Make it as an individual cushion cover, extend the bottom edge and use it for a tote bag, or, if you're really devoted, make a whole quilt top of ribboned packages. Use a small-scale, irregular print, such as this vintage style floral, for the wrapping "paper" so that the seam lines will be unobtrusive.

A
B
C

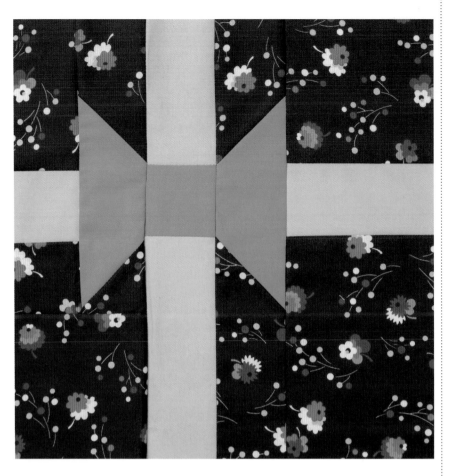

Fabric quantities

- Medium turquoise fabric A: 7 x 9 inches
- Light turquoise fabric B: 7 x 9 inches
- Dark purple print fabric C: 11 x 15 inches

Prepare the patches

Rotary method
- From fabrics A and C, make two 6½ x 2½-inch short boats (see page 17)
- From fabric A, cut one 2½-inch square
- From fabric B, cut one 6½ x 2½-inch rectangle, two 4½ x 2½-inch rectangles, and one 2½-inch square
- From fabric C, cut one 6½ x 4½-inch rectangle, two 4½-inch squares, two 4½ x 2½-inch rectangles, and three 2½-inch squares

or

Template cutting
Using the 6 x 6 templates (pages 278–83):
- From fabric A, cut 2 short boats and 1 small square
- From fabric B, cut 1 medium rectangle, 2 short rectangles, and 1 small square
- From fabric C, cut 1 wide medium rectangle, 2 large squares, 2 short rectangles, 3 small squares, and 4 small triangles

Template piecing

With right sides together, pin and sew the fabric C small triangles to each diagonal edge of both fabric A short boats; press seams over fabric C.

Make the block

Piece the left column Sew a fabric C short rectangle to the top edge of the fabric B small square; join a fabric C small square to the bottom edge. Press seams over fabric C. Sew a fabric C small square to the top of a short boat. Join strips along the long edge with the short boat on the right and facing inward; press seams open. Join a fabric C large square to the bottom edge; press seam open.

Make the center column Sew a fabric B short rectangle to the top edge of the fabric A square; join a fabric B medium rectangle to the bottom edge. Press seams over fabric A. Sew a fabric C small square to the top edge of the second short boat; add a fabric C short rectangle to the bottom edge. Press seams open. Join strips along the long edge, with the short boat on the right and facing inward; press seam open.

Make the right column Sew the large fabric C square to the top edge of the remaining fabric B short rectangle; join the remaining fabric C rectangle to the bottom edge. Press seams over C.

Complete the square With right sides together, pin and sew the right and left columns to the center column, carefully matching seams; press seams open.

emma's puzzle

The seam allowance is ¼ in throughout

Adapted from a popular eight-point star patch, a different color is used for each quarter square in this block. You could replace the flying geese rectangles with half-square triangles.

A
B
C
D
E

Fabric quantities

- Light purple fabric A: 5x 9 inches
- Dark pink fabric B: 5 x 9 inches
- Medium orange fabric C: 5 x 9 inches
- Medium purple fabric D: 5 x 9 inches
- White fabric E: 9 x 20 inches

Prepare the patches

Rotary method

- From fabrics A and E, fabrics B and E, fabrics C and E, and fabrics D and E, make one 6½ x 3½-inch flying geese rectangle (see page 17) each

- From fabrics A and E, fabrics B and E, fabrics C and E, and fabrics D and E, make two 3½-inch half-square triangles (see page 12) each

or

Template cutting
Using the 4 x 4 templates (pages 269–73):

- From fabrics A, B, C, and D, cut 1 medium triangle and 2 small triangles each

- From fabric E, cut 16 small triangles

Template piecing

With right sides facing, pin and sew each fabric A small triangle to the long edge of a fabric E small triangle to make one half-square triangle; press seam over fabric A. Repeat to make another fabrics A and E half-square triangle, then make two half-square triangles each from fabrics B and E, fabrics C and E, and fabrics D and E.

With right sides together, sew a fabric E small triangle to each short edge of a fabric A medium triangle to make one flying geese rectangle; press seams over the small triangles. Make another three flying geese rectangles, one each from fabrics B and E, fabrics C and E, and fabrics D and E.

Make the block

Piece four patches Join matching half-square triangles in vertical pairs, so the top white triangle points down and right and the bottom one points down and left; press seam away from E. Join the matching flying geese rectangles to the right edge of each pair of half-square triangles, making sure it, points outward.

Sew two rows With right sides together, join the light purple patch to the dark pink patch, making sure the points of the medium triangles meet in the center; press seam open. Repeat with the medium purple and orange patches.

Complete the square Join the rows, matching seams and points; press seam open.

cubes

This seemingly three-dimensional block has a 1960s Op Art look, but similar geometric optical illusions can be found in the decorative arts of the medieval and earlier Roman eras. The top right corners of the cubes are pieced from half-square triangles to avoid sewing complicated set-in seams. Pick three distinctly light, medium, and dark fabrics for the cubes and set them against a white background for maximum visual effect.

A
B
C
D
E
F

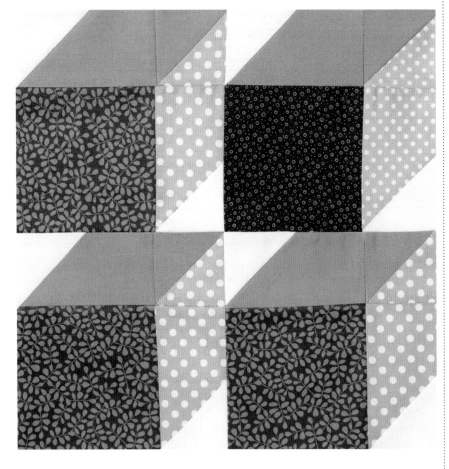

Fabric quantities

- Medium purple fabric A: 9 x 12 inches
- Light purple print fabric B: 9 x 9 inches
- Medium purple print fabric C: 4 x 9 inches
- Dark purple print fabric D: 5 x 15 inches
- Dark brown print fabric E: 5 x 5 inches
- White fabric F: 8 x 8 inches

Prepare the patches

Rotary method
- From fabrics A and F, make four 4½ x 2½-inch left tapered rectangles (see page 16)
- From fabrics B and F, make three 4½ x 2½-inch right tapered rectangles (see page 16)
- From fabrics C and F, make one 4½ x 2½-inch right tapered rectangle
- From fabrics A and B, make three 2½-inch half-square triangles (see page 12)
- From fabrics A and C, make one 2½-inch half-square triangle
- From fabric D, cut three 4½-inch squares
- From fabric E, cut one 4½-inch square

or

Template cutting
Using the 6 x 6 templates (pages 278–83):
- From fabric A, cut 4 left tapered rectangles and 4 small triangles
- From fabric B, cut 3 right tapered rectangles and 3 small triangles
- From fabric C, cut 1 right tapered rectangle and 1 small triangle
- From fabric D, cut 3 large squares
- From fabric E, cut 1 large square
- From fabric F, cut 8 small triangles.

Template piecing

With right sides together, join a fabric F small triangle to the diagonal edge of each tapered rectangle; press seams away from fabric F.

With right sides together, sew a fabric A small triangle to the diagonal edge of each fabric B small triangle to make three half-square triangles; press seam over fabric A. Repeat to make one half-square triangle with fabrics A and C.

Make the block

Piece the quarter patches With right sides together, sew a fabrics B and F right tapered rectangle to the top edge of a fabric D large square; press seams open. Join a fabrics A and B half-square triangle to the matching short edge of a fabrics B and F left tapered rectangle; press seams open. Matching purple fabrics, join the strip to the right edge of the patch; press seams open. Sew this strip to the top edge of the patch.

Repeat to make another two identical patches. Then repeat using the fabrics C and F right tapered rectangle, the fabrics A and C half-square triangle, and the fabric E large square.

Sew two rows With right sides together, join a lighter patch to the left edge of the darker patch, carefully matching seams; press seam open. Join the remaining patches, making sure all of the medium purple tapered rectangles are pointing in the same direction; press seam open.

Complete the square With right sides together, pin and sew the two rows together, matching seams and points; press seam open.

windmill square

The seam allowance is ¼ inch throughout.

A bright and breezy windmill variation with plenty of movement, this block is quick to piece. Choose a large-scale print for the rectangles to make the "sails" really stand out against the muted background squares.

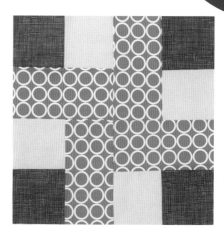

Fabric quantities

- Dark purple print fabric A: 8 x 8 inches
- Light purple fabric B: 8 x 8 inches
- Medium pink print fabric C: 7 x 16 inches

Prepare the patches

Rotary method
- From fabrics A and B, cut four 3½-inch squares each
- From fabric C, cut four 6½ x 3½-inch rectangles

Template cutting

Using the 4 x 4 templates (pages 269–73):
- From fabrics A and B, cut 4 small squares each
- From fabric C, cut 4 short rectangles

Make the block

Piece four patches With right sides together, join each fabric A small square to a fabric B small square; press seam over fabric A. With fabric A on the left, sew a strip to the top edge of each fabric C rectangle; press seam over fabric C.

Sew two rows With right sides together, pin and sew two patches together so that the fabric C short rectangles are perpendicular, meeting in the center; the fabric A small squares should be in the upper corners. Press seams open. Repeat to make the second row.

Complete the square Flip the bottom row. Carefully matching seams, join the two rows so that the short ends of the fabric C rectangles meet in the center; press seam open.

---

scrappy nine-patch chain

The seam allowance is ¼ inch throughout.

Making this block is a good way to use up the ends of precut jelly roll strips or any other small scraps; try to find eight different plain and patterned fabrics for the small squares and a bright print for the large center square. Join multiple blocks with white sashing strips and colored corner squares to continue the chain, or edge to edge, to make four-patch squares where the blocks meet at the corners. This scrappy block is easily made using the rotary method.

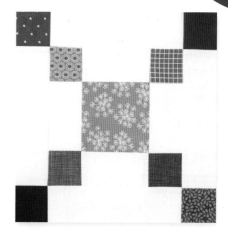

Fabric quantities

- 8 different medium and dark pink and purple solid and print fabrics A: 6 x 12 inches in total
- Medium pink print fabric B: 5 x 5 inches
- White fabric C: 12 x 14 inches

Prepare the patches

Rotary method
- From fabrics A, cut eight 2½-inch squares
- From fabric B, cut one 4½-inch square
- From fabric C, cut four 8½ x 2½-inch rectangles and four 4½ x 2½-inch rectangles

Make the block

Arrange the squares Find a pleasing balance of color and patterns.

Piece the center panel With right sides together, sew a shorter fabric C rectangle to each side edge of the fabric B large square; press seams over fabric B. Join a fabric A small square to each end of the remaining two shorter fabric C rectangles. Sew the strips to the top and bottom edges of the patch.

Complete the square With right sides together, sew a longer fabric C rectangle to each side edge of the center panel; press seams inward. Sew a fabric A small square to each end of the remaining fabric C rectangles; join the strips to the top and bottom edges of the panel. Press seams open.

tic-tac-toe

A historic block with a country feel, the two small nine patches resemble the grid for playing tic-tac-toe. At the center lies a white butterfly, or hourglass, square, which seems to be framed by white sashing and blue shoofly squares. When the block is repeated edge to edge, this effect is emphasized, and a square sashing grid can be seen across the surface of the quilt. Try combining Tic-Tac-Toe with Snowballs and Shooflies on page 194. As with other blocks made from 2½-inch squares, you can use jelly roll strips to reduce the time you spend cutting.

Fabric quantities

- Light blue print fabric A: 8 x 11 inches
- Dark purple print fabric B: 6 x 15 inches
- White fabric C: 13 x 19 inches

Prepare the patches

Rotary method
- From fabrics A and C, make eight 2½-inch half-square triangles (see page 12)
- From fabric A, cut two 2½-inch squares
- From fabric B, cut ten 2½-inch squares
- From fabric C, cut sixteen 2½-inch squares

or

Template cutting
Using the 6 x 6 templates (pages 278–83):
- From fabric A, cut 2 small squares and 8 small triangles
- From fabric B, cut 10 small squares
- From fabric C, cut 16 small squares and 8 small triangles

Template piecing

With right sides together, sew a fabric A small triangle to the diagonal edge of a fabric C small triangle to make one half-square triangle; press seam over fabric A. Repeat to make another seven half-square triangles.

Make the block

Piece two shoofly squares For the top and bottom rows, with right sides together, pin and sew a half-square triangle to each side of a fabric C small square, with the blue triangles pointing inward. For the middle row, sew a fabric C small square to both side edges of a fabric A square. Flip the bottom row, then join the top and bottom rows to the center row, with the blue triangles pointing inward; press seams open. Repeat to make another shoofly square.

Piece two nine-patch squares For the top and bottom rows, sew a fabric B small square to each side of a fabric C square. For the middle row, sew a fabric C small square to each side edge of a fabric B small square; press seams away from fabric C. Sew the top and bottom rows to the middle row; press seams open. Repeat to make another nine-patch square.

Complete the square With right sides together, pin and sew the shoofly squares and nine-patch squares in pairs. With right sides together, pin and sew the pairs together, with identical squares diagonal to one another and carefully matching seams; press seams open.

indian star

The seam allowance is ¼ inch throughout.

A combination of a ditsy allover print with a bold geometric fabric, set against a plain background, adds impact to the this striking block.

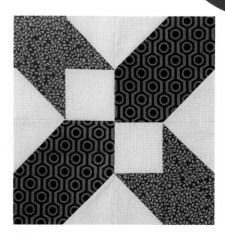

Fabric quantities

- Dark purple print fabric A: 12 x 12 inches
- Dark purple print fabric B: 7 x 14 inches
- Light purple fabric C: 12 x 14inches

Prepare the patches

Rotary method

- From fabrics A and C, make four 3½-inch half-square triangles (see page 12)
- From fabrics B and C, make two 6½-inch hexagon squares (see page 15)
- From fabrics A and C, cut two 3½-inch squares each

or

Template cutting

Using the 4 x 4 templates (pages 269–73):

- From fabric A, cut 2 small squares and 4 small triangles
- From fabric B, cut 2 hexagons
- From fabric C, cut 2 small squares and 8 small triangles

Template piecing

With right sides together, sew a fabric A small triangle to the long diagonal edge of each of the fabric C triangles to make four half-square triangles; press seam over fabric A.

With right sides together, sew a fabric C triangle to each diagonal edge of the fabric B hexagons, pressing seams over fabric B.

Make the block

Piece two arrow squares With right sides together, sew a fabric A small square to the left edge of two half-square triangles, matching purple prints and with the fabric C triangles pointing down and left; press seams open. With right sides together, join a half-square triangle to the left edge of each fabric C small square; press seams open. Join strips in pairs with points of the fabric A small triangles meeting in the center of the arrow patch; press seams open.

Complete the square With the arrow pointing up and left, join an arrow patch to the left edge of a hexagon square; press seam open. Repeat to make the second row. Join the rows, matching seams and points; press seam open.

---

homeward bound

The seam allowance is ¼ inch throughout.

This straightforward arrangement of squares and rectangles has a naive charm of its own. Sashed together with white strips and purple corner squares, it makes an effective and easily stitched quilt top. Using a different fabric for the large squares on each block would give it an old-fashioned, scrappy look.

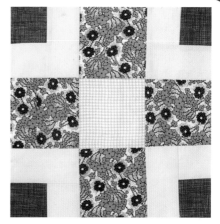

Fabric quantities

- Medium purple print fabric A: 6 x 6 inches
- Medium blue print fabric B: 10 x 10 inches
- Light blue print fabric C: 5 x 5 inches
- Light blue fabric D: 8 x 12 inches

Prepare the patches

Rotary method

- From fabrics A and D, make four 4½-inch three-patch squares (see page 11)
- From fabric B, cut four 4½-inch squares
- From fabric C, cut one 4½-inch square

or

Template cutting

Using the 6 x 6 templates (pages 278–83):

- From fabric A, cut 4 small squares
- From fabric B, cut 4 large squares
- From fabric C, cut 1 large square
- From fabric D, cut 4 short rectangles and 4 small squares

Template piecing

With right sides together, join a fabric A small square to a fabric D small square; press seam over fabric A. Sew the strip to the long side of a fabric D short rectangle to complete a three-patch square; press seam open. Repeat to make another three three-patch squares.

Make the block

Sew three rows For the top row, with right sides together, sew a three-patch square to each edge of a fabric B large square, with the fabric A small squares in the outside corners; press seams over fabric B. Repeat for the bottom row.

For the middle row, sew a fabric B large square to each side of the fabric C large square; press seams over fabric B.

Complete the square With right sides together, pin and sew the top and bottom rows to the middle row, matching seams; press seams open.

missouri

This block is really two designs combined into one: a pinwheel within a windmill. The four flying geese that make the "sails" are made up of two half-square triangles in closely matched colors, which gives the block an intense, vibrant look.

A
B
C
D
E

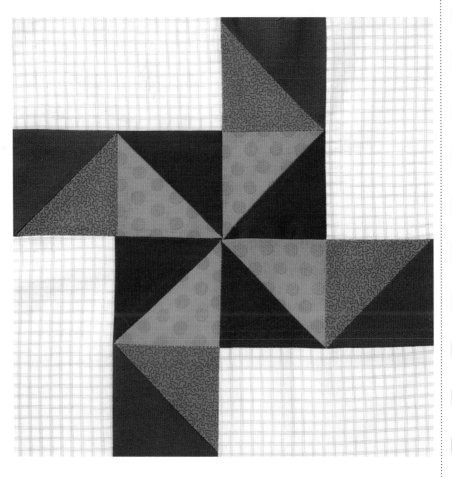

Fabric quantities

- Medium purple fabric A: 5 x 10 inches

- Dark pink print fabric B: 5 x 10 inches

- Dark orange print fabric C: 5 x 10 inches

- Dark purple fabric D: 5 x 10 inches

- Light purple print fabric E: 8 x 14 inches

Prepare the patches

Rotary method
- From fabrics A and B and fabrics C and D, make four 3½-inch half-square triangles (see page 12) each

- From fabric E, cut four 6½ x 3½-inch rectangles

or

Template cutting
Using the 4 x 4 templates (pages 269–73):
- From fabrics A, B, C, and D, cut 4 small triangles each

- From fabric E, cut 4 short rectangles

Template piecing

With right sides together, sew a fabric A small triangle to the long diagonal edge of each fabric B small triangle to make four half-square triangles; press seam over fabric A. Repeat with fabrics C and D small triangles to make another four half-square triangles.

Make the block

Piece four patches With right sides together, pin and sew a fabrics A and B half-square triangle to each of the fabrics C and D half-square triangles, with the fabric B and fabric C triangles meeting in the center; press seam open. With the new triangle pointing upward, sew a fabric E rectangle to the top edge of each strip; press seams over fabric E.

Sew two rows With right sides together, join two patches so that the half-square triangle strips abut in the center; the fabrics C and D half-square triangles should make half of the pinwheel. Press seam open. Repeat to make the second row.

Complete the square Flip the bottom row. With right sides together, join the rows together, making sure the fabrics C and D half-square triangles form a pinwheel in the center of the block; press seam open.

double z

Other names for this nineteenth-century block include Devil's Claws, Framed X, and Brown Goose—look for a goose's head and neck in the colored fabrics.

The seam allowance is ¼ in throughout

A
B
C

Fabric quantities

- Dark purple print fabric A: 7 x 16 inches
- Dark purple fabric B: 7 x 16 inches
- White fabric C: 8 x 16 inches

Prepare the patches

Rotary method
- From fabrics A and C and fabrics B and C, make two 6½ x 3½-inch flying geese rectangles (see page 17), one 6½ x 3½-inch right diamond rectangle (see page 16), and one 6½ x 3½-inch left diamond rectangle each

or

Template cutting
Using the 4 x 4 templates (pages 269–73):
- From fabrics A and B, cut 2 medium triangles, 1 right diamond, and 1 left diamond each
- From fabric C, cut 16 small triangles

Template piecing

With right sides together, sew a fabric C small triangle to each short edge of the two fabric A medium triangles to make two flying geese rectangles; press seams over fabric C. Repeat to make another two flying geese units using fabric B medium triangles and fabric C small triangles.

With right sides together, pin and sew a fabric C small triangle to each diagonal edge of the fabric A and fabric B diamonds to make four diamond rectangles; press seams inward.

Make the block

Piece four squares With right sides together, pin and sew a flying geese rectangle to the top edge of each of the matching left and right diamond rectangles; press seams open.

Sew two rows With the flying geese rectangles pointing up, join the purple print right diamond patch to the left edge of the dark purple left diamond patch; press seam open.

With the flying geese rectangles pointing down, join the purple print left diamond patch to the left edge of the dark purple right diamond patch; press seam open.

Complete the square With right sides together, join the two rows, making sure the white triangle form an hourglass in the center of the block; press seam open.

rows of bow ties

The large Bow Tie on page 161 is a stand-alone block, but this smaller version is designed to make an allover design of diagonal bow ties. Repeat in rows, rotating alternate blocks by 90 degrees, to create a pattern of bows and diamonds.

A
B
C

Fabric quantities

- Medium pink print fabric A: 8 x 10 inches
- Medium purple print fabric B: 8 x 10 inches
- White fabric C: 10 x 15 inches

Prepare the patches

Rotary method
- From fabrics A, B, and C, make three 4½-inch hexagon squares (see page 15)
- From fabrics A, B, and C, cut two 4½-inch squares each

or

Template cutting
Using the 6 x 6 templates (pages 278–83):
- From fabrics A and B, cut 2 large squares and 3 small triangles each
- From fabric C, cut 2 large squares and 3 hexagons

Template piecing

With right sides together, sew a fabric A small triangle and a fabric B small triangle to the diagonal edges of each fabric C hexagon; press seams open.

Make the block

Sew three rows For the top row, with right sides together, sew a fabric C large square to the left edge of a fabric A large square; join a hexagon square to the right edge of the strip, with the fabric A triangle pointing down and left. Press seams open.

For the center row, sew a fabric B square to the left edge of a hexagon square; join the fabric A large square to the right edge of the strip, with the fabric A triangle in the hexagon square pointing up and right. Press seams open.

For the bottom row, sew a hexagon square to the left edge of a fabric B large square; join a fabric C large square to the right edge of the strip, with the fabric C triangle pointing down and left. Press seams open.

Complete the square With right sides together, join the top and bottom rows to the center row, matching seams and points; press seams open.

spool block twist

The seam allowance is ¼ inch throughout.

This is a variation on the traditional Spool Block, made with two squares and two triangles in each corner instead of the usual long hexagon. The original design is an interesting example of how the names of blocks continue to evolve and change. Quilter Setsuko Inagawa exhibited a spectacular Spool Block quilt in Tokyo in 2011, which fired the imaginations of makers worldwide, and it is now a popular block for quilt-alongs and quilt swaps. The design is now usually known as Japanese X in her honor. This block is most accurately made from templates for a finished 12-inch square.

Fabric quantities

- Medium blue print fabric A: 10 x 10 inches
- Light blue print fabric B: 6 x 6 inches
- Medium purple print fabric C: 6 x 6 inches
- Medium red print fabric D: 6 x 6 inches
- Medium red fabric E: 6 x 6 inches
- Dark purple fabric F: 3 x 3 inches
- White fabric G: 10 x 10 inches

Prepare the patches

Template cutting
Using the 5 x 5 templates (pages 274–7):
- From fabrics A and G, cut 8 small triangles each
- From fabrics B, C, D, and E, cut 4 small squares each
- From fabric F, cut 1 small square

Template piecing

With right sides together, sew a fabric A small triangle to the long diagonal edge of each fabric G small triangle to make eight half-square triangles; press seam over fabric A.

Make the block

Piece four corner squares With fabric A small triangles pointing down and left, sew a half-square triangle to the right edges of two fabric B small squares; press seams open. With the fabric A triangles pointing down and right, sew a half-square triangle to the left edges of the remaining fabric B squares; press seams open. Repeat with the remaining half-square triangles and the fabric C small squares.

With right sides together, pin and sew one of each strip together, with the fabric A triangles meeting at the center to form an hourglass; press seams open.

Sew three rows Sew the fabric D and fabric E small squares together in pairs to make four strips. With right sides facing, join a corner square to each long edge of one strip, aligning the fabric C small squares with the fabric E small squares; make sure the fabric B small squares are in the outer corners. Press seams over the strips. Repeat to make the bottom row.

Join a strip to the right edge of two corner squares, aligning the fabric E small square with the fabric C small square; press seams over the strips.

Sewing along the fabric E edges, join the remaining fabrics E and D strips to each side of the fabric F small square; press seams over the square.

Complete the square Flip the bottom row. Carefully matching seams, join the top and bottom rows to the center row, making sure the fabric B small squares are in the outside corners and the fabric E small squares frame the fabric F small square; press seams open.
.

boxed pinwheel

The seam allowance is ¼ in throughout

This block, with its bold colors and geometric design, is inspired by the distinctive quilts made in South Wales during the nineteenth century. Many of them were made from locally woven flannel with an old blanket for the filling. The distinctive bright red flannel was also a favorite for Victorian petticoats.

A
B
C

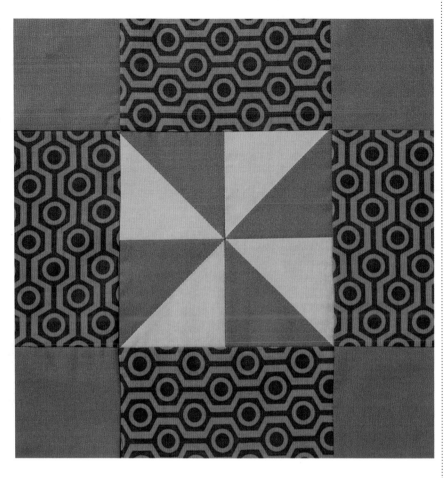

Fabric quantities

- Dark red fabric A: 9 x 14 inches
- Dark purple print fabric B: 7 x 16 inches
- Light gray fabric C: 5 x 10 inches

Prepare the patches

Rotary method
- From fabrics A and C, make one 6½-inch pinwheel square (see page 13)
- From fabric A, cut four 3½-inch squares
- From fabric B, cut four 6½ x 3½-inch rectangles

or

Template cutting
Using the 4 x 4 templates (pages 269–73):
- From fabric A, cut 4 small squares and 4 small triangles
- From fabric B, cut 4 short rectangles
- From fabric C, cut 4 small triangles

Template piecing

With right sides together, sew a fabric A small triangle to each diagonal edge of the fabric C small triangles to make four half-square triangles; press seams over fabric A. Join two half-square triangles together along a light and dark edge; press seam toward darker fabric. Repeat to make the second row. Join the rows along the long edge, with light fabric touching dark fabric and lining up seams, to complete the pinwheel square; press seams open.

Make the block

Piece the center row With right sides together, sew a fabric B short rectangle to each side edge of the pinwheel square; press seams over fabric B.

Complete the square Sew a fabric A small square to each short edge of the remaining fabric B short rectangles; press seams over fabric B. Sew the strips to the top and bottom edges of the pinwheel square, carefully matching seams; press seams open.

philadelphia pavement

The seam allowance is ¼ inch throughout.

The center shoofly motif in this block is scrappy and made of pink and purple fabrics in lighter shades than the frame. Combine it with other shoofly blocks, such as Shoofly (see page 116), Puss in the Corner (see page 170), Snowballs and Shooflies (see page 194), and Tic-Tac-Toe (see page 250), for a sampler quilt. This geometric block is made easily using the rotary method.

Fabric quantities

- 4 different dark and medium pink and purple print fabrics A: 8 x 8 inches in total
- Medium pink print fabric B: 5 x 5 inches
- Dark pink print fabric C: 9 x 12 inches
- Dark purple print fabric D: 6 x 6 inches
- White fabric E: 8 x 14 inches

Prepare the patches

Rotary method
- From fabrics A and E, make four 2½-inch half-square triangles (see page 12)
- From fabric B, cut one 4½-inch square

- From fabric C, cut four 8½ x 2½-inch rectangles
- From fabric D, cut four 2½-inch squares
- From fabric E, cut four 4½ x 2½-inch rectangles

Make the block

Piece the center panel With right sides together, sew a fabric E rectangle to each side of the fabric B large square; press seams over fabric B. Sew a half-square triangle to each end of the remaining fabric E rectangles, fabric A small triangles pointing inward and down.

Flip one strip, then join strips to the top and bottom of the square, triangles pointing inward; press seams open.

Complete the square With right sides together, sew a fabric C rectangle to each side edge; press seams over fabric C. Sew the fabric D small squares to each end of the remaining fabric C rectangles; join strips to the top and bottom edges; press seams open.

welsh diamond

The seam allowance is ¼ inch throughout.

Like Boxed Pinwheel on page 256, this design was inspired by the historic South Wales quilts from Pembrokeshire and Carmarthenshire. The original was a small crib quilt stitched from a mixture of striped shirting and floral dress fabrics, probably salvaged from outworn garments belonging to the baby's family members. Recycling fabric from parents and siblings is a charming tradition to continue if you're making a quilt for a newborn.

Fabric quantities

- Dark purple print fabric A: 12 x 13 inches
- Light gray print fabric B: 10 x 12 inches
- Medium purple fabric C: 6 x 12 inches

Prepare the patches

Rotary method
- From fabrics A and B, make four 2½-inch half-square triangles (see page 12)
- From fabrics B and C, make four 4½-inch half-square triangles
- From fabric A, cut four 8½ x 2½-inch rectangles

Make the block

Piece the center panel With right sides together, sew the four fabrics B and C half-square triangles together so fabric C forms a diamond at the center; press seams open.

Complete the square Join a fabric A rectangle to each side edge of the center panel; press seam over fabric A.

Sew a fabrics A and B half-square triangle to each end of the remaining fabric A rectangles, with the fabric A triangles in the outside corners. With right sides together, pin and sew the strips to the top and bottom of the block; press seams open.

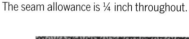

kitchen workbox

The seam allowance is ¼ in throughout

Using two shades of the same solid color within a patchwork shape adds interest to a block. The Grape Basket on page 261 has a lighter green square in the center of the basket; here, a darker red is used at the corners of the center square.

A
B
C
D

Fabric quantities

- Dark purple print fabric A: 6 x 8 inches
- Medium red fabric B: 6 x 10 inches
- Dark red fabric C: 6 x 6 inches
- White fabric D: 11 x 13 inches

Prepare the patches

Rotary method
- From fabrics A, C and D, make four 4½-inch triangle-and-square blocks (see page 15)
- From fabrics B and D, make four 4½-inch rectangle squares (see page 11)
- From fabric A, cut one 4½-inch square

or

Template cutting
Using the 6 x 6 templates (pages 278–83):
- From fabric A, cut 1 large square and 4 large triangles
- From fabric B, cut 4 short rectangles
- From fabric C, cut 4 small squares
- From fabric D, cut 4 short rectangles and 8 small triangles

Template piecing

To make one triangle-and-square block, join the short edge of two fabric D small triangles to the top and left edges of a fabric C small square; press seams over fabric C. Join the patchwork triangle to a fabric A large triangle along the diagonal edge; press seams over fabric A. Repeat to make another three triangle-and-square blocks.

With right sides together, join a fabric B short rectangle to each of the fabric D short rectangles along one long edge to make four rectangle squares; press seams over fabric B.

Make the block

Sew three rows With right sides together, join a triangle-and-square block to each end of a rectangle square, aligning the dark red squares with the red rectangle; press seams open. Repeat to make the bottom row.

Sew a rectangle square on each side of the fabric A large square, joining the red edges; press seams open.

Complete the square Flip the bottom row. With right sides together, join the top and bottom rows to the center row, carefully matching seams to make a red frame in the center of the block; press seams open.

double pinwheel

The dancing motif on this block is exactly like the windmills that generations of children have made from cut and folded paper, a long pin, and a stick.

A
B
C

Fabric quantities

- Dark pink print fabric A: 8 x 14 inches
- Dark purple fabric B: 8 x 8 inches
- Light gray print fabric C: 11 x 16 inches

Prepare the patches

Rotary method
- From fabrics A, B, and C, make four 6½ x 3½-inch flying geese rectangles (see page 17)
- From fabric C, cut four 6½ x 3½-inch rectangles

or

Template cutting
Using the 4 x 4 templates (pages 269–73):
- From fabric A, cut 4 medium triangles
- From fabric B, cut 4 small triangles

- From fabric C, cut 4 short rectangles and 4 small triangles

Template piecing

With right sides together, sew a fabric B small triangle to the left short edge of a fabric A medium triangle. Sew a fabric C small triangle to the right short edge of the triangle to complete one flying geese rectangle; press seams across the small triangles. Repeat to make another three flying geese rectangles.

Make the block

Piece four patches With the fabric A medium triangle pointing upward, sew a fabric C rectangle to the top edge of each flying geese rectangle; press seams over fabric C. Arrange the four squares so that the fabric A triangles meet in the center.

With right sides together, pin and sew two patches together making sure the flying geese rectangles are perpendicular. Repeat to make the second row; press seams open.

Complete the square With right sides together, pin and sew the two rows together, forming a pinwheel in the center of the block; press seam open.

---

sashed pinwheel

White motifs always stand out dramatically against dark backgrounds. You can use this block alternately with one of the other sashed designs, such as Forest Paths on page 133 or Framed Windmill on page 24, to make a quilt top.

A
B
C
D

Fabric quantities

- White fabric A: 8 x 8 inches
- Dark gray print fabric B: 12 x 12 inches
- Light purple fabric C: 9 x 12 inches
- Dark pink print fabric D: 6 x 6 inches

Prepare the patches

Rotary method
- From fabrics A and B, make four 4½-inch three-quarter square triangles (see page 13)
- From fabric C, cut four 8½ x 2½-inch rectangles
- From fabric D, cut four 2½-inch squares

Make the block

Piece the pinwheel With right sides together, join two three-quarter square triangles along a dark and light edge, making sure the white triangles appear to be rotating clockwise; press seam open. Repeat to make the second row of the pinwheel. Join the two rows, carefully matching the center seams; press seam open.

Complete the square Sew a fabric C rectangle to each side edge of the pinwheel patch; press seams open.

With right sides together, join the fabric D small squares to the ends of each remaining fabric C rectangle. Join these strips to the top and bottom edges of the pinwheel; press seams open.

diamond in a square

The seam allowance is ¼ in throughout

A simple block, Diamond in a Square creates a quilt with strong diagonal movement when multiples are set edge to edge. You can add emphasis by using just four, or even two, colors in the diamond square instead of the five shown here.

A
B
C
D
E
F

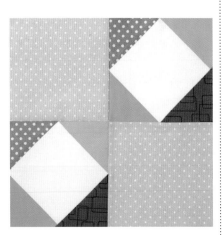

Fabric quantities
- Light purple print fabric A: 7 x 14 inches
- Medium purple print fabric B: 4 x 4 inches
- Light turquoise fabric C: 4 x 4 inches
- Dark purple print fabric D: 4 x 4 inches
- Light green fabric E: 4 x 4 inches
- White fabric F: 7 x 14 inches

Prepare the patches
Rotary method
- From fabric A, cut two 6½-inch squares
- From fabrics B, C, D, E, and F, make two 6½-inch diamond squares (see page 15)

or

Template cutting
Using the 4 x 4 templates (pages 269–73):
- From fabric A, cut 2 large squares
- From fabrics B, C, D, and E, cut 2 small triangles each
- From fabric F, cut 2 diamond squares

Template piecing
To make the diamond squares, with right sides together, pin and sew one each of the small colored triangles to the edges of each fabric F diamond square, from top left clockwise: first fabric B, then fabrics C, D, and E. Press seams over fabric F.

Make the block
Sew two rows With right sides together, pin and sew a fabric A large square to the left edge of a diamond square, joining the fabrics B and E triangles to the square; press seam open. Repeat to make the bottom row, with fabrics C and D triangles joined to the fabric A large square.

Complete the square With right sides together, pin and sew the two rows together, matching seams and points; press seam open.

four-patch corners

The seam allowance is ¼ inch throughout.

This might be one of the simplest blocks in the book, but the use of two completely contrasting colors—found directly opposite each other in the color wheel—give it a vivid, crisp look. Join multiple blocks edge to edge for a checkerboard pattern with a difference.

A
B
C
D

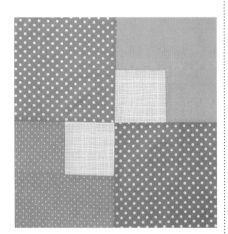

Fabric quantities
- Medium orange fabric A: 4 x 11 inches
- Light blue print fabric B: 4 x 8 inches
- Medium orange print fabric C: 4 x 11 inches
- Light purple print fabric D: 7 x 14 inches

- From fabric B, cut 2 small squares
- From fabric D, cut 2 large squares

Prepare the patches
Rotary method
- From fabrics A and B and fabrics B and C, make one 6½-inch three-patch square (see page 11) each
- From fabric D, cut two 6½-inch squares

or

Template cutting
Using the 4 x 4 templates (pages 269–73):
- From fabrics A and C, cut 1 short rectangle and 1 small square each

Template piecing
With right sides together, join the fabric A small square to a fabric B small square; press seam over fabric A. Join the strip to the long side of the fabric A short rectangle to complete a three-patch square; press seam open. Repeat with fabric B and fabric C.

Make the block
Sew two rows With right sides together, join a fabric D large square to the left edge of the fabrics A and B three-patch square with the blue small square in the center; press seam open. Repeat to join the second fabric D large square to the right edge of the fabrics B and C three-patch square.

Complete the square Flip the bottom row. With right sides together, join the rows, carefully matching seams and making sure the points of the blue squares meet in the center; press seam open.

grape basket

The seam allowance is ¼ in throughout

This nineteenth-century fruit basket is made in a naturalistic color palette. The grapes are traditionally made from purple or green fabric and the basket from a contrasting plain or print, but the triangles can be cut from any color. This block is most accurately made from templates for a 12-inch square.

A
B
C
D

Fabric quantities

- Light purple print fabric A: 10 x 15 inches
- Medium green fabric B: 10 x 20 inches
- Light green fabric C: 4 x 4 inches
- White fabric D: 23 x 23 inches

Prepare the patches

Template cutting
Using the 5 x 5 templates (pages 274–7):
- From fabric A, cut 7 small triangles
- From fabric B, cut 8 small triangles
- From fabric C, cut 1 small square
- From fabric D, cut 2 medium rectangles, 3 small squares, and 15 small triangles

Template piecing

With right sides together, sew the fabric D small triangles to the long edge of each of the fabric A small triangles to make seven half-square triangles; press seams over fabric A. Repeat to make another six half-square triangles from the fabrics B and D small triangles.

Make the block

Piece four rows Lay out all the patches as shown above. Sew the half-square triangles and squares in four rows. For the first row, join a white small square, two purple half-square triangles with the fabric A triangles pointing down and left, and a green half-square triangle with the fabric B triangle pointing down and right.

For the second row, join a purple half-square triangle with the fabric A triangle pointing up and right, two more purple half-square triangles with the fabric A triangles pointing down and right, and a green half-square triangle with the fabric B triangle pointing down and right.

For the third row, join a purple half-square triangle with the fabric A triangle pointing up and right, a purple half-square triangle with the fabric A triangle pointing down and right, a fabric D small square, and a green half-square triangle with the fabric B triangle pointing down and right.

For the fourth row, join three green half-square triangles with the fabric B triangles pointing down and right and the fabric C small square. Carefully matching seams, join the rows to make a square; press seams open.

Complete the square With right sides together, sew a green half-square triangle to the right short end of each fabric D medium rectangle, with the fabric B triangle pointing up and left. Sew one strip to the right edge of the square, matching the green fabrics; press seam open. Join the fabric D small square to the right end of the remaining strip and join to the bottom of the square; press seams open.

violet

In the traditional language of flowers, the violet traditionally symbolizes faithfulness, so this block would be ideal to use for a wedding or anniversary quilt.

A
B
C
D
E

Fabric quantities

- Dark purple print fabric A: 3 x 6 inches
- Medium yellow print fabric B: 5 x 5 inches
- Medium purple fabric C: 10 x 10 inches
- Medium green print fabric D: 6 x 6 inches
- White fabric E: 10 x 16 inches

Prepare the patches

Rotary method
- From fabrics A and B, make one 4½-inch diamond square (see page 15)
- From fabrics C and E, make four 4½-inch house squares (see page 14)
- From fabrics D and E, make four 4½-inch three-patch squares (see page 11)

or

Template cutting
Using the 6 x 6 templates (pages 278–83):
- From fabric A, cut 4 small triangles
- From fabric B, cut 1 diamond square
- From fabric C, cut 4 houses
- From fabric D, cut 4 small squares
- From fabric E, cut 4 short rectangles, 4 small squares, and 8 small triangles

Template piecing

To make the diamond square, with right sides together, join the fabric A small triangles to the diagonal edges of the fabric B diamond square; press seams over fabric B.

To make four house squares, join the fabric E triangles to each of the diagonal edges of the fabric C houses; press seams over fabric C.

To make a three-patch square, join a fabric D small square and a fabric E small square; press seam over fabric D. Sew the strip to the long side of a fabric E short rectangle; press seam open. Repeat to make another three three-patch squares.

Make the block

Sew three rows With right sides together, pin and sew a house square to each side of the diamond square, with the roofs pointing out; press seams over fabric C.

For the top and bottom rows, sew a three-patch square to each side of the remaining two house squares, with the fabric D small squares inwards at the bottom edge; press seams open.

Complete the square With right sides together, pin and sew the top and bottom rows to the center row, matching seams; press seams open.

clay's choice

The seam allowance is ¼ in throughout

Clay's Choice is named in honor of Henry Clay, a popular nineteenth century U. S. politician who spoke out against slavery. This traditional block feels modern when made with crisp solids and a slightly retro print.

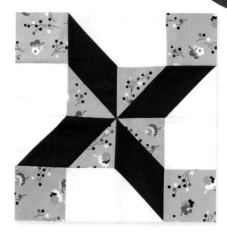

Fabric quantities

- Medium purple fabric A: 7 x 16 inches
- Medium gray print fabric B: 10 x 13 inches
- White fabric C: 8 x 12 inches

Prepare the patches

Rotary method
- From fabrics A, B, and C make four 6½ x 3½-inch left diamond rectangles (see page 16)
- From fabrics B and C, cut four 3½-inch squares each

or

Template cutting
Using the 4 x 4 templates (pages 269–73):
- From fabric A, cut 4 left diamonds
- From fabrics B and C, cut 4 small squares and 4 small triangles each

Template piecing

With right sides together, pin and sew a fabric B small triangle to each left diagonal edge of the fabric A left diamonds; press seams open. Join the fabric C small triangles to the right diagonal edges; press seams open.

Make the block

Piece four patches With right sides together, pin and sew a fabric B small square to each of the fabric C small squares; press seams over fabric B. Join a strip to each of the left rectangles, making sure the gray print square meets the purple diamond, to make four square patches; press seams open.

Sew two rows With right sides together, pin and sew two patches together, making sure the gray print small squares are in the outside corners. Repeat to make the second row; press seams open.

Complete the square Join the two rows, carefully matching seams and making sure the gray print small triangles meet in the center of the block; press seam open.

quick cross

The seam allowance is ¼ in throughout

Living up to its title, this block comes together quickly—and there are only two seams at the center that need to be matched up exactly. A directional print has been used for the main cross; however, an allover floral or other small-scale pattern would work just as well, and a pattern would also make the seam lines within the cross less apparent. This geometric block is easily made using the rotary method.

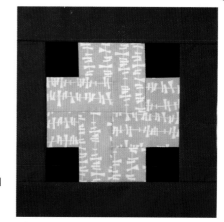

Fabric quantities

- Light beige print fabric A: 9 x 12 inches
- Dark purple fabric B: 6 x 6 inches
- Medium purple fabric C: 12 x 13 inches

Prepare the patches

Rotary method
- From fabrics A and B, make four 4½-inch three-patch squares (see page 11)
- From fabric C, cut two 12½ x 2½-inch rectangles and two 8½ x 2½-inch rectangles

Make the block

Piece the center panel Arrange the three-patch squares so that the fabric B small squares are in the outer corners. With right sides together, sew the three-patch squares in pairs, then join the pairs together, matching seams; press seams open.

Complete the square Join a shorter fabric C rectangle to each side edge of the center panel; press seams over fabric C. Sew the longer fabric C rectangles to the top and bottom edges; press seams open.

sawtooth pinwheel

The seam allowance is ¼ in throughout

The familiar pinwheel motif is used on an unexpectedly large scale at the center of this block and given a sawtooth edging made up of small triangles.

A
B
C
D

Fabric quantities

- Dark purple fabric A: 16 x 19 inches
- Light purple fabric B: 16 x 16 inches
- Medium purple fabric C: 6 x 12 inches
- White fabric D: 6 x 12 inches

Prepare the patches

Rotary method
- From fabrics A and B, make sixteen 2½-inch half-square triangles (see page 12)
- From fabrics C and D, make four 4½-inch half-square triangles
- From fabric A, cut four 2½-inch squares

or

Template cutting
Using the 6 x 6 templates (pages 278–83):
- From fabric A, cut 4 small squares and 16 small triangles
- From fabric B, cut 16 small triangles
- From fabrics C and D, cut 4 large triangles each

Template piecing

With right sides together, sew a fabric A small triangle to the diagonal edge of each fabric B small triangle to make 16 half-square triangles; press seam over fabric A.

With right sides together, sew a fabric C large triangle to the diagonal edge of each fabric D large triangle to make four half-square triangles; press seam over fabric C.

Make the block

Piece four patches For each patch, with right sides together, join two small half-square triangles on a short edge so the fabric B triangles point down and left; press seam open. Join the strip to the top edge of a large half-square triangle, with the fabric C triangle pointing down and left; press seam open. Join another two small half-square triangles together with the fabric B triangles pointing down and right; add a fabric A small square to the right edge. Sew the strip to the left edge of the patch, with the fabric A small square in the top left corner; press all seams open. Repeat to make another three patches.

Complete the square Lay out the patches so the medium purple triangles meet in the center. Join the top pair, matching seams; press seam over fabric C. Repeat with the bottom pair. Sew the top and bottom rows together, matching the center points; press seam open.

fair and square

A plain and simple block, Fair and Square can be made from solid or patterned fabrics. You can join multiple blocks with sashing and corner squares in another color to create a pattern made up of alternate rows of nine-patch squares and diamond squares.

Fabric quantities

- Medium purple fabric A: 4 x 8 inches
- Medium blue fabric B: 4 x 8 inches
- Dark purple fabric C: 4 x 4 inches
- Dark blue fabric D: 5 x 8 inches
- Dark pink fabric E: 4 x 4 inches
- White fabric F: 11 x 15 inches

Prepare the patches

Rotary method
- From fabrics A, B, D, E, and F, make one 6½-inch diamond square (see page 15)
- From fabrics A, B, C, and D, cut one 3½-inch square each
- From fabric F, cut four 6½ x 3½-inch rectangles

or

Template cutting
Using the 4 x 4 templates (pages 269–73):
- From fabrics A, B, and D, cut 1 small square and 1 small triangle each
- From fabric C, cut 1 small square
- From fabric E, cut 1 small triangle
- From fabric F, cut 4 short rectangles and 1 diamond square

A
B
C
D
E
F

Template piecing

To make the diamond square, with right sides together, pin and sew the fabrics A, B, D, and E small triangles to the diagonal edges of the fabric F diamond square; press seams over fabric F.

Make the block

Piece the center row With right sides together, sew a fabric F short rectangle to each side of the diamond square; press seams over fabric E.

Sew the top and bottom rows For the top row, join the fabric A and fabric B small squares to each end of a short rectangle; press seams over fabric F.

For the bottom row, join the fabric D and C small squares to each end of a fabric F short rectangle; press seams over fabric F.

Complete the square With right sides together, pin and sew the top and bottom rows to the center row, making sure the fabric A and small square and small triangle are in opposite corners; press seams open.

tulip ladyfingers

The seam allowance is ¼ in throughout

This traditional block, with an enchanting name, can also be made with a small square at the center and white short rectangles instead of squares.

Fabric quantities

- Medium purple fabric A: 11 x 16 inches
- Light purple fabric B: 11 x 16 inches
- Medium purple print fabric C: 5 x 5 inches
- White fabric D: 10 x 10 inches

Prepare the patches

Rotary method
- From fabrics A and B, make eight 2½-inch half-square triangles (see page 12)
- From fabrics A and B, cut four 2½-inch squares each
- From fabric C, cut one 4½-inch square
- From fabric D, cut four 4½-inch squares

or

Template cutting
Using the 6 x 6 templates (pages 278–83):
- From fabrics A and B, cut 4 small squares and 8 small triangles each
- From fabric C, cut 1 large square
- From fabric D, cut 4 large squares

Template piecing

With right sides together, sew a fabric A small triangle to the diagonal edge of a fabric B small triangle; press seam over fabric A to make one half-square triangle. Repeat to make another seven half-square triangles.

Make the block

Piece four tulip patches Sew a fabric B small square to the left edge of a half-square triangle with the fabric A triangle pointing down and left. Sew a fabric A small square to the right edge of a half-square triangle with the fabric A triangle pointing up and right. Sew strips along the long edges; press seam open. Repeat to make another three patches.

Complete the square Arrange the patches in three rows of three, with the fabric C large square in the center and the tulip patches in each corner, as shown above. Join the patches in rows; press seams open. Join each row, matching seams; press seams open.

amish chain

The seam allowance is ¼ inch throughout.

This block is inspired by the quilts made by the Amish community of Lancaster County, Pennsylvania, which are characterized by squares and rectangles set in contrasting light and dark colors. This geometric block is easily made using the rotary method.

Fabric quantities

- Light green fabric A: 6 x 9 inches
- Medium turquoise fabric B: 6 x 9 inches
- Medium purple fabric C: 12 x 14 inches

Prepare the patches

Rotary method
- From fabrics A and B, make one 4½-inch four-patch square (see page 11)
- From fabrics A and B, cut four 2½-inch squares each
- From fabric C, cut four 4½ x 2½-inch rectangles and four 8½ x 2½-inch rectangles

Make the block

Piece the center panel With the fabric A small squares at top left and bottom right, sew a fabric C short rectangle to each side of the four-patch square; press seams over fabric C.

Sew a fabric A small square and a fabric B small square to the opposite sides of a shorter fabric C rectangle; press seams over fabric C. Repeat to make a second strip. Join the strips to the top and bottom edges of the center panel, matching the fabric A and fabric B squares; press seams open.

Complete the square Join a longer fabric C rectangle to each side edge; press seams over C. Join a fabric A small square and fabric B small square to the opposite ends of the two remaining longer rectangles; press seams open. Join the strips to the top and bottom of the square, matching the fabric A and fabric B squares; press seams open.

blockade

The seam allowance is ¼ inch throughout.

Although dramatic as a single block, Blockade works best when several are repeated edge to edge. It then forms a pattern of on-point hourglasses with solid diamond frames, which alternate with pinwheels. This block is best made from templates.

A
B
C

Fabric quantities

- Light purple fabric A: 12 x 12 inches
- Dark pink print fabric B: 12 x 12 inches
- Medium purple fabric C: 8 x 16 inches

Prepare the patches

Template cutting
Using the 4 x 4 templates (pages 269–73):
- From fabrics A and B, cut 4 medium triangles and 2 small triangles each
- From fabric C, cut 4 diagonal boats

Template piecing

With right sides together, join a fabric A medium triangle and a fabric B medium triangle along one short edge with fabric A on the left. Sew the patchwork triangle to the long edge of a fabric C diagonal boat. Join the long edge of a fabric A small triangle to the short side of the diagonal boat to complete the boat square. Repeat to make another diagonal boat square. Using the fabric B small triangles, repeat to make another two diagonal boat squares.

Make the block

Sew two rows With right sides together, join two diagonal boat squares so the straight, short sides meet at the top and the fabric A small triangle abuts the fabric B small triangle; press seam open. Repeat to make the bottom row.

Complete the square Flip the bottom row. Join the two rows, carefully matching seams and forming an hourglass in the center of the block; press seam open.

----

greek cross

The seam allowance is ¼ inch throughout.

This cross is an old variation on the nine-patch theme, and works well with large-scale fabrics. It is constructed in the same way as Churn Dash (see page 152), but with different placement of light and dark fabrics. When multiple blocks are set edge to edge, diamond squares appear between them.

A
B
C

Fabric quantities

- Dark purple fabric A: 6 x 12 inches
- Dark pink print fabric B: 8 x 11 inches
- Light purple fabric C: 11 x 12 inches

Prepare the patches

Rotary method
- From fabrics A and C, make four 4½-inch half-square triangles (see page 12)
- From fabrics B and C, make four 4½-inch rectangle squares (see page 11)
- From fabric B, cut one 4½-inch square

or

Template cutting
Using the 6 x 6 templates (pages 278–83):
- From fabric A, cut 4 large triangles
- From fabric B, cut 1 large square and 4 short rectangles
- From fabric C, cut 4 large triangles and 4 short rectangles

Template piecing

With right sides together, sew a fabric A large triangle to the diagonal edge of a fabric C large triangle to make one half-square triangle; press seam over fabric A. Repeat to make another three half-square triangles.

To make four rectangle squares, join the long sides of the fabric B and fabric C short rectangles; press seams over fabric B.

Make the block

Sew three rows Arrange the patches in three rows of three, with two half-square triangles on each side of a rectangle square in the top and bottom rows, and two rectangle squares on each side of the large fabric B square in the center row, as shown above. With right sides together, pin and sew the squares in each row; press seams open.

Complete the square Making sure the pink rectangles join the center square, join the top and bottom rows to the center row; press seams open.

darting minnows

A
B

With a traditional name that suggests a shoal of fish swimming in the clear water of a sunny stream, this block dates back to the nineteenth century. The isosceles triangles which create the sharp points mean that this block is most accurately made from templates.

The seam allowance is ¼ in throughout

Fabric quantities

- Dark purple print fabric A: 10 x 10 inches
- White fabric B: 10 x 20 inches

Prepare the patches

Template cutting
Using the 6 x 6 templates (pages 278–83):
- From fabric A, cut 4 right half triangles and 4 left half triangles
- From fabric B, cut 5 large squares and 4 isosceles triangles

Make the block

Make the triangle squares With right sides together, sew a fabric A left half triangle and a fabric A right half triangle to each diagonal edge of the fabric B triangles to make isosceles triangle squares.

Sew three rows For the top and bottom rows, sew a fabric B large square to each edge of an isosceles triangle square with the long edges of the fabric A half triangles adjoining the fabric B square; press seams open.

For the middle row, sew two isosceles triangle squares to each side edge of a fabric B large square with the short ends of the fabric A triangles adjoining the fabric B square.

Complete the square With right sides together, pin and sew the top and bottom rows to the middle row, matching seams, making sure all of the white isosceles triangles point toward the center of the block; press seams open.

string-pieced block

The seam allowance is ¼ in throughout

If you stitch all 365 blocks in this book in numerical order, as you approach the last few, you may have accumulated an enormous bag of narrow scraps along the way. Use some of them for String-Pieced Block to give them a new lease of life. Keep a ragbag in the corner of your sewing cupboard or trunk as you work on all your projects and use it to store even the smallest scraps. This scrappy block is made easily using the rotary method.

Fabric quantities

- Random selection of print and solid fabrics A: 6 x 2 inches each

Prepare the patches

Rotary method
- Cut all the fabrics A into 1-inch wide strips, between 2 and 6 inches long

Make the block

Piece the scraps Chain piece (see page 19) the fabric A strips in pairs, then chain piece the pairs. Continue doing this until you have just one long strip, about 7 yards long. Cut the strip into twenty-four 12½-inch lengths; press all the seams in one direction.

Complete the square Chain piece pairs of 12½-inch lengths along the long edges, then join the pairs. Snip apart and continue chain piecing until you have a square of at least 12½ inches wide. Trim the block to size.

4 x 4 templates

All of the 4 x 4 blocks have a base unit of 3 x 3 inches—the size of the small square patch.

Four of these units fit across the width of a 12-inch square block.

Key

⟷   Line this arrow up with straight grain of the fabric

⬆⬆   Place this edge along the folded edge of your paper

∕   Each template includes a ¼-inch seam allowance: the
∠ ─   finished size of the patch is indicated by this broken line

See page 9 for a detailed explanation of how to cut out and use the templates.

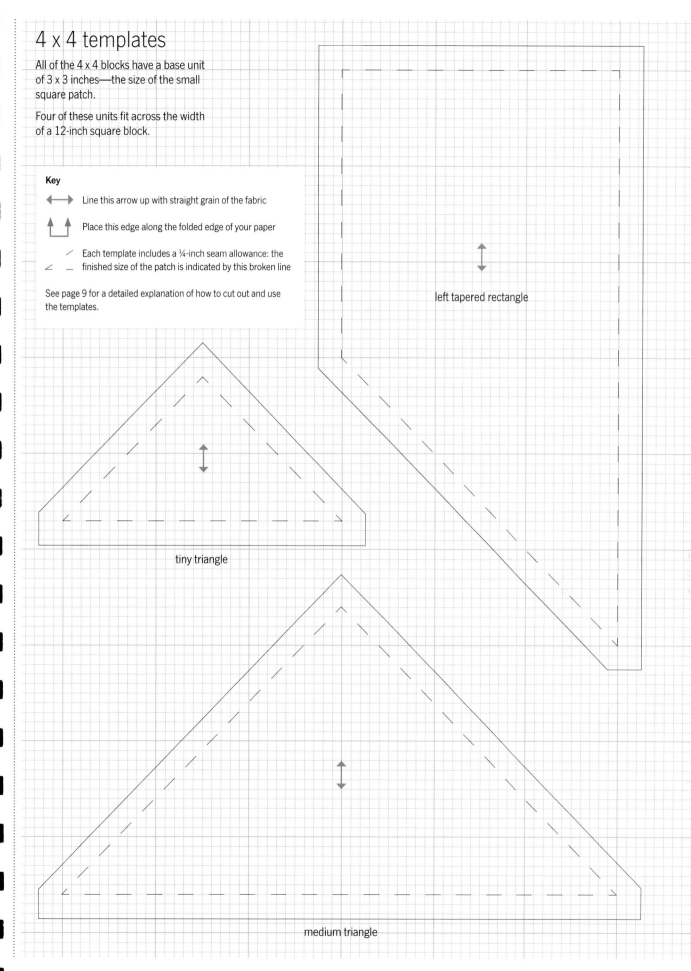

left tapered rectangle

tiny triangle

medium triangle

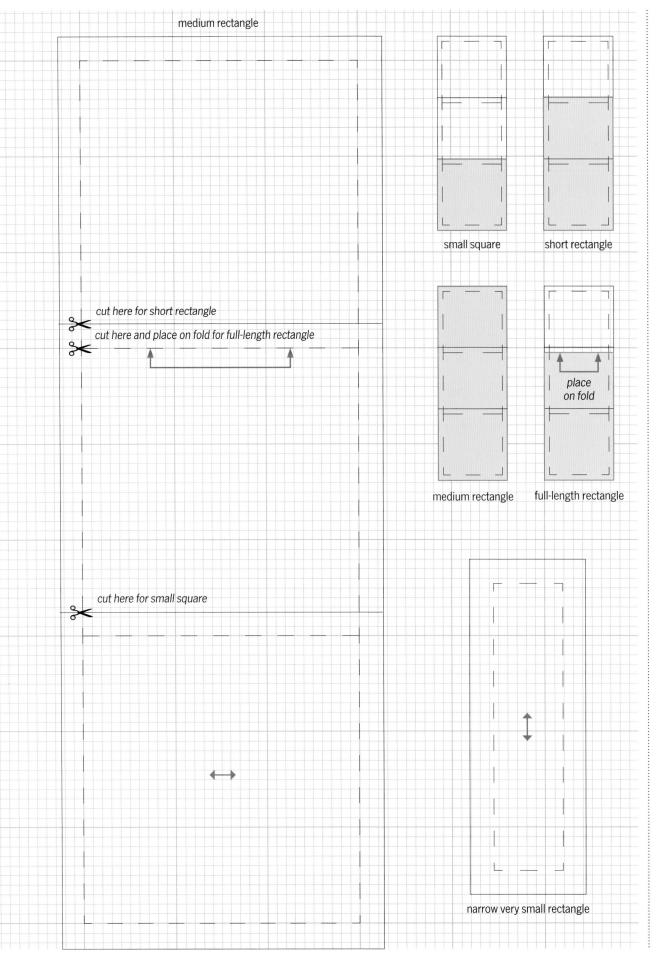

medium rectangle

cut here for short rectangle

cut here and place on fold for full-length rectangle

cut here for small square

small square

short rectangle

medium rectangle

full-length rectangle

place on fold

narrow very small rectangle

large triangle

small triangle

diagonal boat

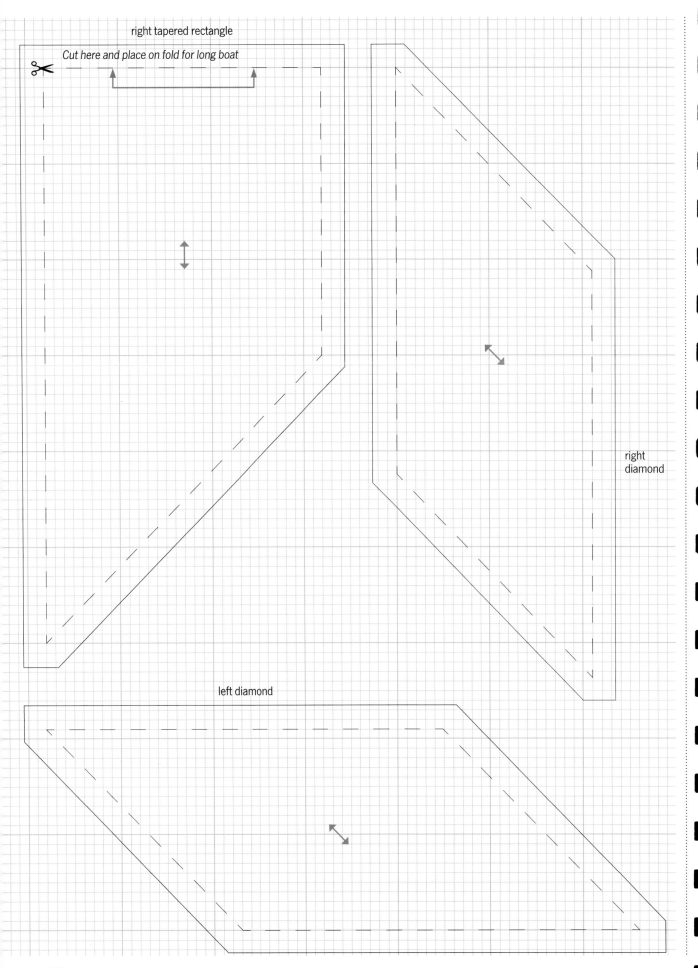

right tapered rectangle

Cut here and place on fold for long boat

right diamond

left diamond

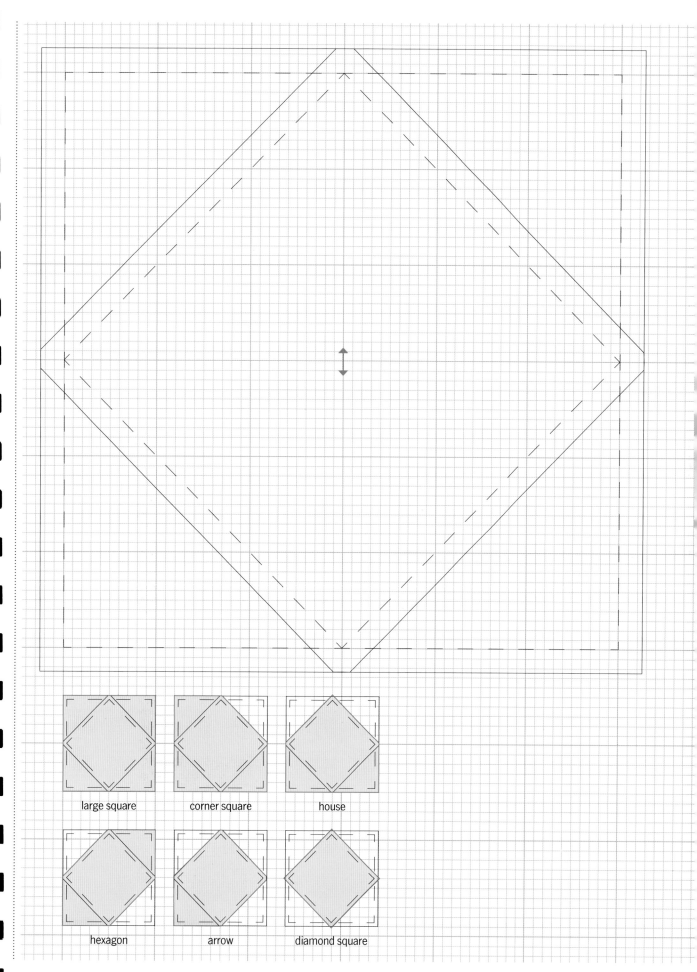

large square   corner square   house

hexagon   arrow   diamond square

5 x 5 templates

All of the 5 x 5 blocks have a base unit of
2.4 x 2.4 inches—the size of the small
square patch.

Five of these units fit across the width of a
12-inch square block.

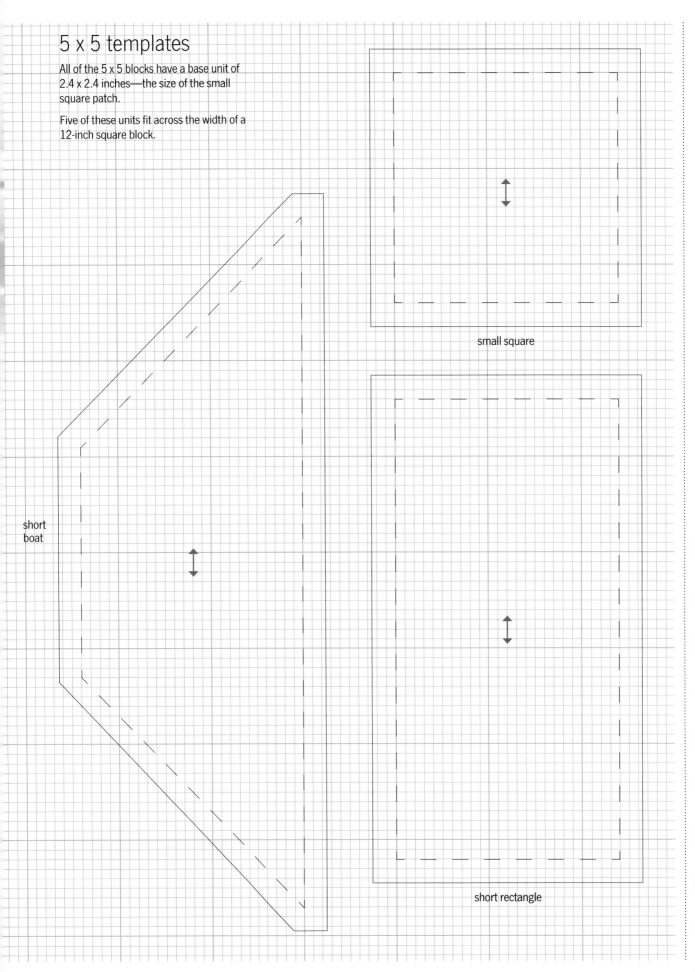

small square

short
boat

short rectangle

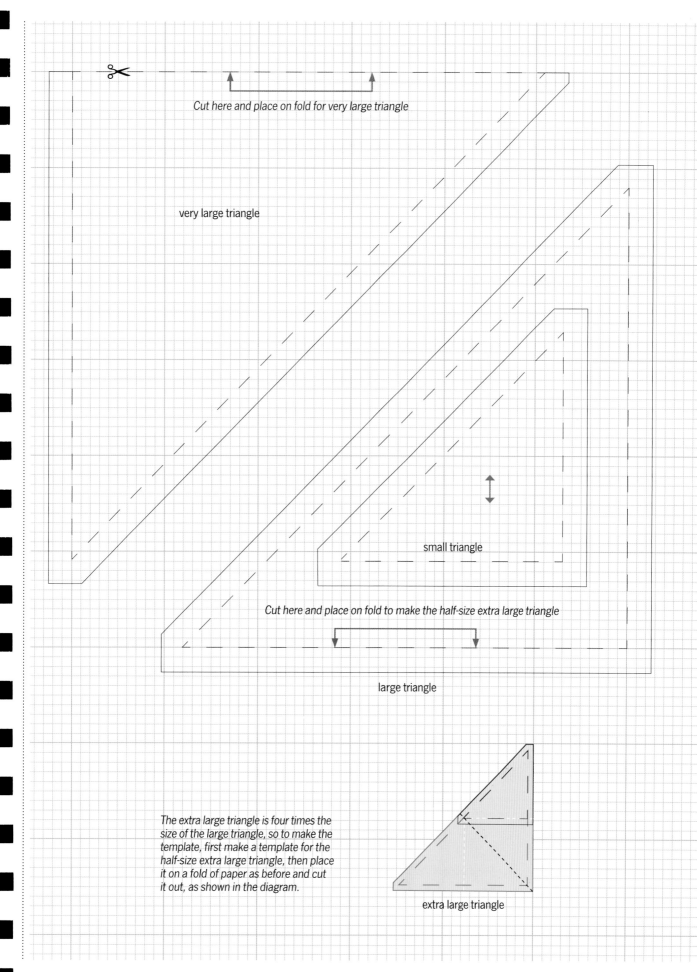

✂ Cut here and place on fold for very large triangle

very large triangle

small triangle

Cut here and place on fold to make the half-size extra large triangle

large triangle

The extra large triangle is four times the size of the large triangle, so to make the template, first make a template for the half-size extra large triangle, then place it on a fold of paper as before and cut it out, as shown in the diagram.

extra large triangle

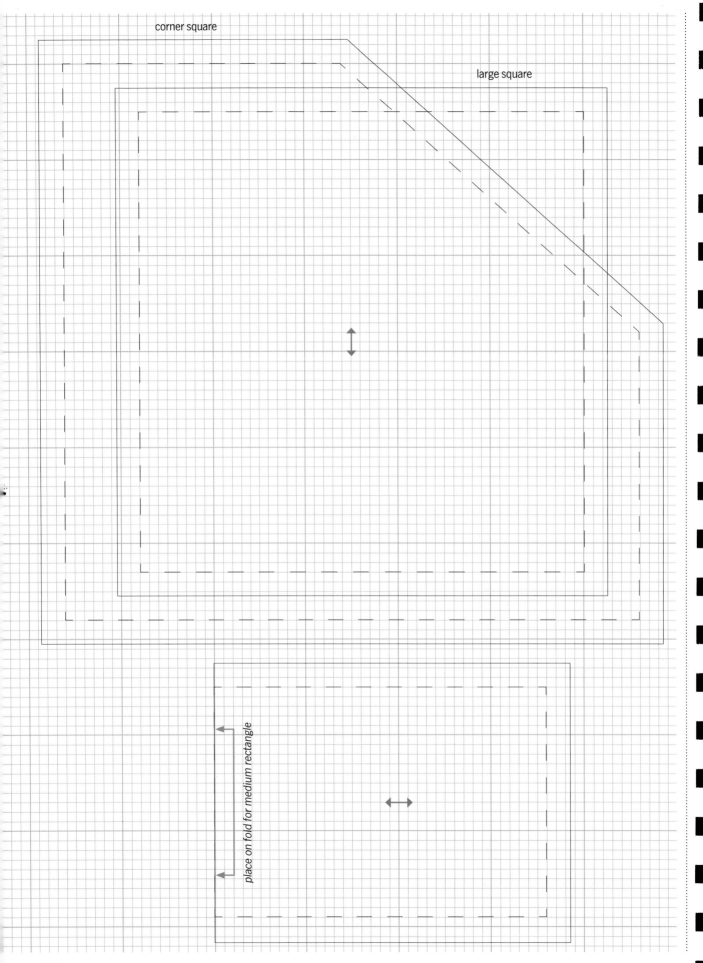

corner square

large square

place on fold for medium rectangle

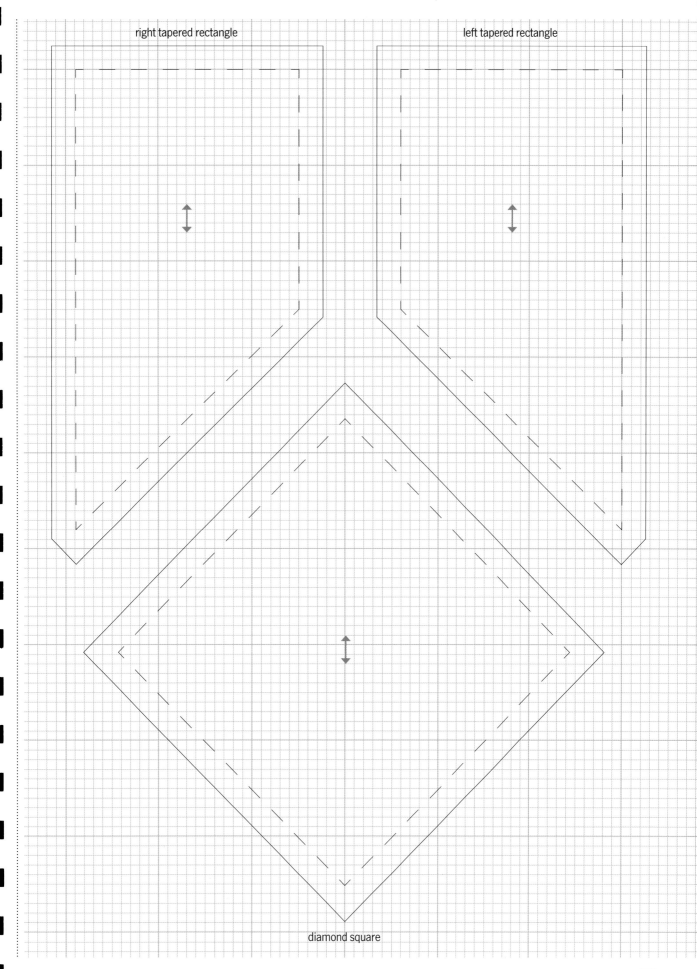

right tapered rectangle

left tapered rectangle

diamond square

6 x 6 templates

All of the 6 x 6 blocks have a base unit of 2 x 2 inches—the size of the small square patch.

Six of these units fit across the width of a 12-inch square block.

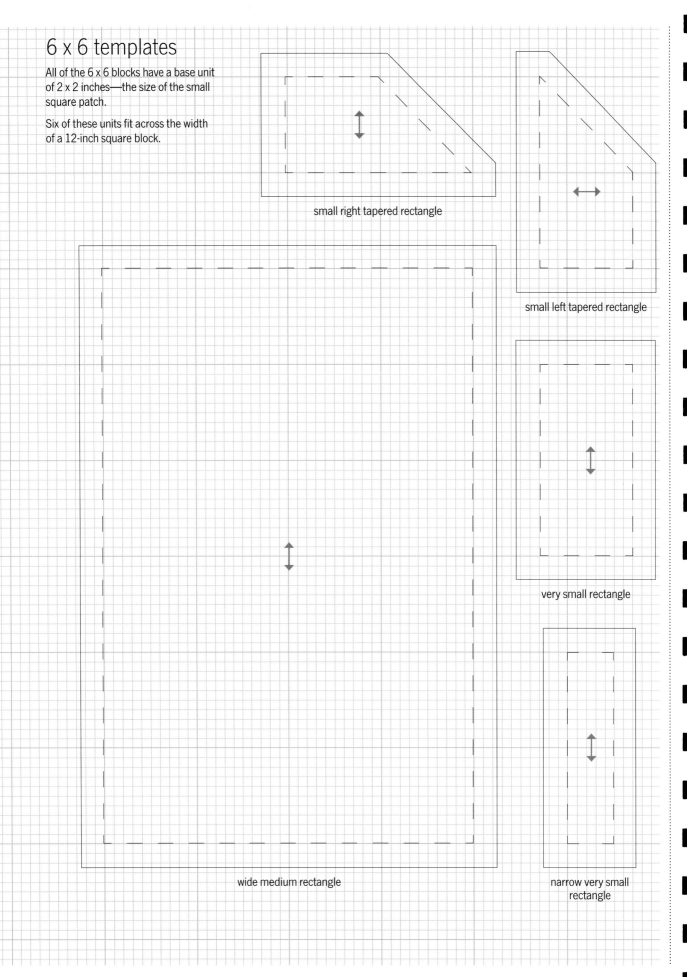

small right tapered rectangle

small left tapered rectangle

very small rectangle

wide medium rectangle

narrow very small
rectangle

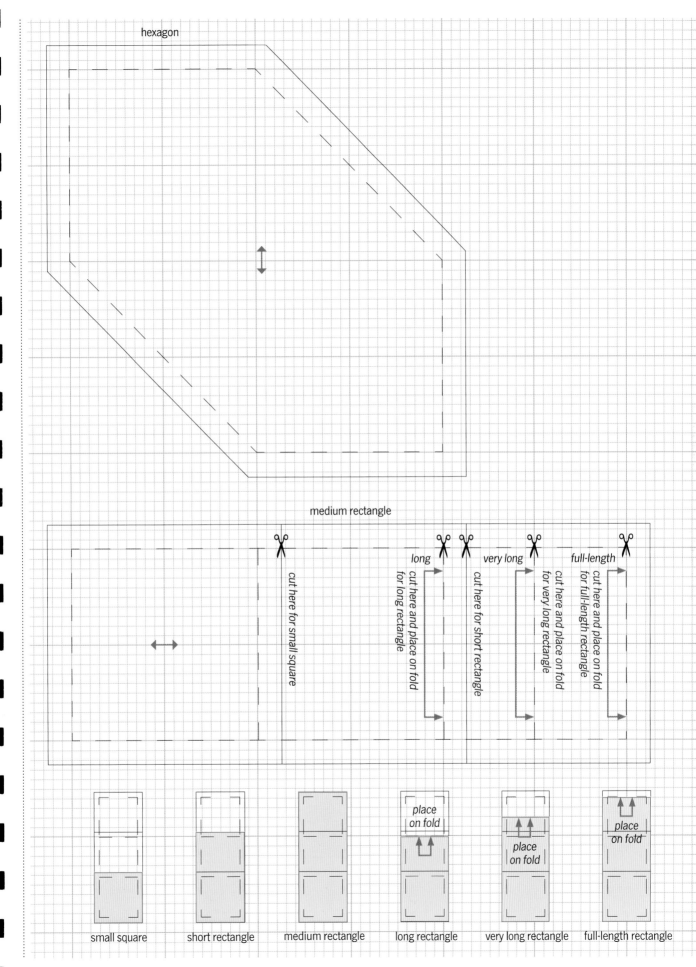

hexagon

medium rectangle

cut here for small square

long
cut here and place on fold
for long rectangle

cut here for short rectangle

very long
cut here and place on fold
for very long rectangle

full-length
cut here and place on fold
for full-length rectangle

place on fold

place on fold

place on fold

| small square | short rectangle | medium rectangle | long rectangle | very long rectangle | full-length rectangle |

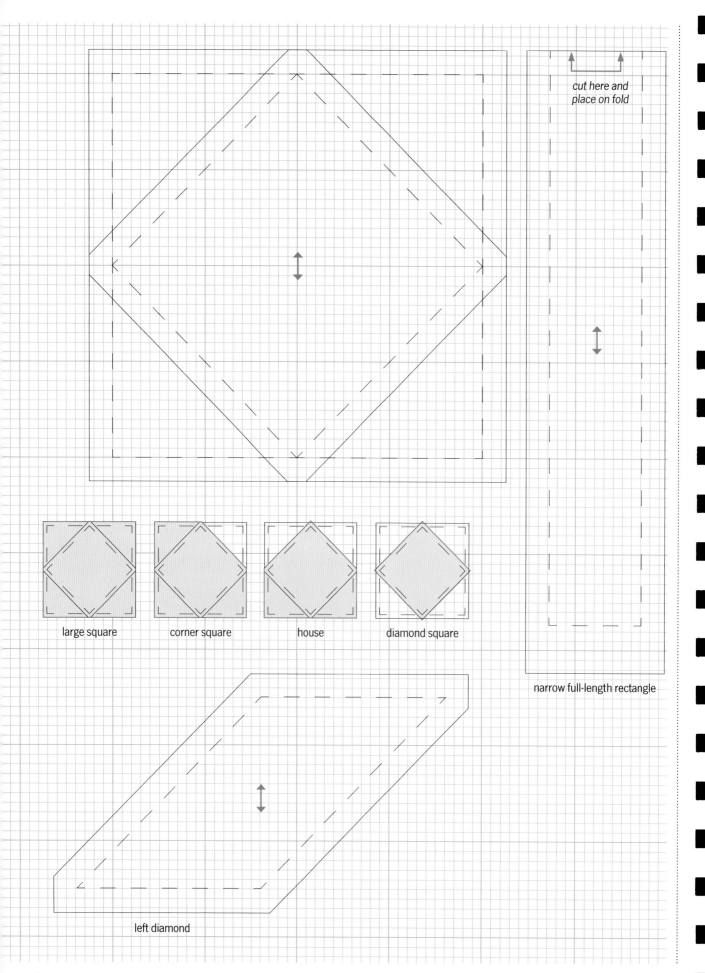

cut here and
place on fold

large square

corner square

house

diamond square

narrow full-length rectangle

left diamond

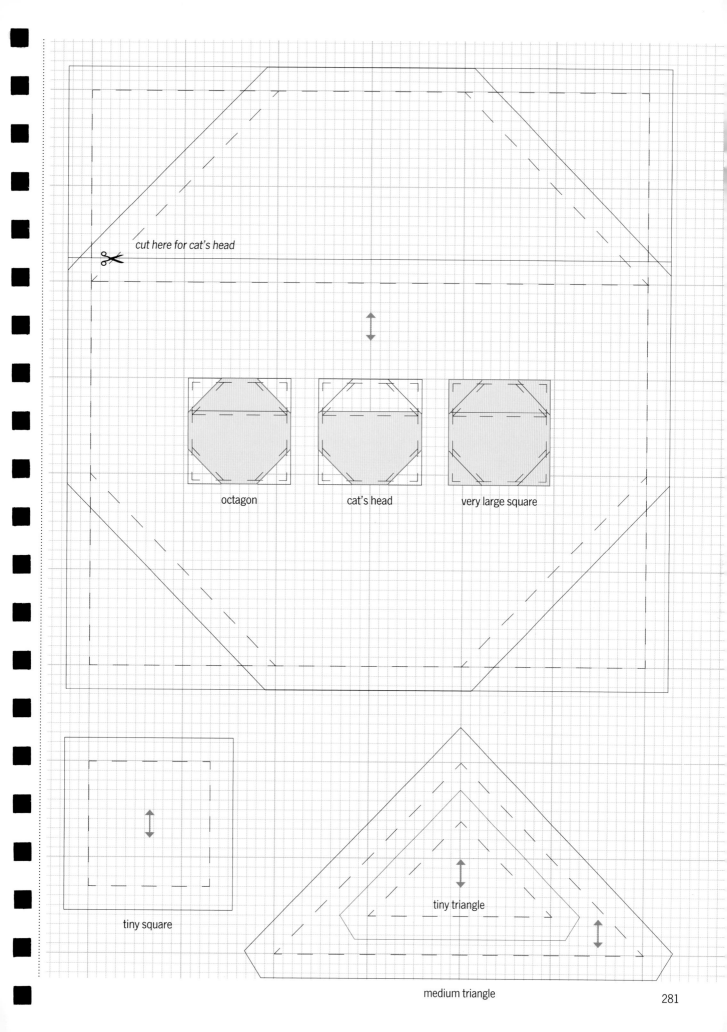

cut here for cat's head

octagon

cat's head

very large square

tiny square

tiny triangle

medium triangle

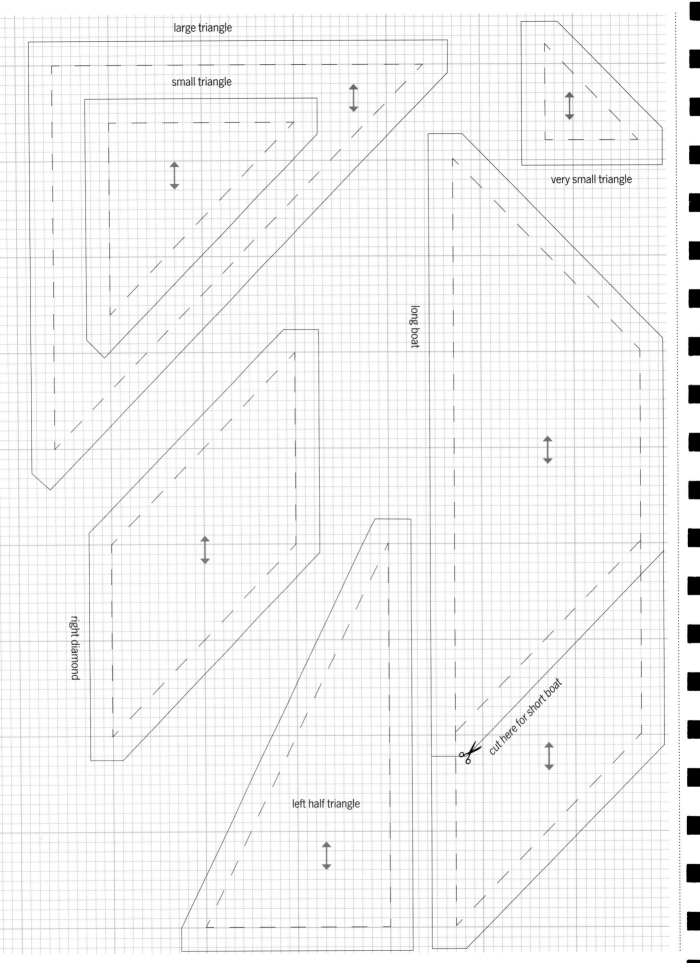

large triangle

small triangle

very small triangle

long boat

right diamond

left half triangle

cut here for short boat

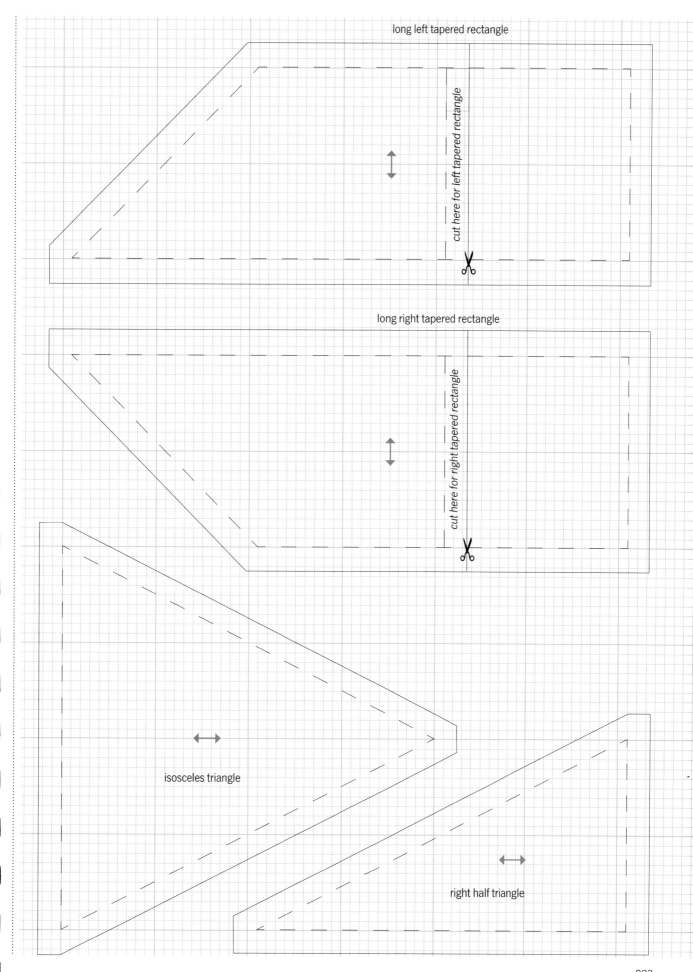

long left tapered rectangle

cut here for left tapered rectangle

long right tapered rectangle

cut here for right tapered rectangle

isosceles triangle

right half triangle

7 x 7 templates

All of the 7 x 7 blocks have a base unit of
1.7 x 1.7 inches—the size of the small
square patch.

Seven of these units fit across the width
of a 12-inch square block.

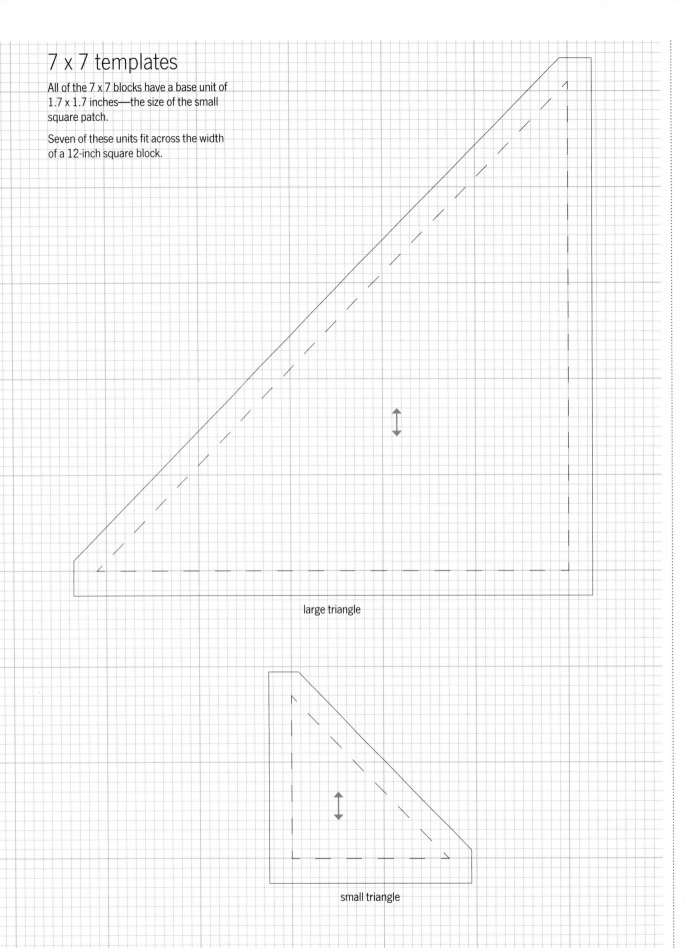

large triangle

small triangle

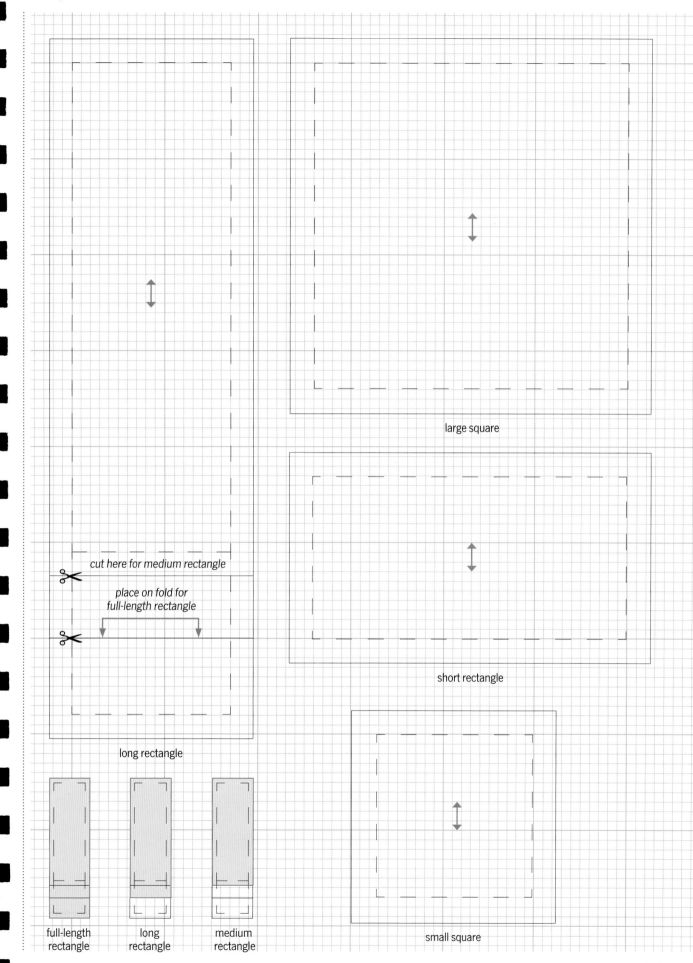

cut here for medium rectangle

place on fold for
full-length rectangle

long rectangle

large square

short rectangle

small square

full-length
rectangle

long
rectangle

medium
rectangle

Additional templates

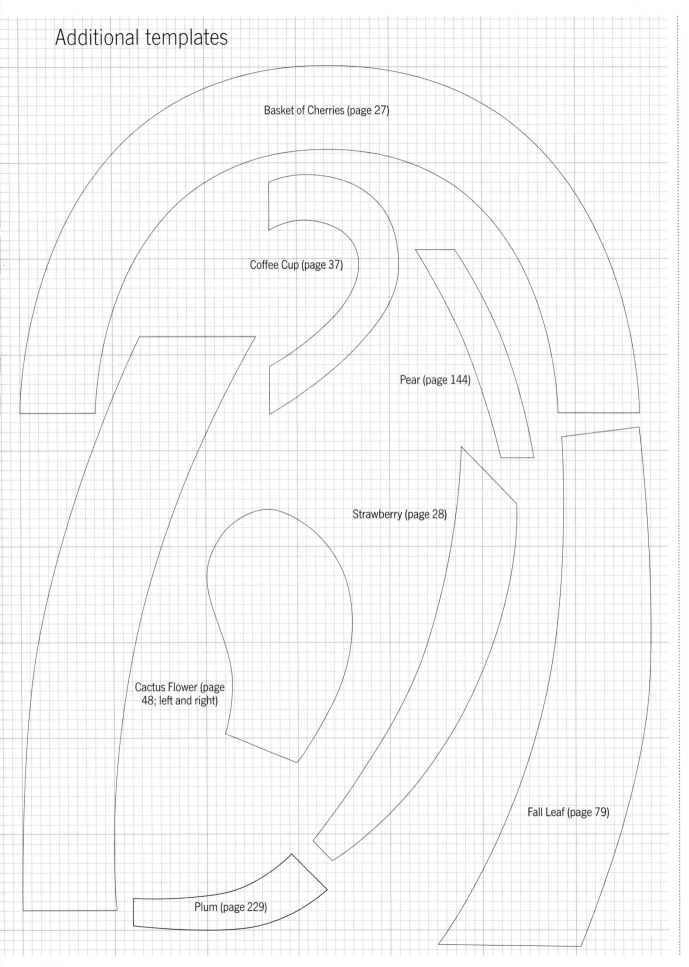

Basket of Cherries (page 27)

Coffee Cup (page 37)

Pear (page 144)

Strawberry (page 28)

Cactus Flower (page 48; left and right)

Fall Leaf (page 79)

Plum (page 229)

index

a

alaska homestead 170
alexander's star 204
all square 73
alternate stripes 77
amish chain 266
antique tile 231
anvil, the 118
appliqué 20
arkansas snowflake 180
arrow block 59
arrowheads 135
arrow square 14
at the window 207
aunt eliza's star 59
autograph 202
autumnal leaf 79

b

balancing blocks 93
banded stripes 163
basket of cherries 27
bauhaus 103
beach huts 167
bear's paw 76
bias seams 19
big bow 191
big flower 187
bird flock 73
bird's nest 185
birthday present 246
blockade 267
boat square 13
bookshelf 218
bordered checkerboard
    104
bow tie 161
boxed pinwheel 256
brave new world 147
brave world 70
breezy bunting 176
brick wall 96
bricks and mortar 204
broken dishes 178
broken dishes diamond
    148
bubble and squeak 213
buckeye beauty 52
butterfly block 111
butterfly star 237

c

cactus flower 48
cake stand 98
calico puzzle 92
candies 88
card trick 235
cat's head 17
chain and hourglass
    115
chain piecing 19
checkerboard 31
checker square 236
checker star 142
checks 118
chicken 80
chinese coin 87
chinese coin stacks 173
christmas forest 153
christmas stocking 29
churn dash 152

churn dash quarters 132
circle 154
city grid 242
clay's choice 263
coffee cup 37
cogwheel 199
color 6, 7
color wheel 91
colorado beauty 78
concentric squares 52
corn and beans 94
corner cross 114
corners 68
corner square 14
corner star 66
cotton reel 124
counterchange 43
country lanes 148
crazy house 196
cross 208
crossbow 180
cross check 178
cross patch 111
crossroads 196
cross weave 42
crown of thorns 41
cubes 248
cutting mat 8
cutting 9–10, 11–19
    fussy see fussing
        cutting
    rotary see rotary
        cutting
    template see template
        cutting

d

dancing pinwheel 183
dandy, the 103
darting minnows 268
diagonal cross 120
diagonal nine patch 49
diagonal seams 19
diagonal square 15
diagonal squares 150
diagonal triangles 110
diamond in a square
    260
diamond pinwheel 56
diamonds 89
domino 169
double butterfly 50
double four patch 74
double hourglass 226
double nine patch 46
double pinwheel 259
double propeller 223
double x 243
double z 253
duck and ducklings 72
dutchman's puzzle 207

e

easy four patch 155
eight-point star 121
eight-point triangle star
    240
emma's puzzle 247
end of the day 125
equal stripes 39
equipment 8

f

fabric markers 8
fabrics 6, 7–8
    fussy see fussing
        cutting
    rotary cutting see
        rotary cutting
    sizes 7
    template cutting see
        template cutting
faceted diamond 127
faceted square 191
fair and square 265
faraway tree, the 157
fast forward 63
fields of green 150
figure eight 162
fireflies 182
five of diamonds 54
five square 177
floating pinwheel 53
floating square 113
flower basket 137
flying cross 69
flying dutchman 244
flying geese 105
flying geese rectangle
    17
flying geese square 15
flying out 95
flying squares 245
forest paths 133
four patch 90
four-patch corners 260
four-patch friendship
    star 184
four-patch square 11
four square 184
four ways 181
fourth of july 25
frame 162
framed checkerboard
    72
framed four patch 84
framed nine patch 143
framed pinwheel 43
framed square 65
framed windmill 24
freewheeling star 125
friendship square 109
friendship star 71
fruit basket 186
fussy cutting 9

g

garden path 228
gingham 24
go-between, the 200
goose star 67
goose tracks 159
grandmother's cross
    123
grape basket 261
greek cross 267
grid stripes 242

h

half-square triangle 12
harlequin triangles 60
hen and chicks 83
hexagon chain 215
hexagon path 172

hexagons and
    hourglasses 60
hexagon square 15
hidden nine patch 225
hidden star 199
hole in the barn door 42
hole in the corner 195
homeward bound 251
hourglasses 29
hourglass square 13
house square 14
h squares 241

i

indian star 251
indigo flower basket
    224
indigo windmill 212
interlocked cross 243
interlocking crosses 64
ironing 8

j

jacob's ladder 230
japanese lattice 210
jeweled crown 107

k

kew gardens 217
keyboard 236
kitchen workbox 258
kitten 75
knot block, the 226
knot garden 232

l

large and small geese 57
leaves 160
left diamond rectangle
    16
left tapered triangle 16
light and shade 85
linked squares 220
little basket 188
little bows 58
little boxes 211
little cherry basket 239
little log cabin 221
little prairie house 35
little yacht 169
log cabin corner 41
log cabin square 65
long boat 17
lost ship, the 149
love-in-a-mist 214
lucky horseshoes 209

m

maltese cross 154
maple leaf 86
massachusetts 44
matchine seams 19
matching triangles 133
merry kite 174
midsummer 100
mississippi spin 172
missouri 252
monkey wrench 93
mosaic 104

n

needles 8
nelson's victory 216
nine patch 203
nine-patch chain 158
nine-patch cross 66
nine-patch snowballs 89
nine-patch square 34
north star 95

o

ocean wave 168
octagon 49
octagon check 115
octagon frame 119
octagons 101
octagon square 18
octagon star 216
offset squares 106
oh! susanna 212
oh! susanna framed 140
old maid's puzzle 179
old windmill, the 158
open star 63
orange tree 61
oregon 131
overlap 113

p

paint swatches 136
patchwork dog 146
patience corner 145
pear 144
pennants 47
perspective square 18
philadelphia pavement
    257
pig pen 238
pine trees 139
pineapple 108
pins 8
pinwheel 87
pinwheel check 70
pinwheels 234
pinwheel square
    (project) 134
pinwheel square (rotary
    cutting) 13
plaid check 99
plain blue check 161
plum 229
poppy 26
posy basket 54
practical orchard 151
pressing seams 20
puss in the corner 170

q

quarter cross 245
quick cross 263
quick susanna 129
quilter's rulers 8
quilting fabrics 6

r

rail fence 147
rainbow circle 22
random roads 151
random squares 233
rectangles 119
rectangle square 11

red, white, and blue
    185
reels of cotton 197
ribbon tail star 163
richmond square 192
right diamond rectangle
    16
right tapered triangle 16
road to california 128
road to oklahoma 175
robbing peter to pay
    paul 40
robin 36
rocky mountain puzzle
    106
rolling stone 222
roman square 238
roman tees 145
rooster 81
rotary cutter 8
rotary cutting 10,
    11–19
    arrow square 14
    boat square 13
    cat's head 17
    corner square 14
    diamond square 15
    flying geese rectangle
        17
    flying geese square
        15
    four-patch square 11
    half-square triangle 12
    hexagon square 15
    hourglass square 13
    house square 14
    left diamond
        rectangle 16
    left tapered triangle
        16
    long boat 17
    octagon square 18
    perspective square
        18
    pinwheel square 13
    rectangle square 11
    right diamond
        rectangle 16
    right tapered triangle
        16
    short boat 17
    stitch and flip 14
    three-patch square
        11
    three-quarter square
        triangle 13
    three-stripe square
        11
    triangle-and-square
        block 15
row of geese 46
rows of bow ties 254

s

sailboat 165
sashed pinwheel 259
sawtooth 68
sawtooth pinwheel 264
sawtooth star 55
scottie dog 32
scrappy nine patch 83
scrappy nine-patch
    chain 249

index

scrappy star 223
seam allowance 19
seams
  bias 19
  diagonal 19
  matchine 19
  pressing 20
seaside 97
seated cat 171
secret star 206
sewing 19–20
  appliqué 20
  seam allowance 19
sewing machine 8
shaded squares 152
shadow cross 92
shoofly 116
shoofly square 128
shoofly star 112
short boat 17
simple diamond
  pinwheel 190
single irish chain 155
single pinwheel 114
single wedding ring 138
sliver strips 33
snowballs and shooflies
  194
southern belle 164
spectrum stripe 100
spinning heart 23
spinning star 217
split nine patch 109
spool block twist 255
square blocks 126
square cross 203
squared star 227
squared up 45
square lock 219
square propeller 233
squares and crosses
  135
square upon square 173
spray starch 8
stacked rectangles 82
stacked squares 33
stacks 241
star flower 55
starry night 205
steps 126
stitch and flip 14
stonemason's puzzle
  215
strawberry 28
stretched nine patch 39
string-pieced block 268
string-pieced squares
  34
striped rectangle 134
summer tree 141
sunburst 102
sunny hill 198
sunrise 116
sweet heart 189

t

tall ship 195
tee block 38
template cutting 9
template sizing 5
thread 8
three-patch square 11

three-quarter square
  triangle 13
three squares 50
three-stripe square 11
thrift block 84
thrift four patch 183
thrift stripes 99
thrifty 234
through the square
  window 129
tic-tac-toe 250
tools see equipment
trafalgar 219
triangles 31
triangle-and-square
  block 15
triangle tree 156
true blue 201
tulip ladyfingers 266
turbo prop 120
twist 131
two-way star 62

V

variable star 112
village 193
village square 143
violet 262

W

watermill 123
weather vane 117
welsh diamond 257
whirligig 122
white diamond 90
wild waves 192
windmill 40
windmill box 96
windmill sails 164
windmill square 249
winter pines 140
wishing ring 82
woven cross 130
woven heart 51

y

yankee puzzle 77

z

zigzag 166
zigzag border 74
zigzag stripe 71

bibliography

Atkins, Jacqueline M and Tepper, Phyllis A., *New York Beauties: Quilts from the Empire State* (Dutton Studio, 1992)

Beresford, Laura, and Hebert, Kate, *Classic Quilts from The American Museum in Britain* (Scala Publishers Ltd, 2009)

Beyer, Jinny, *The Quilter's Album of Patchwork Patterns: More than 4050 Pieced Designs for Quilters* (Breckling Press, 2009)

Bywater Cross, Mary, *Treasures in the Trunk: Quilts of the Oregon Trail* (Rutledge Hill Press, 1993)

Colby, Averil, *Patchwork* (Batsford, 1958)

Cripps, David, *Quilt Treasures: The Quilters' Guild Heritage Search* (Deirdre McDonald Books, 1995)

Eaton, Linda, *Quilts in a Material World: Selections from the Winterthur Collection* (Harry N. Abrams, 2007)

Eddy, Celia, *Quilted Planet: A Sourcebook of Quilts from Around the World* (Mitchell Beazley, 2005)

Goodman, Liz, and Joiner, Susan, *Creative Patchwork: A Golden Hands Book* (Marshall Cavendish, 1971)

Gutcheon, Beth, *The Perfect Patchwork Primer* (Penguin, 1974)

Ickis, Marguerite, *The Standard Book of Quilt Making and Collecting* (Dover Publications, 1959)

Malone, Maggie, *Classic American Patchwork Quilt Patterns* (Sterling Publishing Co, 1979)

Osler, Dorothy, *Amish Quilts and the Welsh Connection* (Schiffer Publishing Ltd, 2011)

Peck, Amelia, *American Quilts and Coverlets in the Metropolitan Museum of Art* (MQ Publications, 2007)

Pellman, Rachel, *Traditional Amish Quilts: Over 30 Beautiful Patterns to Make* (Bell & Hyman Ltd, 1986)

Prichard, Sue, *Quilts 1700 to 2010: Hidden Histories, Untold Stories* (V&A Publishing, 2010)

Rae, Janet, *The Quilts of the British Isles* (Dutton Adult, 1987)

Short McKim, Ruby, *101 Patchwork Patterns* (Dover Publications, 1962)

Warren, Elizabeth V, *Quilts: Masterworks from the American Folk Art Museum* (Rizzoli, 2010)

author biography

Lucinda Ganderton studied Fine Art Textiles at Goldsmiths' College, London and now works across a range of textile media. She is an experienced author who has written over thirty-five books on embroidery and needlework, as well as creating a number of block quilts for her own pleasure. Her most recent publications are *The Liberty Book of Simple Sewing*, undertaken with Liberty of London, and *The Maison Sajou Sewing Book*, for the Parisian haberdashery Maison Sajou.

acknowledgements

No author writes—or sews—in isolation, and this book is the result of dedicated work from the inspiring editorial and creative teams at Ivy Press, with whom I have been fortunate to work. Heartfelt thanks go to Sophie Collins for commissioning me in the first place, and for being so resolutely supportive for many months, as well as to Tom Kitch, Theresa Bebbington, and Judith Chamberlain-Webber for their understanding and exemplary editorial skills. Leslie T. O'Neill and Alison Korleski wrote the steps for each patch with precision and care, and Sara Cook helped to check the patterns. I am also incredibly grateful to Wayne Blades, whose impressive creative vision defines the look of the book, to Ginny Zeal who put the pages together, and especially to Andrew Perris who photographed all 365 blocks. As ever, my family has always been there when I have needed them. This book is for my son Alexander Haydn-Williams, with love.